INDIGENOUS KNOWLEDGE INQUIRIES

Praise for Indigenous Knowledge Inquiries

This is a monumental work; there is nothing comparable in the literature.

— David Brokensha

Indispensable for those working at the sharp end of the development sector, who don't have the benefit of an anthropological background, and need reassurance that their choices and compromises in practical people-centered approaches are sound.

— Graham Haylor
Director of the Asia Pacific STREAM Initiative

The Bangladesh Resource Centre for Indigenous Knowledge has very successfully implemented IK projects and conducted research using this excellent book as a guide. This book will greatly help anyone in any part of the world who intends to conduct work on IK.

— Dr. Mahbub Alam
Independent University of Bangladesh

This splendid book provides a comprehensive overview of current approaches and methods, and will be essential reading for all those with interests in the use of indigenous knowledge in the context of development.

— Douglas Nakashima
Head, Local and Indigenous Knowledge Systems (LINKS)
UNESCO, Paris

INDIGENOUS KNOWLEDGE INQUIRIES

A Methodologies Manual for Development

Paul Sillitoe, Peter Dixon
and Julian Barr

PUBLISHING

Published by ITDG Publishing
Schumacher Centre for Technology and Development
Bourton Hall, Bourton-on-Dunsmore, Rugby, CV23 9QZ, United Kingdom
www.itdgpublishing.org.uk

First published in 2005

ISBN 1 85339 571 4

This edition of the book is published jointly with The University Press Limited,
Dhaka, Bangladesh.

A catalogue record for this book is available from the British Library.

ITDG Publishing is the publishing arm of the Intermediate Technology
Development Group Ltd. Our mission is to build the skills and capacity of people
in developing countries through the dissemination of information in all forms,
enabling them to improve the quality of their lives and that of future generations.

Published by The University Press Limited, Red Crescent House
61 Motijheel Commercial Area, Dhaka-1000, Bangladesh.

Contents

List of Tables		vii
List of Figures		ix
List of Photographs		xi
List of Boxes		xii
List of Abbreviations		xiii
Acknowledgements		xvii
1	**Introduction to Indigenous Knowledge Projects**	**1**
	1.1 Introduction	1
	1.2 Definition	2
	1.3 Background	7
	1.4 Justification	12
	1.5 Methodology	18
2	**Design and Management of Indigenous Knowledge Projects**	**27**
	2.1 Design and Management of Projects	27
	2.2 Project Design Considerations	28
	2.3 The Indigenous Knowledge Cube — A Decision Framework	52
	2.4 The Cube Axes	58
	2.5 Eight Indigenous Knowledge Project Scenarios	60
	2.6 Project and Team Management	71
3	**Tool Box of Methods for Indigenous Knowledge Projects**	**85**
	3.1 Tools and Analysis for Indigenous Knowledge Projects	85
	3.2 Participant-observation	87
	3.3 Interviewing/Discussion	95
	3.4 Wealth Ranking/Well-being or Vulnerability Ranking/Social Mapping	111
	3.5 Mapping	124
	3.6 Venn (or Chapati) Diagramming/Institution Analysis	130
	3.7 Farmwalk	133
	3.8 Transect	137
	3.9 Seasonal Calendar/Pattern Chart	142
	3.10 Taxonomies	154
	3.11 Webbing	158

3.12 Flow Chart/Process Diagram   161
3.13 Historical Comparison/Time Lines   164
3.14 Group Discussion/Focus Groups   176
3.15 Participatory Technology Analysis   184
3.16 Strengths and Weaknesses   188
3.17 Sorting and Ranking   191
3.18 Matrix   195
3.19 Five Questions   202
3.20 Problem/Option Census   204
3.21 Brainstorming   211
3.22 Assessment Workshops/Envisioning   215
3.23 Data Analysis Tools   222

4 Further Sources and References for Indigenous Knowledge Projects   **239**
4.1 Some Key References   239
4.2 Some Indigenous Knowledge Newsletters   239
4.3 Some Indigenous Knowledge Websites   239
4.4 Some Participation Websites and Handbooks   240
4.5 Bibliography   241

Index   **279**

List of Tables

1.1	Indigenous knowledge compared with science	5
1.2	The contrasts between scientific research and IK research	5
1.3	Participatory versus transfer of technology paradigms	10
1.4	Typology of participation in research	11
1.5	Types of collaborative research	12
2.1	Staff factors that relate to the project design criteria of Resources, Time and Objectives	33
2.2	Types of staff that may undertake an IK-NR investigation	35
2.3	Contrasts in institutional backgrounds of IK researchers	36
2.4	SWOC matrix for potential staff on NR-IK Projects	37
2.5	Key to Table 2.6 and Table 2.9	41
2.6	Inputs and outputs of different types of staff	41
2.7	Visual and verbal compared	46
2.8	Framework for trustworthiness of qualitative data	47
2.9	IK data collection and analysis tools	49
2.10	Time and cost factors for various PRA techniques	50
2.11	IK project design variables and logframe OVI quantifiers	53
2.12	Amount of research staff time purchased with five different budgets	54
2.13	Type of IK study appropriate to a range of project durations	56
2.14	Three tiers of IK complexity	57
2.15	Summary of sub-cube inputs/outputs	60
2.16	Descriptions of team research, using the STRAP framework	73
2.17	Considerations in forming a project team	74
2.18	Belbin's profiles for team members	75
2.19	Pros and cons of different forms of team communication	82
3.1	Contrasts in learning and location	90
3.2	The shift from an objectivist to constructivist view	92
3.3	Variation in interview instrumentation	99
3.4	Key indicators of well-being and poverty among rural labouring children	112
3.5	Indicators of household prosperity in rural Java	113
3.6	Some criteria for wealth and poverty given by Tanzanians in wealth ranking exercise	114
3.7	Criteria for households best able to cope, Masaka District, Uganda	119
3.8	Criteria for households least able to cope, Masaka District, Uganda	120
3.9	Wealth ranking exercise, Bangladesh	121
3.10	Translation confusions	156
3.11	Time-line analysis of Lake Khabbaki, Punjab, Pakistan	167
3.12	Comparison of changing community needs	170

3.13	Time series analysis of the experiences of Chandavana village, Junagadh, India	174
3.14	A sickle knife	188
3.15	Matrix ranking of crops against reasons for preferences	193
3.16	A way of presenting analysed matrices from different participants	196
3.17	Criteria for evaluating plant species mentioned by graziers and by researchers	198
3.18	Pairwise ranking of development problems in Miputu, Ndola District, Zambia	200
3.19	Problem ranking matrix using stone counters	201
3.20	A comparison of the needs of different primary stakeholder groups	206
3.21	Problem census results according to stakeholder groups, Bangladesh	207
3.22	Workshop timeline for INTRAC NGO PRA training in Central Asia	219
3.23	Problems and opportunities chart, Mbusyani, Kenya	220
3.24	Options assessment chart, Mbusyani, Kenya	220
3.25	Suitability of CAQDAS for use by different types of researcher	233
3.26	The use of factual codes to monitor the distribution of interviews	233

List of Figures

1.1	Main project design elements	3
1.2	The knowledge continuum	6
1.3	Arnstein's Ladder	11
1.4	Map produced in participatory mapping exercise	18
2.1	The project cycle	29
2.2	A series of linked project cycles creating a project wave	30
2.3	Options for synchronising IK and NR Component Studies	31
2.4	Hypothetical depth and reliability of understanding of IK issues by two staff types vs. project budget	55
2.5	IK project design variables as continua	58
2.6	IK project design variables as axes of a cube	58
2.7	Eight key IK project design scenarios	59
2.8	Common group learning	77
2.9	Model of multi-disciplinary research	78
2.10	The 'integration by leader' model of interdisciplinary research	78
2.11	The 'negotiation among experts' model of interdisciplinary research	79
2.12	The modelling approach to interdisciplinary research	79
2.13	Information flow between team members	80
2.14	Model of idealised communication pathways for integrated scientific and IK study of soil resources	84
3.1	Etic versus emic views	93
3.2	Types of interview	98
3.3	Interviewing and triangulation	109
3.4	Types of household drawn by South African women in PPA exercise	116
3.5	Map showing division of land units by gender, Kenya	125
3.6	Map of Madah area	126
3.7	Water resource map of Kamatchipuram, S. India	127
3.8	Influence and importance of different organisations in Titupara, Bangladesh	132
3.9	Evaluation of Sexual Health Clinic leaflet using an evaluation wheel	132
3.10	Monitoring changing livelihoods in Kenya	135
3.11	A transect across farm land	138
3.12	Transect from Cavite region, Philippines	142
3.13	Transect of land in Gandara region, Philippines	143
3.14	Rainfall calendar for typical and atypical years	144
3.15	Seasonal calendar from Mbusyani, Kenya	146
3.16	Calendar of market prices	147
3.17	Hunger and abundance calendar	148
3.18	Seasonal calendar for women's work	149

3.19 Daily routine diagram for rural and urban women in Gaza   150

3.20 Daily routine task chart for one season   151

3.21 Seasonal calendar for a village in northern Pakistan   153

3.22 Sample seasonal calendar matrix   154

3.23 Grazier classification of rangeland plants   157

3.24 Web of Cogon weed problem, Philippines   159

3.25 Three-level web indicating biophysical causes and socio-economic constraints   160

3.26 Male villagers understanding of the steps in producing crops, Bassenko village, Ougadougou   162

3.27 Before and after integration: bioresource flows between natural resources, Philippines   163

3.28 Bioresource flow model, wet season, Philippines   164

3.29 Farm transect with wet season monitoring data, Philippines   164

3.30 Trend lines from Mbusyani, Kenya   168

3.31 Historical matrix comparing coping strategies in times of crisis, Senegal   168

3.32 Transect through time illustrating land use trends, Eastern Java   171

3.33 Changes on a farm in the Philippines through adoption of upland farm management technology   171

3.34 Spatial patterns of change in the economic importance of rainfed farming, livestock production and cotton farming in the Hadeija-Jama'are floodplain, Nigeria 1971-1992/3   172

3.35 Quality of design   186

3.36 Ranking of food crops   193

3.37 Gender division of plants and tree products from joint tree management, Kenya   197

3.38 Pairwise ranking matrix, Kenya   202

3.39 Using the fingers to enumerate the five questions   203

3.40 Concept map of malnutrition: lactating mothers' group, Accra, Ghana   212

3.41 Pie-diagram for livelihood analysis, Central Asia   222

3.42 Participatory environmental evaluation of forest resources, Kenya   223

3.43 Calculating values of forest resources, Kenya   224

3.44 Screen shot of QSR NUD*IST showing code list, documentation list and code tree   226

3.45 The process of using CAQDAS for making IK accessible to scientists   227

3.46 Coding text units in two interview transcripts for IK on soil properties   228

3.47 Partial coding structure for referential content of transcripts, with examples of search Bengali terms for land and soil   229

3.48 'Matrix' querying of IK transcripts for intersection of local soil names and soil properties   231

3.49 Screen shot of WinAKT showing basic statements about soil texture   237

List of Photographs

1.1	Bangladeshi fisherman with small boat	2
1.2	Ploughing a paddy field	4
1.3	Man checking betel crop	9
1.4	Participatory mapping exercise	16
1.5	Learning by doing: threshing rice	23
2.1	Boatmen	27
2.2	Women taking part in problem census workshop	30
2.3	Monsoon flooding around homesteads	32
2.4	Spear fishing from raft	35
2.5	Briefing during workshop	44
2.6	Women working on chart during PRA workshop	48
2.7	Rice harvest	51
2.8	Collecting sun-dried cow dung for fuel	53
2.9	Fishing boats drawn up at edge of *beel* lake	56
2.10	Threshing rice	80
3.1	A banana market	86
3.2	Fishing with push nets in water hyacinth	91
3.3	Taking notes	99
3.4	Wealth ranking, bottom of the pile: rickshaw pullers	115
3.5	Taking part in problem census	128
3.6	Drawing a map	129
3.7	A farm walk with wading in Bangladesh: harvesting rice	136
3.8	View across *beel* lake and farmland in Bangladesh	141
3.9	Fishing in *beel* lake: pulling in net	143
3.10	Shaking grain from straw	146
3.11	Fishing in *beel* lake	147
3.12	Dramatic seasonal change in Bangladesh, monsoon flooding	149
3.13	A pot seller carrying his wares	149
3.14	Daily routine, a woman cutting up rice straw	151
3.15	Marketing vegetables on the roadside	167
3.16	Spreading grain to sun dry	173
3.17	Focus group discussions	181
3.18	Ploughing a paddy	185
3.19	A seller of various knives	190
3.20	Harvesting rice in dry season	194
3.21	Women sorting preferences during PRA exercise	197
3.22	Conducting a problem census	206
3.23	Listing issues on flipchart during workshop	212
3.24	Ice-breaking exercise	218
3.25	A problem census	225

List of Boxes

1.1	Previous approaches to development	8
1.2	Recent approaches to development	8
2.1	Project wave series of projects (1)	29
2.2	Project wave series of projects (2)	31
2.3	National natural sciences graduate	42
2.4	National social sciences graduate	43
2.5	UK immigrant anthropology undergraduate	44
2.6	Senior academic staff	45
2.7	NR academic staff	45
2.8	Types of output from IK research	52
2.9	The three key IK project design questions	52
2.10	The three key IK project design variables	52
2.11	Definitions of the eight key IK project design cubes	59
2.12	The STRAP framework for assessing research team complexity	72
2.13	Team leader qualities for participatory NR research	74
2.14	Ten tips for team management	78
3.1	Background steps for wealth ranking within a large target population	121
3.2	Issues in the social theoretical critique of GIS	129
3.3	A combined approach to GIS	130
3.4	Livelihood mapping — demand for products in Mokwalto township, Vredefort	134
3.5	Retrospective community mapping (RCM)	166
3.6	Advantages and disadvantages of focus groups	178
3.7	A strengths, weaknesses, opportunities and constraints analysis	189
3.8	Four stages of group development	213
3.9	The main features of WinAKT	235

List of Abbreviations

APFT	Avenir des Peuples des Forêts Tropicales
APO	Assistant Project Officer
ASCII	American Standard Code for Information Interchange (computer code)
BARCIK	Bangladesh Resource Centre for Indigenous Knowledge (Bangladesh NGO)
BRAC	Bangladesh Rural Advancement Committee (Bangladesh NGO)
BRRI	Bangladesh Rice Research Institute
CAQDAS	Computer Aided Qualitative Data Analysis Software
CDR	Complex, Diverse and Risk-prone (of environments)
CGIAR	Consultative Group on International Agricultural Research
CIKARD	Centre for Indigenous Knowledge for Agriculture and Rural Development (at Iowa State University, USA)
CIRAN	Centre for International Research and Advisory Networks (part of Nuffic)
CNRS	Centre for Natural Resources Studies (Bangladesh environmental NGO)
COMPAS	Comparing and Supporting Indigenous Agricultural Systems (programme managed by ETC, Netherlands)
CPR	Common Pool Resource/Common Property Resource
CRDT	Centre for Rural Development and Training (University of Wolverhampton, UK)
CV	Curriculum Vitae
DFID	Department for International Development (UK) (formerly ODA)
ESRC	Economic and Social Research Council (UK research funding council)
ETC	action group on Erosion Technology and Concentration (formerly RAFI)
FAO	Food and Agriculture Organisation (of the United Nations)
FFL	Farmer First and Last (extension approach)
FPR	Farmer Participatory Research
FSR	Farming Systems Research
GIS	Geographic Information System
GO	Governmental Organisation
HTML	Hypertext Markup Language (computer code)
HYV	High Yielding Varieties (of cereal crops)

ICAF	Industrial College of the Armed Forces (National Defence University, Washington D.C., USA)
IDR	Inter-Disciplinary Research
IDRC	International Development Research Centre (Canada)
IDS	Institute of Development Studies (Sussex University, UK)
IFPP	Indigenous Food Plants Programme (Kenya)
IIED	International Institute for Environment and Development (UK research centre)
IIRR	International Institute of Rural Reconstruction
IK	Indigenous Knowledge
INTRAC	International NGO Training and Research Centre (Oxford, UK)
ITK	Indigenous Technical Knowledge
IUCN	International Union for the Conservation of Nature
IWGIA	International Work Group for Indigenous Affairs
LWI	Land Water Interface (programme of DFID's NRSP)
MDR	Multi-Disciplinary Research
MS Word	Microsoft Word (word processing software)
NARS	National Agricultural Research
NASA	National Aeronautics and Space Administration (of USA)
NGO	Non-Governmental Organisation
NR	Natural Resource(s)
NRI	Natural Resources Institute (University of Greenwich, UK)
NR-IK	Natural Resource-Indigenous Knowledge (of projects)
NRM	Natural Resource Management
NRSP	Natural Resources Systems Programme (of DFID)
NRSP-SEM	Natural Resources Systems Programme-Socio-Economic Methodologies (DFID Programme)
NSW	New South Wales (Australia)
Nuffic	Netherlands Organisation for International Cooperation in Higher Education
NVIVO	Computer qualitative data analysis software (from QSR International)
ODA	Overseas Development Administration (now DFID, UK)
OVIs	Objectively Verifiable Indicators
PALS	Participatory Approaches Learning Study (of DFID)
PAR	Participatory Action Research
PCM	Project Cycle Management
PI	Principal Investigator (research project leader)
PLA	Participatory Learning and Action
PM&E	Participatory Monitoring and Evaluation

PPA	Participatory Poverty Assessment
PRA	Participatory Rural Appraisal
PRSP	Poverty Reduction Strategy Paper (of World Bank)
PTD	Participative Technology Development
QQT	Quality, Quantity and Time
QSR NU*DIST	Qualitative Solutions and Research's Non-numeric, Unstructured Data * Index and Searching Technology (Qualitative data analysis software from QSR International)
R&D	Research and Development
RA	Research Assistant
RAFI	Rural Advancement Foundation International (Canada)
RAMSAR	Convention on Wetlands (signed in Ramsar, Iran 1971)
RCM	Retrospective Community Mapping
RRA	Rapid Rural Appraisal
RSS	Reconnaissance Social Survey
SARL	Sustainable Agriculture and Rural Livelihoods (programme of IIED)
SAS	Statistical Analysis Software
SEAGA	Socio-Economic and Gender Analysis (programme of the FAO)
SIDA	Swedish International Development cooperation Agency
SPSS	statistical analysis software
SSC	Statistical Services Centre (at Reading University, UK)
STEP	Social, Technical, Economic, Political (analysis tool, also known as STEPS where S means Sustainability, or as PEST)
STRAP	schema for assessing complexity of research projects
SWAps	Sector-Wide Approaches (technical assistance approach)
SWOC	Strengths, Weaknesses, Opportunities and Constraints (also known as SWOT where T means Threats)
T&V	Training and Visit (extension approach)
TOR/TORS	Terms of Reference (for a research project)
ToT	Transfer of Technology (technical assistance approach)
TQM	Total Quality Management (business management approach)
UK	United Kingdom
UNDP	United Nations Development Programme
UNESCO	United Nations Educational, Scientific and Cultural Organization
USAID	United States Agency for International Development
VRMP	Village Resource Management Plan
VSO	Voluntary Service Overseas (UK NGO)
WID	Women in Development (social development approach)
WinAKT	Agroforestry Knowledge Toolkit for Windows (computer software)
WWF	World Wildlife Fund

Acknowledgements

We could not have produced this book without the teamwork and intellectual contribution of all those involved in two Department for International Development (DFID) research projects — these comprised two closely related projects funded under the Natural Resources Systems Programme, one under the Socio-Economic Methodologies component (Project R6744) and the other under the Land-Water Interface component (Project R6756). We received help and hospitality from many persons — both project staff and many local people at the field sites. It is invidious to name individuals, but we wish to acknowledge here those most closely involved with the IK component of the projects. They are our Bangladeshi colleagues Mahbub 'Pial' Alam and Gour Pada Ghosh, Dr. S.B. Naseem (BRRI) and Professor M.I. Zuberi (Rajshahi University); M. Moklesur Rahman and Anisur Rahman (Center for Natural Resource Studies, Dhaka). Also our natural resource science colleagues who generously agreed to act as our guinea-pigs Dr. Robert Payton and Alice A. McGlynn (University of Newcastle), Drs Graham Haylor and Colin Bean (onetime University of Stirling). We also thank Sukanta Sen of the Bangladesh Resource Centre for Indigenous Knowledge (BARCIK), and volunteers Ben Angell, Anna Miles, Matt McLennan and Jane Stokoe who worked with BARCIK in Dhaka helping to establish an indigenous knowledge network for Bangladesh. We gratefully acknowledge the painstaking design work of Babul Chandra Dhar. We also thank Louise Shaxson (onetime DFID) and Elizabeth Warham (DFID) for their support and interest in the project. The views expressed are those of the authors and not necessarily DFID.

1 Introduction to Indigenous Knowledge Projects

1.1 Introduction

This methodology is intended for development programme managers and project leaders who wish to incorporate an Indigenous Knowledge (IK) element into their work. It is not a single methodology, but a continuous spectrum of approaches and tools, from those of use to persons seeking a quick and limited IK component, to those interested in a more long term and thorough-going IK investigation. It is not prescriptive. We recognise that different persons and situations will demand a range of different options. But we do try to signal the pitfalls and shortcomings of various alternatives, some of which severely limit the results that can be expected and their reliability.

In Chapter 1, we aim to answer the following questions:

- What is indigenous knowledge? A definition of the field covered by this methodology.
- Why has indigenous knowledge become an issue in international development? A brief review of indigenous knowledge in the context of the participatory movement.
- Why bother about indigenous knowledge in development programmes? The added value of indigenous knowledge in international development.
- How do you go about incorporating indigenous knowledge into development programmes and projects? An introduction to the methodology.

It should be noted that the aim is not to provide a guide to the design and management of projects in developing countries *per se*. Such information is available in for example, the UK Government's Department for International Development (DFID) Office Instructions and volumes such as Cusworth & Franks (1993) and other texts on Project Cycle Management (PCM). Nonetheless, it has been reported that the formal project management approach can be at odds with stakeholder participation (INTRAC, 1999). This also applies to IK investigations. These guidelines, by making reference to PCM in the context of natural resources indigenous knowledge projects, present options for reducing the conflicts and more effectively including the views of primary stakeholders in the project cycle. While this book focuses on Natural Resources (NR) research projects, as the field in which the authors have experience, the principles it outlines for incorporating IK into development apply to any field (e.g. health, education, business etc.).

This book draws on key texts that relate to indigenous knowledge research in development (see references) and interdisciplinary work in natural resources research. It also draws heavily on the authors' experience from DFID NRSP-SEM[1] project R6744, *Methodological research into the incorporation of indigenous knowledge into natural resources research on Bangladesh floodplain production systems*. Particular topics,

---

[1] Department for International Development Natural Resources Systems Programme — Socio-Economic Methodologies. We thank DFID for funding our research.

such as Computer Aided Qualitative Data Analysis Software (CAQDAS) and the use of cross-cultural research staff, are covered in more detail than others because the project studied them in some depth. The methodology is grounded in anthropological and development research, and attempts to be critically aware of contemporary reflective practice. We realise that we have not covered all issues relating to IK research methods — indeed many are still under development at this time as this dynamic new field of research establishes itself. We also anticipate that many readers may have specific questions which book such as this cannot answer, particularly relating to their field of work — for example what can IK contribute to research into pests or crop breeding or soils or veterinary science? For these reasons we append an extensive bibliography, which we hope will serve as a useful further resource.

Photograph 1.1: Bangladeshi fisherman with small boat

This guideline is set out as a normal linear document, but the design and management of IK projects involves making decisions about many closely interrelated subjects. For example if a certain budget is decided, that will limit the type of staff that can be employed to undertake the IK study, and that in turn will constrain the type of data collection and data analysis methods that can be used.

Figure 1.1 summarises the main elements of IK project design and management. The principle design issues are Cost, Time, and Scope of objectives. These issues impact on staffing as the main expenditure in IK projects. The type of data collection and data analysis methods are associated with staff, depending on the disciplines in which they are qualified. Indigenous knowledge investigations are normally undertaken as part of a wider research project; the success of the project depends heavily on how well the team functions.

1.2 Definition

- **What is indigenous knowledge? A definition of the field covered by this methodology.**

The meaning of the term 'indigenous knowledge' is by no means clear, particularly at this time when its use is growing rapidly in development circles. There are currently a wide range of alternatives used by different writers as they argue over the content of,

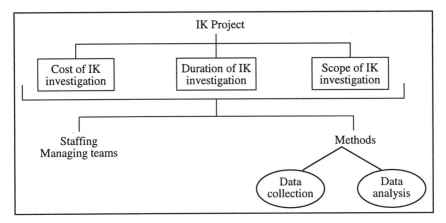

Figure 1.1: Main project design elements

and approaches to this field. Nonetheless they all share a certain common semantic load and address the same broad issues.[2] They relate to any knowledge held collectively by a population, informing interpretation of the world.

The following definitions from the indigenous knowledge literature give a broad, although not entirely accurate indication of the field:

- "Indigenous knowledge — the local knowledge that is unique to a given culture or society — contrasts with the international knowledge system which is generated through the global network of universities and research institutes" (Warren, Slikkerveer and Brokensha 1995:xv).
- "The unique, traditional, local knowledge existing within and developed around specific conditions of women and men indigenous to a particular geographic area" (Grenier 1998:1).
- "Indigenous knowledge is the knowledge that people in a given community have developed over time, and continue to develop. It is based on experience, often tested over centuries of use, adapted to local culture and environment, and dynamic and changing" (IIRR 1996:7).

Indigenous knowledge may relate to any domain, particularly in development currently that pertaining to natural resource management. It is conditioned by socio-cultural tradition, being culturally relative understanding inculcated into individuals from birth, structuring how they interface with their environments. It is community based, embedded in local cultural traditions. Its distribution is fragmentary. Although more widely shared locally on the whole than specialised scientific knowledge in Western society, no one person, authority or social group knows it all. There may be a certain asymmetry here, some clustering of certain knowledge within populations (e.g. by gender, age etc., or according to specialist status, maybe reflecting political or ritual power). It exists nowhere as a totality, there is no grand repository, and hence no coherent overall theoretical model, although it may achieve some coherence in cosmologies, rituals and symbolic

---

[2] All manner of other terms are to be found in the literature for indigenous knowledge, such as rural people's knowledge, indigenous technical knowledge, traditional environmental knowledge, local agricultural knowledge. We think that we should use indigenous knowledge as the one of widest currency in contemporary development debates.

discourse (which are notoriously difficult to access convincingly). It is equally skill as knowledge, transmitted orally and through experience, and repetitive practice characterises its learning across generations. It is the heritage of practical everyday life, with its functional demands, and is fluid and constantly changing, being dynamic and subject to ongoing negotiation between people and their environments. According to this definition, indigenous knowledge research equates largely with anthropological research, only focused on development defined problems not academic ones.

Indigenous knowledge is commonly contrasted with international scientific knowledge, often unfavourably. But some writers argue that to conflate others' knowledge traditions into an indigenous category and contrast it with western scientific knowledge is insupportable because it overlooks differences within each tradition and similarities between various indigenous and scientific perspectives. The distinction also has an unpleasant political edge, with connotations of superiority and inferiority. It is undeniable that there are substantial similarities and overlaps in the contents of various knowledge systems, that they may use certain similar equally objective methods to investigate reality (local farmers regularly engage in experimentation, and science is no less culturally rooted than other knowledge traditions). Nonetheless different cultures have varyingly formulated and expressed understandings of the world, although with the current explosion in communications and associated accelerated process of globalisation, hybridisation is occurring and blurring distinctions between scientific and other knowledge on socio-cultural grounds.

Regardless of globalising trends, we currently find people in different regions have unique cultural traditions and histories, which continue to condition in significant regards their views of the environment, life and so on. They concern different issues and priorities, reflect different experiences and interests, and will be codified in different idioms and styles, which we come to understand to varying currently debated extents. They are informed by cultural repertoires that have evolved over generations, albeit not in isolation, being influenced by others, having some points of similarity and overlap, yet maintaining a distinctiveness; the contrast between different traditions correlating closely until recently with geographical distance. While not replicating one another, individuals share a sufficient indetermined amount in common to comprise a distinct cultural order with common historical tradition, values, idioms and so on.

Photograph 1.2: Ploughing a paddy field

It follows that the scientific 'we' and indigenous 'them' dichotomy is inescapable in some measure and to argue in effect that we should not distinguish between different intellectual cultures is unrealistic. The distinction between indigenous and scientific, local and global knowledge is defensible, differences within, and similarities between knowledge traditions notwithstanding. What is made of the differences apparent between indigenous knowledge and science depends on one's view of development. The transfer of technology, 'normal science' and 'normal professionalism' approaches all emphasise difference; whereas the 'farmer first', 'revolutionary science', and 'new professionalism' all downplay difference encouraging an open, interdisciplinary approach. But the stark discrimination between the scientific and indigenous that characterises current development literature, where two column tables are popular, one listing the traits of the science category compared with the indigenous one is inadequate, if not misleading as to the relationship and distinction between the two, even where it argues for a reversal of the relationship between them in favour of participation and indigenous knowledge (Table 1.1).

Table 1.1 Indigenous knowledge compared with science

Features	Indigenous	Scientific
Relationship	Subordinate	Dominant
Communication	Oral Teaching through doing	Literate Didactic
Dominant mode of thought	Intuitive	Analytical
Characteristics	Holistic Subjective Experiential	Reductionist Objective Positivist

(after Wolfe *et al.* 1992)

We think that from the perspective of this methodology the distinct features of Western science and the scientific method that may be usefully contrasted with indigenous knowledge and participatory/ethnographic methods are as follows (Table 1.2).

Table 1.2 The contrasts between scientific research and IK research

Indigenous Knowledge	Scientific

Inside structure
  Community dynamics: power, knowledge
  variability (common, shared, specialised).
  Participation (Collegiate)
  Local (specific)
  Process
	Outside structure
	  Research team dynamics:
	  interdisciplinarity
	  Directive (Top-down)
	  Universal (generic)
	  Blueprint

It is not particularly helpful however to contrast indigenous knowledge with science in this way. They do not occupy the clear polar positions that this typology appears to demonstrate, as argued by Agrawal (1995). We are not talking about two tenuously connected knowledge traditions separated by a cultural-epistemological gulf, but rather a spectrum of relations.

In this methodology we conceive of the relation between scientists and farmers as comprising a continuum. This novel perspective better reflects the current position, and takes us to the heart of the debate over the definition of indigenous knowledge, and its correctness. At one end of the spectrum we have poor farmers who have no formal education, whom we may take to be as close as we might hypothetically come to 'real' indigenous knowledge, derived from their own cultural tradition. At the other end of the continuum we have Western scientists, who are trying to incorporate some empathy with local perceptions and practices into their work, wrestling with the problems of interdisciplinary research. In between we have various intergradations of local insider and global outsider knowledge depending on community of origin and formal education. Each potentially influences the other, in which process indigenous knowledge research tries to mediate.

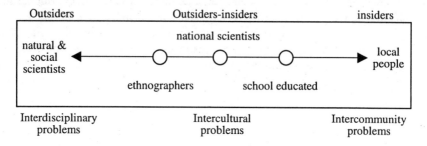

Figure 1.2: The knowledge continuum

As we pass along the continuum, starting from poor persons whose entire experience is of their locality, we come to local people who have received some formal schooling, and have some passing acquaintance with science, which they will blend with their locally derived knowledge and cultural heritage. Their education informs not only their own understanding but also that of their uneducated relatives and neighbours, to whom they will in some measure impart their foreign derived knowledge. All of them will also be subject to extension advice, either first or second hand, received from government agencies, non-governmental organisations and so on, messages based on scientific advice, and received increasing through the mass media.

When we pass further along we come to the more advantaged members of communities who may progress through school to college and university, some to study agricultural subjects, environmental science, geography and so on. We have our national collaborators on research and development projects, whom we might take to be mid-way in some senses along the continuum. They have an extensive formal scientific background, with higher degrees and some occupy senior university posts, but they also have a familiarity with the indigenous culture, as native speaking members of its metropolitan society. This gives a unique perspective, with its own potential insights and blind spots. Some of them may come from rural families, a further conduit of scientific understanding into local communities. They inevitably pass on some of their learning to relatives and friends when they return home, even if they do not themselves engage in the local economy. Social scientists researching local communities, particularly anthropologists, may fall somewhere near the centre of the continuum too, often, though not exclusively, serving to connect the two poles, brokering indigenous knowledge between them.

All knowledge potentially passes into the local pool, is blended with what is known to inform today's understanding and practice. Rural peoples' understanding of natural resource management issues is a mix of knowledge from various sources, which it is difficult to disentangle. It is syncretic knowledge. There is no repository of traditional indigenous knowledge, it is in constant process of change being continually influenced by outside ideas. In indigenous knowledge research we are trying to facilitate some communication along the continuum and beyond to policymakers, and so on. The idea of a continuum extending from poor local resource managers to research scientists should help us to overcome the pernicious side of the 'we' and 'them' divide by uniting us all.

We need to have a methodology that mediates effectively between the contradictions that characterise the promotion of scientific research from an indigenous knowledge perspective. We are trying to bridge between the poles of the indigenous-to-scientific-knowledge-continuum. Local indigenous knowledge contrasts with global scientific understanding. The one is more narrowly culturally contextualised whereas the other is cosmopolitan and has universal theoretical aspirations. The methods of the indigenous practitioner are more inductive with a 'weak' model of the world underlying the knowledge tradition, which to outsiders involved in development is largely unknown (even unknowable according to postmodern thinkers), whereas the methods of scientists are more deductive with a 'strong' model of the world and established methods for investigating it. Consequently, we cannot assume that the one will be congruent with the other, rather we have to seek the contrasts and parallels. We need beware of the 'stronger' scientific view coming to dominate the 'weaker' local one. We have to reconcile indigenous knowledge which is wide holistic knowledge and systemic understanding, with scientific knowledge which comprises the narrow and in-depth understanding of highly trained specialists, and in so doing promote cross-culturally informed research.

In distinguishing between indigenous and scientific knowledge traditions, we need to beware of privileging one above another. It is questionable to privilege scientific discourse as its costs, both environmental with pollution, non-sustainability etc., and social with redundancy, alienation etc. become increasingly evident. Nor should we put local knowledge in the "driving seat". It is undeniable that scientific knowledge underpins technological change, allowing human-beings to interfere with, and extend considerable control over nature, and that it is the dissemination of this technology for the betterment of humankind that underpins the notion of development. It is the wish of the majority of the populations of lesser developed countries to share in this technological advance, not just to increase their standard of living, but sometimes to stave off starvation, sickness and death, particularly with the relentless expansion of some populations.

It is difficult territory. Advocates of local knowledge in development argue that we should aim to play off the advantages and disadvantages of different perspectives to improve our understanding of problems. But conflict is inherent because we are not just talking about furthering understanding but of employing knowledge to effect some action, and sometimes the values that inform them are not readily reconcilable. Perhaps the aim should be equitable negotiation, which is a central tenet of participatory development. The negotiations become far more complex but the development initiatives are more likely to be appropriate for more people and hence more sustainable. It will involve the reconciliation of tensions evident between the natural and social sciences, conveying local knowledge to natural scientists such that they can appreciate its relevance. This is the objective of this methodology.

1.3 Background

- **Why has indigenous knowledge become an issue in international development? A brief review of indigenous knowledge in the context of the participatory movement.**

The history of indigenous knowledge enquiries stretches back, strictly speaking, to the start of anthropology. But as it relates to natural resources, and more specifically to development work, it has a considerably shallower pedigree. Its beginnings in development are dated to the appearance of some provocative works around the early 1980s — although some pioneering applied work predates these.

The emergence of local knowledge ideas and practice has depended crucially on a sea-change recently in the paradigms that structure conceptions of development. The dominant development paradigms until a decade or so ago were modernisation, the classic transfer-of-technology model associated with the political right, and dependency, the Marxist informed model associated with the political left. They are both blind to local knowledge issues.

Box 1.1: Previous approaches to development

The **modernisation** approach — not only dismisses local knowledge but also views it as part of the problem, being non-scientific, traditional and risk-adverse, even irrational and primitive.

The **dependency** approach — portrays poor farmers as helpless victims, local knowledge is again side-lined, this time as the view of the powerless.

The new bottom-up oriented development paradigms that have recently emerged to challenge these top-down perspectives are the market-liberal and neo-populist, both giving more credence to local perspectives but otherwise mirroring the same political divide, the former associated with the political right, and the latter associated with the political left.

Box 1.2: Recent approaches to development

The **market-liberal** approach — although it accords more attention to local knowledge, it is largely as market information relating to available technical options, how this knowledge will influence choice and the appropriateness of the various options to farmers' environments and households.

The **neo-populist** approach — The participatory focus gives potential prominence to local knowledge, which is taken seriously and afforded a role in problem identification, research and so on.

The shift to the bottom-up view and the end of the so-called Cold War are improbably coincidental, overseas aid no longer being imposed so blatantly to advance hegemonies in different parts of the world with the collapse of one of the superpowers, allowing for the potentially more politically volatile expression of poor peoples' views.

These different development approaches do not exclude one another. They are often combined in programmes. Regarding the more recent grass-roots approaches that advocate local knowledge research, both technological and socio-political issues feature to an extent, inextricably entwined. The mixing is applaudable, striving to reach a consensus. There is perhaps nothing new here, with the association on the one hand of technological advances and improvements with natural scientists and hard systems, and on the other of empowerment of the poor and disadvantaged with social scientists and soft systems approaches. And while there is nothing new in supporting attempts to encourage a rapprochement between these positions, as this methodology aims to do by promoting debate and furthering understanding of the issues, we should not underestimate the difficulties and frustrations of such work, which at root come down to differences in values and priorities.

Indigenous knowledge research has many similarities and common roots and objectives with other development approaches, notably farming systems research and participatory NR research. Awareness of the contribution that local knowledge insights might make in development has grown in part out of **farming systems research**, which emerged in the 1970s when the complexity of natural resource management in diverse and risk-prone environments was realised. It promoted, together with agroecology etc., a more comprehensive understanding of production. It introduced a systems perspective and went on-farm, realising that farms are more complex than any experimental station. The systems emphasis is anthropological in tone. In taking trials on-farm, it sought to address problems under farmers' management constraints, and understand their practices and calculations to advance technologically more acceptable interventions. There are many variants but broadly speaking farming systems research features multidisciplinary teams documenting and analysing the complex components — environmental, socio-economic, agronomic etc. — that comprise farm-household livelihoods, informing their members' multiple objectives, acknowledging their dynamic nature and capacity for change. Agronomists and agricultural economists have dominated, concentrating largely on the collection of data suitable for statistical investigation and model building. But considerable problems have emerged with the farming systems approach in development.

Photograph 1.3: Man checking betel crop

It is criticised for being too ambitious in trying to understand complex systems. The implication that researchers have to encompass the entire system is reflected in an inability to focus tightly on identified researchable constraints, and promote meaningful problem-centred, interdisciplinary co-operation. It is data-hungry and data-extractive, preoccupied with documentation not analysis. Its idea of system is limited, as illustrated by its narrow farm focus and tendency not to see beyond the farm boundary. It has confined research largely to professionals, limiting farmer participation, focusing too exclusively on optimising production through the intervention of 'experts'. In denying users' perspectives a place, it promotes a western conception of farming and privileges scientific analysis. Its conception of farming systems, as static structures, not allowing for change and farmers' manipulations, hinders appreciation of lived experience, which is central to different user groups' understanding where farming strategies are diverse. A large flaw from an anthropological viewpoint is the short time frames in which it was thought research could be conducted to achieve understanding of highly complex socio-cultural systems. This contributed to the perceived failure of farming systems research to address development issues pertinently.

Many recommendations have consequently proved largely irrelevant to resource-poor farmers. In response to criticism farming systems research has encompassed participatory methods and farmer decision-making, moving from commodity perspectives towards a better accommodation of farm complexity. It increasingly recognises that in any complex system involving humans, different stakeholders will have a range of perspectives informed by their differing aspirations, viewpoints and goals. Acceptance of participatory approaches has introduced a new analytical dimension — the generation of qualitative data requiring interpretative analysis. Many methodological problems remain, for example how can scientists focus in on constraints of a researchable kind without losing the overall systems view? There is a key role for local knowledge here, it being embedded by definition within the wider context.

The other strand in the emergence of local knowledge in development comprises the **participatory approaches** which have affinities with farming systems research. They are a growing family of techniques with associated battery of daunting acronyms, which have emerged as an attempt to bring development practice nearer to people, arising from growing dissatisfaction with expert-led top-down approaches (Table 1.3). They are a flexible and fast evolving suite of methods, intended to enable local people to take part in research and decision making to plan, act on and evaluate development proposals. They encourage them to analyse their own problems and facilitate the communication of their thoughts to others, furthering understanding of the poor through involvement. Those in favour argue they promote a better fit between proposed research and technological interventions, more effectively identify constraints on the poorest and better adjust projects to prevailing environmental conditions through on-farm work. The joint enterprise, or stakeholder participation approach poses some of the most challenging and stimulating problems in development today.

Table 1.3 Participatory versus transfer of technology paradigms

	Farmer-first	Transfer of Technology
Main objective	Empower farmers	Transfer technology
Needs assessed by	Farmers, facilitated by outsiders	Outsiders
Target farm types	Complex, diverse, risk-prone	Simple, uniform, controlled
Transferred by outsiders to farmers	Principles, methods, basket of choices	Prospects, messages, package of practices

(after Chambers 1993)

Several systems exist that classify and contrast different approaches to participatory development and participatory research for NR development. Perhaps the most well-known are those of Chambers (1993), who uses a polar model to emphasise difference (Table 1.3), and Biggs (1989), who shows grades of participation (Table 1.4), but the earlier work of Arnstein (1969) is also pertinent with his ladder idea (Figure 1.3) which shows grades of participation.

Table 1.4 Typology of participation in research

Type of Participation	Type of Relationship
Contract	Research contracts farmer to provide specific land and services.
Consult	Researchers consult farmers, diagnose their problems and find solutions for them.
Collaborate	Researchers and farmers are partners in the research process.
Collegiate	Researchers encourage and support farmers' research.

(after Biggs 1989)

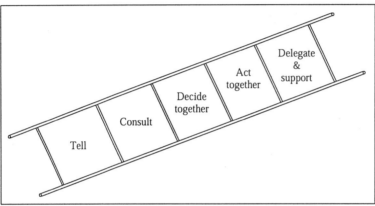

Source: After Arnstein 1969.

Figure 1.3: Arnstein's Ladder

A major issue is how to facilitate meaningful participation. This problem comprises two parts: firstly, determining what technological alternatives might be culturally and environmentally appropriate, and secondly, informing people about these, and the possible social, ecological and other consequences of any choices. Local knowledge research can, and should, play a key role in both stages. It is not always clear in farmer participatory development how the link is established and operates between our scientific research capacity with its technological possibilities, and the experimenting farmers with their problems and ideas, although all manner of methods have been pioneered. They are methodologically eclectic, mixing semi-structured interviews with observation, particularly favouring techniques that draw people in (ranging from participatory mapping with all manner of media, and diagrams and calendars using stones, beans, and twigs, to game play and theatricals, to more conventional paper and pen participatory surveys — see Chapter 3 of this book). They aim to involve a range of people from any community, seeking to include those who may be marginalised such as the very poor and women.

Participatory methods seek to combat the domination of urban-based development professionals and reverse some of their work practices. The emphasis is on listening and learning from people, not lecturing to them, on informality and sensitivity. They encourage farmers' experimentation, encouraging them to amend and design trials. The outsider team, preferably comprising a range of disciplinary backgrounds to promote different perspectives on problems, seeks to catalyse and facilitate reflective action, and act as a conduit to report the findings to policymakers, planners and politicians. The further it can withdraw and hand over to the community the better, allowing people to follow their own lines of enquiry. The approaches vary widely in the scope they afford farmers to participate (Table 1.5), from consultation (outsiders retaining control), to collaboration (co-operation as equal partners), to collegiate (insiders making research decisions). A number of problems attend participatory approaches, including lack of compatibility between farmer-led and scientific approaches and data analysis quandaries with unorthodox experiments, difficulties in selecting participants (preventing wealthier and more powerful community members dominating and directing research to their benefit), and the limited influence that farmers have over policy decisions. The methods employed — maps, diagrams and so on — are not culturally neutral but subject to manipulation, failing to access local knowledge with the subtlety demanded by anthropological experience. Furthermore, deciding what to highlight is also an individually informed judgement, the drawer, game-player or whoever controlling the representation and manipulating it according to their interests.

Table 1.5 Types of collaborative research

Unidisciplinary	Multidisciplinary	Interdisciplinary	Transdisciplinary
Independent	Co-ordination	Joint activity	Common set of axioms
Autonomous	Co-operating	Collaboration	Integration
Single responsibility	Conferring	Shared responsibility	Joint thinking
			(after Sands 1993)
Directive	Consultative	Collaborative	Collegiate
			(after Biggs 1989)

We are now trying to forge **indigenous knowledge approaches** to development, drawing on the experiences of farming systems and participatory research. This method-ology seeks to contribute to this process. Many persons with disciplinary backgrounds other than anthropology are engaging in this work (agricultural economists and human geographers, even foresters and plant pathologists). It is difficult as a consequence to define the intellectual stance of local knowledge studies, which are currently very heterogeneous in their approaches, reflecting a healthy interest in any academic approach if relevant to enquiries and developmental problems, although the majority feature straight ethnographic accounts. The result is that local knowledge research currently lacks methodological coherence, indeed it is caught in a battle of perspectives as practitioners tussle in arguments characterised as right versus left, natural versus social science, hard versus soft systems and so on.

1.4 Justification

- **Why bother about indigenous knowledge in development programmes? The added value of indigenous knowledge in international development.**

It is increasingly acknowledged that other people have their own effective 'science' and resource use practices, and that to assist them we need to understand something about their knowledge and management systems. These assumptions underlying indige-nous knowledge research are unexceptionable. The proposition that **an understanding**

and appreciation of local ideas and practices will further development work is beyond dispute. And by paying attention to local perceptions and practices, it is increasingly realised that development initiatives are more likely to be relevant to people's needs and generate sustainable interventions. Indigenous knowledge research sets out explicitly to make connections between local peoples' understandings and practices and those of scientific researchers and development practitioners, notably in the natural resources and health sectors. By furthering our understanding of other's agricultural, forestry and fishing regimes, IK research aims to contribute in the long term to gainful development and positive change, by promoting culturally appropriate and environmentally sustainable adaptations acceptable to people as increasingly they commercially exploit their natural resources.

A premise of indigenous knowledge research is that we need to adopt a more modest stance and allow others to teach us about their understanding of their natural resources, and **generate solutions to jointly perceived problems**, not attempt to impose inappropriate outside ideas because no matter how elegant a solution, scientific or otherwise, if people reject it on cultural grounds it will meet with local disinterest or opposition. While it is increasingly acknowledged as sound sense in development contexts, that where we think that we can offer technical assistance elsewhere based on the scientific approach, people are more likely to respond to it positively if presented sympathetically with regard for their knowledge and understanding, this is a position that has still to be comprehensively validated to be widely accepted. This methodology furthers this objective. One of the central methodological issues of the indigenous knowledge and participation debate is facilitating meaningful communication between scientists and local people to establish what research may have to offer, informing natural science with ethnographic findings about people's knowledge of, and management of their environments and realising the comparative advantages of each, to generate opportunities for synergy.

A central problem with indigenous knowledge in development, is **bridging the gap between our scientifically founded technology and local awareness and practices**. Indigenous knowledge research should serve as a two-way link between local peoples' perceptions and aspirations and scientific technocrats' research agendas. Somehow people need to be aware of the possible alternatives available and the local milieu into which they might be adopted. We think that by informing development with an indigenous knowledge perspective, we might better help people to improve their technologies and natural resources management practices. It is accepted that the scientific tradition has something to contribute to the development process, and that indigenous knowledge needs to be conveyed to natural scientists such that they can appreciate its relevance. The notion of technology transfer remains, not as a top-down imposition but a search for jointly negotiated advances. Participatory approaches seek to accommodate a more systematic role for indigenous knowledge enquiries in the search for scientifically researchable constraints, as opposed to a hit-or-miss strategy in which researchers glean snippets of information during their work, or hear of ethnographic findings elsewhere that they think might apply to their problems too.

How can people be expected to participate, when they do not know, scientifically speaking, what the alternatives and researchable possibilities are facing them? This can only be achieved so far as awareness, knowledge and socio-political barriers will allow. It relates to **informing people about the scope of scientific research** and what it might offer them, so that they can better understand the alternatives available in addressing their problems as they perceive them. It is the promotion of more effective participation in the identification and tackling of researchable constraints, fostering a partnership in decision-making, planning, and so on. A problematic assumption of participatory research is that local people can frame their problems in a manner intelligible to natural resources scientists, which presupposes that they know the range of possible options that face scientists and the techniques and skills which they might bring to bear on their difficulties. Projects need to acquire an informed and sympathetic understanding of the farmers' position through ethnographically informed research, and then seek technological alternatives that comply with their understanding and practices.

Another potential problem with the participatory search for appropriate technological solutions: it may appear to limit people's options to what they perceive of as second best. If scientific expertise is to be brought to bear on their problems, it demands **informed diplomacy to promote participation** and facilitate potential uptake. If farmers are unable to comprehend the economic and environmental constraints on their choices, they may think that they are being deprived of high-tech solutions and fobbed off with cheap intermediate-technology-like alternatives. This is a potential danger if indigenous knowledge and farmer participatory research fail to link up effectively with large-scale renewable natural resources research. They will be perceived to promote only 'low-tech' alternatives, which is not to argue that intermediate technology has no place, for it patently has given many farmers' circumstances, but to point out the dangers of appearing not to offer the opportunity of ever achieving some degree of modern material affluence. The result will be considerable inducement problems, convincing people that there are other alternatives worth trying out.

These issues relate to **informing extension with a local view**. There has been a shift of emphasis from the top down delivery of extension messages prepared by outside experts, persuading and inducing people to adopt procedures that often appear alien and sometimes deprive them of control over their own activities, to consulting more and giving space to local ideas in the research and development process. Any resulting technology will be framed in more familiar contexts, tailored to problems as people perceive them, so that they can assess its worth. The aim is to allow local populations to make informed decisions by informing of alternatives and constraints, promoting information flow in both directions, towards research and development agencies, and towards farmers in technical messages disseminated by extension officers. But the various revisions of extension strategies, like the Training and Visit system, have fallen short of expectations, often because they have failed to bridge successfully between knowledge traditions.

The implication of considering indigenous and scientific perspectives side by side is *not* that we can translate another culture's conceptions about the environment into scientific discourse, nor necessarily that we should test them according to its canons. They both **jointly further understanding of ecological and developmental implications** of human activities, relating to peoples' thoughts about their practices as agents and outsiders perceptions as observers. It is the contention of indigenous knowledge that the two perspectives taken together help us to achieve a more rounded and better understanding of natural and cultural environments, and sustainable development potentials. The objective is not naively to assess the veracity of local idioms against scientific ones, both are relative, but to enrich our overall understanding of environmental interactions and development opportunities within cultural context. The interpretation and assessment of indigenous knowledge against scientific criteria is a contentious issue, related to emerging 'hybrid' studies, an aspect of what others have called the knowledge interface.

Evaluation may be dubious. Science only has a partial and particular knowledge of the complex agro-environmental phenomena to which indigenous knowledge relates, against which to assess it. Nonetheless, **science may complement indigenous knowledge**. It is conceivable that local knowledge may 'get it wrong' according to scientific canons. While there are many examples of indigenous knowledge facilitating peoples' skilful management of their natural resources, we need to guard against any romantic tendency to lionise it. It may be inadequate. This is particularly likely when rapid change occurs, for example population growth making practices inadequate, or when crises occur. This relates to the local nature of indigenous knowledge, a significant barrier to its incorporation into the development process. Some interpret indigenous knowledge enquiry narrowly as identifying such gaps in others' understanding as constraints on production and targeting scientific research and extension to fill them.

There is a possibility, on the other hand, that scientific assessment of indigenous knowledge and practices will vindicate them according to its positivistic canons. It is possible that **indigenous knowledge may advance scientific understanding** of environmental processes. Not only is the need to build on people's perceptions and practices and not do violence to them, increasingly acknowledged, but also the heretical idea is gaining currency that these people may have something to teach us about their environment and its sustainable exploitation. The cross-cultural study of others' knowledge can serve the useful function of challenging the concepts and models of agro-ecological science, although predicting such advances is extremely difficult (e.g. to satisfy funding agencies and justify proposed research programmes). Indeed the potential of indigenous knowledge research has so far been somewhat undersold, until undertaken synergistically in conjunction with scientific enquiry the outcomes are unknown. A commitment to indigenous knowledge research presupposes a regard for others' knowledge traditions, that these are not only valid but also that they may contain valuable intelligence unknown to us, and at the very least represent a point of view that we need sympathetically to accommodate.

We need to allow that others have equally effective, perhaps sometimes more appropriate and environmentally sustainable ways of managing resources, and promote development as a two-way process. Indigenous knowledge research should **help avoid expensive pitfalls**. Development initiatives may start from false premises if they fail to pay attention to local opinion. The lack of respect shown by some scientists for others' knowledge traditions, especially in the past, on the assumption that technological superiority implies answers to all difficulties, has been a considerable developmental barrier, leading not only to misperceptions of problems and inappropriate research, but offensive interference in others' lives, denying them a voice. But the idea persists that we have to help 'them' develop. While it is beyond doubt that science has contributed to considerable technical advances over the last three centuries or so, others have made impressive technological adaptations to their environments too. Alarming rates of environmental pollution, resource squandering, feelings of social alienation and so on underline the limitations of applied science.

The contrasting of indigenous with scientific knowledge should **further the empowerment of poor people** through respect for their knowledge and management practices. While the extreme advocacy of the participation lobby may be difficult for scientists and technicians to accommodate to, it is widely agreed that they should heed its central message that people should have a say over plans and activities that affect their futures. According to the current empowerment debate, local people, and the poor in particular, should have a prominent voice in development contexts. This negotiation applies not only to seeking some consensus over the way forward, how development should proceed and whom it should aim to benefit, but also to coming to some shared understanding of the issues at stake. This implies negotiation across the interface between insider and outsider knowledge, not that one should impose itself but that each should achieve some awareness of the other. We have to come to terms with different cultural perspectives and attempt to reconcile differences that conflict regarding development initiatives.

The promotion of interdisciplinary research. One constituency of stakeholders involved in any negotiations will comprise natural scientists working on development issues. Once it is seen that they are inevitably involved this opens the way to accepting the proposal that development should involve negotiation between all parties. But many scientists are currently sceptical, if not hostile to the promotion of indigenous knowledge and participation, perceiving them as an attack on their specialist status. This is counter-productive, interdisciplinary research is difficult enough without starting off with civil war between different disciplines. A priority in advancing an effective indigenous knowledge methodology is to promote a collaborative atmosphere in which neither scientific nor local interests feel threatened, assuring all parties that they have a role in negotiations, with vital skills and knowledge. This implies demonstrating how awareness of indigenous knowledge and accommodating farmer participation will improve the relevance of scientific research.

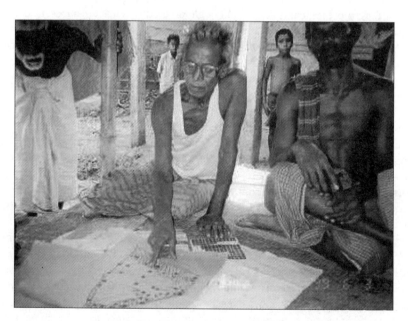

Photograph 1.4: Participatory mapping exercise

We follow an Arnstein's (1969) 'shades of grey' rather than a Chamber's 'black-and-white' approach, and we describe our model of interdisciplinary research involving indigenous knowledge by two sets of continua[3]. There are *interdisciplinarity* issues on

---

[3] Sillitoe has discussed in much greater depth about geometries of knowledge, and the relative positioning of different types of knowledge in three dimensional knowledge space. See Sillitoe, P., Globalising Indigenous Knowledge, in Sillitoe, Bicker & Pottier (2002).

one side and *participation* ones on the other, and linking them together along the continuum is *cross-cultural interdisciplinarity*. Regarding interdisciplinarity Sands (1993) puts forward the continuum below, which corresponds to increasing degrees of inter-personal collaboration. This in turn may be correlated with the participation continuum (Biggs 1989), and increasing interaction between NR users, i.e. farmers and fishers, and researchers or project personnel (Table 1.5). This concept of continua, introduced in defining indigenous knowledge, is a useful overall structuring device for considering the problem of incorporating IK into NR research. As will be seen below (Chapter 2), the concept of continua rather than polar opposites helps to diminish potential conflicts in integrating contrasting knowledge bases, different epistemologies and divergent disciplines, and provide a practical framework for project design.

The participation empowerment debate makes it clear that another aspect of the indigenous knowledge initiative is to **place knowledge in socio-cultural context**. It should not be treated, as some technicians are inclined, as culturally disembodied technical knowledge. The indigenous knowledge perspective advocates viewing natural resources problems in the round, not as isolated constraints to be overcome with techno-logical fixes, because it is rare for production problems to be amenable to straightforward technical solutions subject to scientific investigation for their elucidation. Technical competence can all too easily become technical arrogance, doing damage in development contexts. Development research is not just a question of coming up with technical fixes to others' problems, tackling constraints to production and ameliorating environmental problems by passing over scientifically validated technical information for others to adopt. More often many factors contribute to the perceived constraint, comprising a complex natural and social system. They intimately and unavoidably involve socio-political issues too. Regarding the need for development assistance to be technically apposite, it should be coupled to a cultural awareness. During the negotiation of knowledge process, people will interpret and modify for themselves any scientific-technical information that reaches them in the light of their socio-cultural position and experience. According to the indigenous knowledge approach, scientist-technicians should attempt to anticipate this and facilitate adoption of interventions by developing them in partnership, with an awareness of local social contexts. But this negotiation is demanding, not only because of cross-cultural communication and understanding difficulties, but also because of its inevitable political aspects.

Indigenous knowledge is not locally homogenous. We need to **assess the extent of local variation**. Different interest groups within a country might interpret research findings quite differently, having different perspectives and agendas, and manipulate them accord-ingly, those in more powerful positions attempting to use findings to impose their views on others. Differences will exist along gender, age, class, occupational and other lines, and between individuals of similar social status, although caution should perhaps be exercised overstating the extent to which knowledge varies between people who share a common socio-cultural and linguistic heritage. Whatever, the interpretation people put on shared knowledge may differ, depending on how it affects their interests. There will likely be in-fighting between different interest groups within any community regarding proposed development initiatives. We have to address the issue of whose knowledge we are going to privilege, or can we represent everyone's knowledge, and if so, what is the intellectual status of such all-encompassing knowledge? The privileging of some knowledge above others will extend a degree of power to those who hold that knowledge, or alternatively making it widely known could undermine the position of its holders.

This underlines again that indigenous knowledge research is not socially neutral. The implications of variations in knowledge within local communities demand assessment and the advancement of appropriate methodologies to gauge them.

Indigenous knowledge focused research should also potentially help to **foresee possible social consequences of development initiatives.** Any technical intervention, mediated by indigenous knowledge informed scientific research or not, is likely to have some social impact. The problems are considerably more intractable than they are with pre-intervention indigenous knowledge research, the social sciences having a poor track record when it comes to predicting socio-cultural change. There is a need for considerable methodological research here, to refine social forecasting techniques. If the policy objective is to assist the poor, some idea should be had of how initiatives will impact on current social arrangements, notably relations with the more wealthy and powerful, whose vested interests may prompt them to resist or subvert any changes. The success of facilitatory indigenous knowledge research methods will depend in considerable measure on the appropriateness of options researched, considering the full panoply of socio-political and cultural constraints, through dialogue with specialists in relevant fields and formulated as technical possibilities for farmers, assuming that they are likely to experiment with appropriate alternatives.

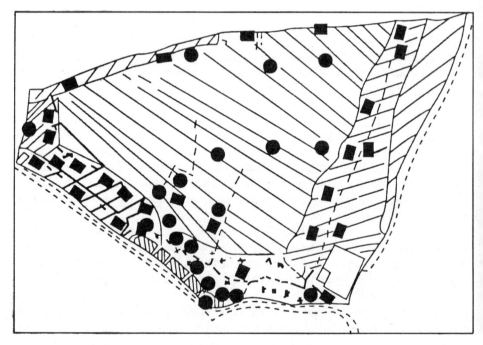

Figure 1.4: Map produced in participatory mapping exercise

1.5 Methodology
- **How do you go about incorporating indigenous knowledge into development programmes and projects? An introduction to methodological issues the methodology.**

If we imagine ourselves at either end of the science to indigenous knowledge continuum, we have two extreme research strategy scenarios. We may have a research team of specialists (e.g. soil scientists) going in with a clear idea of what they think the problem is — e.g. declining organic matter levels. They will arrange a survey of soils and a barrage of physical and chemical tests to demonstrate organic matter status of soils. They may (infected by the participation drive) devise a survey to 'prove'/substantiate their ideas (e.g. asking people about what they use for fuel, plus a leading question about problems finding fuel etc.). They will scratch their heads and come up with a 'solution' to the constraint (but this is frequently divorced from the wider context of the problem). The other extreme is to start with 'free fall' ethnographic enquiries and collegiate participatory methodologies. In this event there is no preconceived idea about what 'the' problem is going to be. The researchers have no control over problem definition, the blueprint notion is redundant, and project management becomes messy and difficult. A wide range of methods may be used to gauge the local situation, and the result is a very complex natural resources systems perspective and cross-culturally informed holistic view. We proceed from this to try and distil out researchable constraints (e.g. for soil scientists, with appropriate experiments etc.). An attempt is made jointly with the local population to puzzle over alternative, appropriate 'development' pathways, sensitive to political game plays etc.

The methodological issue is striving to achieve a productive balance between scientists defining the problem/constraint to be researched (i.e. soil fertility, intercropping or whatever), which is arrogant and ethnocentric (i.e. foreign scientist knows best), and the local people defining the problem/constraint to be researched, when we hit an epistemological brick wall and find scientists unable to cope (their methods are vitiated). We need to devise a methodology that allows both to share the driving seat. How can we go about it? At first sight it seems straightforward enough, we just have to ask some local culture bearers what they think about aphid pests or soil fertility management or tree cultivation or bovine mastitis or fish reproduction or whatever our field of expertise, and problems surrounding it. But the issues rapidly become more complex. We soon run into cross-cultural epistemological problems — that is problems of knowing what we think we know. For example, if we were to ask people in many places about their views of conservation and biodiversity they may look bewildered. They are unlikely to think of these issues in the Rio spirit. A concern for biodiversity is very much an affluent Western preoccupation. If your family is hungry, you are unlikely to give it any priority, even if the issue enters your mind. The implication is not that people fail to consider these issues, but they may do so from a socio-economic position and cultural context quite alien to scientists. It is possible that they may be encompassed in beliefs about spirit forces, mythically expressed preoccupations, and so on. Another issue that complicates the straightforward collection of indigenous knowledge intelligence by 'asking the natives' is that often there is no consensus among the 'natives'. The disagreements may reflect gender, age class and so on, as already pointed out, or they may be less socially structured and randomly ascribed by experience and so on. The local stakeholders are not homogenous, which relates to the socio-political dimension of indigenous knowledge and the significance of wider cultural context. Irrigation in Bangladesh is a case in point. Landowners and sharecroppers are unanimous in their demand for irrigation in the *boro* season, but poor fishermen are less enthusiastic as it reduces the watertable and lowers the levels of perennial waterbodies (the aim of some landowners being to pump them dry for farming, so depriving fishers of a living). The sinking of wells also has political dimensions regarding access to land and water.

We can see from these examples, as already stressed, that one of the central methodological problems facing indigenous knowledge and associated participatory research is facilitating meaningful communication between scientists and local people to establish what research may have to offer, informing natural science with ethnographic findings about people's knowledge of, and management of their environments and realising the comparative advantages of each, to exploit the potential for synergy. A major consideration regarding the incorporation of indigenous knowledge into the development process is producing accounts that relate to other research. We need to avoid the danger of taking the socio-cultural embeddedness issue too far and producing ethnographic accounts which will strike others, notably scientists, as esoteric records which they cannot see having any relation to their work. There is a need to make the connections.

A difficulty with indigenous knowledge research as currently conducted is that it is largely ethnographic reporting of others' productive systems. It is not analytical regarding these systems nor framed to identify and help address scientifically researchable constraints that limit their productivity. It has proved effective in some small-scale NGO work conducted by small teams close to a few communities, notably featuring limited appropriate technology interventions, but has so far had little large-scale impact, failing to inform wider understanding of problems, and regional policy and practice. Even in NGO contexts there is scope for a deeper anthropological awareness among those who advocate both indigenous knowledge and participatory approaches, but in the context of bilaterally and multilaterally funded research and development (e.g. DFID, FAO, USAID etc.) there is an urgent need for it, or else these are in danger of appearing amateurish approaches promoted by social scientists ignorant of technical research. They need a professional edge to penetrate the scientific research establishment. The absence of a coherent indigenous knowledge intellectual framework that might interface effectively with science and technology is a limitation, contributing to natural scientists failing to appreciate it and see how it might inform their research agendas. The up-shot is that indigenous knowledge research appears to contribute to the accumulation of exotic ethnographic documentation and databases which are sterile and undynamic from a developmental perspective, even potentially disempowering people by representing their knowledge in ways inaccessible to them and beyond their control, maybe infringing their intellectual property rights.

The current explosion in database technology will feature prominently in the recording and recalling of ethnographic information and cross-referencing it to relevant development fields, making it readily available to other specialists like foresters, fisheries specialists, soil scientists and so on (discussed in Chapter 3 of this book). The documentation of indigenous knowledge in a manner accessible and congenial to other scientists, such that they can see its relevance to their research, raises considerable methodological problems which should not be underestimated, they are not amenable to any 'quick fix' but require extended and close collaboration between natural scientists and local populations. We need to avoid the jargon-loaded and obscure accounts of some anthropological writing, while not overlooking the advances made, and insights gained by anthropology, into cross-cultural understanding, often in subtle arguments. There is a need to avoid oversimplification of complex issues, inviting distortion and misrepresentation in the search for straightforward accounts of indigenous knowledge phenomena.

It is necessary to get away from the assumption that we can record and document indigenous knowledge and pass it 'up' to interested parties, analogous to the reverse of modernisation's transfer of technological packages 'down' to beneficiaries. The methodology needs to recognise that indigenous knowledge is not static nor uniform, and cannot be documented once-and-for-all, but is subject to continual negotiation between stakeholders. Indigenous knowledge systems are rarely, if ever isolated from the rest of the world, people will incorporate and reinterpret aspects of Western knowledge and practice into their traditions, as pointed out above, an aspect of the on-going globalisation process. Any development project itself should potentially influence indigenous knowledge, the acid evaluation test of success being adoption or modification of local procedures, on the assumption that if worthwhile people will change. The dynamism of indigenous knowledge — that it is continually being renegotiated — increases the difficulties that we face in attempting to represent it. It is a labile process. The negotiated and dynamic status of indigenous knowledge pertains to the theoretical shift in anthropology from a fixed timeless (structural/synchronic) perspective to a fluid historical (process/diachronic) one. But this move from structure to process is proving extremely difficult to operationalise in ethnographic research. It is difficult to break out of the former frame in any field focused ethnographic investigation. And while knowledge never stands still, development aims to accelerate change, dramatically modifying indigenous knowledge systems with scientific perspectives. The time taken to pursue a programme of research into indigenous knowledge and integrate it into a development project will vary with circumstances. It is markedly circumscribed by short time frames. If we hope to accommodate to the dynamic nature of local knowledge we need an iterative research strategy, closely linking natural resources scientists researching production constraints to on-going indigenous knowledge investigations. We discuss this further in Chapter 2 under our notion of the project wave.

The methodological issues are similar seen from the local side, focusing on the promotion of more effective participation in the identification and tackling of researchable constraints, fostering a partnership in decision-making, planning, and so on. This objective can only be achieved so far as awareness, knowledge and socio-political barriers will allow. It relates to informing people about the scope of scientific research and what it might offer them, so that they can better understand the alternatives available in addressing their problems as they perceive them. A problematic assumption of farmer participatory research, as already seen, is that local people can frame their problems in a manner intelligible to natural resources scientists, which presupposes that they know the range of possible options that face scientists and the techniques and skills which they might bring to bear on their difficulties. This relates to indigenous knowledge and extension. It returns us to a central problem with indigenous knowledge in development, namely more effectively connecting along the continuum between our scientifically founded technology at one end and local awareness and practices at the other. Any method needs to promote facilitatory research methods, uniting social science skills with technical and scientific knowledge.

The advancement of interdisciplinary work is central to methodological advances in indigenous knowledge research in development, being critical to combining the empathy of social scientists with the technical know-how of natural scientists, to achieve a sympathetic and in-depth understanding of local farming practices and objectives. But the problems that attend interdisciplinary research are legion, it regularly foundering on the rocks of misunderstanding and unwillingness of specialists to generalise and compromise. This methodology suggests ways to address these problems. A perennial difficulty is communication between specialists. An integrated perspective implies a willingness to learn from one another, in addition to local people. All researchers need to allow indigenous knowledge a place and be willing to learn about local resources management strategies and adapt research programmes accordingly as priorities emerge. The implication is not that the indigenous knowledge component of any research and/or development project should dominate. There must be a genuine two-way flow of ideas and information between all parties. Motivation will depend in considerable measure on fostering consensus decisions, joint ownership and open debate.

The pragmatic foundation of indigenous knowledge means that it is contingent and often local, not systematised and universal, as stressed previously. The ethnographic specificity of indigenous knowledge research and difficulties encountered in formulating generalisations from it applicable on a larger scale present a considerable barrier to its deployment in development. By definition indigenous knowledge research is small-scale, culturally specific and geographically localised, infrequently encompassing regional eco-systems. The scale problem is further exacerbated by the increasing focus of natural resources research and development on marginal and fragile environments away from better endowed regions where high production is achievable, particularly with the advent of high yielding varieties less suited to regions with poorer resources. These marginal and fragile environments are more diverse, making generalisation and the search for widely applicable solutions to production and other problems increasing difficult. This has contributed to indigenous knowledge failing so far to develop an integrated theory relating to its subject matter, indeed why this may not prove possible, for it is difficult to conceive of a single paradigm covering all knowledge traditions worldwide, given their wide variety, their internal variations regarding individuals' unsystematised understandings and their constant revision over time.

There is an urgent need to evolve methods and formulate principles that will facilitate a degree of reliable generalisation from indigenous knowledge research, otherwise we are stuck with the current position of some locally relevant and highly successful project level case studies, which it is not cost effective to replicate in large numbers. These studies contribute to the ethnographic archive amassed by anthropology over several generations but lacking any generic analytical edge will contribute only locally to development efforts. The variation between different societies, even sometimes regions and communities, makes generalisation not only difficult but also potentially dangerous, imputing conclusions that may be incorrect. The experience of comparative studies in anthropology and attempts to uncover cross-culturally universal aspects of human behaviour have been notoriously difficult, and offer little ready guidance. Indeed the problems encountered, and relative lack of success in formulating generalisations about the human condition, suggest that some circumspection may be prudent in the search for generic aspects of indigenous knowledge applicable to development demands.

The methodological task of capturing sympathetically the concepts expressed in local idioms and the import of others' activities is considerable, as anthropologists have long been aware. It is not the scientific component of indigenous knowledge research alone that threatens distortion. In reducing everything to words we constrain understanding. People transfer a deal of environmental knowledge between generations by experiential tradition, one learnt and communicated through practical experience, and are not familiar with trying to express all that they know in words. It is extremely difficult for outsiders to understand convincingly, and to pass on what they learn, particularly within the limitations of a literate intellectual tradition. And employing foreign words and concepts, not just scientific ones, further misconstrues whatever it is that they manage to comprehend about other's views and actions. Heirs to effective systems of natural resource exploitation that have evolved over many generations of experimentation, they follow practices that have agro-ecological implications, sometimes apparently without any need of analytical discourse, articulating a theory of why. Knowledge is passed on by informed experience and practical demonstration, more often shown than spoken, it is as much skill as concept. Knowledge is not codified but diffuse and communicated piecemeal in everyday life, being the product of culturally conditioned events, passed on often by example, transmitted as, and when, events require.

People may also carry environmental knowledge, and transfer it between generations, using quite alien idioms featuring symbols, myths, rites and so on. A sympathetic consideration of such idioms may be central to appreciating some practices and to achieving an understanding of how people manage their natural resources, and their implications for agro-ecological science, regarding intercropping patterns, soil fertility, pest management and so forth. But the methodological problems that attend attempts to access this kind of knowledge, and to convey something about it, are considerable. This is not to suggest that others' knowledge of their environments is expressed in traditions any more esoteric than the scientific one, which is equally impenetrable to many, no less dense than any high priest's liturgy, with its mathematical symbolism and so on! These issues underline the centrality of socio-cultural context in understanding indigenous knowledge, and the misinterpretations invited if it is treated as mere technical information.

Photograph 1.5: Learning by doing: threshing rice

The up-shot is that concepts central to agricultural science may not be appropriate to understanding and documenting local practices. But natural resources development wishes to go further and explain what is happening and what the problems are, and turns to natural science for a theory and concepts. Understanding is inevitably contorted given our unavoidable outsider perspective, although this should not inhibit us from making the effort — we have to accept the inevitable limitations of our research methods, as current 'postmodern' criticism affirms. Any translation of another culture is unavoidably distorting, this development oriented indigenous knowledge work is no different to any other ethnographic enquiry in this respect. It differs in its struggle to combine the hard natural and soft social sciences perspectives in understanding and interpreting other cultures and their environments. This distances it from any fraudulent pretence about achieving an understanding of a foreign population as it understands itself, or worse, better than it understands itself.

While this methodology refers in places to these issues of knowing, it does not explore them in depth. We have discussed them here in the introduction to alert readers to them. And we refer to them further in our discussion of research tools in Chapter 3, as one colleague put it, to serve as a 'health warning' to those unfamiliar with IK research as to how it can go awry in uniformed hands. These issues demand further urgent attention to integrate IK research into the development process. Programme managers who are interested in exploring these contentious issues in more depth are recommended to consult texts on ethnographic method (Agar 1986; Spradley 1980; Werner & Schoepfle 1987a & 1987b; Martin 1995; Bernard 1995 — see bibliography for further reading). It is important that they employ staff on any projects with an IK component who have an awareness of these issues and the methods anthropologists have advanced to handle them.

Any methodology needs to meet the demands of development, although these may compromise anthropological understanding. The time scale involved in ethnographic research is normally considerable which presents problems in development contexts with their short-term orientation and politically driven considerations demanding immediate returns. Whatever approaches are experimented with, one priority should be to convince policy makers, who maleficently drive development with their short-term goals, that indigenous knowledge research is long-term. There is a place for Rapid Rural Appraisal, Participatory Rural Appraisal and so on in some development contexts (and anthropologists *familiar* with a region may be able to undertake such work with a fairly reliable return on their efforts), but these will yield returns quite different to anthropologically informed research. It can take several years, not months or weeks, for someone unacquainted with a region to achieve meaningful anthropological insight into local knowledge and practices, and from this perspective attempt to illuminate technical and other development related problems. The understanding that can be accomplished in a single project cycle will be of a different order. We need to be aware of this point. But it is not to suggest that some sorts of indigenous knowledge research should not be attempted in short time frames. It is necessary to be aware of the possible costs of any necessary compromises, which will entail some intellectual and methodological degradation. It is not just a question of the time it takes to learn language, cultural repertoire, social scenario and so on, but also the investment needed to win the trust and confidence of people who frequently have reason to be extremely suspicious of foreigners and their intentions. These points relate further to contentious ethical issues.

The central anthropological dictum of context (holism) relates to long-term perspective and anticipates the dynamic and negotiated status of indigenous knowledge research. The discipline learnt long ago that it is not possible to predict beforehand which cultural domains might relate intimately with others, and that we need constantly to maintain a broad view, often the least expected practices impinging on one another, for example religious observances influencing certain production activities. While the interconnectivity of issues is acknowledged in development contexts, as evidenced in approaches such as 'integrated rural development' and 'farming systems research', these have fallen foul of the time pressures of development. Any methodology needs to strike a balance between the requirement of achieving a detailed understanding of something, which by definition implies narrowing the field of enquiry, without becoming too narrowly focused and overlooking connections to other issues, distorting understanding. In indigenous knowledge research it amounts to maintaining a broad sociocultural perspective to contextualise the tightly focused view of technical specialists. We discuss these issues further in Chapter 2 using our IK project design cube, which focuses on the key issues of resources, time and aims.

The demands of development present some interesting methodological challenges and invite us to experiment. Perhaps it would prove more time and cost effective in development contexts to employ nationals from any region as indigenous knowledge investigators instead of outsiders. Already familiar with language and culture, they may proceed with the necessary research more quickly and effectively. There are other issues that recommend this strategy relating for example to the contentious matter of intellectual property rights. Adequately briefed indigenous researchers could warn people of the issues and together they could decide on the most appropriate course of action regarding potentially exploitable knowledge without commercially influenced outsider interference. But this approach predictably has pitfalls too. In the first place, there is the danger of creating gate-keepers who accumulate power, influencing overly the lives of others, for instance regarding their rights, although this danger applies equally to outsiders as insiders. In the second place, it may subvert anthropological enquiry which assumes that outsiders 'see' things differently to insiders and ask awkward questions, for example religious beliefs and observances are beyond question to many people. In the third place, finding nationals willing to undertake anthropological research, which may involve living with poor and looked-down-upon members of society for extended periods of time, is a potential problem, with 'loss of face' implications. And poor local people may be even more suspicious of the intentions and motives of a privileged and educated fellow country person than they would be of a less informed and interested foreigner. One answer is a mixture of personnel, with different disciplinary and cultural backgrounds, briefed to consider indigenous knowledge issues as part of their interdisciplinary work, although this raises further potentially tricky issues relating to balance of work, co-ordination, facilitation and so on. It is the option explored further in this methodology, discussed in Chapter 2 under staffing issues. It poses intriguing questions for anthropological method regarding the relatively little explored intellectual implications of cross-cultural academic collaboration, of anthropological outsiders with sociological insiders working together with natural scientists. Furthermore, while any sensitive individual can become acquainted with anthropological research methods — just as anyone can learn technical matters relating to irrigation, soil erosion, plant breeding or whatever — we think that these are best advanced upon within the discipline that has experience of the problems that attend them. It makes sense to proceed from, and so anticipate, mistakes already made, and ethical dilemmas already faced. Hence this methodology is informed by accepted anthropological approaches, on which it attempts to innovate to meet the requirements of natural resources research and development.

It is widely agreed in development circles that it is necessary to appreciate something about local perspectives, the problem is how to achieve this and contribute meaningfully to the development effort. The formulation of appropriate methodologies involves more than the straightforward import of tried and tested anthropological methods into the development research repertoire, of transferring techniques such as participant-observation, sample surveys, case histories etc. (Agar 1986; Spradley 1980; Werner & Schoepfle 1987; Bernard 1995) These are a start, and might be refined to meet development demands, as we attempt in Chapter 3 of this report. We seek to formulate research strategies that meet the demands of development — cost-effective, time-effective, generating appropriate insights, readily intelligible to non-experts etc. — while not compromising anthropological expectations, so downplaying the difficulties as to render the work effectively valueless. We anticipate that managers and policymakers will assess any attempts to innovate on current ethnographic techniques according to their resource effectiveness (time, cost, development relevance, and so on). We stress the need to set these demands against the range of information collected and its reliability, the assessment of which will be central to attempts to demonstrate the effectiveness of indigenous knowledge research in development.

2 Design and Management of Indigenous Knowledge Projects

2.1 Design and Management of Projects

The design and management of projects that incorporate indigenous knowledge is a balancing act, as with so much in life. It is a compromise between what would be theoretically and intellectually the ideal solution and what is feasible given the available resources. The second chapter of the book is focused on the practical and technical issues of designing and managing projects that incorporate an IK component. The aim is to provide guidance on achieving the balance appropriate to individual projects. It is not prescriptive, but provides a range of menus from which a project manager can choose a suitable recipe for a particular project scenario.

Photograph 2.1: Boatmen

This section of the report makes the assumption that the project manager is convinced of the merit of incorporating indigenous knowledge into his/her project, but is uncertain of the how to go about it within certain resource limitations, and requires some guidelines to make informed choices about the techniques and options that are available. The following is designed to guide project leaders and managers through the key issues in this trade-off between the pragmatic and the theoretically ideal by providing them with aids to project design, accompanied by appropriate debate on the consequences of making particular choices.

2.2 Project Design Considerations

We present the design of projects incorporating indigenous knowledge as series of decision cubes. Firstly, we discuss design issues generally such as staffing, methods, results etc. rather than repetitively going over them for each decision cube. Secondly, we present eight cube combinations, referring only to design issues as necessary for each.

The key project design issues are:

1. Project Cycle Management.
2. Staff.
3. Data Collection Methods.
4. Data Analysis Tools.
5. Outputs.

2.2.1 The project

Project Cycle: Project Cycle Management (PCM) is a rigorous approach that drives projects through specific mandatory stages (Figure 2.1), usually at a certain, predetermined rate. It results in well designed projects that should be efficiently executed, with a good chance of success. In DFID and many other donor contexts, it is closely associated with the logical framework PCM tool. One of the problems with this management strategy for IK research is that it tends to be rather restrictive. It inclines towards the 'blueprint' approach to development when IK research demands a more flexible 'process' approach to be effective.

The factors that make IK important in projects, have a similar foundation to those factors which have made participatory approaches to research and development both accepted and desired by funding agencies, as discussed in Chapter 1. Thus the issues raised by DFID's Participatory Approaches Learning Study (PALS) in examining the incorporation of participatory approaches into PCM are similar to those faced in trying incorporate IK into project design. PALS states that:

> In participatory development interventions, the planning phase in a project is essential for establishing links and building trust with stakeholders, learning about the conditions, circumstances and the priorities of those at the primary level, identifying possible projects and developing goals, objectives and strategies that are appropriate, realistic and sustainable within the particular cultural and institutional environment. This suggests an intensive period of consultation, listening and discussion, and sensitive research to establish a baseline for programme planning, monitoring and evaluation. Such a process might include social, gender, risk and stakeholder analysis, participatory needs assessment. Workshops for consulting stakeholders, and similar exercises.

> INTRAC (1999)

In regard to 'normal' PCM, the PALS conclusion was that this type of consultation process (which is analogous in part to an IK study) demands a slower and more far reaching process. It requires greater involvement of primary stakeholders. This has significant implications for the manner in which IK should be included in the design of NR projects and project cycle management. In particular, if primary beneficiaries' views are genuinely considered important, participatory approaches, and hence IK studies should be undertaken:

- over longer time periods;
- in more depth;
- before other activities.

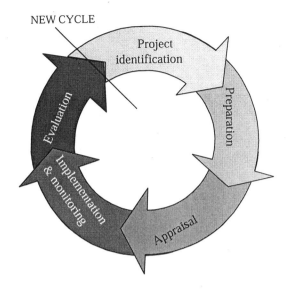

NEW CYCLE

Figure 2.1: The project cycle

In undertaking an IK study and consulting local people prior to commencing Natural Resources (NR), or other research, the IK component becomes either a part of the 'preparation' phase of PCM, or a project in its own right. There is however a difficulty with this chronology. There is a re-occurring and major problem of **synchronisation** in interdisciplinary projects, particularly those that attempt to combine social sciences and natural sciences. It is true that, as indicated by PALS' conclusions, natural science research is likely to be better focused and develop solutions more relevant to local people, if some IK research has been conducted beforehand, at the very least as a scoping exercise. The preferred solution is to commence a cycle of IK study in advance of the NR research. This IK research would produce results that could feed into the project planning phase of the NR research project cycle. We call this arrangement part of the project wave (Figure 2.2).

Box 2.1: Project wave series of projects (1)

The 'projects wave' concept (Figure 2.2) is a series of interlinked project cycles that inform and energise one another. Information flows from one project to another: IK→NR research →NR development. Eventually the wave reaches a point where a new problem is met or IK needs to be re-visited, requiring further IK study and the series starts a second cycle. This does not lead to endless and unaccountable research; monitoring and evaluation are built into component project cycles.

This concept, with IK being re-visited, also relates to IK being a dynamic resource. A weakness of capturing IK into computer databases (see Section 3.22 — Data Analysis Tools) is that the collected IK becomes stagnant or reified. IK collection is unlike, for example soil survey, which can be done once. Local knowledge is constantly in flux, and a project cycle design is required that permits reiteration of research.

Such a project wave is recommended as the ideal solution where resource and time are abundant (Section 2.3: cube 3 and cube 4, and to a lesser extent cube 1 and cube 2). Nonetheless, there are two problems with this approach:

• Development has a demand for prompt answers.

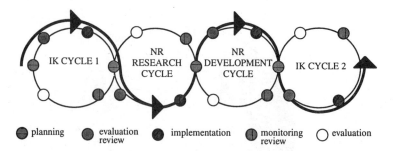

Figure 2.2: A series of linked project cycles creating a project wave

- Scientific understanding of the NR problem is often needed to focus the IK investigation.

The first of these problems — development's demand for answers and new knowledge — relates to the Time dimension of the IK project cube. The project wave scenario is constrained by the pragmatics of programme management. Research programme agendas are driven forward by performance targets that do not currently permit extensive IK investigations. Furthermore, similar agendas drive NR research projects such that NR researchers are not normally able to wait for an IK scoping study to report before commencing their studies. Thus, although the model in Figure 2.3c would be ideal, the model in Figure 2.3a is likely to be more normal, where the various research components run concurrently. This model can function, so long as team members exchange of information effectively (see Section 2.6.1 — Team Communication). One response to this compromise, which is due to Time constraints, is for project managers to lobby for longer project cycles to be adopted, if they think that the trade-offs in the quality/scope of the research due to short time frames are unacceptable. Indeed, the concept of fewer, longer projects is presently being debated within DFID (P. Harding, DFID CRF programme, *pers. comm.*).

Photograph 2.2: Women taking part in problem census workshop

The second problem is the 'chicken-and-egg' variety. A cogent argument has been presented for commencing the IK investigation first. But without NR scientists gaining some understanding of the natural environment through their own baseline research, the IK study may lack focus, and thus proceed as a more open-ended ethnographic investigation. The variable of concern here is thus the Scope dimension of the IK project cube. Where the NR problem is conceived of as more technical or closer to basic science, then a PCM model wherein the NR research commences first is likely to occur (Figure 2.3b). In these circumstances IK is seen as important to the problem only once the NR research has been designed or once uptake of the solution is addressed. Such 'bolt-on' IK is not a recommended approach as the IK is less likely to become integrated into the NR research.

Box 2.2: Project wave series of projects (2)

An IK component can be introduced anywhere on the wave. It is recommended that it precede the NR research (Figures 2.2 and 2.3c). The IK and NR research cycles may have to run concurrently rather than in series (Figure 2.3a). A further variation is undertaking the IK component as a secondary part of a NR project (Figure 2.3b). This would be a small IK cycle as a satellite to the NR research or NR development project cycle, not a precursor. This type of IK study will be brief with limited scope, and able to employ only limited methods.

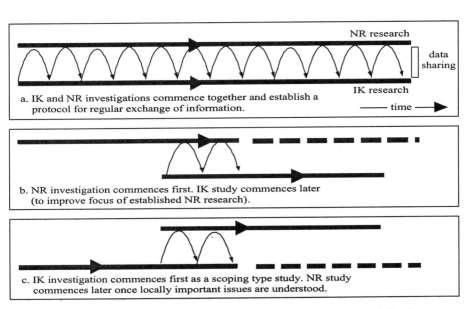

a. IK and NR investigations commence together and establish a protocol for regular exchange of information.

b. NR investigation commences first. IK study commences later (to improve focus of established NR research).

c. IK investigation commences first as a scoping type study. NR study commences later once locally important issues are understood.

Figure 2.3: Options for synchronising IK and NR Component Studies

Project Design: Environmental issues and sustainability are now recognised as important considerations in project design. This prompts demands that projects consider what influence they will have beyond their lifetimes. This highlights the relevance of using local knowledge and building local institutional capacity. This has lead to the recognition that "local knowledge of institutional and farming matters needs to be understood and incorporated into project management practice" (Dennis, 1993). A key issue is how to incorporate IK into the design phase of an NR project. Empowering or 'functional' participatory research faces the same issues — how can local people and local peoples' views be involved at the design stage of a project, instead of involving them as consultees and collaborators once the project has commenced? There are many options for designing an NR-IK study to address these issues, including:

- IK Terms of Reference (TORs) emerge from NR studies. NR research tackles a problem, but brings in an IK component later to address an NR problem. Some field work would be in concert with NR studies, but the IK study would probably be written up as a separate report.
- TORs for IK research are only loosely defined prior to the studies commencing, interaction with NR studies helps define the studies. This assumes as above that the NR research will commence first. The relative chronology of the IK and NR research is considered in depth in the previous section, Project Cycle Management. Field work would be in concert with NR studies, there would be iterative exchange of information, and the output would be a joint NR-IK report.
- IK staff are explicitly included in the NR project design phase, rather than bringing them in later as an after thought, or bolting on IK as side contract. IK will thus be better integrated into the NR project, and the IK TORs will link better to the NR studies.
- IK research would precede any NR study, and it would help to define the NR TORs. IK studies would help local people set NR study agenda, thus the output of the IK study would be used in drawing up NR TORS.

These options will be appropriate in different circumstances. Type (1) IK studies (see page 57) may have the TORs decided in advance by NR personnel, whereas Type (3) studies, featuring greater involvement of local people, will be more responsive to local context. In general, the earlier IK staff are involved, and the more local input there is, the better the quality (in terms of trustworthiness, reliability, rigour, and validity) of the IK outputs.

Whichever model is selected, it should be flexible. The less structured research paradigm of IK studies and anthropological methods do not lend themselves to blueprint approaches. The normal review stages of a process project should be part of the TORs.

Photograph 2.3: Monsoon flooding around homesteads

2.2.2 Staff

It is now routine for a team of researchers to conduct most NR research for development; the team members will usually be selected on the basis of a disciplinary strength plus ability to work in a broad mode, encompassing participatory methods and familiarity with, or sympathy to, socio-economic analysis and the socio-cultural context of the research. This is particularly so given current emphasis on the Sustainable Livelihoods approach. Team members obviously have to be able to work effectively together if the potential synergy of interdisciplinary working is to be realised. The issues in managing research teams are covered in Section 2.6.1 — Team Management. This section addresses the strengths and weaknesses of individuals tasked to undertake the IK component of a project. If we ensure that all team members have some familiarity with participatory methods, staff from a range of disciplinary backgrounds should be able to contribute to some of the IK research.

Staffing Issues: The IK research of a project may be undertaken by staff ranging in experience from novices, such as undergraduates and young field staff, to experts such as senior NGO staff, consultants and university professors. Every type of staff member has their strengths and weaknesses from a project design perspective, such as previous experience in the locality, expertise in IK methods, language ability and cost of hiring them. These strengths and weaknesses are summarised in Table 2.1. In addition to these general characteristics, there will be a number of factors specific to individuals that

Table 2.1 Staff factors that relate to the project design criteria of Resources, Time and Objectives

Staff factor	Resources	Time	Objectives
Gender	–	–	Female staff may face problems in some societies: male staff may find problems accessing IK held by females.
Ethnicity	Local staff often cheaper. Also should know the language of the area, so costs of translation are saved.	–	Local staff may find it difficult to 'step outside the culture' and make impartial analyses or undertake comparative analysis with other countries and regions.
Seniority	Seniority usually equates with cost.	Senior staff are usually busy people – may have little available time.	Seniority usually equates with experience.
IK/ anthropology experience	More experience generally equates to higher day-rates, but the trade-off may be in terms of flexibility to work with NR scientists.	With wider experience of methods, may be able to select more efficient methods.	Methodological experience should ensure reliable outputs, but anthropological training may also drive them towards too much detail or less relevant areas for the NR project.
NR experience	More experience equates to higher day-rates, trade-off is increased ability to address the objectives.	–	IK staff with NR experience are few, but should be able to better address more ambitious TORs.
Local experience	–	Staff who have previously worked in the area should already have knowledge of the cultural, political, economic, etc. basics of the area, and can more rapidly address the project issues.	–

(Contd.)

(Continued)

Staff factor	Resources	Time	Objectives
Language ability	–	Relates to local experience - knowledge of the language speeds up the process.	Knowledge of the language may improve the reliability of the information collected.
Employer	Consultancy staff are usually more expensive than NGO or university staff. Research institutes are usually somewhere in the middle (Table 2.6).	Consultancy staff will be available for the contracted time. University staff may have to juggle availability with term-times, but can often draw-in resources (e.g. research students) above what is paid for.	University staff may be able to call on institutional resources (staff, library, etc.) to give an extra dimension when considering broad objectives.
The 'I' factor	–	–	IK studies in NR projects will by default by undertaken in an interdisciplinary manner. The ability of staff to interact and be interdisciplinary bears very little relation to the other factors – it is a personal attribute that relates to their attitude and approach. This personal chemistry, dubbed here the 'I' factor needs to be considered in selecting staff to include on a successful team, but is difficult to predict.

will affect the value of their project contribution and the results of their research. Team leaders selecting staff for an NR-IK (or any other) research study should consider:

- What level of competition with other projects is there for the individual's time. How heavily committed are they to other projects? Though involvement in several projects can add value and facilitate synergy of methods and ideas, over-commitment can result in chronic under performance with the time committed to any one project being too low.
- What other time commitments does the individual have? In addition to NR-IK research, what other research are they involved in, what teaching (in academia), administration, supervision demands are there? How good are their time management skills to organise these competing demands? Do not over-look time for leave, for family, and for other non-work demands.
- Apart from altruism, what incentives are there for the individual to perform: financial rewards, travel opportunities, equipment budget, research income, professional prestige and recognition, opportunities to further research interests, opportunities to publish, opportunities to attend conferences? Team leaders should aim to ensure that expected rewards are realistic and clear to team members, and that all team members are valued by the team.

These staffing considerations will apply to varying degrees to all potential IK personnel. The following are the most probable types of personnel from which a project manager will have to select staff (Table 2.2).

The majority of these staff will be located within the university/research institute sector, either in the UK and other developed countries, or in the country(s) in which the project is taking place. The senior staff (15-20) and junior staff (7-14) may also be found in the consultancy sector. Academia and consultancy have their own advantages and disadvantages for this type of work (Table 2.3). Other staff (e.g. 3, 4, 8 and 10) may also be based in NGO sector.

Photograph 2.4: Spear fishing from raft

Table 2.2 Types of staff that may undertake an IK-NR investigation

1	village enumerators — trained in IK work by an ethnographer
2	national ethnographer from the study area
3	senior national NGO workers with social science training/experience
4	junior national NGO workers with social science training/experience
5	undergraduate sociologist — national
6	undergraduate anthropologist — foreigner
7	national graduate NR scientist with interest in IK work
8	foreign graduate NR scientist with interest in IK work[1]
9	graduate sociologist — national
10	graduate anthropologist — foreigner[1]
11	national postgraduate NR scientist with interest in IK work
12	foreign postgraduate NR scientist with interest in IK work
13	postgraduate sociologist — national
14	postgraduate anthropologist — foreigner
15	experienced national NR scientist with interest in IK work
16	experienced foreign NR scientist with interest in IK work
17	experienced national social scientist with NR science background too
18	experienced foreign anthropologist with NR science background too
19	experienced sociologist — national
20	experienced anthropologist — foreigner

Note: [1]Might be a VSO-type volunteer.

Those staff more strongly associated with the project locality because they live and/ or work in the area (1-4), have the advantage of more easily accessing local networks. This group also has an advantage for using methods to access IK that follow people-first/empowerment principles, facilitating local people to express and collate their IK themselves. We need to balance against these strengths in IK work various constraints imposed on residents of a locality. They are part of, and influenced by, social norms and mores and by local politics and power issues to a greater extent than external

Table 2.3 Contrasts in institutional backgrounds of IK researchers

Academic	Consultant
Long term engagement with the topic (+)	Applied to topic only for contract duration (–)
Many competing demands on time (–)[1]	Focused on topic throughout contract (+)
Good access to supporting resources (library, IT, colleagues, students) (+)	Isolated (–)
Academic goals may not match with project goals (–)	Goals are the project goals (+)
May tend towards the analytical/theoretical (+/–)	May tend towards the practical/pragmatic (+/–)

Note: [1]Senior academic staff inputs are not always short-term, with commitments to teaching, supervising, publishing, other research, etc. Academic staff may take sabbatical and dedicate themselves wholly to a particular study, or they may charge for their inputs in order to buy in replacement staff to undertake teaching, and so have more time to allocate to the research project.

researchers. In 'Sustainable Livelihoods' terms, the IK they collect may be skewed as a result by 'local institutions', being active players in transforming structures and processes (Scoones, 1998, Ahmed, 2000).

The membership of NR-IK research teams may be dictated by membership of existing teams or research institutes. Where a choice exists, cost, amount of time available to the project and familiarity with different methods will all combine to affect the most suitable staffing for different types of project. The factors to consider in selecting staff can be presented in a modified SWOT analysis — called here the SWOC matrix (strengths, weaknesses, opportunities, constraints) — see Table 2.4. This SWOC analysis should prove a useful tool to appraise project options, as different categories of staff will be appropriate to different types of IK research in NR projects.

We can relate staffing options to the three axes of the IK decision cube for project design. Managers need to appraise the different staffing options according to the resources needed to employ personnel (cost), their availability (time), and their experience and likely expertise with different research methods (scope). While the resources available for the IK study will determine the type of staff that a project can afford and for how long, the manager has considerable room for manoeuvre. The manager has to play off cost against the project's aims and quality of data these demand in relation to staff availability. Some staff options (such as senior academics) may not be available even if the budget is sufficient. These multi-factorial issues are presented in Table 2.6, which is a matrix of budget against experience, availability, methods and quality of eventual outputs.

Some Staff Examples: In our IK and NR research project in Bangladesh, we tried to address some of the staffing issues and concerns in an innovative manner. Worthy of separate mention are experiences with five particular staff types:

1. Bangladeshi environmental science masters graduate, employed as a (para-) anthropologist.
2. Bangladeshi anthropology masters graduate, employed as an anthropologist.
3. UK anthropology undergraduate, of Bengali ethic origin, undertaking an IK dissertation.
4. UK professor with post-graduate degrees in soil and crop science, and anthropology.
5. UK NR research scientists in soil, crop and fisheries sciences.

The project employed two national (Bangladeshi) masters graduates as Research Assistants (RAs), responsible for the day-to-management of the field bases and the

Table 2.4 SWOC matrix for potential staff on NR-IK Projects

Staff Discipline type	Experience/ Qualification	Ethnicity	Gender	Status	Strengths	Weaknesses	Opportunities	Constraints
1. or 4.	1ry/2ry School	National	M	J/M	Immersed in local culture. Local language and dialect speaker. Should know key informants	Lacks comparative experience or outsider's objective view. No formal training. May not be literate.	Issues relating to type of output. Biases.	Can provide long-term contact. No dependent on field visits if living in/is from the village. Bound by cultural mores.
			F	J/M	-do-	-do-	-do-	
8. NR sciences/ +(NR & IK)/ NRM	MSc	Foreign	M	J/M	Some respect as a technological gatekeeper	Not influential (but ? inferred respect from supervisor). Lack of relevant experience. Dependent on others for basics of IK approach	Keen. Has time for focused study.	Culture shock. Language. (illness)
			F	J/M	Some respect as a technological gatekeeper. 'Honorary man'.	Less influential (but ? inferred respect from supervisor). Lack of relevant experience. Dependent on others for basics of IK approach.	Keen. Has time for focused study. May have access to women.	Culture shock. Language. (illness)
10. Anthropo-logy	+ (anthro)/ BA	Foreign	M	J	Basic anthropology training.	Not influential (but ? inferred respect from supervisor). Lack of relevant experience.	Keen. Has time for focused study.	Culture shock. Language. (illness)
			F	J	Basic anthropology training. 'Honorary man'.	Less influential (but ? inferred respect from supervisor). Lack of relevant experience.	Keen. Has time for focused study. May have access to women.	Culture shock. Language. (illness)

(Contd.)

(Continued)

Staff Discipline type	Experience/ Qualification	Ethnicity	Gender	Status	Strengths	Weaknesses	Opportunities	Constraints
10a. Anthropology/Sociology (rural)	+++ (socio)/ BA	Diaspora	M	J	Ethnic local. Local language speaker. Basic anthropology training.	Not influential - difficult to drawn down resources. May speak different dialect.	Keen. Has time for focused study.	Culture shock. Language. (illness). May have to adhere to culture mores. May be directed or protected by blood relations. The experience can lead to questioning own identity and open up post-modern concerns about anthropology.
			F	J	-do-	-do-	Keen. Has time for focused study. May have access to women.	
13. Sociology (rural)	+ to ++ (socio)/ PhD	National	M	J/M	Open-minded – no preconceived ideas of NR structure into which to fit IK	No familiarity with NR leads to long learning curve and risk of irrelevance. Junior – not influential – may find it difficult to hold respondeds' attention.	Native language speaker. Anthropology/ rural sociology training.	Genuinely native to the subject matter. Should adhere to cultural mores; little access to women. Educational system may not have fostered innovative thinking and independent research.
			F	J/M	-do-	-do- may be considered even more junior/ lower	-do-	-do- though has better access to female respondents.
15. NR sciences/ NRM	+to ++ (NR & IK)/PhD	National	M	J/M	Familiar with NR systems.	Closed-mind: NR science training and education fosters a positivist mentality. Has an established framework of knowledge and world view.	Native language speaker. Already familiar with the local NRs and environment.	Educational system may not have fostered innovative thinking and independent research. NR science training may have fostered rigid thinking. Should adhere to cultural mores; little access to women.
			F	J/M	-do-	-do- may be considered even more junior/lower	-do-	-do- though has better access to female respondents.

(Contd.)

(Continued)

Staff Discipline type	Experience/ Qualification	Ethnicity	Gender	Status	Strengths	Weaknesses	Opportunities	Constraints
16. NR sciences/ NRM	+++ (NR & IK)/PhD	Foreign	M	S	Open to new ideas. Familiar with PRA approaches. Has a clear scientific framework for describing natural resources, soils, fisheries, crops, forestry, etc.	Scientific framework is often epistemologically at odds with an IK framework. Works with resource-centred, not people-centred paradigms.	Willing to work with anthropologists/social scientists to develop shared understanding. Familiarity with PRA approaches may lead to lack of real depth in IK approaches.	Language. Short visits. Unfamiliar with open/ethnographic approaches. Access to female respondents.
			F	S	-do-	-do-	-do-	-do- though has better access to female respondents.
17. Sociology (rural)	+++ (socio & NR)/PhD	National	M	S	Experience, familiarity with local culture. Probably hands-on experience with PRA methods and farming systems tools.	Lack of time: multi-tasking work environment.	Understands the language, and historical and cultural context – rapid entree. Has a holistic view.	May be bound by local culture. Access to female respondents. Very few exist – in heavy demand.
			F	S	-do-	(though less of an 'upper')	may be better aware of gender issues	May be bound by local culture. Very few exist – in heavy demand.
18. Anthropology	+++ (anthro & NR)/PhD	Foreign	M	S	Training, experience, multidisciplinary perspective.	Lack of time: multi-tasking work environment. May be viewed Chambers' 'upper' – middle class – foreign academic. Natural scientist cum anthropologist – versed in NR and ethnographic (IK) issues.	Can work more independently if necessary.	Language (in 'home' research region probably fluent). Probably short visits. Few such polymaths exist. Access to female respondents.
			F	S	-do-	-do- (though less of an 'upper'	-do- and may be better aware of gender issues.	Language. Probably short visits. Few such polymaths exist. Access to male respondents.

(Contd.)

(Continued)

Staff Discipline type	Experience/ Qualification	Ethnicity	Gender	Status	Strengths	Weaknesses	Opportunities	Constraints
19. Sociology (rural)	+++ (socio)/ PhD	National	M	S	Experience, familiarity with local culture. Probably hands-on experience with PRA methods.	May not have the same breadth of comparative experience.	Understands the language, and historical and cultural context – rapid entree.	May be bound by local culture. Access to female respondents.
			F	S	-do-	-do-	-do- and may be better aware of gender issues.	May be bound by local culture. Access to male respondents.
20. Anthropology	+++ (anthro)/ PhD	Foreign	M	S	Training, experience, comparative knowledge.	Lack of time: multi-tasking work environment. May be viewed Chambers' 'upper'[1] – middle classes, middle age, white male academic. May not have hands-on experience with PRA tools.	Knowledge of ethnographic methods and comparative studies.	Language (poss. fluent). Probably short visits. Access to female respondents. Respondents may be overly differential. Anthropologists tend to be ethnically or geographically specialised (e.g. 'Africanists').
			F	S	-do-	Lack of time: multi-tasking work environment.	-do- and may be better aware of gender issues.	Language (poss. fluent). Probably short visits. Access to male respondents.

Notes: This table is meant to be generic to various locations and peoples, but is informed by work in Bangladesh, and this is reflected in comments on gender issues, seniority, etc.

Key experience: +++ = 10 yrs +   Age (equates to seniority and respect):   S = Senior

                    ++ = 5 yrs   M = Middle

                    + = 1-2 yrs   J = Junior

---

1 'Upper' is a term used by Chambers (1997) to denote a privileged person.

Table 2.5 Key to Table 2.6 and Table 2.9

Factor	Code	Explanation
Experience	+++	10 yrs +
(in relation to IK)	++	5 years
	+	1-2 years
	–	< 1 year
Methods	S	Simple/easy to use
(ease of use)	M	Moderately easy to use
	D	More difficult to use
	C	Difficult and complex to use
Output quality	H	High
(in relation to IK)	MH	Medium-high
	A	Average/acceptable
	V	Variable
Availability	FT/PT	Full-time/Part-time
(primarily for field work)	1/2/3/4 Q/yr	Part-time input is 0-3, 3-6, 6-9, or 9-12 months a year.
	< 1m/> 1m	In blocks of more than or less than 1 month.
Cost	a	Day rate < £50/day
(based on charge-out)	b	Day rate £50 to £100/day
rates, not salary at Jan	c	Day rate £100 to £250/day
2000 values)	d	Day rate £250 to £500/day
	e	Day rate > £500/day

Table 2.6 Inputs and outputs of different types of staff

Code	Staff type	Experience	Methods (to use)	Output quality/ relevance	Availability		Cost
					Academic	Consultant	
1	Village enumerators – trained in IK work by local ethnographer	- to +	S	V	–	F/P	a–
2	Local ethnographer	+ to +++	S-M	V-MH			a
3	Senior national NGO workers with social science training/ experience	++ to +++	S-D	A-MH	–		a/b-c
4	Junior national NGO workers with social science training/experience	+	S-M	V-A	–		a
5	Undergraduate sociologist – national	–	S	V	PT-1, > 1m	–	a
6	Undergraduate anthropologist – foreigner	–	S	V	PT-1†, >1m	–	a
7	National graduate NR scientist with interest in IK work	+	S-M	V-A	FT		a
8	Foreign graduate NR scientist with interest in IK work[1]	+	S-M	V-A	FT	FT	a
9	Graduate sociologist – national	+	S-M	V-A			a
10	Graduate anthropologist – foreigner	+	S-M	V-A	FT	FT	a/b

(Contd.)

(Continued)

Code	Staff type	Experience	Methods (to use)	Output quality/ relevance	Availability		Cost
					Academic	Consultant	
11	National postgraduate NR scientist with interest in IK work	+ to ++	S-D	A-MH	F/P-3/4, >1m	FT	a
12	Foreign postgraduate NR scientist with interest in IK work	+ to ++	S-D	A-MH	F/P-3/4, >1m	FT	b/c
13	Postgraduate sociologist – national	+ to ++	S-D	A-MH	F/P-3/4, >1m	FT	a/b
14	Postgraduate anthropo-logist – foreigner	+ to ++	S-D	A-MH	F/P-3/4, >1m	FT	b/c
15	Experienced national NR scientist with interest in IK work	+++	S-C	MH-H	PT-1, <1m	FT	a-c
16	Experienced foreign NR scientist with interest in IK work	+++	S-C	MH-H	PT-1, <1m	FT	d/e
17	Experienced national social scientist with NR science background too	+++	S-C	H	PT-1, <1m	FT	b-d
18	Experienced foreign anthropologist with NR science background too	+++	S-C	H	PT-1, <1m	FT	d/e
19	Experienced sociologist – national	+++	S-C	H	PT-1, <1m	FT	b-d
20	Experienced anthropo-logist – foreigner	+++	S-C	H	PT-1, <1m*	FT	d/e

Notes: [1]Might be a VSO-type volunteer or an intern; *(PT-1, <1m) for all academic staff, unless on sabbatical leave or their time is bought out in substantial chunks, e.g. as a secondment; [†]unless on sandwich year, etc., when FT.

collection of much of the primary IK data. These RAs were also both registered as PhD candidates in anthropology at the UK university leading the project. Their PhD theses provided the main analysis of the primary data. Boxes 2.3 and 2.4 reflect on the main issues surrounding this approach to staffing an IK project.

Box 2.3: National natural sciences graduate

One of the RAs had a first degree in botany and masters degree in environmental science. His masters supervisor has a keen interest in IK and ethno-botany, but the formal Bangladeshi science education is a traditional one.

The project aimed to develop a broad understanding of Natural Resource Management (NRM) on the floodplains. It was not directed towards a specific technical or social problem, thus the data collection method was similarly broad. This required him to employ an open-ended ethnographic 'snow-balling' method. This fluid and unstructured method was difficult for this RA, who, coming from a science background, sought a more structured framework of investigation. Taking a science graduate as a field anthropologist or para-anthropologist may be more successful where the topic of study is a more tightly focused technical problem.

The IK was collected mainly through open-ended interviews, which were word-processed into near verbatim transcripts in the evening. Coming from a science background, this

RA tended to transform the IK in the transcripts into scientific terms. For example rather than recording soil as *balu doash*, he would record the farmer as calling the soil a *sandy loam*.

This RA also experienced problems relating to his PhD candidature. Needing to satisfy the university's upgrade committee, he had to produce a thesis draft which met the norms for anthropological study, placing his findings in the context of comparative anthropological work from South Asia. He did not have the background to do this readily. Some NR staff on the project thought that a proportion of his efforts were directed to meeting university demands that did not directly match the requirements of the project, whereas from the perspective of the IK staff he was learning valuable anthropology. These problems relate again to time and disciplinary differences.

Recruiting national natural science graduates to undertake IK work on projects can be problematic, and only outstanding candidates should be considered for work of more ambitious scope. This type of RA may prove adequate in Type (1) or Type (2) studies (see page 57).

Regardless of the problems faced by this RA and the next one, they have both proved the most committed by far of all the project's national collaborators. While tenured academics, short-term consultants and local field assistants have only undertaken work while remunerated (and sometimes even then only half heartedly), these two RAs, investing in their futures with postgraduate qualifications, have worked diligently throughout and beyond the project. One of them intends to return to his field site in the future and pursue further IK research. They have been excellent value for money.

Box 2.4: National social sciences graduate

The second RA had a masters degree in anthropology, and had undertaken some field work as an assistant to a foreign anthropologist.

This RA had fewer problems meeting the requirements of the University upgrade committee, but was genuinely naïve in respect of natural resources. Many of his initial interviews reflect his experience of learning about the basics of farming and fishing. These interviews were elementary as a result, and at a descriptive rather than probing and explanatory level. However, once this RA did become familiar with the NR problems, his data collection was robust and informed by his anthropological training. The data he collected explored issues in depth, and extensively addressed their socio-cultural dimensions (characteristic of a Type 3 study, see page 57), and probed local understanding of NR processes. An important point regarding this staff member was that his understanding of natural resources management was *entirely informed by local Bengali ideas*. Some NR scientists were concerned that this RA's studies ran the risk of becoming 'too ethnographic' and failing to focus on the technical dimensions of the NR research. This RA also faced personal problems in the field interacting with local scientists who perceived of him and his study as lower status than their own technical research. But partnered with someone with an NR science background and an understanding of anthropological methods (e.g. see Box 2.10) an RA with this background should prove excellent value in IK enquiries.

Regarding problems that national social scientists face, see Ahmed (2000) who has some pertinent reflections on the difficulties faced by staff in Box 2.4 and to some extent Box 2.6 — as academics with a foreign anthropological training attempting to undertake field work in their own culture.

Photograph 2.5: Briefing during workshop

Box 2.5: UK immigrant anthropology undergraduate

The Bengali parents of this student had come to Britain when she was an infant and settled in the London area. They are from the Sylhet region of Bangladesh, from where much of the Bengali diaspora in Britain originates. The potential advantages of this student for an IK project were:

- she is an ethnic Bengali, familiar with Bengali culture;
- she is a native Bengali speaker;
- she has a western education;
- she has an academic anthropology training.

The student should have been able rapidly to fit in with and comprehend the local cultural environment, yet make impartial analyses, informed by her western anthropological education. The exercise proved to have serious flaws, as follows:

- being an ethnic Bengali, she was expected to observe cultural traditions, such as *purdah*, which made field work difficult;
- being a lone female in Muslim-Bengali culture presented further cultural problems;
- she was not working in Sylhet, and she did not understand the dialect of the study area, and respondents did not understand her;
- perhaps most seriously, the experience led her to question her own identity. Having been brought up a Bengali, she had a lifetime's exposure to family talk about home. When she experienced Bangladesh for herself, she was surprised at the lives of most Bangladeshis and shocked by the poverty, which she found difficult to accept.

We recommend this approach be employed with care, especially with students. The approach may be more successful using mature expatriates from the countries and cultures where a particular project is operating, as they would cope with the personal identity issues better.

When we turn to UK staff we encounter other problems. Our experiences suggest that a mixed IK research team of nationals and foreigners should work best, staff being more likely to cover for weaknesses in one another. The project tried hard to foster an interdisciplinary research environment with mixed results. On the whole the team worked very well. Many of the problems encountered are attributable to time constraints, not failures of team chemistry.

Box 2.6: Senior academic staff

An interdisciplinarian is "someone who is capable of using the theories, methods, and techniques of two or more of the disciplines that constitute the social and/or natural sciences" (Cochrane, 1976). It has been said that only true interdisciplinarity occurs where all the pertinent disciplines combine in one person (den Biggelaar, 1991). Few examples exist, but this member of the project team does exhibit the necessary multi-disciplinary training and experience. This type of staff member will always be in great demand for NR-IK projects.

In most NR projects, various NR specialists will be employed to undertake particular tasks, and someone else, often an anthropologist, be engaged to undertake the IK work. It is common to pigeon-hole staff according to their discipline. The benefit of having an interdisciplinarian anthropologist on the team should be that the person is able to understand the natural resources research, being able to converse with the natural scientists on their own terms. This can help to break down the epistemological barriers and improve the acceptance of IK. However, our experience in Bangladesh was that although, for example, the soil science could provide a meeting point for IK and NR science, integration did not occur. This is not a criticism of the staff, but more of the design of the project which limited interaction in the field, resulting in most interchange of information in the written word. Although this staff member and the soil scientists had much training in common, epistemological and methodological differences prevented achievement of a major integrated output benefiting from their synergistic interaction. The natural science training of this staff member meant that he was able to work in an interdisciplinary mode without necessarily having to co-operate with other staff members.

The problems faced by NR staff underline the time issue. Many of the NR scientists were heavily committed to other work and failed to meet fully their obligations to the project. There is a danger of trust breaking down in this situation, project members becoming reluctant to commit themselves to work that requires the co-operation of someone else on whom they think that they cannot rely. (The following staff box gives a composite picture of our experiences and, as the novelists say, represents no one living person!)

Box 2.7: NR academic staff

All of the NR staff on the project were initially sympathetic to the idea that IK should feature in the research. Indeed some of them were enthusiastic at the prospect, for a number of reasons. They agreed that many development interventions had gone wrong in the past because little, or no attention was paid to local ideas and aspirations. They anticipated that local knowledge pertaining to their fields might throw new light on their disciplines. They were all at heart part-ethnographers, a fascination with others' lives and cultures being somewhat responsible for them working overseas in development in the first place.

Regardless of these good omens, the project failed to capitalise on them. Several of the reasons are mentioned elsewhere in this book. The IK researchers were unable to supply relevant information to the NR staff in time to inform their research. Consequently, they soon returned to 'business as usual' research mode, using established natural resources research methods and virtually ignored the IK work. They could see no way that IK could deliver information relevant to their work in time for them to use it. The short term contract inputs of some NR staff prevented them from engaging with the IK component of the project, they were focussed on completing their standard contracted input quickly and moving on to the next project. One person described the situation as having too many plates on wobbly sticks. They were in no position to entertain experimenting with non-standard research methods. Some of the academics were likewise over-committed to other work (projects, teaching, administration, publishing etc.) and failed to deliver data on time as they promised the project. If we leave aside personality differences, we had simmering below the surface the natural versus social sciences conflict. Some of the NR staff became chary of the ethnographic methods. One of them was heard to comment that IK research failed to yield 'real' (i.e. quantitative) data. Many of these problems relate to time, agencies demanding too much of researchers in unrealistic time spans, certainly for the meaningful incorporation of IK into projects.

2.2.3 Data Collection Methods

The methods for collection of IK may be classified into two categories:

- long-term, longitudinal ethnographic field work based on participant observation and in-depth interviews;
- short-term methods, often employed by technical scientists wishing to involve rural people in their own development.

These latter methods, with their origins in Rapid Rural Appraisal (RRA), have been further developed ands are now identified under the umbrella term Participatory Rural Appraisal (PRA). These rely heavily on visual techniques, such as diagramming and matrix ranking, rather than verbal ones.

Chambers (1997) favours visual (i.e. diagramming) techniques as they place control of the information generation process with a wider constituency of participants, and are therefore less dominated by the researcher (Table 2.7). In the context of collaborative and interdisciplinary working, methods that rely on visual techniques and graphical outputs have the further advantage of being accessible and easily understood by people

Table 2.7 Visual and verbal compared

Characteristic	Verbal	Visual
Researcher's role	Probing investigator	Facilitating initiator and catalyst
Insider's mode and role	Reactive respondent	Creative analyst and presenter
Investigative style	Extractive	Performative
Insider's awareness of outsider	High	Low
Details influenced by:	Etic categories	Emic categories
Information flow	Sequential	Cumulative
Accessibility of information to others	Low; transient[†]	High; semi-permanent
Initiative for cross-checking	Researcher	Insider
Ownership of information	Appropriated by researcher	Shared; can be owned by insiders
Utility for complex analysis	Low[‡]	High

(after Chambers 1997)

Notes: [†]The aim of CAQDAS (Section 4.4.1 is to make verbal data accessible. [‡]Similarly, CAQDAS facilitates complex analysis of verbal data.

from a range of skills and disciplinary background. But the shallowness of information and the overlooking of individual perspectives (visual PRA techniques favour group work) are drawbacks.

Traditional ethnographic methods have the drawback of being slow to deliver outputs, mainly due to the depth of inquiry. Their typical output is a monograph, which presents IK in a format not immediately accessible to NR scientists, because it is set in a detailed, and often jargon-loaded, ethnographic context. Conversely RRA and PRA are not in-depth methods, and may lead to 'interesting nuggets' of IK being seized upon by researchers, removing that knowledge from its socio-cultural context, leading possibly to its misunderstanding.

Nearly all of these methods yield qualitative IK data, whether in a textual or graphic form. Such qualitative data cannot be analysed using the standard approaches and analytical tools of conventional natural science. This can lead to two problems for natural scientists: it is difficult for them to appraise and utilise the data, and they suspect that the data may not be as 'valid' as their hard-won quantitative data. Analytical approaches which can improve the accessibility of IK to NR scientists are discussed in Chapter 3 (Chapter 3 — Data analysis tools). Some of the doubts about the validity of IK data concern their collection methods, discussed below.

Science applies well recognised statistical methods to measure confidence in data. Commonly experiments are designed to produce data amenable to rigorous statistical analysis, which allow assessment of the reliability of the results. This is also possible to some extent on farmers' data which have been collected through questionnaire and survey methods, but it is not possible on IK data which have been collected through open-ended interview, observation, diagramming, farm walks and so on. Nonetheless faith can be placed in these data if rigorous research methods are employed with frequent triangulation between information to double check. Scientists can trust such research findings within the limits of the methods employed. Pretty's (1995) framework can be used to assess the trustworthiness of qualitative data collected on a project (Table 2.8).

Table 2.8 Framework for trustworthiness of qualitative data

- Prolonged and/or intense engagement between the various groups of people
- Persistent and parallel observations
- Triangulation of multiple sources, methods and investigators
- Expression and analysis of difference
- Negative case analysis
- Peer or colleague checking
- Participant checking
- Reports with working hypotheses, contextual descriptions and visualisations
- Parallel investigations and team communications
- Reflexive journals
- Inquiry audit
- Impact on stakeholders capacity to know and act

(after Pretty 1995, Pretty *et al.* 1995)

Anthropologists have long known that no local community is a homogenous entity, although in development work the realisation appears to be recent (Agrawal & Gibson, 1999). The evidence shows substantial heterogeneity, with asymmetries of skill, interest and power. It is difficult without substantial prior knowledge of a community to identify respondents with differing skills and experience, though there are methods to identify key respondents who may be the locally recognised experts in particular matters (although these assessments can be notoriously unsound if based on a brief acquaintance with a community).

It is important to avoid working with a skewed sample of a village community. There is a risk, especially where the research is short-term and the researchers are male, of talking mainly to middle-age, upper income men. Often these will also be the better educated people in the village, with whom it may be easiest for an outsider to work. Efforts should be made to achieve a balanced spread of informants from the population; they should include both genders, all wealth or socio-economic categories, age cohorts, educational levels, occupations, as well as households in different locations and access to different natural resources. The longer spent in the field the wider the informant sample and the more representative it will be of the whole community. The very poor are likely to be the least accessible members of a population, and identifying them, let alone winning their trust, can take some time.

Photograph 2.6: Women working on chart during PRA workshop

A spectrum of methods — toolbox of techniques — is available to IK research. This toolbox is presented in detail in Chapter 3. The main tools dealt with are summarised in Table 2.9.

In relation to the IK project design cube, the various methods can be assessed according to the three axes, comparing their cost with the time they take to gather IK data with the quality and usefulness of the information to collaborating NR scientists. Regarding the applicability of the different methods to NR research, there will be a trade-off between scope and speed, both of which will affect cost. Ethnographic methods are best suited to Type (3) studies with broad scope, whilst many of the rapid methods in the PRA toolbox are suited to Type (1) or Type (2) studies (see page 57). Chambers has put forward the idea of 'acceptable imprecision' in relation to PRA methods. These methods

Table 2.9 IK data collection and analysis tools

No	Tool	Description	Ease of use
Diagramming tools			
1	Flow Chart/Process diagram	Diagram showing a series/cycle/flow of activities, procedures, events or other related factors.	M
2	Mapping	For collecting spatial information on the distribution of certain resources in a region.	S
3	Matrix	A method for collecting data on the characteristics of a number of specified items such as vegetable or crop types or livestock or fish species either at a one point in time (the present) or over a longer historical period.	M-D
4	Seasonal Calendar/ Pattern Chart	A visual representation of different events over a predetermined time period (such as a year) which the analysts regard as significant to the study being made.	M-D
5	Sorting and Ranking	Sorting: The division of objects/ideas into different categories according to single or multiple criteria.	S-M
		Ranking: The arrangement of objects/ideas into a hierarchical rank order according to single or multiple criteria.	
6	Taxonomies	Classifications of objects and ideas by local people. Classifications may be overt with distinct terminology, or may be implicit.	S-M
7	Transect	A method for collecting information on major land-use zones managed by individuals and households within a community.	M
8	Venn (or Chapati) diagramming/Institutional analysis	A method for identifying and representing both formal and informal institutions within a community and its external environment and the nature of the relationships between them and the informants' community.	S-M
9	Webbing	A method for representing relationships between a situation/problem and the causal factors underlying it.	M-D
Verbal tools			
10	Brainstorming	Group discussion where all participants contribute to discussion and the generation of ideas on a specified topic in a largely unstructured way.	S-M
11	Farm Walk	A walk with informants, either singly or in a group, through an area of NR while discussing the latter with them.	S
12	Group Discussion/ Focus Groups	Discussions with small groups of informants on one or several topics.	M-D
13	Interviewing/ Discussion	Communication between researchers and informants respondents in a variety of mediums (but primarily verbal) around topics of interest to one or both parties.	S-C
14	Participant-Observation	A method for the collection of data through intense interaction by the researcher(s) with respondents in the research setting over the medium to long term.	M-C
15	Problem/Option Census	A method for collecting data on the problems/options that a target population faces in particular sectors or in their overall livelihoods, and the ranking of these according to preference.	M-D
16	Strengths and Weaknesses	A group exercise to list the strengths and weaknesses of a technology, practice, or event and provide additional information concerning this judgement.	S
17	Surveys	(see Interviewing)	D-C
Visual/Verbal tools			
18	Assessment workshops/ Envisioning	Workshop with respondents for the consideration of information, and movement towards a specific output.	D-C

(Contd.)

(Continued)

No	Tool	Description	Ease of use
19	Historical Comparison/ Time Lines	The comparison of conditions, techniques and practices at different historical points.	M-C
20	Participative techno-logy analysis	A means for the participative learning of and about a given technology and the implications the technology has for social organisation, time allocations and the like for social units.	M-C
21	Wealth Ranking/ Well-being or Vulnerability Ranking/ Social Mapping	The participatory identification of social units/individuals within a population/community and their arrangement into a hierarchical rank order according to single or multiple criteria of differentiation (such as gender, age, ethnicity, occupation and the like) which are determinant of differences in wealth, well-being or vulnerability between the identified social strata.	M-D
Other tools			
22	Critical Events	(see Historical comparison/Time lines)	M
23	Five Questions	A method for assessing causal impacts	M
24	Daily routine record/ diary	(see Seasonal calendar/Pattern charts)	S
25	Trend analysis	(see Historical Comparison/Time lines)	M-D
26	Secondary data/ Records/Grey literature		D-C

do miss a great deal of detail, but that imprecision can be balanced against the use that will be made of the data. He cautions against over-collection of data, resulting in a large volume of data that is not analysed or acted on. This caution should apply here — methods and scope should be appropriately balanced.

Sutherland (1998) has estimated the cost of the various steps in undertaking farmer participatory NR research (Table 2.10). Some of the stages in this research may parallel those involved in some initial IK work, and give some indication of resource and time implications of various field activities. It can be seen that these methods require Brief or Short time frames and Pilot or Basic budgets. They are comparatively cheap and quick methods. They collect technically focused data, although they do not gather IK as such. Thus their scope is very limited and collection of reliable quality IK generally requires use of longer term or more expensive methods, particularly where the work involves iteration between data collection and analysis.

Table 2.10 Time and cost factors for various PRA techniques

Activity	Time required	Staffing input	Cost level	Comments
Key informant interviews	2-4 days	1-3 researchers	Low	Careful selection of informants
Key informant farming systems zoning survey	1-6 weeks	2-4 researchers	Medium-high	Inputs depend on area covered and details required
Topical diagnostic survey/PRA	5-10 days	2-5 researchers	Medium	Careful selection of sample area
Broad-based diagnostic survey/PRA	10-15 days	5-15 researchers	Medium-high	Requires experienced team leader and cross-section of disciplines
Planning workshop with farmers	1-2 days	5-20 persons	Medium	Needs careful planning and expert facilitation

Photograph 2.7: Rice harvest

2.2.4 Outputs

One of the aims of IK research must be to avoid a final report that comprises a number of parallel reports on separate disciplinary topics. The objective should be for an integrated output. In this context, the interim or internal outputs of the project should also avoid what we might call Rhoades *et al.*'s (1986) 'multidisciplinary' trap. It is necessary that an NR-IK research team works from the start in what Rhoades *et al.* call an 'interdisciplinary' as distinct from a 'multidisciplinary' way. They characterise this latter as: "wherein team members pursue disciplinary research and pass back and forth jargon-ridden, mutually incomprehensible reports".

The need for interdisciplinarity needs to be thought through during the design phase, and related to the aims of the research. The objective of the IK component needs to be clear, as do the type of output expected and how it will interface with the NR research results. If any misunderstanding occurs among scientists as to what the IK research can deliver, then this can be addressed early on. There is no point in allowing team members to plough on in ignorance, as this will only frustrate and disillusion them.

The Box 2.8 specifies a range of possible outputs. A manager needs to match these to a project's aims.

A manager will need to consider integration of these outputs with the NR research and also subsequent development interventions informed by the research. Interdisciplinarity remains a paramount issue. Other key issues are synchronisation of the research and timeliness of the outputs. There is a danger of IK research falling behind other scheduled work because of the large number of unforeseen factors that can influence this work — hence the need for a process project format. A manager will need to be flexible and innovative as the project proceeds to keep the IK component synchronised with the NR research.

Box 2.8: Types of output from IK research

1. Consultancy report (e.g. RRA report)
2. Team report (e.g. PRA report)
3. Technical report (e.g. ITK report on a target technological issue)
4. Social situation report (e.g. socio-economic review of target region/community)
5. Local demand assessment report (e.g. focus group discussion report)
6. Ethnographic analysis/scholarly monograph
7. Video/film
8. Interactive electronic/internet presentation of data and analysis
9. IK databank (CAQDAS) — integrated with NR databases
10. Artificial intelligence database for NR researchers to use
11. MA or MSc thesis
12. MPhil or PhD thesis

2.3 The Indigenous Knowledge Cube — A Decision Framework

If we now consider the practical issues of project design for projects incorporating an IK component, we can see, following on from the points earlier (Chapter 1), that many of the relevant issues lend themselves to representation in continua, since we are not talking about clear-cut or black and white decisions.

Project managers facing the need to incorporate an IK work package must address three fundamental questions before they can address the detailed decisions about anthropological methods, PRA methods, staffing:

Box 2.9: The three key IK project design questions

1. What budget is available for the IK component?
2. How much time is available to complete the IK component?
3. What depth and breadth of inquiry is required for the IK component?

These three main issues may be summarised as three variables or continua axes:

Box 2.10: The three key IK project design variables

1. Resources (finances available).
2. Time (for IK research component).
3. Objectives/Scope (of IK research).

These three variables have certain parallels with the "Quantity, Quality and Time" quantifiers of the Objectively Verifiable Indicators (OVIs) of logical frameworks, and may be elaborated in these terms (Table 2.11).

- **Quantity/Resources** relates to the financial resources made available for the IK research contribution, i.e. its budget: *"How much?"*
- **Time** is similarly straightforward, and relates to the deadline by which the work contracted should be delivered: *"By when?"*
- **Quality/scope** are more difficult to compare directly regarding the IK task. In guidelines for compiling logical frameworks, 'quality' is described as "a commitment

Table 2.11 IK project design variables and logframe OVI quantifiers

	LOGFRAME TERMINOLOGY	
Quantity ↓	Time ↓	Quality ↓
cost/budget	speed	'quality'
resource requirement	duration	fitness for purpose
		efficacy
		academic gold standard
		trustworthiness/reliability
		rigour/validity
Resources ↑	Time ↑	Scope ↑
	IK TERMINOLOGY	

to being responsive to user requirements".[2] Research quality relates to the trustworthiness, reliability, rigour, and validity of outputs. In academia, quality is judged by peer-review and publication in highly-rated journals and monographs. However these criteria of quality are distinct from quality as defined as 'fitness for purpose'. A practically oriented report may be more appropriate (i.e. a better fit), for some projects' requirements than a learned treatise. If IK is to be accepted and incorporated into NR research, it needs to demonstrate both research quality and 'fitness for purpose'. Project managers may find it difficult to quantify the quality specification for a project along these lines. Therefore is it more straightforward to take the extent of the IK study itself as the design criterion, relating it to the abundance or ambitiousness of the objectives. Are they simple (e.g. technical IK related to a single agricultural tool), or complex (e.g. the social, political and ecological IK of communal management of a common pool resource)? The decision which the manager must take is: "*How ambitious do I want the scope of the IK component to be?*"

Photograph 2.8: Collecting sun-dried cow dung for fuel

2.3.1 Resources

In a project the first task is to specify resources and determine what these sums will finance in IK research terms. How much does IK research cost? The principle cost is staff time. This research has relatively low equipment costs, requiring mainly travel and subsistence costs in addition to salaries. The following table is based on costs of different types of staff; it ignores travel and subsistence costs. Five budget points along a nominal scale of between £1,000 and £250,000 have been selected as representative of the typical range of budgets for most IK projects (Table 2.12).

Table 2.12 Amount of research staff time purchased with five different budgets[3]

	≤£1000 Negligible	≤£10,000 Pilot	≤£50,000 Basic	≤£100,000 Median	≤£250,000 Major
NGO/NARS Research Assistant	4-7 months	40-67 months	17-28 years	33-56 years	83-139 years
NGO/NARS Senior staff	Upto 2 months	7-20 months	3-8 years	6-17 years	14-42 years
Postgraduate[†]	Upto 1 month	8-11 months	33-55 months	6-9 years	16-23 years
Post-doctorate	–	3-5 months	13-24 months	27-47 months	6-10 years
Lecturer/Scientific Officer	–	2-5 months	8-24 months	16-47 months	3-10 years
Professor	–	1-2 months	5-11 months	10-22 months	2-4 years
Consultant	–	1-2 months	3-9 months	7-18 months	1-4 years

Note: [†]Post-graduates must usually be employed for the 3 year term of their PhD. Costs averaged over UK and overseas students.

This table is indicative. It is based on costs at the time of writing. All combinations have been costed for illustration, but clearly some are impractical, such as a project staffed by 139 Research Assistants. Some types of staff, such as post-doctoral researchers and consultants, will be more likely to work on their own, and thus the table gives a good idea of how much of their time might be purchased within the given budgets. Other types of researchers, specifically university-based lecturers and professorial staff, do not routinely charge their time where the project is not a full-time commitment. However in these situations, they will usually supervise a team of more junior researchers or have one or more post-graduate assistants. Most budgets will therefore need to be calculated to cover the cost of a combination of researchers, say 5% of a lecturer's time, a full-time UK research post-graduate assistant plus three NARS research assistants.

---

[3] Costs calculated using the following estimates:

NGO/NARS Research Assistant (£150-250/month)   NGO/NARS Research Officer/Senior RO (£500-1500/month)

UK undergraduate (summer vac. project): airfare + subs   UK Postgraduate (fees £2750/yr, stipend £7500/yr)

O/seas Postgraduate (fees £8000/yr, stipend £7500/yr)   UK Post-doctorate (£17,000-22,500/yr + 50-100% overhead)

UK Lecturer (£17,500-37,500/yr + 50-100% oh/d)   UK Professor (£35,000-60,000/year + 50-100% oh/d)

Consultant (£250-500/day for 22-30 days/mth).

Quality and quantity: Quantity of resources and quality of the research output are not necessarily linearly related. For example, the IK output from 139 research assistants is unlikely to be 139 times better than that from one research assistant, whereas this type of relationship may well pertain when purchasing additional time at a professorial level.

The reliability of IK will increase in an almost linear fashion in relation to the budget of the project, as shown in Figure 2.4, due to the increased amount of staff time spent directly interacting with local people. Reliability is one dimension of research quality, depth of understanding is another. It is the case that the short contact periods achievable on poorly resourced projects (e.g. $\leq$ £50,000) will result in a shallower level of understanding of local knowledge systems. A certain threshold of time needs to be spent on the project, meeting local people and reflecting on their IK, to achieve a minimally acceptable understanding of local issues, beyond this threshold understanding progresses to deeper levels.

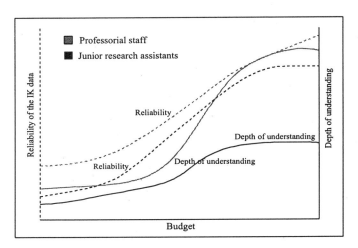

Figure 2.4: Hypothetical depth and reliability of understanding of IK issues by two staff types vs. project budget

Better resourced projects can also afford more senior staff, with the experience to push understanding of local knowledge to deeper levels. This will probably only occur in projects with abundant resources; projects with limited resources will produce descriptive IK without real depth of understanding. In summary, well resourced projects are able to afford 'quality time'. There is no substitute for achieving reliable results.

A caveat to the above discussion of depth of understanding of IK is that expenditure needs to be balanced against project scope. If the scope is narrow — e.g. collecting Indigenous Technical Knowledge (ITK) on one very limited aspects of technology — funding a 'major' project will probably not deliver value for money.

Finally, it should be noted, that although IK research is generally not equipment intensive, better resourced projects are necessary where other than written data will be required. This is particularly relevant in the context of Computer Aided Qualitative Data Analysis Software (CAQDAS), which needs desktop computers, laptop computers for the field, e-mail connections, and the use of transcription services. Where new developments such as digital audio are employed, costs will increase further. These costs can climb even more if digital video and anthropological film making equipment are used.

Photograph 2.9: Fishing boats drawn up at edge of beel lake

2.3.2 Time

1. IK research time — the days/weeks/months taken to complete an IK study.
2. Project cycle time — how an IK study fits into the project cycle and project cycle management (PCM).

IK Research Time: As noted above, the expectations of research quality change as researchers can afford to spend longer on their field work and in analysing their data. Thus quality and time are linked in the same manner as quality and cost. This leads to the question, how long does IK research take?

It can be seen in Section 2.2.1 — Project Cycle Management, which deals with relative project time, that there are good arguments for extending the timeframe for projects beyond traditional three year cycles. However, in the context of defining the time axis of the IK design cube, points can be selected along a nominal scale of between 3 months and 3 years as representative of the typical time spans budgeted for most IK projects in the NR area (Table 2.13).

Table 2.13 Type of IK study appropriate to a range of project durations

3 months Brief	6 months Short	12 months Medium-short	2 years Medium	3 years Extended
ITK on a specific technology		In-depth IK research ↑ scope with greater duration ↑ quality (depth of understanding) with greater duration		

IK studies with very limited scope (e.g. collecting indigenous technical knowledge on one very limited technology, as above) can be completed in short time frames — 3 to 6 months. Beyond this, and where budget permits, more time will result in an improved project. Short time frames have a number of implications for IK research quality:

- Shallow interaction with farmers.
- Little opportunity to become part of the NR project team.
- Inhibits meaningful commitment by researchers.

- Encourages short-term employment contracts.
  - lack of staff continuity.
  - chronic job insecurity limits building an institutional team.
- Encourages focus on short term goals.
- Limits data collection methods to the more rapid options.
- Limits options for data analysis; CAQDAS not suited to short projects.

Project Cycle Time Frame: Time as governed by the project cycle is discussed in Section 2.2.1 – Project Cycle Management.

2.3.3 Scope/Objectives

How ambitious and encyclopaedic are the objectives of the IK research? What are their scopes?

We can distinguish three tiers of IK complexity and scope (Table 2.14).

Table 2.14 Three tiers of IK complexity

	1 Basic technical	2 Ethno-science	3 Socio-nature
Type of IK	ITK*	– IK of production – IK of biological and physical processes	– IK of complex environmental issues – IK of access to natural resources
Example of subject matter	fishing gears	– agroforestry; crop production – crop pests; soil erosion	– management of CPRs[†] – catchment management – land degradation (the environment × poverty nexus)
Definition	Extracted 'nuggets' of IK	– IK *systems*, mainly relating to NR sector	– Holistic, socially and politically contextualised IK of NRM[‡]

Notes: [*]ITK = Indigenous Technical Knowledge. [†]CPRs = Common Pool Resources. [‡]NRM = Natural Resources Management.

Type 1 projects have the most limited scope and are concerned with obtaining decontextualised indigenous knowledge of technical issues, this may be seen as extracting 'nuggets' of IK. Sillitoe (1998) cautions against studies this narrow as the IK loses all of its social, cultural and political context. To treat IK as a piece of transferable and globally relevant information, akin to western scientific knowledge, is to misunderstand IK, and thence potentially to misuse it. Narrowly scoped ITK research is often focused on generating a catalogue or database of local technologies for dissemination. This raises intellectual property issues. In limited circumstances, Type (1) ITK research can improve NR research, but we should recommend project managers to strive for resources and time to undertake Type 2 ethno-science investigations.

Type 2 ethno-science investigations represent the majority of IK studies undertaken to date in development contexts. Studies of IK of agroforestry (Thorne *et al.*, 1997; Sinclair & Walker 1998), crop pests (Bentley & Andrews, 1991; Shaxson & Riches, 1998), and soil erosion (Lamers & Feil, 1995; Zimmerer, 1994) are typical of this type of IK study of production and natural processes. It is in this is type of study that the major advances in incorporating IK into NR research have been made to date. Type (2) studies avoid the pitfalls of ITK, yet maintain a technical focus with which NR scientists are able to engage. This is essentially problem-focused IK, and for many NR projects is exactly what is demanded. In these projects, the cope of Type (3) studies would be overkill and may reduce the accessibility of the IK to NR scientists and thence reduce its incorporation.

Type 3 research with broad and complex scope parallels normal ethnographic research and is closer to anthropology than the type of IK research normally undertaken within NR projects. Nonetheless, as NR research moves to tackle more complex problems, and development moves to adopt a Sustainable Livelihoods paradigm and its associated holistic perspective, Type (3) IK studies will become more common. Projects need to be carefully designed to incorporate studies of this complexity, and need to be resourced and given the time to undertake them.

Whatever the scope of the IK research, the principal objective is to make local people's views, ideas and practices accessible to other development practitioners, especially NR scientists. The demand for ready accessibility means that some structure must be given to the IK data. This in turn implies a middleperson 'speaking' on behalf of local people, interpreting the data into accessible format for others (i.e. translated into their scientific culture's idioms). In Type (1) studies, the distortion of this translation process is extreme, to the extent that it separates the farmer and the knowledge. The increasingly anthropological methods used as we move from Type (2) to Type (3) projects should reduce this third party role, reducing translation distortion.

2.4 The Cube Axes

We can see that Resources, Time and Scope are continuous variables, which returns us to our idea that the interface between IK and scientific knowledge comprises a continuum. We can likewise represent these project design variables as existing along continua (Figure 2.5).

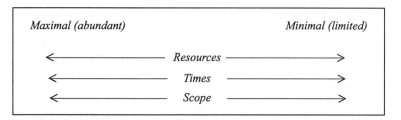

Figure 2.5: IK project design variables as continua

These three continua may be represented as the three edge axes of a cube, which gives us our IK decision cube (Figure 2.6).

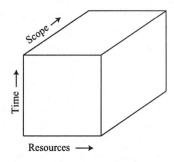

Figure 2.6: IK project design variables as axes of a cube

We need scales on the cube axes. We identify only two points: abundant and limited, because with more points, the cube combinations become too cumbersome for presentation. Here we discuss maximal and minimal values for resources, time and objectives. The cube axes need definition and quantification, using quantities that are realistic and meaningful in terms of NR project design and management and IK objectives. Project managers will need to establish values appropriate to their aims, for example, time could run from 1 week to 3 years in weekly time steps, and resources could run from £100 to £1,000,000 in £100 increments. For simplicity, we present the cube with just two units on each axis. In this scenario there are either abundant or limited amounts of each variable, resulting in a cube comprising eight smaller cubes located at each corner, like a Rubik's cube. Each one of these smaller cubes represents a combination of variables that gives a distinct IK project scenario.

This gives us the following combinations of these three critical project design variables arranged as eight smaller cubes or IK project scenarios (Figure 2.7).

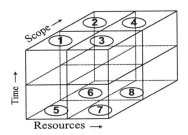

Figure 2.7: Eight key IK project design scenarios

Box 2.11: Definitions of the eight key IK project design cubes

1. abundant time/limited resources/limited scope
2. abundant time/limited resources/abundant scope
3. abundant time/abundant resources/limited scope
4. abundant time/abundant resources/abundant scope
5. limited time/limited resources/limited scope
6. limited time/limited resources/abundant scope
7. limited time/abundant resources/limited scope
8. limited time/abundant resources/abundant scope

This IK cube comprises the first point on the project design decision tree. The cube device may be used in two ways:

i. Could be used from the start of a project to design the IK element as an integrated component, with budget, timeframe and objectives commensurate with delivering an output that fits with the NR components.

ii. Could be used in projects which have already been largely or completely designed, and an IK component is bolted-on as an additional item. In these circumstances, budget and time frame are likely to be already set. The project manager can then jump to one cube (say No. 5: limited budget, limited resources, limited scope) and quickly see what staffing, research approaches and type of output is likely to be appropriate, and what are the consequences of this combination.

This cube approach is summarised in Table 2.15, and discussed in more detail in Section 2.5.

Table 2.15 Summary of sub-cube inputs/outputs

Cube	Time	Resources	Scope	Who (Staffing; Table 2.10	How (Methods & Tools; Table 2.11	What (Outputs; Table 2.4)
1	H	L	L	– to +	S	Limited ITK
2	H	L	H	+ to ++	S-D	ITK-IK systems
3	H	H	L	+ to ++	S-D	ITK
4	H	H	H	+++	S-C	Holistic NRM IK
5	L	L	L	– to +	S	Limited ITK
6	L	L	H	++ to +++	S-D	ITK-IK systems
7	L	H	L	+ to ++	S-M	ITK
8	L	H	H	+++	S-C	Holistic NRM IK

The conditions set within each cube put limits on the available IK options. In Cube 5, the project manager is unlikely to be able to employ a University Professor on a full-time basis or obtain an in-depth ethnographically based study on local environmental knowledge of a certain region.

2.5 Eight Indigenous Knowledge Project Scenarios

This section examines each of the eight IK project design cube combinations, and outlines the methodological options and project management implications for each of the following:

1. design,
2. staff,
3. methods (toolbox),
4. management issues,
5. outputs.

These are illustrated with examples of the type of project and IK study that might occur in each of the eight cubes.

2.5.1 Cube Scenario One

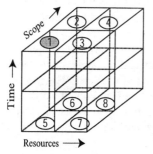

Resources ⟶

Abundant time/limited resources/limited scope: A project with these design criteria will be primarily concerned with collecting ITK on a basic technical issue. Although the budget for this will be limited, say less than £10,000, there will be at least a year, and probably two or three in which to collect this information.

The budget is the key factor in this sub-cube, and it dictates the staffing options. A limited budget would buy about one month of a consultant or senior academic's time, less than a year of a post-graduate's time, but would purchase several person-years worth of local staff time. Therefore this type of project would be best let as a contract to a local organisation, such as a local NGO or a local university department. This scenario may involve a limited number of more senior staff or would be most likely to utilise a senior staff member in a principal investigator role, with a team of junior staff and local enumerators. However there are two risks associated with a project that uses entirely local staff, especially if the local staffing includes a high proportion of village enumerators:

- Tacit knowledge: Locally recruited staff may overlook some knowledge as being so obvious to them as to be not worth recording. Such tacit knowledge may however include knowledge that would be critical to outsiders, such as NR scientists or development project personnel, in using the IK or implementing a technology project on the strength of it.
- Local power brokers: When researchers first come into an area, they normally approach the local office holders (e.g. village chairman) first. Alternatively well-educated and influential people are often the first to approach outsiders (cf. Ahmed, 2000). This may result in family members of the locally influential people, or people aligned to these power-brokers being put forward as suitable to work with the project. Alternatively people within the power-brokers' sphere of influence may be recommended as key informants. The result of such circumstances is that IK may be skewed towards or dominated by the power-brokers. Thus by default it may exclude the poor and misrepresent their interests and their knowledge. Since local enumerators are part of the local culture, they are influenced by it and may not be the best interpreters of it. This interpreter role is highly important as it is also a gatekeeping role between local people and outside agencies who want to utilise IK. Project leaders should aim to use triangulation and cross-checking to ensure IK is faithfully collected by village enumerators, that it is not covertly biased by local politics and that the gatekeeper acts in good faith.

The alternative to contracting a local organisation on this budget would be to identify a senior academic or consultant with previous experience in the specific locality of the study and knowledge of the technical problem (the chances of this are likely to be quite slim). They could undertake a rapid appraisal study and produce an ITK report. This option also relates to Cube 5.

Having a narrowly focused ITK scope, the research can be presented in an output that is either a technical report on the target technological issue or a catalogue/database of local technologies.

Collection of ITK means that IK is de-contextualised from its social and cultural context. This can result in conclusions being drawn about IK that are not relevant or in IK being utilised in a manner inappropriate to its socio-cultural context (Sillitoe, 1998). This scenario is overtly an ITK study. Thus with suitable cautions about the provenance and use of ITK, decontextualisation this is not a key issue. Therefore methods that extract simple ITK descriptions will be appropriate. Questionnaires, short semi-structured interviews, focus group discussions, field observation/farm walk, participation in activities, and photographic records are all suitable.

None of the approaches to undertaking this type of IK study lend themselves to use of computer-based data analysis. Both CAQDAS and expert-systems are costly because they require large time inputs from medium or senior level staff. Though the abundant time in this scenario suits the time consuming nature of these tools, there will probably not be the level of skills in local organisations to utilise them. One exception is the example of use of the WinAKT expert-system software by a local research organisation in Nepal (Walker *et al.*, 1997). In this instance there was a prior training element as one of the local staff had done his PhD in the UK using WinAKT. Where a local organisation had already received the training, the software could be used, however if the training cost must be included, the cost of the IK study as a whole will be above the budget for this scenario.

2.5.2 Cube Scenario Two

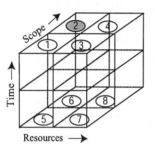

Resources ⟶

Abundant time/limited resources/abundant scope: A project with these design criteria will probably be concerned with the IK of production or the IK of biological and physical processes (a Type 2, ethno-science study). However it may have a more ambitious scope, such as the IK of managing common pool resources (e.g. grazing lands). It will be working on a limited budget, say £10,000 to £25,000 and will have a duration of two or three years.

The budget is a key factor in this sub-cube, as in Cube 1. In Cube 1 budget dictates which staffing experience × cost options are feasible, with a focus on cheaper local staff options. Because the scope of the Cube two scenario is broader, methods also become an issue.

The broad scope, especially if closer to a Type 3 study, argues for inputs from senior staff who will have experience to address more ambitious IK research. However the budget will not cover much time from experienced staff, particularly foreign ones. An experienced national sociologist, preferably with some NR science background, or a senior national NGO worker with social science training/experience would be appropriate leaders in this scenario. Leadership, guidance or advice might also from might come a post-graduate undertaking thesis research on the area and topic or from periodic short inputs from a foreign academic. However, as with Cube 1, this is essentially a locally resourced endeavour, and the small budget will probably be best spread thinly across the broad scope by liberal use of cheap local NGO staff, village enumerators and other villagers. The caveats from Cube 1 about a project with a high proportion of village enumerators therefore apply here. Resources will need to be set aside to train the local NGO and village staff in the varied data collection methods (see below) and further resources should be assigned to external quality assurance and monitoring progress in this longer-term scenario.

An ethnographer resident in the area for the duration of the study, using methods such as participant observation and open-ended interviews would address the scope of the study, but would probably be too expensive for this scenario. Thus in relation to methods, the resource limitations point towards use of a range of triangulating participatory techniques, largely taken from the PRA tool box, and implemented in the field by junior NGO staff with enumerators. The range of methods needs to be selected so as to cover the complexity of both the NR focus and the socio-cultural factors associated with it. Methods such as Venn/chapatti diagrams, institutional diagrams, social mapping, wealth ranking, and historical timelines are needed to give an understanding of the socio-cultural context. Methods such as flow charts, farm walks, mapping, matrices, problem census, participative technology analysis, seasonal calendars, taxonomies, and transects can be used to provide insight into the IK of the NR issue(s) of concern. Both sets of methods can be supplemented with focus group discussions and interviews, but the emphasis should not be placed on these due to the difficulty/cost of analysing many interviews on complex subjects. CAQDAS and expert-systems deal with this type of interview data well, but, as for Cube 1, are unlikely to suitable for use in this Cube 2 scenario.

Given the abundant time for this study, it may also be possible to experiment with some path-breaking and innovative participatory methods, such as participatory or community video. Methods such as these would require some of the limited budget to be diverted into equipment and training in the use of that equipment. Participatory video has been found to be successful both at presenting complex local knowledge, such as that which relates to management of the grazing commons, and at empowering local communities to influence development initiatives. One example is the use of community video by Maasai people for relating their on their knowledge and concerns about grazing issues in relation to wildlife concerns in the Ngorogoro Conservation Area in Tanzania (Johansson 1998 in the *Forest Trees People Newsletter*).

In methods such as participatory video, the researcher's gatekeeper/interpreter/ translator role, normally required to make take local peoples' IK and present it to an outside audience, is greatly diminished. Such an approach genuinely attempts to confront the post-modern conundrum that faces anthropology. The 'objective outsider' does not exist, all outsiders bring their ethnocentricity, viewing other societies through an optic that is a reflection of their ethnic background, their education, their belief system and their preconceptions about what it is they are researching. Thus most of these cube scenarios, which use people from outside the locality to collect and present IK, subjective outsider bias affects the IK. A method such as outlined above can avoid this.

Closely related to this is the issue of intellectual property. As noted in Section 3.22 — Evaluation of CAQDAS for IK projects — much analysis of IK is done away from the where it is collected, in a linear collection-analysis sequence. This extractive approach to IK separates the intellectual property and its interpretation and use from the owners of that intellectual property. Approaches such as participatory video reduce this exploitation of local peoples' intellectual property rights, and thereby empower the community. However, caveats regarding hijacking of IK collection processes by locally influential people pertain here as in Cube 1.

The outputs from this type of study may be unusual, such as a participatory video. Or they outputs that are difficult for NR scientists to readily integrate with their research. For example a PRA report collating outputs from many techniques, rich with visual/ diagrammatic results, which are difficult to relate to technical results. Other outputs may include social situation reports (e.g. socio-economic review of the target community), reports on community workshops, reports on taxonomic studies (e.g. indigenous taxonomies of soil types), and MA or MSc theses.

2.5.3 Cube Scenario Three

Abundant time/abundant resources/limited scope: A Cube 3 project will be characterised by its focus on the technical IK (ITK) related to a narrowly-defined subject. However it will typically have more than a year, often two or three years, to research this narrow topic, and it will have a generous budget, probably in excess of £50,000, with which to undertake it.

This scenario is thus rather imbalanced: a well-resourced, long duration project, studying a narrow topic. This argues for querying the purpose of the IK in relation to

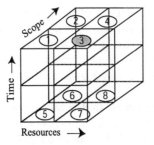

the NR topic. Might the relevance of the IK to the NR topic be improved by some broadening of the scope towards a Cube 4 scenario?

In Cube 1, which is overtly an ITK study because of its budget limitations, the issue of extracting 'nuggets' of technical IK from their social and cultural context is mentioned. The cultural decontextualisation of IK is a much more significant issue in this scenario because of the time and resources which are directed towards a very narrow topic. A very substantial amount of ITK could be collected and elaborate outputs produced, but there is a risk that the findings might have an unreliable basis because of a scope which that ignores the social implications of the narrow, technical IK. Unless the study is undertaken by an experienced person, who knows the society intimately, the research may yield dangerously distorted conclusions (for example Sillitoe 1998).

If the scope remains narrow, the study should be staffed that type of researcher who understands the social issues surrounding ITK, i.e. somebody with a social science background, and ideally experience in the locality. Thus appropriate staff include:

- senior national NGO workers with social science training/experience
- graduate sociologist – national
- graduate anthropologist – foreigner (might be a VSO-type volunteer or an APO)
- postgraduate sociologist – national
- postgraduate anthropologist – foreigner
- experienced national social scientist with NR science background too
- experienced foreign anthropologist with NR science background too
- experienced sociologist – national
- experienced anthropologist – foreigner

As for Cube 1, methods that extract simple ITK descriptions will be appropriate. These include questionnaires, short semi-structured interviews, focus group discussions, field observations, farm walks, and participant observation. In a Type 1 study, they would aim to collect information on what a local technology is, and how local people believe it works. Commonly ITK studies produce catalogues of local technologies, with short descriptions of each and a photograph or sketch. For example, ten different agricultural implements for cultivating paddies. The underlying assumptions is that these local technologies can passed horizontally to other societies so they can adopt the technologies, or passed vertically to extension agencies to promote in other places.

Given the abundant resources of the project, the normal catalogue of ITK could be considerably embellished. The technologies being considered could be photographed or illustrated, or video of them in use could be taken. These could be used in more expensive output formats such as a book or a documentary video.

So far the narrative about this scenario has included much implied and explicit criticism due the weaknesses of ITK compared to culturally contextualised IK. However one of the strengths of this scenario is the time available to the IK researchers for interaction with NR scientists and iteration back to informants. With an IK study of similar duration to the parent NR project, there is opportunity for increased synergy between the parts. If the components run in parallel, the IK staff should be involved in the design, implementation and analysis phases of the NR and IK components, ensuring integration of what ITK is produced. Furthermore, a two or three year study permits several cycles of data collection, analysis and reflection. There is time for queries and data gaps to be addressed by re-visiting the field and collecting more information from farmers. There is time to present results to NR scientists, canvas their opinion and use their NR-oriented queries to go back to the field to collect further rounds of more targeted data. These features of a medium or extended duration project considerably improve the quality of the data, and will act to offset some of the objections against ITK versus IK.

With this level of budget and time, the conditions are suitable for using either CAQDAS or an expert-system. However in relation to an ITK study, the effort of coding raw data into CAQDAS and then sorting and structuring is unlikely to reward the investment of time. CAQDAS could be used as a data storage system, a glorified filing system, but again the effort may not be worthwhile. The simple descriptive data collected in a Type 1 ITK would be amenable to breaking into unitary statements and inclusion into a WinAKT type expert system. However the knowledge base built on these statements could produce distorted outputs due to the simple scope of the project and the simple data collected for it.

2.5.4 Cube Scenario Four

Abundant time/abundant resources/abundant scope: A Cube 4 scenario is the optimum for a high quality IK study. It will have a broad scope, but will have two or three years to address it, and a budget of £100,000 or more with which to do it.

A project of this type has three distinct advantages:

- It can afford to employ skilled staff for extended durations, who can use a range of methods to collect IK of high quality in terms of its depth of understanding and data reliability.
- It has the time to maximise interactions between team members, and develop a multi-tiered communication strategy between IK and NR staff to promote both day-to-day exchanges and major information sharing.
- The resourcing allocated to the IK component indicates the importance placed on IK in the project as whole. It is therefore likely to be possible to implement the project in a 'projects wave' scenario (Figure 2.2), with the IK component commencing prior to the NR studies (Figure 7.3).

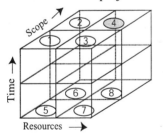

Projects with limited budget and limited time scenarios have to make constrained 'and-or' choices about staff and methods. This is not the case for a Cube 4 project. The project has the resources to establish a layered team of researchers, including senior and junior staff from different types of institution and from both the local country and overseas. Similarly, this mix of staff is conducive to the use of multiple, triangulating data collection methods that require both short and extended contact with local people.

A staff team for a project with a Cube 4 design scenario might include:

- an experienced sociologist or anthropologist as team leader. The budget would cover a minimum of 12 months of their time over the course of the project, and may be sufficient to cover their full-time involvement solely on this project for the duration.

- an experienced NR scientist with interest in IK work as a senior partner.
- a small number of number mid-level researcher from overseas or the study country. These might be university lecturers or research associates, or NGO staff.
- a team of field-level staff, constituted by junior NGO staff with social science training or experience, local social science graduates or post-graduates recruited specifically to the project, and village enumerators trained in IK work.
- one or more students undertaking studies for a higher degree. These may undertake a short, focused study for a Masters degree or be thoroughly immersed in the project for the duration as their PhD thesis is based very closely on the project.

A complex team such as this will mean that managing information flows and building and maintaining the team will be important. These tasks will be important at two levels; they will be a significant task for the senior staff member managing the IK study, and they will be an even more substantial task for the overall manager of the combined NR-IK project.

Sections of this book that are relevant are:

a. Section 2.6.1 — Team Composition and Team Building, wherein key advice on team building includes:
- undertake an initial team field visit, including PRA-type exercises.
- try to establish a residential field base, as this fosters time spent with other team members in the field.
- strong interpersonal relations facilitate team learning. Thus schedules should incorporate time for social interaction.

b. Section 2.6.2 — Models of Communication, which indicates an optimum communication strategy for the main phases of a team research project:
1. During the planning and inception phases:
- face-to-face meetings and joint field work (facilitate interaction and team building).
2a. On-going during the research (smaller issues and day-to-day problems):
- A project website, quarterly administrative reports, ad hoc e-mail.
2b. On-going during the research (significant exchange of information):
- Regular face-to-face meetings, co-incident field work, topic specific e-conferences.
3. Towards the end of the project, during writing up:
- An intensified programme of meetings and exchange of reports.

Cube 4 projects should draw on a combination of methods. As in Cube 2, a range of methods are needed to cover the complexity of both the NR focus and associated socio-cultural factors. A Cube 2 scenario could utilise Venn/chapatti diagrams, institutional diagrams, social mapping, wealth ranking, and historical timelines to collect data on the socio-cultural context. It could then use methods such as flow charts, farm walks, mapping, matrices, problem census, participative technology analysis, seasonal calendars, taxonomies, and transects can be used to provide insight into the IK of the NR issue(s) of concern. These methods and their uses are all relevant to Cube 4. However, Cube 2 projects can make only limited use of focus group discussions and interviews, because the difficulty and cost of analysing many interviews on complex subjects is beyond their budget. This is not true for Cube 4, which can embrace interviewing and other verbal methods. The pro-longed involvement of senior social scientists and anthropologists means that ethnographic methods such as open-ended interviewing, snow-ball interviewing, and participant observation can be promoted as appropriate methods.

This project scenario facilitates prolonged and in-depth interaction with local people. It should therefore result in highly reliable data and in a deep understanding of local knowledge systems (see Figure 2.4 "Hypothetical depth and reliability of understanding of IK by two staff types *vs.* project budget"). It also favours the use of CAQDAS and the building of knowledge bases for use with expert systems. The primary logistical criticisms of CAQDAS and expert systems (see Section 3.22 — Data Analysis Tools) are their luxurious demand for time inputs, and hence their relatively high cost. In addition they require a certain level of computer literacy and need data collection methods to be well defined at the outset so that all data are suitable for CAQDAS coding or WinAKT-type deconstruction. These weaknesses are largely overcome in Cube 4 projects. Most importantly these projects can employ mid-level researchers for large periods of time or post-graduate research assistants full-time. Section 3.22 shows these type of staff to be best suited for using CAQDAS. Large Cube 4, team NR-IK projects can thus potentially reap the benefits of computer-based data analysis tools.

A Cube 4 project can aim to produce a combination of outputs to satisfy a number of different demands for IK. Initially it could produce a social situation report (e.g. a socio-economic review of the target community). As indicated in Section 2.2.1 — Project Design, where an IK study precedes the NR study, the IK study can help define the Terms of Reference (TORs) for the NR research. Thus an output of the IK studies would be the NR TORS. Once the NR research has commenced, at the very least the IK research should aim to contribute to a joint output with the NR scientists — an integrated final team report on the NR issue being researched, relating it to the relevant IK information and socio-cultural context.

During the course of the IK study, particular NR topics may yield notable or interesting IK, such as IK of soil management or pest control. This could be written up as additional IK report (not an ITK report). There may be the resources to explore some of the more radical, people-first data collection methods, such as participatory video (see Cube 2). Thus output from these may be included from the IK study's total output.

The resources and staff on Cube 4 projects are favourable for the use of CAQDAS and expert-system software to analyse IK. Thus outputs may be produced from these tools, such as:

- IK databases (CAQDAS) or IK knowledge bases (WinAKT); these might be integrated into NR databases. Through the software, these IK databases can be interrogated by NR researchers. These databases could be established in the study country for on-going use and entry of fresh data by local IK researchers.
- Interactive electronic presentations of data and analysis. These may be put on to the internet for wider dissemination. An example of this is the Centre for Computing in Anthropology at the University of Kent at Canterbury project on interactive databanks for teaching anthropology.

Projects of this nature will often include one or more students studying for a higher degree of one sort or another. Thus an output from the IK study may be one or more thesis for an MA, MSc, MPhil or PhD degree. The drawback of the PhD thesis is that it is unusual for these to be completed within three years. They will normally be completed in three to four years. Thus the output would only come available after the IK project has concluded, and possibly after the NR project has also concluded. See Boxes 2.4 and 2.5 for further discussion of higher degree theses as project outputs.

Finally, the in-depth involvement of senior university-based anthropologists means that in addition to outputs specific to project requirement, there may be more academically oriented outputs. These may include ethnographic analyses, scholarly monographs and papers in peer-reviewed journals. These may appear during the life of the project, or after its conclusion once the researchers have had more time to reflect on their findings.

2.5.5 Cube Scenario Five

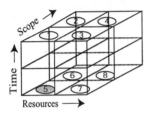

Limited time/limited resources/limited scope: A Cube 5 scenario calls for a miniature IK project. It is a project with a narrow, ITK scope, which must be addressed in a Brief or Short time frame (3 to 6 months), on a budget of about £10,000 or less.

Where this combination of design factors combine, one of three situations is likely:

- The IK component of an NR-IK project has been conceived of by someone who does not understand what IK research entails.
- This is emergency, fire-fighting, IK. A traditional NR project is nearing completion and has had the sudden realisation of a need for IK component, or has been told by programme management that an IK component is needed. This is known as a 'bolt-on' approach to IK.
- A very limited IK study is being commission at the outset of an NR project. This may compliment the NR research, but may be being undertaken to 'tick a box'.

The staffing issues for this scenario are similar to those for Cube 1. The budget will cover about one month of an experienced consultant academic's time, but ample junior local staff time. Given the limited project time and limited scope of the IK, this type of project could be undertaken by a consultant, if a suitable one could be found. The short time frame would mean that someone with some general familiarity with the area and subject matter should used. Alternatively, as for Cube 1, this type of project could let as a contract to a local NGO or a local university department. If this is the case, the caveats in Cube 1 regarding local/village staff apply.

The data collection methods that would be most suitable in this type of project are those that extract simple ITK descriptions. As for Cube 1, these include questionnaires, short semi-structured interviews, focus group discussions, field observations, farm walks, participation in activities, and photographic records. The data collected through these methods can be presented in an output that is either a technical report on the target technological issue (if a consultant is employed) or a catalogue/database of local technologies (where a local organisation is used). This is an ITK study and the limitations of utilising these ITK outputs, as discussed in Sillitoe (1998) and Cubes 1 and 3, should be observed.

As indicated above, this is likely to be a project that is being driven by NR researchers and others at the research scientist end of the IK — NR continuum presented in Chapter 1. The weaknesses of ITK in relation to socially contextualised IK may not be obvious to these staff, who have thus conceived of a project of limited scope. Similarly, they may not be aware of the limitations in depth of understanding and data reliability consequent to a study that only has the time and resources to skim the surface of the subject matter. In order to prevent the occurrence of fundamentally flawed IK projects as presented in a Cube 5 scenario, there is a need to involve IK staff at the design phase of projects. In relation to Project Cycle Management (PCM), IK inputs are needed at the project identification and preparation stages. In relation to 'bolt-on' IK studies, there is a need to better synchronise the IK and NR components of NR-IK projects.

2.5.6 Cube Scenario Six

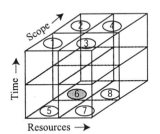

Limited time/limited resources/abundant scope: This sub-cube is the least favourable scenario. Short time frames and pilot scale budgets are allocated to research the complexities of interactions between social and natural systems.

Probably the only way to achieve an acceptable output is if the substantive research has already been undertaken. Thus the project manager must identify and recruit a senior and experienced social science researcher or anthropologist who has previously studied the area, and preferably the topic, in question. One of these staff types is required as long as their experience is relevant:

- experienced national social scientist with NR science background too
- experienced foreign anthropologist with NR science background too
- experienced sociologist – national
- experienced anthropologist – foreigner

With the budget limitations, only a few months of staff time can be purchased, so field work will be limited. Therefore data collection methods will be limited to some interviewing and some use of PRA tools. However neither of these will be able to provide the level of information needed for a Type 3 study, so the researcher will have to rely on data previously collected and secondary sources. The output will have to be an IK report a consultancy type report or an ethnographic analysis. There will be little time to interact with the NR researchers, so the IK report will have to be a stand-alone output.

If a project manager finds the need for an IK study of with Cube 6 characteristics, it is probably best to plan a new IK study. With this number of constraints and the slim chance of finding a suitably experienced researcher to undertake this study, it is probably wisest to be realistic and admit that no meaningful IK component is possible. The project manager should re-visit the IK requirements of the NR project or the resourcing available to the IK component and aim to narrow the scope or increase the resourcing. Any other scenario would be preferable to this one.

2.5.7 Cube Scenario Seven

Limited time/abundant resources/limited scope: An IK project with Cube 7 character-istics will have a narrow, ITK scope, that must be addressed in a Brief or Short time frame (3 to 6 months). However an ample, even generous, budget (+/– £100,000) has been provided to do this.

This scenario is an evolution of Cube 5, wherein a project manager has a (sudden) need for a short-term and targeted IK input. This was termed a 'bolt-on' approach to

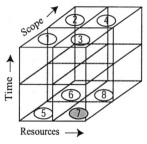

IK. Cube 7 also has the features of a NR project in which the IK component has been bolted-on. An improvement from Cube 5 is that the project was probably designed by a NR project manager who appreciates the merits of incorporating IK, although he/she does not realise the full depth of what IK entails. The advantage of this Cube is that the project manager has understood that IK studies are not necessarily cheap exercises, and thus need to be properly resourced, so a higher budget is available.

Staffing can be generous in relation to the scope of the task. The budget would cover at least 3 years of a post-doctoral staff input, or 12 months of consultancy input. However expending all the budget on senior staff may not be appropriate. A layered staffing strategy as in Cube 4 would be feasible, with a combination of senior, expert staff and junior field staff. The opportunities for post-graduate researchers on this type of project are limited due to its short duration.

Senior staff need not have local experience as the focus is on ITK. However it will be an advantage if these people do have prior experience of the area since the outputs will be improved if the ITK is contextualised in its socio-cultural milieu. In a short study this can only occur if staff are already familiar with the society being studied. The cautions that relate to the distortion in ITK compared to IK, as described in Cube 3, should be noted here.

A short IK study with have fewer opportunities for interacting with NR researchers on the related NR project. This means that the IK is unlikely to be closely integrated into the NR research. It also means that the IK study will probably be out of synchronisation with the NR study. Furthermore this scenario probably will be required to deliver technically-oriented, stand-alone IK outputs.

As in Cubes 1, 3 and 5, data collection methods will focus on extracting simple ITK descriptions. These methods will include questionnaires, short semi-structured interviews, focus group discussions, field observations, farm walks, participation in activities, and photographic records. The outputs may be a technical report or a catalogue or database of local technologies. However as in Cube 3, there are the resources to embellish normal outputs with commissioned illustrations or video.

2.5.8 Cube Scenario Eight

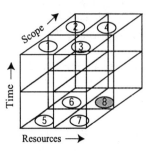

Limited time/abundant resources/abundant scope: A Cube 8 project is overly ambitious in that it needs to complete a complex IK study in a short period. This scenario requires completion of a Type 2 indigenous knowledge system study or a Type 3 holistic, socially and politically contextualised IK study in a 3 to 12 month period. Abundant budgetary resources (+/– £100,000) are available to achieve this project. Nonetheless the imbalance between the broad scope and the short time scale is the key design issue for this scenario.

The IK study in this scenario is similar to any job that has high expectations that need to be met in a short period — the solution is to employ an expert — the best person in the field that can be afforded. The budget for this project should cover the cost of at least 3 years of a post-doctoral staff input, 18 months of professorial staff input or 12 months of a consultant's time. The project requires as much high quality staff time as can be afforded. This might be a team of three or more post-docs for at least six months each, or a small consultancy team working on the project for a few months. Both options would also require a small local support team.

The project requires the researchers to gain an in-depth knowledge of the cultural and social dimensions of the IK. As indicated in Table 2.6 researchers need to spend above a notional threshold amount of time interacting with local people before they gain this in-depth understanding (see Figure 2.4 "Hypothetical depth and reliability of understanding of IK by two staff types *vs.* project budget"). It is doubtful whether a Brief or Short study is long enough for researchers to accumulate enough contact to get beyond this threshold. Thus all limited duration projects will find it extremely difficult to understand local culture and society in depth. Indeed this is the reason that anthropological training has traditionally entailed extended residence in a village setting. This mismatch between scope and project duration can only be solved if the IK staff have already worked in the study area and so already have an in-depth appreciation of the local culture.

Working in this time-bound manner probably means that the IK study is running in parallel to an on-going NR project that has an urgent demand for the IK. The staff should not only be field-experienced anthropologists or rural sociologists, they should also be sympathetic to demands of development and NR researchers. The commissioning project manager will thus be canvassing a rather limit field to find staff for this type of project.

Time will constrain the methods that can be used and the type of outputs that can be produced. Being highly experienced, the staff will be able to manage their interviews to glean large amounts of useful information. Careful selection of key informants and good interviewing techniques will probably be at the core of this type of project. This approach will be supplemented with and triangulated against data collected with judicious use of PRA and ethnographic tools, such as farm walks and participant observation, social and institutional mapping, timelines, and diagramming techniques such as flow charts, mapping and seasonal calendars.

Outputs will probably be stand-alone reports since the project will be too short and demanding to building strong interdisciplinary team linkages. Thus the mostly likely outputs will be a rich and detailed consultancy-type report plus a social situation report of the target communities. There will not be enough 'grassroots' participation with local people to try to produce an output such a participatory documentary. There will be insufficient time to code and structure data with CAQDAS or other computer tools, so databases outputs will not be produced either.

2.6 Project and Team Management

By definition, NR-IK studies will combine more than one discipline. Sands (1993) has provided one framework of polydisciplinarity, ranging from multidisciplinary, through interdisciplinary, to transdisciplinary studies (Table 1.5). Without entering into a semantic debate about these terms, it is necessary to be aware of the differences between multidisciplinary (MDR) and interdisciplinary (IDR) research, as these have a significant impact on the design and implementation of NR-IK research. Both approaches imply a team operation focused on a particular task and both thus require attention to the process of team management (Epton *et al.* 1983).

The differences between multidisciplinary and interdisciplinary research are explained as follows by Michaelis and Rossini *et al.* (cited in Epton *et al.* 1983):

> Interdisciplinary work results from the joint and continuously integrated effort of two or more specialists having a different disciplinary background.

— Michaelis

> Multidisciplinarity is the result of the inter-relation of disciplinary components when they are linked externally only ... interdisciplinarity involves the internal and substantive interlinking of the various disciplinary analyses so that each considers the results of the others in its own development.

— Rossini, Chubin, Porter and *Connolly*

If an NR-IK project opts for MDR, it will commission the IK component as a separate study that will come together with the NR parts of the project only at an advanced stage. This will need to be clear in the initial terms of reference. It will result in a poorly integrated final report. The IK will have little impact on the NR research and vice versa. If a project opts for potentially more insightful, and certainly more ambitious IDR, then the IK component must be commissioned as a tightly integrated part of the NR research, continually iterating knowledge with natural science team members. The project must be established and managed to facilitate this interaction. It presents many challenges to management.

2.6.1 Team Management

It is now increasingly accepted that the problems faced in Natural Resources Management (NRM) should be, indeed only can be, addressed through an interdisciplinary approach (Greenland *et al.*, 1994; Janssen & Goldsworthy, 1996; Syers & Bouma, 1998). The 'systems approach' which has evolved out of 'Farming Systems Research' depends on interdisciplinarity, aiming as it does for an holistic understanding of natural resources management (Ison *et al.*, 1997). A similar integration of disciplines is necessary in working within the currently fashionable Sustainable Livelihoods Framework. Fundamental to all of these approaches is the integration of natural and social sciences.

The management of an interdisciplinary team raises a number of issues for a project, which need careful attention in both the planning and implementation phases. The varied backgrounds and diverse constitution of the project team — increasingly common in research on Natural Resource Management (NRM) — has been characterised by Janssen & Goldsworthy (1996) as an "administrative challenge" or a "research administrator's puzzle". The following discussion draws upon the STRAP schema, devised by Chubin *et al.* (1986), for analysing complexity of research projects. The factors that underlie this schema are:

Box 2.12: The STRAP framework for assessing research team complexity

1. **S** – the level of intellectual skills in the project (substantive knowledge) (*s or S*)
   - *S*: Groundbreaking – new knowledge – high level professional
   - *s*: Routine – textbook level understanding
2. **T** – the range of techniques needed (*t or T*)
   - *T*: Expert level techniques
   - *t*: Technician level sufficient
3. **R** – the range of intellectual skills in the project (*1 to 3*)
   - *R1*: Single discipline (e.g. agronomy)
   - *R2*: Closely related disciplines (e.g. agricultural sciences)
   - *R3*: Diverse disciplines (e.g. anthropology, agricultural sciences, fisheries)

4. **A** – Complexity of the <u>a</u>dministrative unit (research team) (*1 to 3*)
 – *A1*: Single unit
 – *A2*: Multiple linked units, reporting to same high level administrator (e.g. teams within a single University)
 – *A3*: Multiple, dispersed units)
5. **P** – <u>P</u>ersonnel (*1 to 3*)
 – *P1*: Single individual
 – *P2*: Quasi-permanent team (e.g. a lab or a FSR team in a CGIAR or NARS institute)
 – *P3*: An *ad hoc* team, assembled for a particular project

Those responsible for team management must appreciate the problems that inherently follow from interdisciplinary projects designed to undertake IK research as outlined in this book. Key points to note are:

S – Substantive knowledge
 • will frequently require expert inputs and the generation of new knowledge. It could be argued that, by definition, IK is never routine or 'textbook'.

T – Range of <u>t</u>echniques
 • consideration needs to be given to use of techniques for both natural science and social science/IK investigation - these are broadly quantitative and qualitative respectively. Consideration must also be paid to their integration.

R – Range of intellectual skills
 • a wide range of intellectual backgrounds is required in NR-IK team research.

A – Administrative complexity
 • physical separation means that the administration overhead to maintain information flows becomes very high.

P – Personnel
 • there is often a large inertia to overcome to encourage the team to gel before exchange of ideas and information can start to happen.

Use of the STRAP framework in the project design phase should assist in the allocation of appropriate levels of resources to managing the research team, and that suitable arrangements are made for administration and communication in relation to the complexity of the project.

If we start with the first two S/s and T/t factors, a project will range from *st3*, at the simplest level, to a *ST9*, at the most complex (Table 2.16). The nature of projects that involve IK routinely require team members from different disciplines. Therefore NR projects with an IK component are likely to be either *st9* or *ST9* type projects.

Table 2.16 Descriptions of team research, using the STRAP framework

Code	Description
sT3	Project can be accomplished by routine knowledge and technical skills in a single discipline. The team is a single person at one institute.
sT6	Project can be accomplished with routine knowledge but requires high level technical skill. The team work in closely related disciplines, in associated administrative units, and normally work together as a team.
sT9	Project requires new knowledge generation and expert technical skills in diverse disciplines. The team is spread across administrative units and has been put together for this particular piece of research.

Box 2.13: Team leader qualities for participatory NR research

- Strong leadership qualities: having an overall vision (the 'big picture'), inspires others, good communicator, able to delegate, able to forward plan, good time manager, fair-minded, approachable, able to criticise constructively, good people-manager.
- Experienced manager.
- Experience with range of methodologies and approaches, qualitative and quantitative.
- Holistic grasp of NR issues.
- Able to integrate and synthesise information from different disciplines.

(after Sutherland and Martin 1999)

If we move onto the R-A-P criteria, we find that teams can vary widely depending on institutional arrangements. Teams in CGIAR and NARS institutes are quasi-permanent, and because of the primary commodity focus of most institutes, are often from associated disciplines. According to the R-A-P criteria, they will often score between 3 and 6. Teams from universities are more often dispersed and may be ad hoc, and bidding for research projects funded from competitive sources (such as research councils and DFID) will score closer to 9 on these criteria. We can see that the combined STRAP scores of NR projects with an IK component are going to be high — they comprise Janssen & Goldsworthy's (1996) "administrative challenges".

Team Composition and Team Building: The key factors to consider in recruiting a team for an interdisciplinary research project incorporating an IK component are:

Table 2.17 Considerations in forming a project team

Factors	Refer to
An appropriate mix of relevant skills and experience	Staffing (Section 2.2.2)
Members who have a convincing track record in the field	Staffing (Section 2.2.2)
Demonstrable value for money	Resources (Section 2.3.1)
Members who function effectively as a team	see below

We have discussed the characteristics of individual team members in Section 4.2 — here we discuss the mix of skills required in recruiting a team, and the desirable personal attributes in addition to professional competencies.

The best known work on personal attributes for team personnel is Meredith Belbin's work, based on psychometric profiling (Belbin, 1981). Belbin identified that the ideal team needs a mix of personality types to ensure the undertaking of innovative, thorough and competent work. He identified nine personality types that should be represented on a team (see Table 2.18).

Not all nine types of team member are necessary for a team, but a team with a range of profile-types is most likely to be successful. In this context it is noteworthy that an IDS Workshop (1989) recommended that smaller teams, with a stable composition, integrate best — assuming that the members are compatible. A team containing only shapers is likely to feature high levels of conflict, whereas a team containing several specialists (an ever present risk in academic research) may be unable to integrate and work in an interdisciplinary mode. Psychometric testing and profiling for personality types can be, and is, used for recruiting people into teams, but may not be wise in the sort of project contemplated here. Mutual respect is the key, for one another's intellectual

Table 2.18 Belbin's profiles for team members

Team Member	Description
The Computer-finisher	Pays attention to detail, deadlines and schedules; catches errors and omissions
The Co-ordinator	The natural chairperson; promotes decision making; elicits contributions from all team members
The Fixer	Extrovert; good networker; explores opportunities
The Implementer	Workhorse; reliable and logical; puts ideas into practical actions
The Monitor-evaluator	Analytical and introvert; good at deeply and thoroughly analysing large volumes of data
The Spark	The ideas person; creative, imaginative; unorthodox
The Specialist	Source of specific knowledge and skill; single-minded; dedicated to a narrow discipline
The Shaper	Self-elected leader; dynamic; positive; argumentative; a pressuriser; seeks ways around obstacles
The Team worker	A counsellor; promotes harmony; valuable in crisis; social and perceptive of others

(after Belbin 1981 and Pretty 1995)

and personal contributions to the team, all seen as necessary to its success. It is preferable to allow a realistic period of time for team recruitment and bedding down — which is not something that current development funding arrangements allow with their politically driven demands for immediate action.

Analysing team organisation in a military context, ICAF (n.d.) state that high-performance teams seem to possess the following characteristics:

- "higher levels of camaraderie
- increased levels of interdependence
- greater collective learning and adaptive capabilities
- closer identification with team outcomes than the average team".

The report concludes that "at the core of a high-performance team's capability is the team members' ability to use interpersonal relations to facilitate team learning and performance". These high levels of interpersonal linkages within the team serve to:

- accelerate mutual learning in the team
- maintain focus on team objectives.

The emphasis is on minimising internal politics while stressing team identity and prioritising team goals. In a military context, senior officers encourage collective action by establishing standards for individual commitment, promoting accountability to the group and encouraging the team to constantly self-monitor.

What is interesting and relevant in this military comparison is the weight placed on intangibles such as camaraderie and interpersonal relations, and the recognition that interdependence is fundamental to success. In more academic terms, what this report stresses is the need to build social capital within the team. This is often overlooked in putting together research teams, where individual member's track records and disciplinary skills are evaluated, but not necessarily their potential contribution to the team's social capital. It is not something that can be assessed from CVs but requires a trial period in a team. As stated in Table 2.4, ability to bond within a team is largely a personal attribute, and this personal chemistry (dubbed the 'I' factor) is difficult to predict. A person may get on very well in one team but prove a disaster in another. The intangible social cohesion has also been referred to as the team's "internal chemistry" (Bouma and Hoosbeek, 1996). The project manager should not overlook this point. Activities should be designed so as to foster cohesion in the team, and the research managed to promote interdependence.

A number of researchers have noted the fruitful interaction that occurs within a team when they work together in the field (IDS Workshop, 1989). Joint participation in interviewing, mapping, transect walks and so on renders disciplinary specialisms less dominant — albeit these are important to provide each researcher with a particular perspective to contribute to the interpretation of the data. It is therefore recommended that projects incorporate:

- an initial team field visit, including PRA-type exercises (Sutherland and Martin, 1999)
- a residential field base is established (where cost permits) as this will foster time spent with other team members in the field
- time for social interaction.

Most authorities agree that it is how the team is managed at the start of the project that is most important, this defines how the team members interact, and affects how well they bond as a team. Team building activities and good communication at the planning and inception phases will ensure that team members:

- have a shared ownership of project goals
- share a frame of reference for the project (Sutherland and Martin, 1999)
- are aware of the 'big picture' of the project.

2.6.2 Team Communication

Having the right mix of skills and Belbin personality types does not automatically result in an NR-IK team that will function effectively. Good communication within the team is essential from the outset.

Charles Handy (1985) has written widely on business management and the team. He has characterised the operational steps of team building as (see Box 3.9):

forming

storming

norming

performing

According to this schema, a team must come together, go through some stages of tension or conflict before normalising, at which point it can start to realise the synergy of team working. The tension and conflict stage is also noted by Rhoades *et al.* (1986). In IK projects the 'forming' and 'storming' stages can be crucial as there will be some fundamental differences between the NR and IK team members. They will not "share the same set of professional norms and values" (Janssen and Goldsworthy, 1996). This must be recognised and addressed if the team is to function. The absence of a common set of disciplinary principles and lack of a shared perspective on the world is particularly extreme in teams, such as those in NR-IK research, that bridge the social science-natural science boundary. Therefore part of the 'norming' stage is establishing clear lines of communication between team members across this boundary. This is the bridge that unites the team together and is necessary if 'performing' is not to disappear down the disciplinary gulf.

Two factors are important here:

1. Models of team communications
2. Operational protocols for team communication

Models of Communication: A number of models of team communication exist. It is important to be clear which model the NR-IK project will be following as this helps to establish roles and modalities for intra-team communications. Noting that some tension between disciplines is likely to be the norm rather than the exception — indeed some intellectual tension is necessary for creative research — a model which facilitates closer contact between team members near the start of the project should improve the quality of the NR-IK output. Models which rely too heavily upon NR and IK team members interfacing only towards the end of a project when they have collected data and are at the analysis stage, run the risk of leaving too little time for the team to 'norm and perform'. The most frequently followed model of team interaction 'Common Group Learning', falls into this trap.

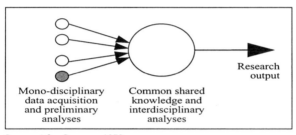

Source: After Swanson 1979.

Figure 2.8: Common group learning

The 'Common Group Learning' approach is better than the multidisciplinary one (Figure 2.9) (Rhoades *et al.* 1986). Competing demands on researchers' time, especially in academia currently, increase the risk of projects following this model. We strongly advise project managers to avoid this interactive model because they will fail to realise the potential synergy of team research. The IK component in particular is likely to be side-lined by the 'stronger' natural science partners.

'Common Group Learning' assumes a peer-based or collegiate approach to the research. This mode of research requires a focussed project co-ordinator. In reality, a project leader or principal investigator (PI) drives most research in development. Figure 2.10 depicts a team depending on the PI to integrate the different disciplinary streams of knowledge. This is intellectually very difficult to achieve. It assumes a polymath — a very rare person in today's highly specialised research world — and places heavy pressures on the PI. It is likely in situations where staff may be on short-term contracts or contracted to provide limited inputs to a number of projects (as is currently the position for many hard pressed university Research Assistants), or where consultants produce an output after a single intensive period of work on a project. The 'integration by leader' model is not recommended for NR-IK research. Nonetheless, where a project puts a PI in this role, the person appointed will require certain qualities to be successful (see Box 2.14).

The approach recommended for NR-IK research is a 'flatter' structure which promotes equal interaction between all research staff during the course of the project. It assumes

Box 2.14: Ten tips for team management

- Select team co-ordinator carefully — should be open-minded and able to resolve team conflicts.
- If necessary train the team leader to provide skills in participatory planning, conflict management and facilitation.
- Conduct team activities, such as PRAs, at the start of the project.
- Plan and set goals as a team activity.
- Hold regular team meetings, and share work schedules and outputs.
- Hold regular resources allocation meetings and maintain financial transparency.
- Consult with individual team members about inputs and incentives.
- Share responsibilities to avoid team leader overload.
- To achieve both productive and interaction, resource levels should be set so that no team member is independent, yet resourcing does not impede progress.
- Project design should be flexible to allow creative management of incentives.

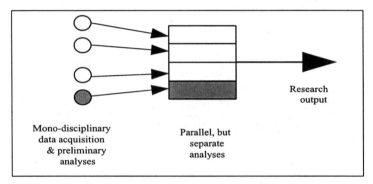

Figure 2.9: Model of multi-disciplinary research (after Rhodes et al. 1986)

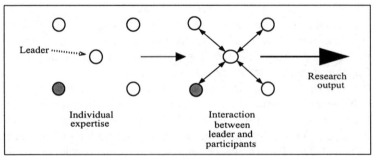

Source: After Swanson 1979.

Figure 2.10: The 'integration by leader' model of interdisciplinary research

mutual respect between team members, not only for their disciplinary contributions, but also what they contribute personally to the team's internal chemistry. This 'negotiation amongst experts' model of interdisciplinary research (Figure 2.11) should be what a project manager aims for, and is the model used when discussing operational protocols for team communication below (Table 2.18).

Finally, in discussing approaches to NR-IK research, consideration should be given to research that relies on modelling to advance understanding of it. This is increasingly

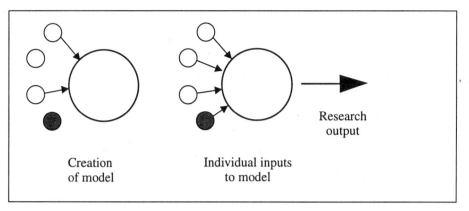

Source: After Swanson 1979

Figure 2.11: The 'negotiation among experts' model of interdisciplinary research

becoming a standard method of researching NR problems and identifying interventions, usually featuring computer-based modelling. While it is currently difficult to integrate IK research into such models, they merit consideration as they provide a framework that can break down disciplinary communication barriers and help develop a willingness to share knowledge, absorb others knowledge and incorporate the acquired insights into the emerging model (Patten, 1994) — namely promote interdisciplinary research. The latest graphical interfaces offer easily understood ways to communicate complex information in an accessible format (Fedra, 1995) and can support open debate between disciplines. The scheme in Figure 2.12 depicts a situation in which NR scientists create the model without reference to IK researchers. However, advances are being made in using computer databases in IK research (see Chapter 3), and serious consideration should be given to integrating an IK component at the model creation stage.

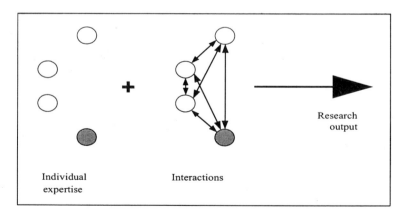

Figure 2.12: The modelling approach to interdisciplinary research

Operational Protocols for Team Communication[4]: Regular communication and exchange of ideas is necessary, to establish and maintain an effective NR-IK research

---

[4] A related methodological issue is communication with the local population of farmers, fishers, etc. This is discussed in Section 3 of the book — *Tools for Participation*.

Photograph 2.10: Threshing rice

team. This will ensure team members are kept informed of progress and have the information either to integrate IK findings into NR research, or alternatively use NR findings to direct the IK studies. Communication protocols need to be established to ensure a regular flow of information between team members. We can envisage these promoting a vortex of relations which draw the team together through constant interaction and feedback, leading to an integrated analysis and output (Figure 2.13).

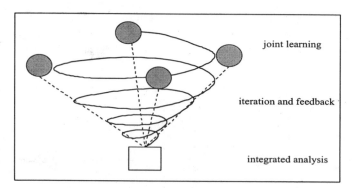

Figure 2.13: Information flow between team members

The guiding principal for team communication should be that members are as parsimonious as possible in their communications, whilst keeping others informed of their findings and progress. There is a danger of over-communication. In other words, the team must avoid snowing itself under with internal memos, e-mails and back-to-office reports. There is a tendency currently towards information overload, especially with the advent of e-mail, for all communications to be sent to all team members. While this ensures that no team members have an excuse for not being aware of what is going on in the project, it risks overloading persons with information of only tangential relevance and may result in team members eventually ignoring most project communication. This is disastrous.

There are a number of ways to avoid this. A project needs to budget for them, as they all involve a considerable administrative burden.

- regular bulletins/digests synthesising the main project news
- a bulletin board where information can be posted and accessed by all
- streaming information according to relevance to team members (create interest groups — but be careful this can work against interdisciplinarity).

It also necessary for a project to avoid the reverse of over communication, namely where some members fail to communicate sufficiently with others. It is a balancing act, and comprises an important part of team formation and performance. Interdisciplinary *work* will only *work* where all team members *work* together. One weak link will cause an integrated team to fail, those who can work will withdraw and concentrate on their own agendas. These points are obvious but frequently overlooked in arranging team research. They come down to trust.

Table 2.18 lists the strengths and weaknesses of various type of text-based and face-to-face team communication. It distinguishes between active and passive receipt of information. Active requires team members to be pro-active to receive information, such as logging on to a web site or attending a meeting. Passive entails team members receiving information without taking any action, such as receipt of e-mails. Both types of participation require action on the part of the recipient to close the communication feed-back loop. Each has its pros and cons. Active participation requires more effort from team members, but once taken, is more likely to result in the information being acted upon. Passive receipt of information ensures that persons receive information, but they are less likely to act on it.

What is the best communication strategy for team research?: It is important to ensure good communication from the planning stage of the project, so that team members achieve a shared ownership and shared frame of reference for the project. It is also critical to revisit the plan regularly and to set short-and mid-term goals and to discuss issues the have emerged in the course of research. These points are demonstrated in Sutherland & Martin's (1999) key points for managing teams (Box 3.2).

We need to remember that:

- No one form of communication is ideal or will serve all of a projects' needs all of the time.
- Projects should employ a combination or sequence of methods according to changing needs.
- Different forms of communication are better suited to certain types of output, e.g. electronic communication may be more favourable for an output that uses CAQDAS since the discussion can also be analysed, such as for differences in understanding between team members from different disciplines (this will make the communication part of the research project and may give team members more of an interest in it).

We suggest a communication strategy for an NR-IK project that uses a combination of methods in sequence, such as follows:

1. During the planning and inception phases of the project:
   - face-to-face meetings - facilitates interaction and team building
     - Round-table meetings for planning
     - Field-based meetings with PRA exercises during the inception phase

Table 2.19 Pros and cons of different forms of team communication

Type of communication	Frequency	Type of participation to receive communication	Advantages	Disadvantages	Comments
e-mail	*ad hoc*	Passive	Text-based systems are better where telecomms poor easy to manage	Difficult where poor telecomms – disadvantages developing country team members. Can cause information overload	Need PC and internet connection. Can create selective distribution lists
e-mail	regular	Passive	Reduces information overload	Recipients may skim 'newsletter' type communication. Does not stimulate feed-back	-do-
e-group	*ad hoc*	Passive/Active (messages sent as e-mail or read via browser)	Can be set to send weekly digest. Messages can be 'threaded'	Team members may not log-in. Digests may be skimmed. Does not stimulate feed-back	Need faster telecomms link, www is more graphical (thus slower)
e-commerce	*ad hoc* for short intensive communication	Passive/Active	Good for in-depth debates on specific topics. Where technology is available, an ideal forum for many team members to debate an issue over a number of weeks in real depth.	Need advance warning and preparation, as with any conference	Need PC and internet connection
Bulletin board	–	Active	Low-tech interaction. Message threading and archiving	Team members may not log-in	-do-
Web page	–	Active	Message threading and archiving. Can store project documents, e.g. longer reports	Team members may not log-in. Does not stimulate feed-back	Need faster telecomms link, www is more graphical (thus slower)
Phone – one-to-one	–	Passive	Quick, good for solving specific problems	Expensive and Selective. Usually needs e-mail or paper-based follow-up.	–
Phone – conference call	–	Passive	–	Expensive. Difficult with large teams	Best where teams well know to each other. World Bank and WWF use weekly transatlantic team conference calls. Improved by video-conferencing.

(Contd.)

(Continued)

Type of communication	Frequency	Type of participation to receive communication	Advantages	Disadvantages	Comments
Broad-cast fax	–	Passive	Works where PCs not available	Not interactive[2] Expensive	–
Paper-based newsletter	regular, monthly quarterly	Passive	Cheap Works where PCs not available	Not interactive	–
Paper-based report	regular, quarterly	Passive	Cheap Works where PCs not available	-do-	–
Paper-based report on specific topic, e.g. IK of fishing	ad hoc	Passive	A good way to communicate complex information to many team members to start a debate or sharing of disciplinary results	Difficult to programme as a regular communication device. Risk of Rhoades et.al.s (1986) 'multidisciplinary'	Someone need to ensure other team members do respond, not just read the report and file it.
Round-table meeting	regular, weekly, monthly	Passive/Active (need to attend)	Good for single institute teams. Face-to-face meetings are the best way to bond the team	Not suited to multi-site teams.	Specific team members can be tasked with presenting a specific disciplinary issue for debate at each meeting.
Round-table meeting	infrequent: annual	Passive/Active (need to attend)	Very good way to review progress and, with presentations, to share findings and questions the originating researchers. Good for iterative enquiry and mutual learning.	Needs much preparation. Need to ensure several days commitment from all team members.	Travel and subsistence expensive for multi-site teams
Field-based meeting	ad hoc or infrequent: annual	Passive/Active (needs to attend)	Team members can easily interact with each other and farmers. Good for iterative enquiry and mutual learning. Good for establishing team spirit	Need much preparation. Need to ensure several days commitment from all team members.	Travel and subsistence expensive for multi-site teams

Notes: [1]For example: http://www.egroups.com/; http://www.onelist.com/; http://www.mailbase.ac.uk. [2]Need to tread the thin line between communication and the team leader engaging in 'Socratic dialogue' (Popper, 1963), i.e. one-way information flow.

2a. On-going throughout the research phase of the project (to deal with smaller issues and day-to-day problems):
- A project web-site containing key project documents for reference
- Quarterly administrative reports copied to all team members
- *Ad hoc* e-mail with parsimonious copying
- *Ad hoc* one-to-one meetings (including phone calls)

2b. On-going throughout the research phase of the project (to handle significant exchanges of information):
- Six monthly face-to-face meetings of all the team to review findings
- Arrange co-incident field work whenever possible
- A small number of 1 week e-conferences (e.g. mid-project), focused on specific research topics. Conference catalysed by a topic-specific report as a discussion document.

3. Towards the end of the project, during writing up:
- An intensified programme of meetings and exchange of reports. Preferably using computers to assist rapid exchange of information.
- A formal workshop or conference towards the end of the project, to focus team members on common output for discussion in public domain.

Figure 2.14 illustrates such a communication strategy for IK research on soils, involving interaction with soil scientists, showing the three phases of communication.

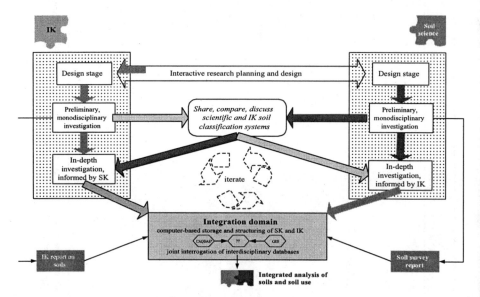

Figure 2.14: Model of idealised communication pathways for integrated scientific and IK study of soil resources

3 Tool Box of Methods for Indigenous Knowledge Projects

3.1 Tools and Analysis for Indigenous Knowledge Projects

Project cycles are normally presented in linear form. However, as NR research has moved to become more participatory and process-oriented, the need for ongoing iterations of data collection, analysis and validation, reflection and re-evaluation, and further data collection has increased. It should therefore be noted that many of the tools in this chapter can be used at different times and on a number of occasions throughout the project cycle. The order in which they are presented is informed by the overall goal of the UK government's White Paper on International Development (1997) which is to create knowledge which will lead to sustainable improvements in the livelihoods of the poor.

Firstly, in the light of the participatory movement and of increased concern with the IK of the end-users of NR research and development, attention is given to the act of participant-observation, and to the process of IK data collection ('Interviewing'). We point out that the interface between researchers and respondents is not 'neutral' and that attention therefore needs to be paid to the process of data collection and analysis. Thus these two sections do not deal with the practicalities of doing participant-observation and interviewing (which have been detailed in a number of texts elsewhere and are listed at the end of this book), so much as with identifying some of the issues involved.

The second chapter deals with means for identifying the poor. With a recommitment to the goal of poverty elimination and to listening to the beneficiaries of development, the need to identify the latter and access their IK is a priority. The tool ('Wealth/Vulnerability ranking') could be use to identify social groups other than the poor, while it is suggested that because there are interdependencies between the livelihoods of the poor and those of other stakeholder groups, there is a need to identify these as well.

An approach which stratifies the population according to various criteria is taken as fundamental to understanding the dynamics of poverty. Earlier development approaches such as 'trickle down', Farming Systems Research (FSR) and even sustainable livelihoods approaches are holistic but have tended to be politically neutral (see Ashley and Carney 1999:27). For example, as Ravnborg has said (1992: 3), (early) "FSR constructs a coherent but fictive system, and thus masks differentiation between resource-rich and resource-poor." Such approaches have assumed all farmers in the research area to have similar needs and capacities, which is in fact not the case. These approaches also mask the fact that the wider system of which different livelihoods are part is a negotiated outcome in which the power (or lack of it) of the various parties plays a critical role (see Long and Long 1992). Thus, if we seek to intervene in the system so as to improve access to opportunity for the resource-poor, we need to make a political decision to support the latter (see Biggs and Farrington 1991; Colclough 1993; Ashley and Carney 1999). This requires us to identify who the poor are, what the characteristics and causes of their 'poverty' are, and what the resource-poor themselves identify as their needs. Acknowledging and responding to social diversity is critical and, as Norton and Bird 1998) note, presents a new challenge to development professionals in the context of Sector-Wide Approaches (SWAps) and Poverty Reduction Strategy Papers (PRSPs).

The third chapter deals with understanding the local context in which the livelihoods of the poor are set (the development context), and in particular with the linkages between the economic, environmental, social and institutional patterns. The anthropological contribution here is to provide data on social relations ('institutions') — including those involving 'power' — or individual and group motivations — both economic and non-economic- and the role of these in livelihoods. A socially disaggregated approach which stratifies populations according to various criteria is taken as fundamental to understanding the dynamics of poverty.

The fourth chapter deals with learning about different stakeholder groups' livelihoods, about the assets they have and the vulnerabilities they face, and about the interdependencies between different groups. Here it is accepted that the poor (and other stakeholder groups) are likely to have 'portfolios' of livelihood strategies and that a holistic rather than 'sectoral' approach to knowledge should be taken. It is also accepted that the knowledge gained will be a resource shared between researchers (and policy-makers), local stakeholder groups and the community in what is a Participatory Learning and Action (PLA) process.

Photograph 3.1: A banana market

Some development professionals (see for example Abbot and Guijt 1997) express worries about the compromises made between planners and policy-makers working at the macro-level and their need for information (and therefore for the use of 'extractive' methodologies) and those of development professionals working at the micro-level with local people. The two groups tend to view 'participation' rather differently; the former interpreting it as primarily being about 'consultation' with local people to inform the policy and planning process, while proponents of the latter see it as a means for empowering local people to manage their own development. While recognising the need for the consultative approach, the authors stress the need for greater attention to more action-oriented research and development in which collegiate participation and learning take precedence.

The fifth part deals with learning about the poor (and other stakeholders') priorities for development and for working with them to achievement improved sustainable livelihoods. This entails learning from them about what technical, economic, social and political constraints there are to their livelihoods and what opportunities they see for enhancing livelihood strategies. It also entails working with individual groups and at the community level to develop action plans to take the process forward towards an 'envisioned future.' Here local stakeholders with their IK are seen as working in partnership with researchers and their scientific knowledge (and extension agencies with their own local expertise) to create new knowledge designed to have practical and beneficial outcomes for the poor.

This toolbox part of the book concludes with a review of the use of computer software in IK research, and a brief mention of other tools of possible use in IK research with some references. We score each of the methods discussed according to cost (low, middling to high), time needed (low, middling to high), reliability of data collected (low, middling to high), the perspective researched (individual or group knowledge), expertise required by investigators (low, middling to high), and control exerted over the process by researchers (low, middling to high).

3.2 Participant-observation

Cost	L-H	Individual/group perspective	I/G
Time	L-H	Expertise required (social and nat. scientist)	M/H
Data reliability	L-H	Observer bias	L-H
		Control of process (directive)	L-H

Definition: A method for the collection of data through intense interaction by the researcher(s) with respondents in the research setting over the medium to long term.

Purpose: To understand and validate field data within a culturally-specific but holistic context through accessing local actors' knowledge and perspectives.

3.2.1 The 'Field'

A shift by NR researchers from rapid to more 'relaxed' participatory appraisal techniques has led to renewed interest in the ethnographic field method of participant-observation. In social studies participant-observation is an omnibus-activity with an all-inclusive methodology. It primarily refers to the longer term immersion of the researcher in the 'field' situation under investigation — a context in which the researcher may use a limited or very wide range of investigative tools. The 'field' can range from an institution in any community (as in Organisational Management or Social Administration studies) to a rural or urban community (as in Anthropological and Sociological studies). What primarily denotes the 'field' in social studies and distinguishes it from much natural science is that it is a 'natural' setting (e.g. 'on-farm') as opposed to a controlled/experimental setting (e.g. the experimental station, survey or focus group). Secondly the researcher is concerned with accessing the knowledge (IK) of the different actors (primary stakeholders) in the research setting, understanding things from their perspectives, and grasping the nature of the social relationships which exist on a number of levels between actors and social units. The researcher observes and participates in the everyday affairs of the actors in the research setting without attempting to manage that setting or influence how events unfold. For this reason such studies have generally been termed 'naturalistic enquiry', with the intention generally being to produce 'rich' data (i.e. multifaceted descriptions) rather than reducing the complexity and diversity of social life to a limited number of variables.

3.2.2 Research Traditions

The rationale for longer-term immersion in the field is the cardinal principle of qualitative researchers (e.g. ethno-methodologists) that background and context are crucially important to the understanding and interpretation of human activity systems. That is an interpretation of the behaviour of people in another culture must be adequate at the level of meaning — in essence the interpretation of their behaviour should be in terms that would make sense to them (see Winch 1958) — and this principle lies behind the holistic rather than reductive approach taken by anthropologists to field data. Ethno-methodologists maintain that an element of culture cannot be removed from its context and retain the same meaning — a point forgotten for example by early feminist and Women in Development (WID) approaches which repeated the errors of empiricist anthropology which in the 1940s tried to measure and compare largely incommensurable concepts such as 'marriage' and 'divorce' cross-culturally. (To compare, measure, quantify requires a neutral 'language'. But which language — English, mathematics, Mongolian — is to be used, and what happens to the data when one language is privileged over others? Of course it is possible to construct formal measures (see for example poverty indicators) but the difficulty comes in determining whether like is being compared with like.) In contrast ethno-methodologists maintain that the meaning of each element of another culture is to be understood in relation to other elements of that culture, not in comparison with elements of another culture — that is it is to be understood systemically. For example, what is meant by 'mother' and the appropriate behaviour towards that personage is only to be understood in relation to 'son' and 'daughter' and is specific to a culture. These in turn are embedded in a collection of terms (such as 'father,' 'brother,' 'sister,' 'cousin,' 'uncle' and so on) which we recognise as a kinship system — again specific to a culture. A culture is a collection of a myriad of sub-systems, and anthropologists have expended considerable effort in understanding these (see e.g. Douglas 1975, Leach 1976) (see also Section 3.10: Taxonomies).

Natural scientists have no problem with the concept of a system and of sub-systems within it, but possibly because they have to label the natural world (since it does not come ready labelled) and do so in their own terms, they tend to forget that other people may also denote the natural world as a result of their own experience. Rationalist (positivist) natural and social scientists have tended to ignore such denotations, maintaining that it is possible to know that something is true or false (i.e. through deductive reason) without reference to the observer's own conception of it. In doing so they separate observer and the observed but (unwittingly) privilege their own interpretations over those of others. By contrast with this position, interpretivist social scientists hold there are no universal criteria for choosing between theoretical frameworks, that instrumental values play a big part in their choice, and that there is no privileged observer status. Interpretivists hold that 'knowing something' (i.e. forming knowledge) is only possible through concepts which are social in character.

Importantly, while positivists assume human behaviour has universalist characteristics, interpretivists maintain that behaviour is in large measure socially determined, and that positivists ethnocentrically impute causal meaning to behaviour and action. Positivist researchers measure human behaviour, discover patterns in the data, and form hypotheses as to the causal factors underlying that behaviour. But this cannot tell us actors' reasons for behaving as they do. To discover this, the researcher must grasp the (implicit or explicit) social 'rules' actors are following and which makes the behaviour meaningful (or not) for them (see Winch 1958; Lieberson 1985:99-101; Hughes 1990:58). This means establishing adequacy at the level of cause. (On these different approaches to social enquiry see Keat and Urry 1982; Hughes 1990.)

Interpretivist researchers rely upon inductive methods (moving from the particular to the general) rather than deductive ones (moving from the general to the particular). Our purpose here is not to champion one method over another — it is likely that in everyday social and scientific life, if not in logical philosophy, people use both deduction and induction. For example, people act according to prior experiential knowledge (apply general 'rules of thumb' to particular situations) but adjust these in the light of experience (build 'rules of thumb' from case study experience). (Consider for example, the resource-poor farmer in a risk prone environment whose cropping practice is more likely to be 'performative' than planned (Richards 1990; Dixon *et al.* 2000). Our purpose is rather to stress that longer-term engagement with another culture is necessary to learn about the different perspectives and behavioural tenets of, and the interdependencies between, the groups that comprise it. Our purpose is also to suggest that supply-driven development approaches (underpinned by deductive logic) are flawed because they take insufficient account of the experience of NR users (the 'customers') and of their IK (which can operate as 'feedback' promoting 'fit' between product and context of use).

Anthropologists have historically been as guilty as any natural scientist in naively imputing meaning to actors' behaviour. While there is still room for etic analysis, the development of interpretivist, Liberal, Marxist and Feminist approaches over the last 40 years has made social scientists far more aware that the experiential world is open to interpretation from many different 'standpoints'. Marxism and Feminism in particular have been influential in undermining the privileging of etic perspectives and making heard the voices of the disadvantaged (women, children, the poor, those with disabilities). Additionally they have highlighted the political nature of the representation of the views of actors. These theoretical developments have led researchers to seek to understand the world — NR opportunities and constraints, the social and institutional environments in which livelihoods are set, and individuals' goals, and capacities — from the perspectives of different social groups. As Abbot and Guijt note (1997:29) in development studies there is a growing appreciation of the value of local knowledge and the dangers of interpreting realities when unfamiliar with the locality.

In development studies this shift is archetypically represented by Robert Chambers' many writings in which he insists on the need to reverse the traditional relationship between researchers ('experts') and NR users. That is the claim of researchers to having privileged knowledge about the world which must be communicated to NR users who lack it — a pedagogic (political) relationship — is rejected. Researchers have specialist knowledge, but so too do NR users (particularly of the socio-economic and biophysical context in which their livelihoods are set, and of their own goals and capacities), and it about these that researchers must learn. The Farmer First and Last (FFL) paradigm, as Chambers stresses (1985:19-20) "entails reversals of explanation, learning and location ...," while "The reversal of learning requires that scientists start by systematically learning from farmers ..." (see Table 3.1).

Table 3.1 Contrasts in learning and location

	TOT	FFL
Research priorities and conduct determined by	needs, problems, perceptions and environment of scientists	needs, problems, perceptions and environment of farmers
Crucial learning is that of	farmers from scientists	scientists from farmers
Role of farmer	'beneficiary'	client and professional colleague
Role of scientist	generator of technology	consultant and collaborator
Main r&d location	experimental station	farmers' fields and conditions
Physical features of r&d mainly determined by	scientists' needs and preferences, including statistics and experimental design	farmers' needs and preferences
	research station resources	farm-level resources
Non adoption of innovations explained by	failure of farmer to learn from scientist	failure of scientist to learn from farmer
Evaluation	farm-level constraints, by publications, by scientists' peers	research station constraints, by adoption, by farmers

Source: (Chambers and Ghildal: 1985:21).

Whether by reason of 'empowering' actors or by reason of 'functionality' (ensuring better uptake of r&d technologies), the development community has widely accepted the need for demand-led r&d. This means recognising livelihood diversity — that there are many different NR user groups ('stakeholders') with different perspectives, goals and capacities in most communities. The 'community' is not socially homogeneous, and may therefore be disaggregated according to different social indices (such as age, gender, well-being, poverty, occupation, religion, ethnic group and so on).

3.2.3 Observer-Bias

Observation is a key part of scientific methodology. However, it is not as unproblematic as it might first appear. *Pace* positivists there is no position of neutral observer; observation is made in terms of conceptual categories; measurements are made in terms of socially derived scales. A simple example is given by wealth indicators (see Section: Wealth ranking/Well-being or Vulnerability ranking/Social mapping). Formal monetary indicators have historically been used to measure wealth across different communities. These were originally developed in Western societies where income and financial assets are good indicators of wealth or its absence. The validity of their use in non-Western societies has been questioned on the basis that the understanding of 'wealth' may be based on a mix of monetary and non-monetary 'assets' (for example 'social capital'). McCracken *et al.* (1988:19, 21) give an example. As they say:

> Some of the more innovative forms of direct observation rely on carefully chosen indicators. These are events, processes or relationships which are easily observed or measured but can be used as an indicator of some other variable that is more difficult or impossible to observe.

They then present a table (from Honadle 1979) giving low, medium and high measures of prosperity in rural Java as indicated by the characteristics of housing (e.g. material built from, number of rooms, roofing material, source of light) and other indicators such as water source, toilet facilities, transport, and the refreshment served to visitors. However, they also warn that care must be taken when transferring indicators from one location to another. For example:

> ... large well-built houses are generally taken as a sign of agricultural prosperity. However, in typhoon belts in the Philippines farmers tend to invest their wealth in other forms that are not susceptible to natural disasters, and in Northeast Thailand large houses are more usually an indication of off-farm sources.

Photograph 3.2: Fishing with push nets in water hyacinth

The lesson here is that researchers have to be careful with their 'instrumentation' so that the data generated are valid and are not a 'quixotic' outcome of the observational procedures. This is something that quantitative social science has paid considerable attention to (e.g. the pretesting of survey questionnaires), but is a matter for qualitative social scientists as well if their data, and conclusions drawn from them, are to be considered robust (see Kirk and Miller 1986). This means, for example, that if the researcher is trying to capture local perceptions of wealth and well-being as opposed to measuring individuals and households against a standard measure of wealth, (s)he has to pay attention to local categories. The majority of the world's population is poor when measured against a western standard of wealth, but measuring this tells us little about differences in wealth and well-being at the local level or the processes reproducing poverty and lack of well-being.

Secondly the extent to which a researcher can observe events in their natural setting without influencing the measurement of them has been a matter of debate in the natural and social sciences for some considerable time (e.g. ever since the Heisenberg Uncertainty Principle was proposed in physics early in the last century). Perfect validity is not attainable. Post-positivist social scientists accept that the nature of the measuring instrument — in this case the participant-observer — inevitably influences understanding and does so because (s)he comes to the field already 'socially situated' — with an existing social status (age, gender, ethnicity, etc.), culture (e.g. English) and observational framework (pre-existing social and theoretical ideas). Unreflective researchers have assumed that IK represents an objective body of knowledge, a literal account of which can be easily incorporated into western knowledge. But knowledge has to be constructed. Thus knowledge has historical and sociological aspects (see for example Kuhn 1962; Foucault 1972; Feyerabend 1975; Douglas 1979, Latour and Woolgar 1979; Knorr-Cetina 1981).

Much work has been done in anthropology, sociology, and the sociology of science since the early 1960's on the social construction of the 'life world' (to use Schutz's phrase) and the implications of the constructivist approach for data collection and knowledge formation; less has been done in NR development studies. As a number of development anthropologists now recognise (see Long 1989; IIED 1993; Cornwall *et al.* 1993; Scoones and Thompson 1994), there is a need to go beyond the acceptance of the relationship between researcher and actor (between observer and observed) as neutral, and to see this relationship as structured by both parties' world views and therefore as inevitably 'political'. Some of the implications for NR research and development of the shift from an objectivist to a constructivist epistemology are captured in Table 3.2.

Table 3.2 The shift from an objectivist to constructivist view

	Populist: Farmer First	Beyond Farmer First?
Assumptions	Populist ideal of common goals, interests and power among 'farmers' and 'communities'.	Differentiated interests and goals, power, access to resources between 'actors' and 'networks'.
	Stock of uniform, systematised, local knowledge available for assimilation and incorporation.	Multi-layered, fragmentary, diffuse knowledges with complex, inequitable, discontinuous interactions between (local and external) actors and networks.
Process	'Farmers' or 'community' consensus solutions to identified problems.	Bridging, accommodation, negotiation and conflict mediation between different interest groups.
	Managed intervention, designed solutions and planned outcomes with farmer involvement in planning and implementation.	Process learning and planning with dynamic and adaptive implementation of negotiated outcomes; collaborative work requiring dialogue, negotiation, empowerment.
Role of 'outsider'	Invisible information collector, documentor of RPK; Planner of interventions: Manager of implementation; More recently, facilitator, initiator, catalyst.	Facilitator, initiator, catalyst, provider of occasions; Visible actor in process learning and action.
Role of 'insider'	Reactive respondent; passive participant.	Creative investigator and analyst; *active* participant.
Styles of investigation	Positivist, hard systems research (FSR, AEA, RRA, PM&E, some PRA, FPR & PTD).	Post-positivist, soft systems learning and action research; PAR; increasingly FPR, PRA &PTD.

Source: IIED 1993:7.

While there is a need for researcher awareness concerning the political nature of the researcher-respondent relationship (and question-answer linkage in questionnaires), and of the potential for bias/'hidden agendas' in both parties' standpoints, there are techniques for arriving at more robust data. A variety of triangulation techniques may be used to improve the 'reliability' of the data (see Section: Triangulation). Nevertheless observer- and participant-bias is an ever-present danger where time and resources are scarce. Naturalistic enquiry seeks to minimise the observer-effect as far as possible, for example through being as unobtrusive as possible, and through oblique rather than direct questioning on sensitive subjects (e.g. income and savings matters). This raises ethical issues (e.g. about openness with informants, confidentiality, and who might have access to and use the data). More importantly it needs to be linked to greater reflexivity on the part of the observer if 'expert' perceptions are not to unwittingly intrude, while research interests are still likely to remain those of external agencies rather than respondents.

3.2.4 Stances of the Participant-Observer

The term 'participant-observation' then, can cover a variety of stances by the researcher (as a 'situated agent') to the field context. At one end of a continuum there is the stance of 'onlooker' (or 'development tourist'), where the researcher has no grasp of the ways in which the actors understand their world and observes and measures their beliefs and behaviour entirely according to her/his own ontological standards and criteria of causality. Understanding here is entirely observer-driven, and produces etic (outsider) explanations of actors' behaviour. It is this stance to others' behaviour that interpretivist social scientists have criticised in the approach of positivist natural (and social) scientists with an inordinate focus on quantitative measurement.

At the other end of the continuum is the stance of 'actor' — the local participant with her/his socially-derived attitudes towards and for acting in the world, and who monitors it and the responses of others with a view to changing beliefs and/or behaviour as appropriate. Since actors' perspectives and behaviour are — like the 'onlooker's' — also inflected by their social position (age, gender, ethnicity etc.) and social context, the potential for bias is considerable here too — particularly when representing the perspectives of other social strata in their own culture to outsiders. This is one reason why researchers should not rely solely on key informants but seek views on potential technological and policy-interventions from different stakeholders and carry out participatory social and environmental impact analysis prior to implementation (see Sections: Problem-census; Village-workshops exercises).

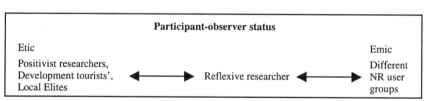

Figure 3.1: Etic versus emic views

A naturalistic researcher may interact with the 'field' as a participant-observer at any point between the two extreme positions of onlooker and actor. S(he) can always be an onlooker, but can never entirely become an actor if the intention is to represent the latter's views and behaviour in the terms of the researcher's society. The act of translation, of the representation of verbal and non-verbal behaviour in the categories of another culture, proscribe this. Data collection (and quality) are also constrained by the social status of the researcher (age, gender, ethnicity, etc.) and by personal capacity (see Chapter 2 for a qualitative analysis of the implications of these characteristics for qualitative data). In general the naturalist researcher tries to see the world as far as is possible from the (emic) perspectives of the actors and uses multiple sources of infor- mation to validate and cross-check findings. Simple observation can produce a significant amount of data on who does what, where, when and how, but real insight into why people act as they do — what the rational underlying their actions is — requires a good grasp of and discussion with actors in the local vernacular. This is not readily achieved by the outside researcher in the short term, though local interpreters can help here.

A failing of many qualitative approaches (including PRA), and partly caused by staffing, time and resource constraints, partly by a lack of reflexivity and partly by pressure to legitimise findings, is that researchers do not sufficiently clarify their own limitations as 'measuring instruments' and the limitations of the spatio-temporal contexts in which the measurements are made. Both social and natural statistically-oriented researchers and policy-makers are concerned that data be robust — that it should be valid and reliable and that findings based on it should have a wider applicability than the local context in which it is gathered. Qualitative researchers have sought to address these issues through a variety of triangulation techniques and through mixing qualitative and quantitative methods, but a prime issue in naturalistic research remains the confidence that can be placed in the measuring instrument — the researcher. Making transparent ('operationalising') the status of the participant-observer in the research act is therefore of some importance in judging the quality of data and interpretations deriving from it.

3.2.5 Outputs and Issues

The output of naturalistic enquiry is 'rich' data — that is the researcher describes the experiences of the actors in depth and in terms which are acceptable to them. This requires a holistic picture of the field situation — the context in which events occur. In doing so the qualitative researcher seeks to enable outsiders to understand the world as seen by the actors, and to understand their behaviour from their perspective. In doing so no test (or judgement) of the truth or falsity of actors' ideas of causality is made, they are merely presented as they are. The approach is primarily an inductive one making sense of a situation without the imposition of pre-existing expectations, and builds towards general patterns rather than absolute scientific laws (see Glaser and Strauss 1968; Patton 1980). As such, analysis is interpretation rather than explanation. At the same time, and because the goal is poverty elimination, the researcher is concerned with analysing the social processes which are causative of social exclusion.

Adaptive natural science has increasingly gone on-farm to develop and evaluate technologies (e.g. cereal varieties) in their natural setting. Scientists increasingly recognise that uptake is dependent not just on the biophysical qualities of the technology, but the evaluation of these qualities by clients in relation to their overall livelihood strategies and the social milieu in which they live and work. Thus natural scientists increasingly recognise that the technologies they develop lie at the interface between the natural and the social. Natural scientists with a narrow production-led focus on a particular technology domain (e.g. developing rice cultivars, or improved livestock species) may feel that they only need to use a few of the tools mentioned in this book (such as matrices, ranking and scoring, taxonomies) to identify production constraints and opportunities for improvements. However, they need to note that new technologies are generally not socially neutral but have impacts upon and change social relations between social units (i.e. intra- and inter-household/group, and between men and women). 'Early' FSR did much to analyse biophysical relationships on client-farms and identify opportunities for diversification and intensified recycling of nutrients. However, in general, insufficient social impact analysis was done, and there were biases in the distribution of benefits from the technologies introduced. 'Later' FSR, recognising the intricacies in relations between the biophysical and the social, has adopted a 'soft systems' approach — a concern for 'human activity systems' — where different stakeholder groups may have very different needs and divergent perspectives on a particular technology. Here natural scientists themselves (or with anthropologists and other specialists) are concerned to explore in greater depth the social context in which new technologies, extension services or policy measures may be introduced. To do so they have shifted from RRA to 'relaxed' and participative (PRA) techniques — such as the medium to longer-term participant-observation mentioned here.

3.3 Interviewing/Discussion

Cost	L/H	Individual/group perspective	I/G
Time	L/M	Expertise required (social and nat. scientist)	L/H
Data reliability	L/H	Observer bias	L/H
		Control of process (directive)	L/H

Definition: Communication between researchers and informants/respondents in a variety of mediums (but primarily verbal) around topics of interest to one or both parties.

Purpose: The generation of information relating to a single or multiple topics by researchers and informants in order to learn more about topics of interest to them or with a view to the clarification of, or deepening of, knowledge gained in other contexts and through other methods, to its analysis by outsiders, or to its use in joint learning and the generation of new knowledge with respondents.

3.3.1 Interviews

The interview, in its broadest sense, lies at the heart of almost all tools detailed in this publication. Most PRA methods, with the exception of ones such as pure observation, require a variety of sensory exchanges between researchers and respondents which range from the chance encounter, through 'chats' and discussion, to informal and more formal interviews as they are generally understood. Where the focus is on IK, verbal exchanges with respondents is *de rigour*.

Research Traditions

In the social sciences the interview/discussion has historically been used by researchers for accessing knowledge held by informants/and/or for exploring their behavioural characteristics. In this use of the method, researchers determine what the object of investigation is and the methods by which data concerning it is to be collected. Informants/respondents are those from whom data are collected (they 'respond' to verbal cues) but do not have a role in the research design. This use of the method owes much to the early history of the social sciences which, after Descartes, modelled themselves on the natural sciences with their logico-deductive experimental methodology.

With the decline of logical positivism and the development of systems theory and cybernetics, the nature of the interview — like other observational techniques — was increasingly recognised as more problematic. Whereas previously it was thought that the observer and the observed phenomena were discrete, it became increasingly clear that they were part of the same system, that there was feedback and feed forward between the observer and the object of observation, and in particular that the observer (as a 'measuring instrument') had a considerable influence on what was observed and what the outcome of observation was (i.e. what 'measurements' were taken). System effects were exacerbated in the social sciences through the investigation of phenomena (social beings) who monitor their external world closely and, for a variety of reasons, adapt their responses accordingly (see below).

As in the natural sciences, so in the social sciences, considerable efforts were made to standardise measuring instruments in order to 'hold steady' the variables under investigation. This led to the development of structured interview procedures (e.g. the standardised questionnaire format) designed to allow comparison of data from different spatial and temporal contexts, and from which in turn it was hoped to develop generic models of social behaviour. The later realisation that the 'closed' questionnaire (like the experimental station) did not capture the natural (e.g. on-farm) situation of respondents (i.e. measurements might be reliable but not valid — of which more anon), led to the development of questionnaires with a mix of standardised ('closed') and more multiple choice and open-ended questions which would allow respondents flexibility in determining their responses, and then to the unstructured interview. In brief, the control of the observer was increasingly relaxed in an effort to achieve greater validity through leaving space for more of the variables which respondents have to take into account in their daily lives. This process of relaxation has gone furthest in anthropology (and in sociology with ethno methodology) where the fieldwork tradition stresses a dedication by the fieldworker to 'non-directive' encounters with respondents and participation in their daily lives (see Section: Participant-observation).

Anthropologists have traditionally made much of participant-observation and the comparative method. Their reasons for doing so have to do with issues of validity — a concern with measurement and the proper labelling of phenomena. Anthropology became a field-work based discipline at the beginning of the 20th Century because of concerns that the analysis of secondary data (from explorers, missionaries and the like) could not derive valid accounts of the social organisation, beliefs and practices of the peoples these observers wrote about due to the latters' cultural biases. For early anthropologists the answer to this was to observe other cultures themselves at first hand and, as the century progressed, increasingly to participate in those cultures.

Immersion in another culture over an extended period (characteristically a year or more) is the method of anthropology today, and the reason for it lies in trying to understand a culture in all its facets from the actors' point of view — that is learning to act in a wide range of contexts as local actors would do. To do so involves learning from different actors about appropriate behaviour in different contexts, the room for manoeuvre that one has, the different stratagem available, the different goals, values, ideals that are appropriate, the different vulnerabilities one faces, and the different social, natural, intellectual (IK) and other assets that are or are not accessible for one's livelihood.

This social learning involves an ongoing 'conversation' (informal and unstructured interviewing, questioning, mimicry and trial-and-error behaviour) in a great variety of contexts and with an openness to correction (i.e. feedback) from members of that culture. This process involves a gradual movement by the researcher from the status of 'observer' where sensory information (IK, activities, behaviour) is either 'puzzling' or is made sense of according to the researcher's own categories, to the status of 'participant' where the researcher has 'cultural competence' — (s)he behaves appropriately through having grasped the local meaning of this information (see Winch 1958). At this point the researcher can be said to have confirmed the internal validity of the data. (For more about participant-observation see Section: Participant-observation). The shift by rural sociologists from 'rapid' to more 'relaxed' data collection suggests a similar concern — in a post-Transfer-of-Technology age — with the validity of the data (though this can have resourcing and timetabling implications for time-bound projects; see Chapter 2).

3.3.2 Cultural Bias

How far anthropologists (and other social researchers) ever can set aside the mores of their own culture is a moot point. Since they do not enter the field as *tabula rasa*, they are more like 'go-betweens' representing other cultures in terms which can be understood in their own. It is also the case that, being actors with specific social characteristics themselves (gender, age, religion and so on), they are unlikely to capture more than a 'slice' of another culture — that is a particular perspective on what is a multi-facetted and changing whole. (A number of anthropological controversies where two observers of the same society have produced different accounts, and which suggest that one or other's account is unreliable, may actually be resolved by accepting that the research was done at different historical periods between which the observed cultural practice changed, and/or that the observer's social and theoretical characteristics predisposed them towards participant-observation in certain domains of social life and precluded them from others. The apocryphal story of blind men each describing an elephant according to that part of its body they are touching, reminds us that we all have a tendency to reductionism even when we are trying to be holistic! (Anthropologists and rural sociologists, for example, have a tendency to project a questionable diachronic and spatial validity to their data even though their research is done at a specific historical period and in a determinate geographical location.) Sound natural and social science is pluralistic in its methods — both in order to seek internal, external and diachronic validity and in order to identify variance. These are reasons for repeating research in experimental science, and for having more than one observer and/or multidisciplinary teams in NR research — the latter giving more than one perspective on the same object/problem/issue and assisting a more holistic understanding.

However, it is important to note that anthropologists consider that faithful representations (i.e. reliable and valid 'measurements') are dependent upon *longer term encounters* with other cultures. That is they explicitly recognise that where the participant-observer is the main measuring instrument, it is only through continuous experimentation and testing of his/her theories and beliefs about another culture in that culture that there can be a better calibration of the instrument. This comparative method is designed to improve the reliability and validity of the data — that is to establish findings as independent as possible from the accidental circumstances of the research, and which are interpreted in the correct way.

For anthropologists close involvement in the lives of people of other cultures normally requires a good grasp of the vernacular. Without this, there is abundant room for misunderstanding not only what people are saying and doing, but also why they are doing it. In particular, and unless researchers cross-check 'findings', they are likely to rely heavily on observation and attach interpretations from their own cultural and theoretical experience to the observed events and behaviour. (Fairhead and Leach's work (1996) on the forest islands of the West African savannahs and Sillitoe's (1996) work on soil management in New Guinea illustrate how listening closely to local people and accessing their IK can lead to a radical re-interpretation of NR issues). It is recognised that with time and resource constraints it is not normally possible for NR scientists to gain a good facility in a local language, and that they will have to rely heavily on local interpreters. However, it is important to recognise that this involves trade-offs in terms of data quality and reliability (see Chapter 2), and that there will be a greater need for cross-checking data. It is also important to recognise that while information may be translatable, translations make it less easy to grasp the organising principles that lie behind data — that is there can be a tendency for scientists to again impose their standards of rationality, of evidence and the like on the data rather than grasp the principles according to which respondents are acting (see Richards 1990).

With the above in mind we can now say something about the different kinds of interview/discussion.

3.3.3 Interviews can Vary Along a Number of Axes

They may vary in terms of those taking part, with one or more persons interviewing/discussing with one or more local informants. Either party may have relatively homogenous or relatively heterogeneous social characteristics. (For example a small team of social and natural scientists with different theoretical perspectives may explore the IK of a number of individuals from a similar social background — e.g. the young wives of poor fishermen). The interview may be self-contained and a 'one-off' (as in a social survey) or consist of a number of short, informal encounters over an extended period with one or more persons in which themes are gradually progressed as new information comes to light. The interview may vary in degree between the informal and the formal, and between being unstructured to highly structured. That is it may vary from casual conversations without structure or interviewer control, through unstructured interviews with a 'topic guide', and semi-structured interviews based on a more ordered list of topics, to the structured interview based on a questionnaire or interview schedule. The setting for the interview may also vary according to whether it takes place in the public or private domain.

3.3.4 Interview Control

One of the main axes on which the interview is structured is that of the *degree of control* exercised over the responses of informants by the interviewer(s). There is a continuum from being non-directive to being directive, but the continuum can be broken down into 4 main types; informal interviewing, unstructured interviewing, semi-structured interviewing, and structured interviewing (see Bernard 1995; Dohrenwend and Richardson 1965; IIRR 1996:44; Patton 1990:288-9).

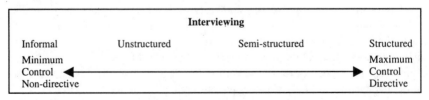

Figure 3.2: Types of interview

Patton (1990: 288-9, also in Mikkelsen 1995:102-3) provides a typology of their different characteristics, strengths and weaknesses, which we reproduce (with adaptations) below.

Photograph 3.3: Taking notes

Table 3.3   Variation in interview instrumentation

Type of Interview	Characteristics	Strengths	Weaknesses
1. Informal/conversional	Questions emerge from the immediate context with no preset question topics.	Increases salience and relevance of questions; interviews emerge from observations; they are matched to individuals and situations.	Different questions to different informants mean different data and difficulties in data organisation and analysis.
2. Unstructured (Topic guide)	Topics specified in advance in outline form; sequence and working of questions varies to suite the flow of the interview.	Data collection is reasonably systematic yet flexible; logical gaps in data can be anticipated and closed; interviews conversational and situational.	Salient topics may be inadvertently omitted; flexibility in question sequencing and wording may lead to different interviewee responses and reduce comparability.
3. Semi-structured (open-ended interview)	Sequencing and working of questions preset; all interviewees asked the same basic questions; questions are open-ended.	Comparability of responses is high facilitating data comparability; interviewer biases reduced where several interviewers used; researchers better able to review quality of instrumentation.	Little flexibility in relating interview to individuals or situation; standardisation of questions limits naturalness and relevance of questions and answers.
4. Structured (closed quantitative questionnaire)	Sequencing, questions and response categories preset.	Comparability is high; data easily aggregated and analysis is simple.	Respondents must fit their experiences and feelings to researcher's categories with potential for bias; may be perceived as impersonal, irrelevant and mechanistic; may lead to similarly mechanistic or bogus responses.

'Farmer First' PRA (see e.g. Chambers 1983; 1993) has made much of the fact that structured interview schedules/questionnaires, as in early RRA, are based on a hierarchical relationship between scientific 'expert' and NR user where outsiders' notions of relevance, validity, and 'authority' take precedence. As the authors to the *Proceedings of the 1985 International Conference on Rapid Rural Appraisal* stated at the time, 'There is a feeling that many RRA techniques are in their present stage of development too "outsider-oriented", relegating farmers to the passive role of respondent to questions of the researchers' choice' (Khon Kaen University 1989:20). Here questions are generated by scientific concerns (the interview is highly structured), there is little room for NR users to influence the encounter, and the data (their answers) are organised according to scientists' standards of validity and reliability. As suggested above, however, the data may be reliable but have poor validity because it does not capture informants' real-world situations. Farmer-First approaches seek to reverse the 'normal' relationships between interviewer and interviewee through more 'relaxed' appraisal (more informal discussion in surroundings familiar to the respondent) to give space for NR users to bring out their own IK and NR management perspectives.

However, as Beyond-Farmer-First approaches stress, Farmer-First practitioners are mistaken in assuming that, because the research setting is more 'natural', the encounter is neutral, (see Scoones and Thompson 1994; Cornwall *et al.* 1993). Reducing the degree of interviewer control can reduce the impact of the questioner's own cultural frames on the data generated, but it is a mistake to assume the same with regard to respondents. In reality both the interviewer's questions and the respondent's answers are influenced by their particular intellectual interests and skills and their social position and by what they are not. (For example, a young female social scientist focusing on social inclusion in health-care provision will ask different questions of, and find different significance in answers provided by, the wives of young fishermen than would a natural scientist focusing on the technical aspects of fishing and directing his questions to an elderly male fisher. But the fishermen's wives may give different responses to the same questions collectively in public to what they might say individually in private, they may be more forthcoming with a young female researcher than they would with an older male researcher, and they may give different answers to the same question at different times! Again the elderly fisherman's responses may well differ in private to what he may maintain in public and in response to different interviewers. Finally all respondents may be categorical about what they do (asserting prescriptive/normative rules of behaviour, i.e. giving 'the party line'), while actually behaving quite differently.

In sum all forms of interaction between parties have implications for the kind of data that is generated. The data is structured (implicitly or explicitly) by the interests, capacities and values of the parties involved, the (shifting) relationships between them, by the questions asked (and not asked), by the physical setting in which the interview takes place (in particular public vs. private), by the unfolding process of the interview(s) and by wider socio-political and historical concerns. In brief an interview/discussion is a social encounter in which data is socially constructed. As such the encounter is not neutral, and researchers need to be aware of the potential for bias according to the following: who is asking the question and why; what is being asked, how and in what context; and who is responding, how and why, and in what context.

Participatory methods make use of the range of interview techniques from unstruc-tured, through semi-structured to structured. There is an emphasis on the use of interview techniques which are salient to the situation of respondents — that is informal and unstructured interview techniques. Even when more structured techniques such as matrix ranking and the problem census are used, normally in focused or sector-specific ways (e.g. addressing NR issues only), they may be used in a non-directive way — allowing respondents to prioritise choices from their own livelihoods' perspectives. This can, however, cause difficulties for researchers whose expertise may be limited to a particular field (e.g. NR) when respondents rank other elements from other sectors (e.g. financial, health, education) as more critical to their needs.

Since informal and unstructured interviews give most opportunity for respondents to contribute their IK to the research enterprise, we say more about these methods here, though much has been written about them in qualitative social studies over the past 50 years (see e.g. Merton *et al.* 1956; Kahn and Cannell 1957; Lofland 1971; Pelto 1971).

3.3.5 Unstructured Interviews

1. The unstructured interview can be used in many research contexts — for eliciting primary data, developing formal topic guides for semi-structured interviews, or for learning what questions to include or not in a questionnaire. It is also excellent for building rapport with respondents before moving to more formal interviews or for eliciting information from respondents who balk at formal interviews (e.g. women), or from key informants who may feel friendship is compromised by such formality.

2. The intention of unstructured interviewing is to derive information from the respondent in as natural a setting as possible. This usually means striking up conversations in surroundings that the respondent(s) are at ease in (such as their own home, the market) and on topics which they have an interest in or activities that they are currently engaged on (such as weeding a field). Interviews in an office or field house are usually too formal, imply hierarchy, and may inhibit responses unless the respondent is a key informant familiar with the interviewer.

3. As PRA practitioners point out (see Chambers *et al.* 1990; Chambers 1993), adopting a learning attitude and communicating to the respondent that you wish to learn from them is crucial. All social research is designed to generate data in response to the questions Who, What, When, Where, How, To/With Who, and Why, but to do this in a way which minimises interviewer impact on the data proffered by the respondent. Being as non-directive as possible is crucial. The intention here is to 'let the informant lead'; the interviewer defining the focus of the interview, the respondent defining the content. Thus while the interviewer needs to keep a conversation going, and on topics in which s(he) is interested, the respondent must be given room to determine what they think it is important the interviewer should know concerning the topic under investigation. What may seem like digressions to the interviewer may not be so from the perspective of the respondent. 'Shy' and reserved respondents (such as women in many cultures) may not volunteer information readily and may need encouragement. At the same time the interviewer should not 'fill space' left for the respondent by making suggestions as to possible replies. Putting words into the mouth of the respondent is to lapse back into the Yes/No format of the (directive) questionnaire. Remaining silent after a question and giving the respondent time to reply is called 'the silent probe' by Bernard (1995:215), and is one of a number of techniques for keeping an unstructured interview flowing — for example 'the echo probe', 'the Uh-huh probe', the 'phased assertion' (see Bernard 1995:215-9).

There are occasions when an interviewer may ask what seem to be leading questions. In general these are questions to elicit clarification from a respondent — particularly a key informant — who may assume the interviewer has the same 'cultural competence' as the respondent does and therefore 'abbreviates' his replies. Other respondents may rehearse a normative or 'party-line', or say what they think the interviewer wants to hear. On these occasions it may be necessary to ask some direct questions to investigate whether they personally accept/agree with what they are reciting, and to check later as to whether or not their behaviour accords with what they assert. For example, women may say they know nothing about a particular topic because it lies in the male or public domain. Early RRA techniques in the NR sector had, amongst a number of biases, an implicit male bias in data collection. Yet sympathetic and confidential interviewing techniques (frequently with female interviewers) can reveal that women possess IK which may or may not be gender-specific, and that women have their own perspectives on NR problems and issues and traditional and potential technological interventions. Gender-disaggregated social research methods — whether survey, interview, problem census or matrix exercises — consistently reveal differences in needs between the sexes.

4. Unstructured interviews can be held with groups as well as with individuals. These can be more like debates, can elicit considerable information in a short time, and can reveal differences between individuals which can be investigated subsequently (either with individuals or groups through 'in-depth' techniques) to see whether they correlate with social status. An 'exploratory' interview may be almost completely unstructured and be held with a random (heterogeneous) sample of respondents. The intention is to get a general idea of the range of IK and opinions (the similarities/differences) on the topic under investigation.

   The difficulty for the interviewer, however, is keeping track of conversations where more than one person may be speaking and where group members 'abbreviate' information on the assumption that others know what they are talking about. For this reason group numbers normally need to be kept small, the interviewer needs to keep all respondents focused, and needs to control the process more than s(he) would with an individual. In-depth group interviews are frequently semi-structured with the interviewer using a topic guide in order to cover in the time available the issues the researcher has determined are relevant — the issues having previously been identified through other methods.

   The interview group may be formed from a random or representative sample of respondents (to form a heterogeneous group) — for example a village workshop — in order to investigate the range of IK and opinion in the group on the discussion topic, or it may consist of a purposive stratified sample (to form a homogenous group). Heterogeneous group-interviews are good for eliciting a range of data and opinions, though some members (e.g. women, children, the poor) may be reluctant to contribute due to being socially disempowered. Homogeneous group-interviews are good for eliciting information from such individuals, and for validating the generic nature of data generated in interviews with individuals. Group interviewing techniques have given rise to 'Focus group' interviewing which, in the hands of a skilled moderator, can produce remarkable results. (See Section: Group Discussion/Focus Groups).

5. In all interview contexts the researcher needs to look out for, and attempt to minimise or compensate for, 'response effects' — biases in the data generated due to the characteristics of informants, interviewers and environments. A considerable number of sociological studies have shown that personal characteristics of the respondent and interviewer — such as race, sex, age, accent, funding source, level of experience, cultural norms, asking controversial vs. neutral questioning, socio-economic differences between the parties — can all influence the presentation and interpretation of the data. There are also 'deference effects', where

respondents tell the interviewer what they think (s)he wants to know, and 'expectancy effects' where 'there is a tendency for researchers to obtain the results they expect not simply because they have anticipated nature's response but rather because they have helped to shape that response through their expectations' (Rosenthal and Rubin 1978:377). (For examples of the above effects see Bernard 1995:229-233.)

Guidelines for successful interviewing are provided in a number of the publications mentioned and are not reproduced here. A short and succinct list is given in McCracken *et al.* 1988: 23-4) (see also Peil 1982).

3.3.6 Structured Interviewing

Structured interviewing involves exposing all respondents in a sample to the same stimuli, the intention being to control the input triggering each informant's responses so that the latter can be compared later. 'Holding variables steady' reduces the chances of random external stimuli being the cause of variability (or similarity) in responses and thus improves the *reliability* of the data. This reliability is not something which can be easily achieved through unstructured methods. However, the trade-off is that the *validity* of data produced by the structured interview may be poor.

The structured interview may consist of respondents being asked sets of questions (the commonest form of structured interview is the questionnaire), being asked to construct lists (names, photographs, plants, crop varieties and so on) or sort or rank them. The commonality lies in the method of administration — all respondents are systematically asked the same questions in the same order. Unlike questionnaires (which are 'consultative'), most of these latter techniques rely on ('collegiate') participation by respondents — and people enjoy the exercises — and as such the techniques can elicit IK on a wide variety of topics and reveal what people think, how they think it and how they organise the material. Their systematic nature means that data can be readily checked for reliability, while their participatory nature means that validity is also likely to be high. In addition the visual presentation of data assists analysis and the communication of ideas to others (for example data collected in small socially stratified group contexts to plenary workshops) (see Miles and Huberman 1994). Sorting, ranking, matrices, problem censuses, paired comparisons, and the like are structured interview techniques which are dealt with elsewhere in this book and as such will not be referred to again in this section.

Questionnaire and Survey Research

The social survey, using a structured questionnaire, is the method most commonly associated with the highly structured format. The social survey has a bad image among PRA practitioners for a variety of reasons (see e.g. Chambers and Jiggins 1986; Chambers *et al.* 1990). Firstly because it is seen as costly to administer and produces data 'overkill'. Secondly because it is has historically been 'non-participatory', extractive, and driven by external agendas and ToT approaches in NR research ('normal professionalism'). Thirdly because 'scientists based in commodity or disciplinary programmes typically display impatience with investigation of farmers' system constructs', even though these constructs would seem crucial to the understanding of individuals' decision-making (Chambers and Jiggins 1986:12). As the latter authors argue, in the light of scarce resources, the ecological and social complexity and diversity of resource-poor farming systems can only be covered by avoiding large surveys and massive data bases and reducing dependence on multidimensional teams.

Despite these criticisms, there can nevertheless be a role for the social survey, and it can be used for accessing IK. Participatory approaches stress the importance of learning from respondents, but the rational for research methods (whether qualitative or quantitative) is learning about respondents and their livelihoods. The survey method is historically modelled on the logico-deductive methodology of the natural sciences. As such it has primarily been used for investigation of individual behaviour or for determining the characteristics of social groups. And this is where the real difference between the older use of the survey and its present use lies. Historically, scientists have (positivistically) made universalist assumptions about human behaviour (e.g. economism) without exploring how far these are projections of their own social and historical condition, and in consequence have constructed surveys and analysed data on other cultures ethnocentrically. In the new use of the survey method there is far greater sensitivity to the behavioural categories of local people, and it may be used in a limited role as just one of a number of methods for learning about and from respondents.

The great majority of surveys are cross-sectional — the measurement of some variables at a single point in time. The analyses of data from such surveys suffer from the same drawback as participative ethnographic analyses — there is no way of knowing from the data itself whether or not the sample period has any greater representativeness. In order to validate this, it is either necessary to conduct the same survey at different time points — that is by using a longitudinal survey instrument (and there is no way of knowing whether informants will respond in the same way to the same questions or whether the characteristics of the sample have changed) — or by use of other methods (e.g. participative time lines, see Section: Historical Comparison/Time Lines).

Investigating trends is of great importance in poverty and livelihoods research. For example researchers wish to know whether target groups are climbing out of or slipping into poverty, whether this is likely to be temporary or longer term, and whether particular livelihood strategies are environmentally sustainable. Panel studies, in which a sample consisting of the same people is interviewed periodically, can be of great value here in monitoring outcomes and identifying potential trends. Hansen (1988) (also mentioned in Bernard 1995:282) gives an example of the usefulness of the method in identifying that, due to a number of factors, a far higher number of women in Malawi are likely to become heads of agricultural households at different periods of their lives than the 20% indicated by cross-sectional surveys. If female-headed households are more vulnerable than others, then "recognising that more women cycle through this phase increases the importance of working with women who are not now heads of households but who might occupy that decision-making status in the future" (ibid.).

At base the survey method consists of exposing all respondents to the same stimuli (e.g. questions), recording their responses, comparing these, and forming hypotheses concerning the definition of the objects of investigation, their characteristics, and/or their behaviour on the basis of patterns (frequencies) and correlations revealed in the data. For example, where a research project focuses on identifying the opportunities and constraints to the livelihoods of target groups, a survey may be made of a random sample of households/individuals. Indicators are chosen which will discriminate between members of the survey population and reveal characteristics and behaviour which may correlate with respondents' social status. The indicators may be based on etic categories, on emic ones or on a combination of both. Thus when investigating the well-being status of disabled persons, a researcher may use formal indicators which have a wide acceptability in health studies, or may use ones which are based on local understandings of 'disability' to identify the target group, or a mix. (For an example of a combination of etic and emic indicators see Section: Wealth ranking/Well-being or Vulnerability ranking. In a project in Bangladesh a reconnaissance social survey using national indicators of wealth and poverty based on size of landholdings was used to identify different stakeholder groups and to improve the external validity of the data collected. A smaller participatory wealth-ranking exercise accessing emic categories was administered to test the internal validity of the etic categories used in the survey).

Question construction is clearly vital to the type of information obtained. A questionnaire can be highly structured (with closed questions) or it can be semi-structured (with open-ended questions). A question such as "Have you suffered any of the following symptoms in the last six months?" (followed by a list) will generate data which is structured by etic categories (even if the respondent answers untruthfully). Questions such as, "Have you been ill in the last six months?" and "List your illnesses", give the respondent the opportunity to provide IK — that is to reveal their own understanding of 'illness' and what counts as 'illness'. For example, Blaxter's study of health and lifestyles in the UK (1990) indicated that many older people who, in medical terms may have chronic illnesses, regard themselves as being 'in good health for their age'. As Blaxter's study also shows, the understanding of 'being in good health' and 'being in poor health' also varies according to other social characteristics besides age (e.g. gender, socio-economic class, marital status).

One of the reasons for having a highly structured questionnaire is for ease of data analysis (i.e. in order to compare like with like) (see Patton's 1990 typology of variations in interview instrumentation given earlier in this section). However, while respondents must fit their experience to the researcher's categories, this does not necessarily mean that this severely distorts what respondents really mean or experience. For example other techniques may be used in order to gain a general understanding of local categories of health or wealth status prior to the administration of a questionnaire survey based on these. The survey can then be used to investigate the incidence of this IK in the population or amongst particular target groups. In this instance the survey can show a sensitivity to the local context approaching that of the unstructured interview (it can have a high degree of validity). In addition it may be argued that the data and conclusions based on them have greater reliability since the survey instrument usually allows a greater gross number of respondents from a wider social spectrum to be consulted than does the unstructured interview which is time and personnel intensive. However, some methodological research indicates that the data may be less reliable since more informants respond (e.g. tick boxes) to items listed on a closed survey than respondents mention the same items in open ones (see Schuman and Presser 1979). (The lesson here is that, as with unstructured interview techniques, the researcher must remain vigilant to 'response effects' — to the potential for data to be an outcome of the method rather than a reflection of underlying reality.)

There are a variety of methods for the administration of a survey questionnaire: personal face-to-face interviews; self-administered questionnaires; telephone interviews. The first two methods can be combined — part of a face-to-face interview being unstructured and another part being self-administered while the interviewer stands by to clarify potentially ambiguous items. The pros and cons of the different methods are detailed in Bernard 1995: 258-267). Bernard also gives a list (1995:268-275), with examples, of general rules that survey researchers follow to construct good questionnaire items. These rules of thumb apply to face-to-face interviews as well as questionnaire surveys, but whereas adjustments can be made immediately with the former in the light of feedback from respondents, this is not easily done with survey questionnaires. The gist of the general rules is given here, but interested researchers should refer to Bernard (1995).

3.3.7 General Rules

1. Questions should be unambiguous. Ambiguity is the source of most response errors in closed questionnaires. The appropriate phrasing of questions is difficult enough in English, but the potential for ambiguity is compounded when questionnaires are translated into another language. Having the questions translated into the other language by a bilingual person from the culture under study and then translated back again by another person (preferably from your own culture) can help reduce ambiguity. The original and the back translation should be a close match. If not, something was lost in one of the two translations and needs to be attended to. Finally pretesting the questionnaire with respondents who will not form part of the sample population will help to eradicate ambiguities. However, when analysing the data, the researcher needs to be aware of possible misunderstandings by individual respondents.

2. The phrasing of questions should be appropriate to the competence-level of respondents. When the survey is of a specific population segment this is relatively easily established through ethnography and pretesting, but is more difficult to achieve when surveying a large population.

3. Respondents need to know enough about the topic of investigation to be able to respond to questions. Again many people cannot recall with any accuracy many of the quantitative details that NR researchers are interested in because they do not conduct their lives in that analytic manner. For example, questions about how often a respondent has fished in the last month, or the total weights of different fish species caught over a similar period are unlikely to produce accurate data. Here it is better to seek the data through other methods — such as asking a sample of people to keep diaries over a set period and record those details the researcher is interested in.

4. The questionnaire should be well-planned, not be repetitive and only consist of questions which are strictly necessary (i.e. be parsimonious). Questions on a topic should be bunched together, topics should have an ordered progression, and 'transition remarks' between topics are useful in assisting the respondent to grasp the logic of the shift from one topic to another.

5. Attention should be paid to 'contingency'/filter questions, and to the questions that might lead on from these along diverging 'decision trees'. For example, in investigating fishing the researcher may wish to know how many men in a community fish, whether this is a full-time livelihood strategy, a part-time income generating one, or a part-time subsistence one, and what decisions flow from these different strategies. A method for ensuring all contingencies are allowed for is to build a contingency flow chart as a preliminary to identifying the most parsimonious questions, which will generate the desired data.

6. Questions should be kept short. Ones likely to intimidate respondents should be preceded by an introductory preamble. Emotional and loaded questions should

be avoided since they intimidate respondents to agree (or react) to the question rather than revealing what the respondent really thinks. When asking respondents for opinions on controversial issues, specify the context as far as possible (i.e. give respondents choice) since most people's answers are unlikely to fit a simple binary scale.

7. Scales should be clear and unambiguous. Survey research uses a variety of scales (for examples see Bernard 1995: Chapter 13). Where a sample is large, a scale consisting of 5 categories or more may be possible, but where the sample is small it is likely that the data will need to be aggregated into three categories at most for analysis of findings to be statistically meaningful. Since scales are used as indicators, and not as mechanisms for capturing holistic data, the general rule is to use single indicator measures whenever possible and only to use composite measures when single indicators won't do the job. (For example in a project in Bangladesh, the authors used size of landholding as an indicator of wealth/poverty. The robustness of this measure was tested by means of a participatory wealth-ranking exercise with a small sample of respondents. The measure was found to be generally robust, though there were some respondents (e.g. tubewell owners) who were wealthy but did not own land.) Where the sample respondents are literate/numerate, numbers and phrases can be used; where respondents are illiterate, visual scales (e.g. a smiling <—> unsmiling faces scale) will have to be used. Lastly, while there is a place for the binary scale (Yes/No) — for example, in answer to the question "Are you married?" — acceptance that different people have different needs, assets, livelihoods and perceptions on the world requires multiple — choice response items in order to capture this diversity.

8. When using a self-administered questionnaire, the bundling of questions and the use of scales is desirable in order to cut down the time needed for the respondent to answer them. This will lessen the chance of the respondent becoming bored and abandoning the questionnaire or answering without due thought.

9. Always provide alternatives for responses where appropriate, since most peoples' answers are unlikely to fit a simple binary scale of the Yes/No type. For example some Bangladeshi respondents when asked whether they are fishers or not, prefer to answer that they fish full-time for part of the year but would not regard themselves as fishers since they are primarily agriculturalists or day labourers. (Since the sustainable livelihoods approach recognises that many of the poor have 'portfolios' of livelihood strategies, surveys need to be fine-grained enough to capture the subtleties of difference between livelihoods and how these indicate well-being or vulnerability.)

10. The pretesting of any survey instrument is vital. Even where there has been considerable ethnographic work prior to the design of a questionnaire, there are likely to be unforeseen ambiguities in the wording of some questions, or lack of sufficient choice in the response items, or problems around the administration of the questionnaire. These can only be identified through pretesting and receiving feedback from pretest respondents (preferably face-to-face). The pretest should be done under the same conditions and in the same context and with respondents of the same type as those for the real survey. The pretest should be in another community to that where the real survey will be administered so as to prevent cross-tainting. After the pre-test, those administering the pre-test should evaluate it, so that feedback can improve the survey instrument.

3.3.8 Data Analysis

The design and administration of questionnaire surveys and the analysis of data produced by them is a specialist domain most usually involving sophisticated quantitative manipulation of the data. We do not deal with these methods here. Those interested in quantitative approaches may refer to any of a large number of publications in the field.

NR researchers on DFID projects should note that The Statistical Services Centre (SSC) at the University of Reading provide a biometric advisory and support service to DFID. Among others the SSC also provides a number of Guideline booklets including:

- Guidelines for planning effective surveys (March 1998).
- Statistical guidelines for natural resource projects (March 1998).
- Data management guidelines for experimental projects (March 1998).

Details concerning the SSC's website are provided in the Section: Useful websites.

Content Analysis

We say a few words about this data analysis method since it is one that has become of some significance in qualitative research, and particularly with the development of CAQDAS (computer assisted data analysis software). Content analysis consists of a number of techniques that make inferences from 'texts' from any source. The researcher makes hypotheses about what might be in the text set (e.g. what a sample of NR users are saying to the researcher about their NR base), the set is systematically coded and statistically analysed, and the results interpreted in relation to other ethnographic information. In brief, the information in the text set is reduced to a series of variables which can then be examined for correlations (and then the statistical significance or not of these determined). The method can be used with cross-sectional or longitudinal data sets.

Content analysis is not a new method (see Colby 1966), but computers have considerably increased the potential for dealing with large batches of text by doing word or synonym word searches. Bernard (1995:340-342) gives two examples (by Margolis 1984 and Springle 1986) which illustrate the method. However there are many methodological difficulties with the method which recall those with questionnaire surveys. In particular there are issues surrounding the validity and reliability of coding. Who determines the codes? What checks are there on their reliability and what is their validity from the respondents' perspective? Also if the researcher wants fine discriminations (for example between socio-economic groups as to their IK on the NR base), a considerable amount of primary data will need collecting if the results of analysis are not to be statistically meaningless. Coding is a big task in itself, but improving validity and reliability through using multiple coders and so on is likely to make the method inappropriate and 'poor value for money', in terms of useful information, for most NR research. (For more on CAQDAS see Section: CAQDAS.)

3.3.9 Interviewing, and Data Validity and Reliability

The above sections may seem complex and confusing to scientists who only want some simple answers to their questions. However, the reason for stressing the complex nature of the interview encounter has to do with the validity and reliability of the data generated through it — two areas that are of concern to both natural and social scientists (and to policy makers who wish to develop knowledge-based policy and practice). Thus a number of simple points can be made with regard to the above and which are germaine not only to the interview encounter but to all tools and techniques (matrices, seasonal calendars and so on) by which data is generated:

- The first point is that data/information does not "lie around like sea-shells waiting to be picked up from the sea shore" (as positivists appear to think) but is generated in the encounter. That is why reflecting on the 'interface' between, and the potential 'agendas' of, the parties to such encounters is so important (see Blaikie *et al.* 1996).
- Secondly, knowledge is culturally specific — which means that it may also be specific to the social status of the parties to the encounter and to the social context in which the encounter takes place.
- Thirdly, where there is a development 'problem' (a constraint/opportunity), whether and how it is perceived as being one or the other may vary according to different parties (whether researcher or different NR user), as may potential solutions.

These points require the researcher to reflect on the nature of the data generation and, through comparative methods, check how generic particular items of knowledge are in the culture under study.

- Fourthly, if generic data is sought, there is a need for 'triangulation' to establish the validity and reliability of the data (see Section: Validity and Reliability), it is as well to check the information derived by one method in one context from particular respondents with that derived from other respondents (with similar and contrasting socio-economic characteristics) in other contexts using other methods.
- Fifthly, 'reliability depends essentially on explicitly described observational procedures' (Kirk and Miller 1986:41). Identifying the conditions under which data is generated enables the researcher to form an opinion as to the reliability of the conclusions based on it and, through varying different variables, test how far they hold in different contexts or with different respondents. It also enables the researcher to form a view as to whether data are 'quixotic' (trivial and misleading), 'type 3 errors' (the result of asking the wrong question), the result of a poor measuring instrument (the interviewer) or whether they have 'synchronic' and 'diachronic reliability' — that is are robust. In general structured interview techniques have been considered as producing reliable but not necessarily valid data, while unstructured interview techniques have been considered as producing valid data whose reliability has to be substantiated through triangulation and the detailing of the relevant context of observation (see Figure 3.3).

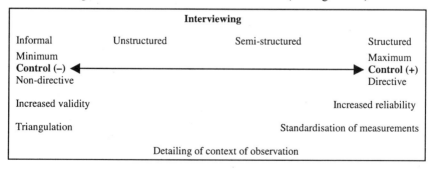

Figure 3.3: Interviewing and triangulation

3.3.10 Issues: Discussion and Dialogue

The trend in academic anthropology over the last century and more recently in NR research has been from observational methods to participatory ones, and for the same reason — the urge to improve the validity of data. Yet the goals of the two disciplines are essentially different and this has an impact on their use of the interview method. The academic anthropologist's goal is to achieve accuracy in the description of the observed social behaviour and respondents' perspectives on reality. With the decline of 'Grand theory', understanding, upon which 'middle-order theory' may be built, has become the superordinate goal of fieldwork (see Glaser and Strauss 1968). The methods used are primarily extractive and static (the capturing of IK and its reification in textbooks). In general this has meant that for academic anthropologists the social formations they study remain unquestioned. By contrast the development anthropologist goes beyond the faithful representation of other cultures to ask 'why is this so' and 'why can't this be different'? (S)he is concerned with identifying the social processes which entrench inequality and lack of access to opportunity, and with 'relaxing' these. Here 'culture' is seen as being as much a constraint as an aid to the livelihoods and well-being of identified social groups. The difference between the two approaches in neatly captured by the title of an article by Sean Conlin in RRA No.2, "Baseline surveys: an escape from thinking about research problems and, even more, a refuge from actually doing anything".

Pace Hobart (1993), while the development goal is resolutely 'modernist', in a post-ToT era it is increasingly driven by the goals of stakeholders in the cultures in which development anthropologists work. Here understanding 'custom' is necessary for providing a baseline for setting out from and exploring with stakeholders the possibilities for resolving constraints to their livelihoods and developing opportunities. Here the generation of new knowledge with (or by) stakeholders represents a shift from 'interviewing' (with its overtone of unequal relationship between interviewer and interviewee) to dialogue and discussion where participants converse on an equal footing, and may question received wisdom and suspend cultural assumptions (as in 'brainstorming' and 'envisioning'). The same tools may be used (matrices, charts, Venn diagrams, interviews and so on), but they are no longer used just for RRA or PRA (where the stress is on 'appraisal') but are integrated into 'action research' (PLA) cycles in which reflective learning (using IK and Scientific Knowledge) is shared by all participants (and where the stress is on action and problem solving) (see Peters and Waterman 1982; Checkland and Scholes 1990; Senge 1990).

In this enterprise, while semi-structured and structured interview techniques may be used to focus in on particular topics and issues (as for example in needs analysis and options ranking through matrices and problem censuses), the preferred methods are informal and unstructured interviews (i.e. dialogue and discussion, for example in workshops with stakeholders), and collegiate rather than consultative working with stakeholders (see Ladder of Participation: Figure 1.3). Validity is improved, though not necessarily easily achieved (since IK may have internal but not external validity), through direct and immediate feedback from the different stakeholders at the level of investigation — local stakeholders (both end-users and extension agencies) with their IK and researchers with their scientific knowledge. Triangulation and sampling using different measuring instruments and in different contexts, becomes important.

3.4 Wealth Ranking/Well-being or Vulnerability Ranking/Social Mapping

Cost	L	Individual/group perspective	I/G
Time	L	Expertise required (social and nat. scientist)	M
Data reliability	M-H	Observer bias	L
		Control of process (directive)	M

Definition: The participatory identification of social units within a population/ community and their arrangement into a hierarchical rank order according to single or multiple criteria of differentiation (such as gender, age, ethnicity, occupation and the like) which are determinant of differences in wealth, well-being or vulnerability between the identified social strata.

Purpose: To identify participatively and rank different social units (villages, quarters, households, individuals) within a population/community according to significant social criteria as a first step in the collection of comparative information on the well-being status of these units and with a view to designing more targeted interventions and monitoring their impact on the livelihoods of these units.

3.4.1 Defining the Target Group: The Poor

Why rank social units? One answer is in order to identify the appropriate end-users of technology development, whether for data collection or extension purposes. In the case of public sector development agencies the end-users are primarily the poorest of the poor. Some writers have drawn attention to the tendency through the 1980s for equity concerns and concerns about resource-poor NR users to be overshadowed by concerns about the environment and participation in development (see e.g. Ravnborg 1992; Lipton and Maxwell 1992:15-16). However, there is now agreement by the international community (as enshrined at the Cairo, Copenhagen and Beijing Conferences) that the reduction of poverty and social exclusion are now the prime objectives of development (see for example ODA 1992; World Bank 1992), and that there are complementarities between poverty reduction, participation and environmental sustain- ability. In the 1990s attention has increasingly focused on seeking a deeper understanding of the causes and consequences of deprivation, and seeking solutions in policy and practice which will lead to its sustained reduction (Brocklesby and Holland 1998:1). But in order to do so it is first necessary to identify who the resource-poor/socially excluded are.

Identifying the Poor

This is not as simple as it might at first seem. As is now accepted (and as the 'poor' themselves point out) 'poverty is not just an economic condition, but is tied in with issues of vulnerability, social exclusion, powerlessness and insecurity. Poverty is complex, context specific, and affected by political, social, gender, seasonal, geographical and environmental factors' (Brocklesby and Holland 1998:ii). As the Human Development Report states 'human poverty is more than income poverty — it is the denial of choices and opportunities for living a tolerable life' (UNDP 1997:5).

Historically, formal economic definitions of absolute poverty have led to whole populations being classified as poor or vulnerable, with development policy and inter- ventions treating them as a homogeneous target group. Supply-side development policy and practice in particular assumed that all NR users in an area were basically alike and that one policy instrument/technology would fit all. But as Grandin notes (1988:3) "By assuming all households are similar, the representativeness of farmers interviewed does not arise". As Chambers has pointed out (e.g. 1983, 1995), this leads to biases in the data collected and to the development of policy instruments/technology which, while they may suite the better-off, are inappropriate to the needs of the resource-poor. For example, in a study of inequality in a Hausa village, Hill (1972) long ago pointed out that, "there are many rich farmers who have entirely different economic aims from many poorer farmers."

In brief, insufficient attention has been paid to social differentiation and relative poverty within populations (e.g. inter- and intra-household differences), to issues concerning the transfer of resources between social units within populations and the effect of development policy and practice in favouring some social units at the expense of others. While earlier development theory assumed the poorest within poor populations would benefit via 'trickle-down', there is compelling evidence of a widening gap between rich and poor in many parts of the world as the poor's access to resources is eroded and as the better-off — favoured by policy and practical initiatives — 'capture' resources to secure their own well-being (see UNDP 1992).

The underlying point here is that a concern with formal measures of poverty and the treatment of whole populations as poor has masked the issue of social inequality within populations. Yet processes of social and economic differentiation naturally take place among NR users operating under similar agro-ecological conditions, and lead to different resource endowments and livelihood strategies. As Mikkelsen (1995: 129) points out, "social anthropologists have long observed that villagers take a passionate interest in the relative household standard of living and do their own subconscious rankings." Thus if we are concerned about social equity, there needs to be criteria for judging between resource-rich and resource-poor social units within a population. We give two examples here from Indonesia. (It should be noted that these are probably local researchers' indicators, based on field experience, rather than respondents.)

Table 3.4 Key indicators of well-being and poverty among rural labouring children

Indicators of Well-being	Indicators of Poverty
Own a pumpset	Fetch water from public pump/well
Own a cow/bullock	
Own farming land	Landless/small piece of dry land
Have regular bank transactions	Own a sheep/goat/hen or nothing
Own a house	Live in leaky thatched house or homeless
Consume rice as staple	Eat *jowar* and *bajra*, but rarely rice
Have stainless steel vessels	Most vessels of mud, rarely stainless steel
Own jewellery	
Purchase groceries on monthly basis	Purchase grocery items daily
Own a radio, TV, cupboard, fan, clock	
Own a motorcycle/moped	
Send children to standard schools	
Own a latrine	Use open air defecation
Own plots locally/in town	
Have a borewell in the house	
Work at a bank/office, run a business etc.	Odd jobs, daily wage, share cropping, construction, agricultural tasks etc.
Wear neatly washed cloths	Cloths not washed properly and may be torn

Source: Narayanasamy *et al.*. 1996.

Table 3.5 Indicators of household prosperity in rural Java

Indicators	Prosperity level		
	Low	Medium	High
House	Bamboo	Combination	Brick and plaster teak
Rooms	1 or 2, small	–	Many, large
Floor	Dirt	Bricks with cement, limestone blocks	Polished cement blocks
Roof	Straw; fronds	–	Tiles
Windows	None	Wooden with slats	Wooden with glass
Bedding	Mats on floor	Bamboo slat beds with mats	Wooden/iron beds with mattress
Lighting	Oil lamps	Kerosene lamps	Home generator
Water source	Neighbour's well, river	–	Own well
Toilet	Outdoor, unenclosed	Outdoor, enclosed	Indoor
Transport	None	Bicycle, draft cart	Motorcycle, truck, van
Entertainment equipment	None	Radio, tape recorder	Battery TV
Refreshment for researcher	None, tea without sugar	Tea with sugar, other	Tea, coffee, plus snacks

Source: Honadle 1979, in McCracken *et al.*, 1988:21.

The definitions of 'poverty' and 'well-being' have also been critiqued for having an ideological bias towards a materialistic interpretation of peoples' livelihoods. As Chambers notes (1995:172), "anti-poverty rhetoric is widespread; indicators are universalistic, as are solutions. Economists' 'realities' predominate — expressed in 'income-poverty', 'employment' and the like — while other indicators of well-being are rarely used. Thus 'income-optimisation' and 'employment' become the end of policy." (See also Ravnborg and Sano 1994).

Current development initiatives accept that, while whole populations may be classified as poor according to formal income-based measures, there are large differences within populations when measured on relative as opposed to absolute scales. The one-dimensional measure of poverty which characterises people as poor according to a fixed point on an income scale (the poverty line), has largely been replaced by criteria which identify 'quality of life', 'well-being', 'vulnerability' and/or 'social exclusion' according to a bundle of characteristics of both a formal and more informal/local nature (see de Haan 1999, Maxwell 1999, Ravallion 1992), and has led to a concern with livelihood security. The research agenda has broadened to a concern with the multi-dimensionality of poverty and vulnerability, an interest in local people's own criteria for the identification of these (see example below), and a consideration of the variability in local people's needs and priorities. As Grandin says (1988:1) where "wealth is defined in terms of access to or control over important economic resources ... wealth inequality is found in virtually every human community ... . As the nature of economic resources varies from community to community, so too will the specific defining characteristics of wealth." But in addition, wealth status has social and political correlates beyond the economic sector. Poverty goes hand in hand with poor health status, exploitation, lack of access to natural, social and economic resources, powerlessness and social isolation, and general vulnerability to shocks and trends. The design of interventions appropriate to their social context and client need is considerably helped by understanding the local character and determinants of poverty, well-being and vulnerability within populations and between social units, and is a prime reason for the disaggregation of a population for data collection purposes. (The example below is based on respondents' criteria, rather than on mixed etic and emic criteria as in the Indonesian examples above.)

Table 3.6 Some criteria for wealth and poverty given by Tanzanians in wealth ranking exercise

	Msombe (Kiponzelo)	Kihanga A (Kihanga)
Criteria for wealth	• having strength to farm	• having full working abilities
	• facing no problems with fertilizers	• getting big harvests which allow for considerable sales
	• cultivating big fields	• using fertilizers, perhaps even twice
	• using ox-plough	• employing needy people as day labourers
	• employing day labourers	
	• having cattle	
Criteria for poverty	• failing to cultivate or cultivating only small fields due to lack of strength or old age	• being old, sick or single
		• failing to get enough food and feeling hunger
	• never managing to get fertilizers	• working for others to get food
	• depending on others for food	• using cash money for food rather than for fertilizers

Source: Ravnborg 1992:7.

3.4.2 *Missing the Poor*

There is a definitional issue concerning the identification of the poor — they may be 'missed' by their being lumped together with other social strata (e.g. small farmers) or with whole populations. But there is also a practical problem on the ground — the most vulnerable may be missed because of project biases which militate against researchers coming into contact with them. Chambers (1983, 1987) long ago pointed out some of the unwitting biases (e.g. 'tarmac bias', 'dry-season bias', 'diplomatic bias', 'elite bias', etc.), and other methodological biases which can lead researchers to focus on the resource-rich rather than the resource-poor (e.g. focus on cash crops, class affinities, convenience of access, risk-acceptance by the resource rich) (see also Leonard 1977; and Chambers and Jiggins 1986:23).

All these biases lead to sampling errors, and can result in what Chambers has called 'rural development tourism' and in the poorest of the poor being missed by researchers and extension agencies alike. For example, Lindberg *et al.* (1993), in a critique of a report to SIDA on the impact of structural adjustment programmes on the poorest groups in Tanzania (Booth *et al.* 1993), suggest that the report's conclusions are suspect because it does not represent the views of the poorest groups — those 'without anything' *(hana kitu)* or 'totally destitute' *(maskini kabisa)* — in the study villages. Indeed details from the report suggest that the study team "never encountered the bottom stratum" ... (p.5) and "... became unduly dependent on what was publicly said about local social stratification" (p.6). The authors note that others such as Grandin (1983) and Pretty *et al.* (1992) have previously shown how easy it is to miss the poor in local studies focused on social stratification, and they stress that even when using wealth ranking and other participatory techniques, and ostensibly focusing on the poor, "precautions must be taken to make sure that the poorest of the poor are included" (p.4). In brief when studying whole communities, researchers need to be careful about establishing the representativeness of the community, of the subgroups which compose it, and of the respondents from which information is sought; and when studying any particular strata within a community to include respondents from that strata.

In addition, we should also note that a focus on the normative 'household' can lead to the most vulnerable (women, children, the aged) being missed altogether. As Mikkelsen notes (1995: 152), historically "Indicative strategies on poverty have not been gender disaggregated and women's heavier exposure to poverty has been disguised". Yet poverty studies which apply gender disaggregated analysis (as in intra-household studies) demonstrate that women more than men are subject to relative as well as absolute poverty (see Wignaraja 1990; Moser 1989; 1993). The same may be even more true for children and the aged in some contexts — that is they may be the most vulnerable to shocks, and may be the most at risk of food insecurity. The experience of recent famines in Africa, for example, suggest that monitoring food security at the household level may be inadequate among populations which consider the very old and the very young as the first social capital items to be expended when the household is faced with disaster.

The perception by researchers that the population they are dealing with are all poor can also be reinforced by what local people say. (Local people may 'ventriloquise' what more 'powerful' or better off 'experts' say in order to gain access to the opportunities which development professionals bring). This is one reason why researchers have moved beyond 'income poverty' to a broader-based definition of 'poverty' which includes vulnerability due to lack of, or access to, NR, financial, social and other resources. A PPA in South Africa by Operation Hunger (see Breslin and Delius 1997) found that participatory exercises to 'identify the poor' were not very useful in getting a greater sense of local processes and perspectives, because participants continually responded that they were all 'poor.' Whatever the (strategic) reasons for them saying this, the PPA team decided that '... instead of using local classifications of poverty as the starting point for discussion, it might be more productive to explore the diverse nature of households ...' Starting from local people's perceptions of what the 'ideal' household was in their context and why, the team were then able to move on to consider which households on the ground resembled this proper household and how they reached this ideal condition, and which households failed to and why. This led to participants (in this case women ranging in age from their early twenties to mid-sixties) drawing pictures to represent the range of households in the village, and in turn led to a group exploration of the range of household dynamics. The exercise in one village led to the depiction of 7 types of household (these are illustrated below) — though there may be more — with a story of how each household survives (see article for these coping strategies).

Photograph 3.4: Wealth ranking, bottom of the pile: rickshaw pullers

It is also worth noting that the perceptions of different categories of participant may also bias the data. In the Operation Hunger PPA, the team held group discussions with participants divided according to age and gender, but found that, "even seemingly homogeneous groups, such as female pensioners, had vastly different development opportunities and constraints" (due presumably to their different 'assets' and social responsibilities, and position within the broader community). Thus there were differing gender and generational perceptions of household and community dynamics, and contrasting development priorities within the village. (On exploring contrasting problems and priorities see Section 3.18 Problem Census.)

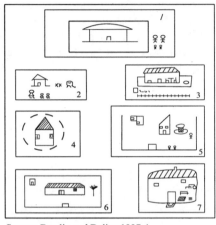

Source: Breslin and Delius 1997:4.

Figure 3.4: Types of household drawn by South African women in PPA exercise

Finally, in sectorally-focused research (such as NR research) there is a particular danger of the resource-poor being defined in relation to the soils-water-topography-vegetation environment rather than by the sum of their personal, social, natural and other resources (see Chambers and Jiggins 1986:23). As Lipton and Maxwell note (1992:15), "agricultural research ... is not yet sufficiently permeated with the new anti-poverty agenda. A growing majority of the poor are labourers, rather than 'small farmers'." While HYV crops do raise demand for labour, much research persists in developing labour-saving production techniques (e.g. mechanisation) while the poor's problems go largely unresearched. An interesting finding from the Operation Hunger PPA was the role of agriculture in households' coping strategies. The women who drew the pictures of the different types of household had been invited to the PPA session to discuss agricultural issues. The defining feature of the group was that some had access to land and were growing food and others did not, but had agricultural piece jobs. Despite this, there was no mention of agriculture, and "the key issue which was constantly reinforced throughout the exercise was wage employment — employment being central to the 'proper household'." Moreover, the loss of employment appeared as a key factor in the undermining of the household" (Breslin and Delius 1997).

To give a hypothetical example of the potential consequences of failure to identify the poorest of the poor. The population of Bangladesh is in excess of 125 million, 90 million of whom lead rural lives. 50% of these are functionally landless (owning less than one fifth of a hectare of land per household) and on international measures the majority of these are poor. Many aid organisations work at this level to alleviate poverty. Yet to identify the poorest of the poor amongst this huge population (say 45 million) requires even finer criteria of discrimination. One such criteria is gender since women are known to be amongst the poorest on international measures (see Section: Gender). (Another is old age). Yet in the drive to lift women's status vis-à-vis men, rural women are frequently lumped together as a group for extension purposes (e.g. micro-credit schemes). Thus the result may again be a bias in favour of those households which are not among the poorest and most vulnerable. Indeed the poorest may only be 1-2% of the total rural population (say 2 million) on measures of extreme vulnerability, and virtually invisible in individual rural communities because their numbers are so thinly spread through the whole population. In consequence when their coping strategies fail — for example during a natural shock such as the prolonged high floods experienced in Bangladesh in 1998 — the death of one in ten of these from hunger and disease is very unlikely to be noticed or recorded — particularly if they are women and/or old persons and even though this may represent about 200,000 people!

A Platform for Discussions

The consideration of absolute versus relative (local) measures of poverty and vulnerability also suggests a second reason for undertaking participatory wealth/vulnerability ranking exercises. As noted above, indicators of poverty have historically been formal (positivist) and may bear little relation to conditions on the ground at the local level. Participative ranking, by contrast, can indicate those social units that local respondents consider most vulnerable and, as importantly, provide the criteria for why they consider them(selves) to be so. Thus the exercise is not just a ranking exercise for identifying those most at risk but provides a platform for further discussion (individual or group) about local coping strategies and where effort might be most usefully directed to reduce vulnerability. Certainly Brocklesby and Holland (1998:5), in their report to DFID on PPAs and Public Services, consider that PPAs (which include wealth ranking and purposive sampling) provide important information on the character and process of poverty for policy makers. For instance in the example from Tanzania given above, 'lack of strength' — particularly associated with being old, sick or single — is not only an indicator but a cause of vulnerability and can lead to a draw-down on cash reserves. Discussion with respondents might reveal that the ideal is to be a successful farmer while young and invest profits in stock, in having many children and cash in the bank to provide for old age and sickness. But what might be done for those who fail to achieve this and thus become vulnerable in old age? Discussion may reveal that there are increasing numbers of older people in the region while their traditional social support mechanisms have deteriorated as their children migrate to the mines or urban areas and 'forget' them. The ranking exercise indicates that farming is no longer an option for these people — they have no 'strength' to do so — but further discussion may reveal opportunities for creating jobs for the young in the area and for supporting less strenuous work-fare activities for the old rather than just targeted safety nets.

Other Criteria of Social Differentiation

The criteria of social differentiation that is chosen for data collection purposes may vary according to the type of data that is required. Major axes of difference within communities may be gender, age, well-being, ethnicity, religion, caste, occupation and so on. Differences in income, employment, health, and educational status and the like may be outcomes of these axes of difference — that is access to opportunities in different sectors may be apportioned differentially according to such social characteristics. Disadvantage is frequently multi-dimensional, with the vulnerability of social units according to one criteria being repeated and reinforced in other sectors. For example women in many developing countries have a poorer educational status than men, and partially in consequence have less occupational and income-generating opportunities, and may in turn have a poorer health status. Their well-being, and that of their children, can be particularly at risk on the death of, or separation from, their husband. However, as the example above indicates, not all women in a population are equally at risk. Other cross-cutting factors, such as age, ethnicity, occupation/wealth of husband (or father), as well as marital status and family size, interact with that of gender to produce gradations in the present/future vulnerability of women. The same is true of social units identified according to other criteria of difference. Understanding the character of well-being and vulnerability in a population is understanding how these different social mechanisms are inter-related and interact to socially produce individuals and groups with particular needs and vulnerabilities. It is also to understand how the relations between the vulnerable and other social units in a population reproduce their social exclusion.

Internal Versus External Validity of Well-being Indices?

Social units can be identified through formal methods (such as surveys) using a range of indicators of well-being and vulnerability and increasingly include a combination of formal and local/culture-specific indicators (see Carvalho and White 1997). This is increasingly common in some sectors -for example health (see Blaxter 1990). Such an approach can provide robust data with validity wider than the survey location.

Participatory Poverty Assessments (PPAs), as promoted by the World Bank and supported by national governments go some way to linking location-specific qualitative information with that which can be used by policy-makers at a wider scale. PPAs have been carried out in a wide range of countries and are designed to gather poor people's perceptions on key issues relating to poverty reduction. "The premise is that involving poor people in the analysis will ensure that the strategies identified for poverty alleviation will reflect their concerns, include their priorities and identify the obstacles to development" (Thompson *et al.* 1996:23). As Brocklesby and Holland state (1998:1), PPAs "have challenged both traditional modes of poverty analysis and subsequent policy development. Through them poor people have demonstrated a hitherto overlooked capacity to analyse poverty and policy. Their analyses have provided a depth and understanding to the notion of poverty, extending and enhancing narrow consumption-or income-based definitions ..."

There are a number of well-documented limitations to PPAs (see Hanmer *et al.* 1996), not least the question of external validity where explanatory depth in a limited number of research sites is emphasised over breadth of coverage, aggregation and standardisation of results, and the data generated is based on opinion rather than measurable behaviour. In consequence Brocklesby and Holland (1998:5) suggest a need for caution in their use. Nevertheless, PPAs enrich the poverty profile through illustrating dimensions which conventional statistical analyses tend to miss, provide indicative ideas about what issues are and are not important to local people, and together with quantitative data can be used as a yardstick against which to compare any location-specific data.

3.4.3 Wealth-Ranking Approaches: Participatory

A second approach to wealth-ranking, growing out of PRA and very common in community-based research, is to rely entirely on local informants' identification of social units and their level of well-being using their own culture-specific measures. There is the difficulty here in achieving the external validity that policy-makers at the macro-level require, but may be appropriate for an intervention at the micro-level. Researchers need to be careful to clearly identify and understand informants' criteria for evaluating well-being, and to have a wide spread of informants across the social spectrum to avoid bias. Perspectives on well-being and vulnerability are inflected by social position and context. For example, if one were researching the risk of HIV/Aids infection among different social strata in an African community, one might find local business-men ranking transport- and migrant-workers as more at risk than themselves (on the grounds that these social strata do not wash as thoroughly as business-men do before casual sexual encounters), while rural women might suggest that all these strata are more at risk of infection than rural men because they frequent 'bad' urban environments. As Brocklesby and Holland note (1998:6-7), local conceptualisations of poverty can be diverse and may vary by level (individual vs. community), geographical area, and particularly by gender and age (for an example see tables below from Seeley *et al.* 1996). As can be seen there can be quite marked differences between men and women on some indicators (e.g. 'Having/not having friends and relatives') which may have implications as to whether an intervention should be directed to increasing social solidarity/capital (a community approach) as opposed to one directed to improving (individual) NR and economic capital. It may therefore be difficult to determine a community-wide measure for a specific vulnerability, but on a basket of measures there is likely to be general agreement on who is most at risk and when (n.b. the impact of seasonality on different social units (see Gill 1991).

Table 3.7 Criteria for households best able to cope, Masaka District, Uganda

Indicators	Responses		
	Women	Men	Total
Own and Cultivate a lot of land	25	26	51
Sell *Matooke/mbidde*	26	20	46
Sell coffee	18	15	33
Own cows from which they get milk (to consume and sell)	18	12	30
Have many friends and relatives	22	5	27
Have many sources of income (traders/taxi drivers/builders)	8	9	17
Own goats/pigs/hens (could be sold in an emergency)	5	2	7
Own rental properties	5	0	5
Sell brew	4	1	5
Are well-educated	3	0	3
Are with few dependants	1	0	1

Source: Seeley *et al.* 1996: 15.

Participatory wealth-ranking can be a relatively rapid and cheap exercise but, being location-specific, lacks external validity without further testing for the representativeness of the sample to a larger population. As Thompson *et al.* (1996:22) and Brocklesby and Holland (1996:5) both note, it is important not to directly extrapolate results from participatory appraisals to a larger population. Grandin (1988: 7-9) gives some guidance for choosing representative communities for FSR. She notes that once researchers have selected a target area, they need to get a general sense of the ecological and social diversity of the area (perhaps from government maps, reports, and other secondary sources), check this on the ground through reconnaissance work with extension agents and local people, and follow it up with exploratory study in a number of communities, before choosing communities to represent the diversity of the zone.

Table 3.8 Criteria for households least able to cope, Masaka District, Uganda

Indicators	Responses		
	Women	Men	Total
Without a permanent job (casual labourers)	21	21	42
Without land or having infertile land	17	9	26
With a very small, poor hut to stay in or are squatters	20	5	25
Without relatives or friends in the area	15	3	18
Who are sick/old/disabled	10	6	16
Who are youth just setting up their households	6	6	12
Who are drunkards	0	8	8
Who are widows (with many dependants)	5	2	7
With no possessions (that they could sell in a crisis)	1	3	4
Who live alone	1	2	3

Source: Seeley *et al.* 1996: 16.

There are, however, two issues here. Firstly, seeking 'the representative community' is to focus on the normative and can lead to inappropriate policy instruments at a wider scale because the diversity of communities and their changing poverty status within a region is 'missed'. Secondly, it should be noted that FSR's starting point is the ecological zone. This prioritises NR and can lead to a focus on those who are not the poorest of the poor (since these may have little or no access to NR). By contrast a poverty approach would seek to identify the poorest percentile in the area's (diverse) communities, draw up (or draw on) a participatory poverty assessment for the target area as a whole, and then determine whether 'the problem' is best addressed through NR or other research and development. However, wealth ranking is still required to identify the target group and to gather poor people's (and other stakeholders') perceptions on key issues relating to poverty reduction. With these provisos in mind we reproduce Grandin's figure (below) of the background steps for wealth ranking within a large target population.

Wealth-ranking Approaches: Participatory with External Validation
Another, midway, approach — participatory, less resource intensive than a formal survey but producing more robust and generically applicable data than community-level wealth-ranking exercises — may be possible in countries with good social statistics. This approach bases local participatory wealth-ranking/well-being exercises on the social categories used in national statistics. For example, a NR project in Bangladesh drawing on land-holding categories routinely used by the national Bureau of Statistics, carried out a reconnaissance social survey and wealth ranking exercises at two sites, in order to test whether a social stratification of natural resource users based on land-holding was valid. The project found that size of land-ownership (or its absence), as a proxy for wealth, was a generally valid indicator of similar livelihood, and provided a good platform on which to base further quantitative and qualitative data collection exercises from representatives of the identified social strata (see Barr *et al.* 2000, Dixon *et al.* 2000).

Box 3.1: Background steps for wealth ranking within a large target population

I. Determine ecological zones in target area
   - surface area
   - human population
   - livestock population
   - natural conditions

II. Within ecological zone, determine community differences
   - distance from town/market
   - distance to road
   - farmer group/development programme
   - age of settlement
   - ethnic groups
   - relative wealth (and why) of different communities

III. Select representative communities
IV. Wealth ranking within community

Source: Grandin 1988:8.

Table 3.9 Wealth ranking exercise, Bangladesh

NR user groups			Problem Census Groups		
Strata no.	Wealth Strata by Land Ownership (acres)		Grp. no.	Problem Census Groups-Ujankhalsi	
1	Landless III	<0.05	1	Landless share croppers and other labourers (Strata 1 & 2)	
2	Landless I & II	0.05-0.49	1	-ditto-	
3	Marginal	0.5-0.99	3	Share croppers and medium farmers (Strata 2, 3 & 4)	
4	Small	1.0-2.49	3	-ditto-	
5	Medium I	2.5-4.99	5	Medium farmers (Strata 5 & 6)	
6	Medium II	5.0-7.49	5	-ditto-	
7	Large	>7.5	6	Rich farmers (Strata 7)	
–	+ Prof. Fishers	normally 0	4	Fishermen and fish culturists	
–	–	–	–	–	
–	–	–	2	Women from poor and very poor HH (Strata 1, 2 & 3)	
–	–	–	7	Women from non-poor HH (Strata 4, 5, 6 & 7)	

Source: Barr *et al.* 2000.

A criticism of the method might be that it relies too heavily on a single, extantly-derived, indicator of well-being based primarily on land-holding and income from land, rather than on local peoples' indicators which are multiple and broader. There are, for example, some rural Bangladeshi individuals/households which are wealthy but whose wealthy is not based on land-holding, but on others' agricultural production from land. An example is the deep tubewell owner who 'share-crops' the plots he supplies with water, but may own no land himself. There are inevitable trade-offs in the choice of methods to use and which approach is taken must depend on the purpose for which the data is generated, issues concerning wider validity, and resource and other constraints which the project faces. However, the international community's need for the comparability of data in the drive to meet internationally agreed development targets may require the sacrifice of local nuances in order to capture the larger picture. That is there is a need for focus in the use of the method (and other participatory tools). A recent DFID publication (DFID 2000) notes "the importance of good statistics and other data, disaggregated by sex, to aid policy formulation and monitor progress ..." (p.11). Targets [and indices] "cannot capture the full richness and complexity of the process ... . But regular public assessment ... against a simple and intelligible standard is essential ..." (foreword).

Thus wealth, well-being or vulnerability ranking is a tool for identifying significant social units for data collection purposes, for designing and implementing targeted aid, and for monitoring the impact of this on identified social units. The tool can generate information from respondents about the criteria they use to identify well-being and vulnerability, and about the social units that are differentiated according to these criteria. The social units can then form the framework from which a stratified sample of respondents can be drawn to provide data on particular topics via other methods (ranging from structured and semi-structured questionnaires, through focus groups, to other PRA techniques — as detailed in this report).

3.4.4 Method of Wealth Ranking

The normal starting point is a map of the households of a community, each of which is individually identified by number. If the community is small, then it may be feasible to rank all the households in it. If the community is large and/or the purpose is the exploration of the criteria respondents use to rank social units and the distribution of characteristics of well-being and vulnerability across different social units, then the ranking exercise can be performed by respondents for a random sample of households. How representative the sample will be of the larger population will be a moot point of course, but the sample can be stratified in order to obtain a cross-section of well-being types, particularly if the intention is to identify those at risk according to specific criteria, target them through an intervention, and monitor their progress against specified indicators. Once a general measure of well-being has been established across a number of households and the criteria underlying the local ranking system are understood, it is possible to establish the approximate rank of any household in a community or wider region by measuring it against the initial ranked sample.

The standard method (see Grandin 1988) is for respondents to sort a pile of cards with the number of each household and name of its head written on individual cards. The cards are shuffled and respondents are asked to arrange the named cards in order according to whether they think each household is better, the same, or worse off than the one on the card next to it. The exercise may be done with individual respondents (say three or four) and their rankings averaged to give a composite score (see Grandin 1988:22-26 for figures) or the respondents might work together to agree a ranking. The households then need to be grouped into a number of wealth strata. Grandin (1988:34) suggests that "for most projects, three groups (rich, average, poor) are sufficient" — though informants may recognise more — and she gives details (p.33-36) on how to derive these. The underlying principle is to seek natural breaks in the averaged scores between one household and another in order to obtain fairly homogeneous groups.

After the ranking exercise, respondents are asked to explain what criteria they are using for ranking the households as they do. The criteria will normally go far beyond simple income and even wealth in the European sense to include such things as money, house, amount of land, livestock, transport and machinery, number of wives and/or children, social status, positions of influence and responsibility, specialist knowledge and so on. Respondents usually assess the well-being of a household (or its vulnerability) according to a bundle of characteristics (or their absence). Characteristics which are valued in one society and are considered as enhancing well-being, for example a large number of children, may be considered as increasing vulnerability in another. So it is necessary to establish the value (or its lack) that respondents put on individual characteristics in relation to others.

As Grandin (1988:12) and Guijt (1998: 71) both note, care needs to be taken to clarify with respondents what 'household' and other social terms mean locally, since the household can take a variety of forms and there can also be considerable variation in definition. Indeed if researchers are seeking to identify the poorest of the poor, they may need to focus on individuals rather than households, on intra-household disparity, or on social units which respondents do not consider 'households'. Since the poor occupy the interstices of the social fabric, 'hiding' in other's households, in public spaces, and non-formal residences, they can easily be overlooked in household surveys.

The second method relies on a social mapping technique where respondents make a map indicating the social units (individuals or households) which are the subject of study. Respondents then compare one unit with others (and adjust as they go along) in order to come up with a rank order in which there are 'blocks' of social units of more or less the same level of well-being. The criteria used by respondents for ranking are noted as are their reasons for establishing discontinuities between the blocks (which represent locally-significant social strata. As with card ranking, social mapping establishes a relative and not absolute ranking of social units, and if external validity is required, the rank order will need to be related to wider scales of well-being and vulnerability.

Well-being Monitoring
Grandin (1988:36) sees wealth ranking as an exercise for identifying significant socio-economic strata for data collection purposes. However, the method is also useful for identifying strata for extension purposes and for monitoring the impact of interventions on the target groups (e.g. the potentially negative impact of structural adjustment policies on the poor). This is in keeping with the 'new poverty agenda' which is not only interested in the character of poverty but is also concerned with poverty as a process, and with establishing indicators for monitoring the achievement (or not) of social and economic targets designed to eradicate poverty (see e.g. World Bank 1992). Thus Guijt (1998: 71-73) includes well-being/social mapping as a useful method for monitoring socio-economic data relating to social units over time, and gives a number of examples. The method "is also useful for establishing local indicators of well-being that can then be monitored more specifically with other methods" (p.71). It can presumably also be used for collecting historical data on social units from respondents using those indicators. One difficulty may be that local indicators of well-being are likely to change over time — in the same way as the constraints that people face in their livelihoods do — since these are perceptual and not observable outputs (see an example in Section: Historical Comparison). (An example is provided by new technology adoption. At one point in time an indicator of poverty may be not having a tin roof on the house. Many years later, even the houses of the poor may have tin roofs, but the poor may not have fridges). Researchers will need to establish a standard with respondents that can hold over time and/or employ a modicum of 'substitutability' in the indices chosen.

3.5 Mapping

Cost	L	Individual/group perspective	I/G
Time	L	Expertise required (social and nat. scientist)	L
Data reliability	H	Observer bias	L
		Control of process (directive)	L

Definition: For collecting information on the spatial distribution of natural and other resources in a region.

Purpose: To identify the distribution of specific resources and topographical features in an area or region and provide a platform for the participative analysis of current and potential future relationships between them.

Maps may show any/all of the resources thought important to natural resource research (e.g. topography, water, soils, forest, property regimes, land-use patterns, human habitation, roads/footpaths, markets, the location of service providers, ritual sites, social and political groupings, the spatial and temporal distances between features, and many more).

Maps may be constructed according to conventional scales and units or according to those habitually used by the informants. Which is used will depend upon the purpose of the map, but if the map is intended to capture IK, participants should be allowed to draw according to local canons and scale and to record only those features which they find significant. It is recognised that the resulting output may then be difficult to interpret by researchers unfamiliar with these canons, but it is important to capture what is valued by participants; the comparison of this with researchers' own 'objective' map, and discussions about the differences, can provide insights into local NR management rationale.

The method has traditionally been used with key informants (those who are knowledgeable about many of the features that researchers wish to record). However, it may be used in individual and/or group sessions with informants drawn from different socio-economic strata (i.e. differentiated according to ethnicity, gender, age, occupational status or socio-economic status). Maps are then constructed from the perspective of the individual, individual household, community or at a larger scale, dependent upon the purpose of the map. For example a map drawn by a household head may indicate where the main NR underpinning the household's livelihood strategies are located. Such resource maps may also be constructed according to gender as a step in investigating the conflicts and complementarities over NR between men and women in a household (see below). The same can be done with different socio-economic/NR user groups. This can reveal differences between groups both in their livelihood strategies and in their perception of opportunities and constraints, and between them and scientists, with regard to their knowledge of, and/or access to, natural and social resources. These can be explored further using other methods.

Mapping may have an end in itself in familiarising researchers with the location of and relationships between available resources in a region. However, it also serves as a way into more extended discussions with target groups concerning opportunities and constraints to their livelihoods as they see them. In Madah in central Tanzania — a rapidly growing community dominated by immigrant farmers — for example, Ostberg found that "Drawing a map of the area and discussing it had a profound effect on the perception of land use for a number of people in Madah" (1996:27). The common opinion expressed by new immigrants to the region was that there were abundant land resources for the community's future needs, while some residents were of the opinion

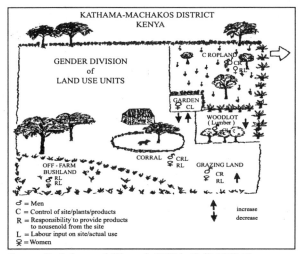

Source: Rocheleau and Edmunds 1997 in Guijt 1998:65.

Figure 3.5: Map showing division of land units by gender, Kenya

that forest clearance for farming was controlled. The mapping exercise and discussion it provoked revealed both of these as misconceptions, and also brought to light other concerns by indigenous people that there were now too many people and livestock in the area. "Different ways of life now meet in the hills ... . The immigrants and the Burunge agree that vacant land still remains in the hills, but they disagree on whether the remaining forests should be cleared or not" (p.26). Thus "participatory mapping helped to focus local interest on the area's natural resources. This enabled the local people to think about land use planning for the future" (p.28).

While it is a spatially-oriented method, mapping can have a temporal dimension. It can be used to collect baseline data, seasonal and historical data, and to monitor future NR patterns and land-use change. As such it can be used to evaluate impact and/or can serve as a platform for extended discussions with target groups about shocks and trends (examples of these uses are to be found in Section 3.12 Historical Comparison).

NR maps may also be developed into bioresource flow diagrams (again in order to investigate the potential for greater integration between the livelihood strategies of identified user groups) (see Section: Bioresource flows). An example of combining methods is provided by Willmer and Ketzis (1998). They combined resource mapping and labour allocation analysis techniques to gain a deeper understanding of intra-household division of control and responsibility for labour and resource-related activities in a small rural community in Honduras. Basic data on 12 households considered representative of various strata in the community (based on wealth, location and characteristics such as female-headed) was obtained through informal interviews. Households were then ranked into three classes according to a wealth ranking exercise (after Grandin 1988) and a household from each class from each community neighbourhood was then selected for the mapping exercises. Resource maps were drawn first, and followed by labour maps which were drawn on tracing paper laid over the resource map with different coloured lines (representing each family member) being drawn from each object on the resource map to/from the house to represent the activity. The exercises provided a visual representation of gender and generational differences between household members' labour allocations (time allocation figures could be added to the lines) and a platform for further discussions about the differences between men's, women's and children's activities. It also provided a platform for an analysis of differences between households according to their wealth.

Source: Ostberg 1996:27.

Figure 3.6: Map of Madah area, (central Tanzania, drawn by participants on the ground and transferred to paper by researcher)

It should be remembered that maps drawn by local people are unlikely to conform to the canons of modern formal cartography based on a Cartesian interpretation of space which have so influenced western researchers' perspectives on and evaluation of the world. Indigenous maps are personal/collective statements with all that that implies. There may be contraction/expansion of features and particularly of the relations between them according to their importance to the informant(s) rather than according to any spatial relationship, and the data recorded (or left out) is inflected by social and personal characteristics. The latter inflection can be overcome through (homogeneous) group exercises, the former is instructive in its own right — maps being particularly informative as regards the systems-boundaries of NR users' primary livelihood strategies. There are no 'objective maps' (see Gell 1992), merely maps from different perspectives, the similarities and differences of which are informative and can give rise to further discussion with local people concerning opportunities and constraints to their livelihoods and the potential impacts of interventions on these and on those of other groups in their community.

As with the collection of all IK, care must be taken in the framing of the questions asked since respondents will respond (or not) in terms of the particular question asked. Questions should be of a general nature, rather than specific, though respondents may then ask for and require some clarification. Leading questions should be avoided since they structure responses in terms of etic and not emic perspectives. Individual responses may well be different to group responses.

As with transects, a drawback to mapping (whether resource mapping or GIS) in the NR sector is its focus on land use and NR rather than on livelihood strategies. There is a danger that researchers may seek optimal production strategies for biophysical zones, rather than exploring client need/concerns in terms of their environmental perspectives, livelihood goals and capital endowments, and the trade-offs they may have to make as a consequence. For example, some individuals/households belonging to less well endowed social strata may have to grow staple crops under sub-optimal conditions because they have little or no access to those zones identified as biophysically most suited to the growing of these crops).

3.5.1 Interpretation of Maps

Caution needs to be taken when developing conclusions based on the data recorded on a map. Maps are partial, constructed according to particular questions and, while they appear to suggest logical answers, this logic can shift in the light of new data added to the map. An example is provide by Anbalagan *et al.* (1997:5) in their investigation of well pollution from tannery effluents in a south Indian village (see below). The authors used a range of methods besides resource mapping (including social mapping, transect walks, chemical analysis of water quality, time line and trend change analysis and focus group discussions). The map identifies water sources (wells, river, ponds and tanks) and distinguishes between wells in use and those no longer in use. The authors state that of the 56 wells located in Kamatchipuram, only 16 wells near the river are uncontaminated while agricultural land has been made unsuitable for crop production because of high saline deposits in the soil. This has had a significant negative impact on agriculturally-based livelihoods and on the health of livestock and humans. The authors are also definite in their attribution of the cause of pollution as the development of the tanning industry in the region over a period of 50 years, and in particular the shift from natural tanning materials to chemical ones and their disposal in streams and fields.

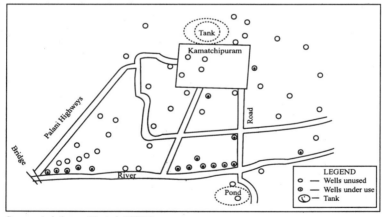

Source: Anbalagan, K. et al. 1997:5.

Figure 3.7: Water resource map of Kamatchipuram, S. India

The authors may well be correct in their attribution of the cause of pollution, though it is not clear from their article whether local people understand 'pollution' in the same terms as the researchers and identify the tanning industry as the cause. There may also be other factors involved in the increasing salinity of the soil and decline in agricultural productivity. The point being made here, however, is that the mapping of some additional elements (such as the location of the tanneries, and contour-lines to gain an impression of land height) together with further discussion on changing population densities, agricultural practices and the importance of agriculture versus the tanning industry over the longer term might reveal a complex of causes for the pollution. The point is that maps may have too little or too much data, and like statistics, require the support of other methods and verbal statements to assist their interpretation.

Photograph 3.5: Taking part in problem census

3.5.2 Participatory GIS

Participatory GIS is becoming popular, and there may be cost benefits from its use when compared with formal mapping techniques. However, there is a worry that as GIS becomes more widely used in spatial decision-making, top-down development planning will be reinforced. There is also the issue again that mapping by NR users and scientists is according to different scales and units, but that priority may be given by planners to that 'objectively' determined by scientists — i.e. to one which they understand. However, it is this difference in perception that is so instructive. As Abbot *et al.* note (1998:27), GIS has 'the ability to bring together selected themes or layers of data and perform a number of spatial analytical operations." In an experimental participatory GIS project in Mpumalanga in South Africa, the overlay of official land type data and IK about soils indicated conflicting representations of land potential. "These discordant understandings are a product of scale, the multiple meanings of agro-ecological potential, and differing farming systems" (p.27).

Again GIS maps 'outcomes', and any relationships hypothesised between elements may be primarily etic unless the method is supported by data gleaned by other PRA techniques. GIS cannot capture the (emic) NRM reasoning behind land use patterns; this has to be explored via other methods. A GIS which maps according to local scales and units might indicate the relationships between elements (as in the participatory resource mapping above), but as a substantive rather than formal representation of reality will require exploration and interpretation by researchers together with informants if they are to gain maximum value from it. As Abbot *et al.* note (1998:32), some of the constraints GIS faces are 'the difficulties of capturing power relations and politics in a spatial database, integrating information derived at small scales from conventional sources with that at much larger scales from exercises such as participatory mapping, and finding an appropriate 'balance' between such widely differing types of data and information ... ." Abbot *et al.* (1998) consider that it can assist in raising awareness across different interest groups, and help to avoid misrepresentations such as using the physical environment to infer lifestyles.

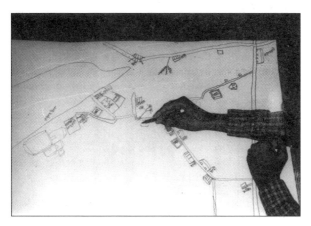

Photograph 3.6: Drawing a map

Some of the criticisms that have been levelled at GIS are summarised in a paper by Harris and Weiner (n.d.) on 'Community-Integrated GIS for Land Reform in Mpumalanga Province, South Africa'. They note that there are those political economists such as Rundstrum (1995) who consider that "Geographical 're-presentations' — topographic maps, GIS, and other exotica — are just part of a much larger world of inscriptions used in Western techno-science to disenfranchise indigenous peoples" (ibid. 51) — i.e. GIS is culturally biased. On the other hand there are those such as Harris and Weiner who believe there is a middle ground and contend that GIS is a contradictory technology that both marginalizes and empowers people and communities simultaneously. The issues surrounding GIS are summarised in Box 3.2, while the Harris and Weiner's counter argument is summarised in Box 3.3.

Box 3.2: Issues in the social theoretical critique of GIS

- the perceived positivism and hegemonic power relations embedded within GIS.
- the claimed value-neutral and objective nature of GIS.
- the apparent pre-eminence given to data and facts and the retreat from knowledge with resultant regional and data inequities.
- the (anti) democratic nature of GIS brought about by the existence of differential access to data and technology.
- the surveillant capabilities of GIS and the trend toward normalisation, knowledge engineering, and the control of populations.
- differential access to GIS data, hardware, software, and humanware.
- data availability, the commodification of data, the movement toward a bureaucratic-informational complex, and the role of spatial data institutions and GIS agencies.
- privacy, confidentiality, and the intrusive role of geodemographics expert 'top down' vs. local knowledge 'bottom up.'

- structural knowledge distortion.
- ethical and responsible uses of GIS.
- digital representations of the world and the map as metaphor.
- GIS epistemologies and multiple realities of space.
- the cultural bias of the technology.
- alternative forms of knowledge representation and qualitative data.
- the pre-eminence of Boolean logic in GIS applications.

Source: Harris and Weiner n.d.

Box 3.3: A combined approach to GIS

'Community-Integrated GIS seeks to broaden the use of digital spatial data handling technologies with the objective of increasing the number and diversity of people who are capable of participating in spatial decision-making. This assumes that the production of GIS is also made more inclusive. As a result, Community-Integrated GIS:

- is likely to be agency-driven, but it is not top down nor privileged toward conventional expert knowledge.
- assumes that local knowledge is valuable and expert.
- broadens the access base to digital spatial information technology and data.
- incorporates socially differentiated multiple realities of landscape.
- integrates GIS and multi-media.
- explores the potential for more democratic spatial decision-making through greater community participation.
- assumes that spatial decision-making is conflict-ridden and embedded in local politics.

Community-Integrated GIS recognises GIS as an 'expert' system but tests the capacity of the technology in the context of people and communities normally peripheral to spatial decision-making processes and politics. In this respect, a Community-Integrated GIS would contain not just the cartographic and attribute information traditionally associated with GIS but would be expanded to become **a forum around which issues, information, alternative perspectives and decisions revolve**.' (emphasis added)

Source: Harris and Weiner n.d.

The debate over the construction of GIS and thus about its operational utility (or not) for development encapsulates the ongoing debate not only about cartographic representation but also about other tools presented here (such as transects, flow diagrams, taxonomies, interviewing, participant-observation and the like). The over-riding lesson that emerges from the debate is that meaning, and representations of that meaning, are relative to their cultural context. That in turn requires that researchers be sensitive to social context, to the multiple meanings and perspectives that co-exist, to the 'political' nature of their engagement with the research context, and to making transparent the basis on which they collect and interpret data. It does not mean that they should not engage with other cultures, or that their own perspective(s) on the world is any less valid. But it does mean that they should not prioritise them.

3.6 Venn (or Chapati) Diagramming/Institution Analysis

Cost	L	Individual/group perspective	I/G
Time	L	Expertise required (social and nat. scientist)	L
Data reliability	M-H	Observer bias	L
		Control of process (directive)	L

***Definition*:** A method for identifying and representing both formal and informal institutions within a community and its external environment and the nature of the relationships between these and the informants' community.

***Purpose*:** To identify and visualise the relative importance of institutions both within and beyond a community which impact upon the livelihoods of target individuals and groups.

The method consists of working with a small group (or groups) of informants representing either a (heterogeneous) cross-section of a community and/or individual (homogeneous) stakeholder groups within it. The aim is to identify and evaluate the relative importance of community and wider institutions (or stakeholder-groups) and their impact upon a target group's livelihood. The exercise is best done using circular pieces of paper (the chapatis) of different diameter (to represent the institutions/stakeholder groups and their relative importance to informants' livelihoods), though it could be done through drawing on a board, or even on the ground while using different objects to represent the differing importance of institutions.

If using 'chapatis', a large one is placed in the middle of the floor/table to represent the community. Participants are then asked to identify the formal and informal institutions, groups and individuals, both within and outside the community or target group which they consider as having an impact upon their livelihoods. These can range from public and private extension services, and regional political and economic bodies (e.g. the local market) to the local magistrate, church/mosque membership, extended kinship grouping, immediate kin group, household residence group, occupational guild, women's sorority, school, traditional healer, and so on.

The participants are then asked to thoroughly discuss and reach a consensus about the relative importance of the institutions and their influence upon the community. They can indicate the importance of an institution by the size of chapati chosen, and the influence of an institution by its distance from the community chapati. (Chapatis representing institutions geographically located in the community should be placed within the community or target group chapati; those representing ones external to the community but with a presence within it should overlap the edge of the community chapati; external institutions with no internal presence should be placed at a distance to the community chapati and at a distance from it in relation to the extent of its influence upon the community; institutions that influence one another or have members in common should overlap with the extent of overlap being in relation to the degree of influence/membership in common).

The participants then — again collectively — write the name of the institution on the corresponding chapati and place it on the diagram in a position which corresponds to their felt consensual evaluation of the institution's influence upon and significance to their livelihoods.

As with Focus group and Village Workshop discussion groups, group dynamics are important. It is therefore important to ensure that all participants contribute to the discussion and evaluation of institutional importance, and to guard against individuals dominating discussions or pressing sectional interests.

3.6.1 Venn Diagrams (Variations)

There are a number of variations upon the chapati diagram which capture the same information. For example varying thicknesses (or colour) of line can be drawn between the community circle and other circles to represent the degree of influence of the institution.

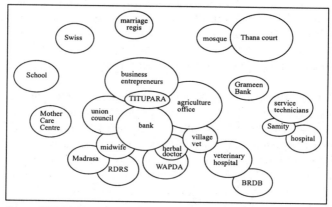

Source: SHOGORIP 1992; and in IIRR 1996:104.

Figure 3.8: Influence and importance of different organisations in Titupara, Bangladesh

Another way is to use an 'evaluation wheel' to indicate the relative importance of each external institution to the community or to a particular stakeholder group within it. This can be particularly useful in representing the 'networks' of different stakeholder groups, and can bring home how little relevance some public service bodies have to the livelihoods of their supposed target clients! The evaluation wheel below was used to evaluate a family planning clinic's sexual health information leaflets in the UK, but it could be adapted to the appraisal/evaluation of a wide variety of items, activities and processes which have multiple criteria.

Another variation is to generate a series of concentric rings around the central community/stakeholder group 'target' and place the institutions within a ring which corresponds to their influence upon informants' livelihoods. Still another is to do a force-field analysis as per business-studies, where there is both input (i.e. influence upon) and output (influence by) the community upon other institutions which it regards as significant. These different methods of representation are given below.

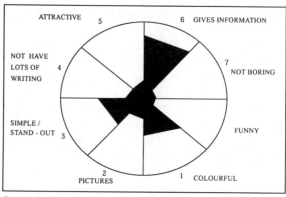

Source: Sellers and Westerby 1996:79.

Figure 3.9: Evaluation of Sexual Health Clinic leaflet using an evaluation wheel

Distribution of stakeholders according to importance: Landless vs. Large and Medium Farmers, Bangladesh. (CNRS, in Barr *et al.* 2000) (n.b. The differences in the quantity of linkages as well as types of linkage between the two groups).

Much development work is done at the level of the community. However, communities are rarely homogeneous, and typically consist of individuals and households belonging to different social strata and having different livelihood strategies. Doing Venn diagramming with different stakeholder groups can be very useful in revealing the differences (and complementarities) between groups as regards those organisations which are of most significance to them. Thus Venn diagramming is a particularly powerful tool for revealing local people's perceptions about the relative importance and impact that various institutions have on their livelihoods. The feedback the method provides can be enlightening for all concerned. External bodies, such as extension services and policy makers are often surprised to find a considerable gap between their own perception of their importance to local livelihoods and that of the people they serve. This can be a useful corrective spurring these bodies to work harder to fulfil the role for which they are mandated. More importantly, visualisation and discussion of the institutional framework in which rural lives are set is a process of systems learning which can clarify for all concerned the potential opportunities and constraints to organisational change which may accompany systems interventions. Historically development specialists have often proposed new institutional arrangements (frequently drawn from their own cultural experience) to accompany community initiatives without evaluating (as part of an overall STEP analysis) the role that *in situ* community and local government institutions might play or the challenge to change that existing institutions might present. Many solutions to natural resource as well as social development 'problems' require partnerships between community and external agencies if they are to be sustainable, and the Venn diagramming method can be an invaluable tool for identifying where strategic alliances might be fostered.

Livelihood Mapping

The above examples illustrate the relative importance of institutions to individuals stakeholder groups and communities. The same diagramming technique can also be used for accessing and representing the relative importance of different livelihood strategies to the 'portfolios' of the individual, the stakeholder group, or the community. We provide a number of examples below (see Box 3.4 and Figure 3.10).

3.7 Farmwalk

Cost	L	Individual/group perspective	I/G
Time	L	Expertise required (social and nat. scientist)	L/M
Data reliability	H	Observer bias	L
		Control of process (directive)	L

Definition: A walk with informants, either singly or in a group, through an area of NR while discussing the latter with them.

Purpose: To collect IK on topics pertaining to natural resources, their management, and related human activity systems, or to validate previously completed formal agroecosystem mapping through PRA techniques.

The intention may be to construct indigenous (emic) 'maps', cross-sectional diagrams, or flow charts of land resources and land use in a particular locality (e.g. soil maps

---

Box 3.4: Livelihood mapping — demand for products in Mokwalto township, Vredefort

LIVELIHOOD MAPPING

Objective
To identify the products/services that the participants consider as very important in the livelihood of their community.

What to do
The participants are asked to list all the products/services that they consider as most important to the community's livelihood. The products/services can be from their homes, workplace or recreation. 'Importance' can refer to necessity for daily use, status or luxury. Participants must mention products/services, and not issues. A participant can be asked to write these products/services on a flip chart. The next step is to have the participants indicate where each of these resources comes from. A target circle representing the community boundary is drawn on the ground or on a flip chart and pieces of paper containing the names of the products/services listed are then placed beside the 'map' of the community. The participants should be able to provide this information through discussion based on the following:

- Whether a particular product/service is available within the community boundary and is sufficient in quantity;
- Whether it is partially available in insufficient quantities within the community;
- Whether it is completely unavailable within the community and has to be acquired from outside.

All the products/services which are available within the community are placed inside the 'map'. All the products/services that are partially available are placed on the border of the 'map'. The resources, which are completely unavailable within the community, are placed outside the 'map'.

Application
Livelihood mapping of a given community is an indirect way to investigate the needs and desires for particular products/services. In this process the participants identify the most important products/services that can be produced or 'imported' and sold in the local community.

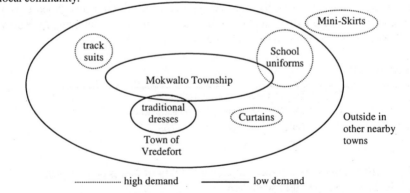

Source: Roos and Mohatle 1998.

detailing the indigenous soil categories, and other significant aspects of the resource base such as slope and hydrology), and to do this in relation to the various social strata identified in a Reconnaissance Social Survey (RSS) and/or Wealth ranking

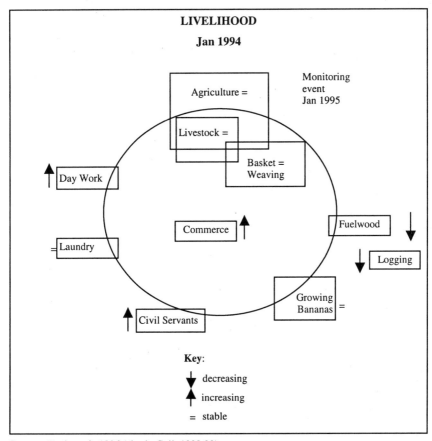

Source: Ford, *et al.*, 1996 (also in Guijt 1998:99).

Figure 3.10: Monitoring changing livelihoods in Kenya

exercises. The data collected may be used to complement and inform a systematic scientific (etic) survey or may be a 'stand-alone'.

The researcher(s) accompanies a local user (or perhaps a small number of local users) on a reconnaissance survey ('farm walk') around the resource base (farm, fishing areas, homestead, etc.) used by them. At various points where the informant has, for example, a plot of land, s(he) is asked to describe the properties of the resource base that are significant to them. For example, when asking about soil on a farmer's plot, the researcher may ask for the local name for that soil type, where it stands in an indigenous ranking of soil types and what its main properties are (friability, texture — which may be expressed as 'easy to plough', 'sticky', and so on.). Other locally significant aspects mentioned by the informant, such as slope and hydrology, should also be recorded.

The farm walk should be a 'relaxed' affair, led by the informant and with the latter doing most of the talking and description. The researcher should be completely open-minded and non-directive, the intention being to capture the informant's perspective on the resource base. The researcher may have a check-list of topics and may prompt the informant with a few select questions to keep the dialogue going, but should be as non-directive as possible and concentrate on listening and recording the informant's knowledge. The intention is not to collect every detail concerning the resource base and land usage at this stage, but to open a dialogue with the informant which can be picked up again and continued over the medium term as different topics are explored. During later discussions (either in the field or in the homestead) information from the farm walk can be used to start more detailed discussions (both on a one-to-one and/or group basis) about specific aspects of the resource base and land use. At this stage the IK recorded should primarily be descriptive (how the informant perceives the natural and human resource base); the analysis (why they manage the resource base in the way they do) can be explored in later discussions. However, if an informant proffers explanations for their management practices, these should be recorded, while researchers may also record their own observations as well — though these should be clearly distinguished from those of the informant.

Farm walks should be undertaken with a number of individuals separately from each social strata identified in RSS/Wealth ranking exercises (and including men and women from households in these strata) both to investigate whether their perspectives and IK may be socially inflected and in order to achieve representativeness. A farm walk should be undertaken on a number of occasions with the same individual through the year since an informant may only express relevant IK, management goals, constraints, etc. at that time and in relation to immediate management issues. (The representativeness of the information gathered can, however, also be validated at a later date through Group Discussion techniques).

The reason for collecting IK from each of the different social strata is so researchers can compare their perceptions of the resource base and their goals regarding resource management with those of other strata and to the model which researchers may have built through formal scientific data collection techniques. These may or may not differ, but it is these which partially determine the different groups success/lack of success in exploiting the resource base. Future resource development can only be assisted by outsiders (the research team) once the potentially competing Human Activity Systems/ Livelihood strategies of the different social strata have been grasped by researchers, and interventions designed in participation with local stakeholders.

Photograph 3.7: A farm walk with wading in Bangladesh: harvesting rice

It is important for researchers to record which informant is providing information, so that their social position and the socio-economic category to which they belong can be clearly identified against wealth/well-being indices; and also to record where and when the information is given and what it relates to, so that it can be cross-referenced to and compared with any formal scientific spatio-temporal data being collected. The researcher should note the date and time of the farm walk, what the informant's plots are being used for at that time (e.g. specific crops), together with any general comments the informant makes. The latter may relate to Strengths, Weaknesses, Opportunities, and Constraints (SWOC) the informant feels s(he) faces at that time (e.g. "I am growing potatoes because the price was high last year, but there are many pests, potatoes require great care, and there is no cold store nearby except one which is expensive to use'). Constraints (or Problems) are of particular interest to researchers because they may be able to suggest technical solutions to them, but care should be taken to allow the informant to express these rather than the researcher directing the discussion to potential problems — for example soil erosion. (The discussion can also range over neighbouring plots not managed by the informant with information about them being validated via discussions with other farmers later, but the researcher must be careful to note who is providing the information when and in relation to where.)

Farm walks with key informants can produce a considerable amount of data. Their strength is that they provide the researcher with a user perspective on the resource base. This perspective is generally livelihoods-based — that is the informant picks out those sections of the resource-base which are of importance to their particular livelihood, and may mention the opportunities and constraints they face in pursuing it. The approach taken is likely to be holistic, with issues being raised which relate not just to the natural resource base but also to human, social, technical and financial capital — that is overall capacity issues — which impact on the informant's livelihood. Since the livelihood system is that of a particular informant, a number of farm walks with different individuals, and from different social strata, are needed to explore how general or strata specific the livelihood strategies and the opportunities and constraints are.

Farm walks are just one method for accessing the IK that local people have. Other methods of both an informal and more formal nature may be required to access knowledge on particular topics and/or to validate data derived from farm walks. The farm walk is particular useful for accessing descriptive data because informants have immediate visual cues which prompt them to give experiential rather than generic data. Drawbacks with the method are that it can be time and resource intensive for the researcher. These can be partially overcome through having farm walks with groups of informants, but the data derived will be different due to group dynamics and because informants are likely to talk in more generic terms rather than in relation to their own specific livelihoods. As with the group discussion/focus group method, the data derived will differ according to whether the groups are formed on a heterogeneous or homogeneous basis.

3.8 Transect

Cost	L	Individual/group perspective	I/G
Time	L	Expertise required (social and nat. scientist)	M
Data reliability	M-H	Observer bias	L-M
		Control of process (directive)	L-M

Definition: A method for collecting information on major land-use zones managed by individuals and households within a community.

Purpose: To provide an easily graspable picture of how the natural resources under a community's management are used by the latter's members/households so as to identify the opportunities and constraints of each zone for target beneficiaries within the community.

The transect (or transects) has traditionally been constructed so that a farm-walk(s) (see Section 3.7 Farmwalk) can be made with a number of key informants along a route which covers all the major ecological and production zones around a community. These zones have previously been identified by informants through participatory mapping techniques (see Section 3.4: Mapping). Information is sought from the respondents on the NR properties, land use and opportunities and constraints of each zone as it is traversed. Once the data has been collected it is presented in a cross-sectional format according to major NR categories — soil, crops grown, trees, forage, animal husbandry practice, and problems and opportunities.

The amount of information that is recorded can vary according to the extent and type of questioning employed, the socio-economic status of the informants and as to whether the latter or scientists are recording the information.

3.8.1 Issues

While the Transect diagram presents data in a tabular form which is easily grasped by the NR scientist, it has limitations which can lead to misunderstandings. It is an idealised representation of reality, and in much of the literature (though see Lightfoot *et al.* 1993) primarily maps NR resources and implicitly assumes that land use is primarily a function of these. As Conway says (in Chambers *et al.* 1990:78) transects "focus attention on the different zones or micro-environments in a watershed, village or farm. In agroecosystems analysis, they are drawn up by researchers who walk from the highest to the lowest point in an environment, accompanied by local people, consulting people in each zone. The main purpose of the transects is to identify the major problems and opportunities of the agroecosystem, and where they are located."

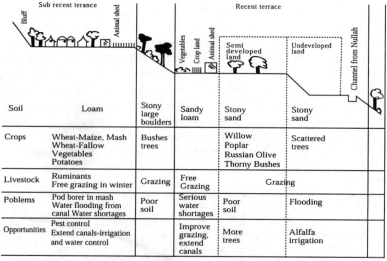

Soil	Loam	Stony large boulders	Sandy loam	Stony sand	Stony sand		
Crops	Wheat-Maize, Mash Wheat-Fallow Vegetables Potatoes	Bushes trees		Willow Poplar Russian Olive Thorny Bushes	Scattered trees		
Livestock	Ruminants Free grazing in winter	Grazing	Free Grazing	Grazing			
Poblems	Pod borer in mash Water flooding from canal Water shortages	Poor soil	Serious water shortages	Poor soil	Flooding		
Opportunities	Pest control Extend canals-irrigation and water control		Improve grazing, extend canals	More trees	Alfalfa irrigation		

Source: Chambers et al. 1990:79.

Figure 3.11: A transect across farm land

A number of criticisms can be made here. Firstly, while NR may be a major determinant of land use in rural agriculturally-based communities, socio-economic factors and externalities may be more significant determinants for some social groups (e.g. women, the disabled, the elderly), and result in significant trade-offs in land use. In brief the question frame from a NR scientist's perspective has tended to be 'What grows here?' This may be a useful first question, but needs to be followed up by a second — 'Why do you use this land for that activity?' (where 'you' stands for a respondent drawn from a specific socio-economic or livelihoods group). The first question is 'consultative' only and tends to leave the attribution of rationale for current land use (and of opportunity for future land-use) up to the external ('objective') observer; the second is more participative and dialogically seeks reasons for land use from the standpoint of a particular user-group and opens up possibilities for the joint exploration of the opportunities and constraints different social groups face to their livelihoods.

A telling example of the very different perspectives that 'experts' and 'local people' bring to transect walks is given by Mahiri (1998). Mahiri notes that experts' approach to the environment stems from a technical and intellectual standpoint. "For example, the foresters attached no special importance to scattered bushes and thickets. Yet, as was established during the walk with 'locals', bushes serve as reservoirs for wood for multiple uses". The dominance of expert knowledge in the policy process has led to the clearing of the bush to create space for mechanised cash-cropping with dramatic consequences for livelihoods systems of local people. Mahiri contrasts the different perspectives thus:

'Experts'	'Locals'
1. Clear the bushes and plant trees to get fuelwood and wood for timber building poles.	1. Retain the bushes to get fuelwood, sticks for building, and browse for small ruminants.
2. Plant two trees where you cut one.	2. Manage coppice growth from tree stumps.
3. Working on the fuelwood problem.	3. Use wood from farm trees, sisal leaves, crop residues, cow dung.

Source: Mahiri 1998.

In the above example Mahiri treats the local community as though it were homogeneous — which it is very unlikely to be. Inter- and intra-household differences can be quite marked, even in rural areas where the population appear to outsiders to be uniformly poor compared with researchers — and even where they define themselves as uniformly poor in comparison with researchers (See Breslin and Delius 1997). Since the women's movement of the 1980's and policy initiatives such as Women in Development, a concern for gender differentiated needs analysis has been increasingly integrated into research. It is easy for outside researchers to identify men and women, but they should remember that neither gender strata represents an homogeneous group. Similarly the anthropological tendency to label rural communities as either 'hunter-gather', 'pastoralist', 'agricultural', 'fishing' and so on, reveals a normative and 'evolutionary' bias. It disguises the fact that all these activities may be being pursued severally or jointly by different individuals and/or households from the same community as strategies in their 'livelihood portfolios' (see Ellis 1998). The members of both genders, just like households, may be distinguished according to wealth/well-being, occupation, livelihood portfolio and so on, and have very different needs and capacities. Their evaluation and exploitation of NR may be quite different

Thus transect walks with different NR user groups (e.g. men vs. women; hunters vs. pastoralists vs. agriculturalists) in the same community/region — and in particular with those most 'at risk' (as identified perhaps through a PPA and well-being ranking exercise) — is likely to reveal significant differences in perceptions of the environment and NR use between the groups (see for example Ministry of Agriculture, Water and Rural Development: Namibia 1998: Chap. 3). From a livelihoods perspective, doing transect walks (and constructing transect diagrams) with informants from a number of identified user groups may reveal disparities between the groups as regards access to particular NRs. For example, poorer families may only have access to fuelwood from a CPR some distance from the homestead (and which may be the first to be cleared to make way for commercial cash cropping by a government parastatal!). Again, constructing seasonal transect diagrams may reveal very different patterns in the use of materials for fuel and interdependencies between the different social groups that make up a community (see Harvey 1998).

Secondly, the Transect method is limited by its focus on specific livelihood strategies involving NRs (i.e. farming, fishing, herding) to the exclusion of other livelihood strategies which may also be important in individuals/households' overall portfolio of livelihood strategies. This prioritises NR strategies and biophysical opportunities and constraints and downplays/ignores livelihood strategies based on other resources and capital assets, and skews the analysis away from a livelihood approach towards a production focus. In doing so it focuses on production issues (optimising return from NR) whereas client-need in terms of their overall portfolio of livelihood strategies may suggest alternative land use outcomes. It also prioritises NRs, such as soil and water and their associated properties, over socio-economic aspects of the landscape (e.g. distance from the village, ease of access) which may be more important determinants of land use to particular categories of person/household. Indeed such an approach may miss the poorest altogether, since they may have few/none of the NR (land, trees, stock, fishing gear, etc.) which natural scientists have traditionally focused on. Thus while biophysical properties of a zone may suggest that particular crops may be best grown there rather than elsewhere in order to optimise yields, individuals and households — because of their varying socio-economic needs and capacities — have to make trade-offs preventing them from optimising zonal NR properties.

Thirdly, as an idealised representation, a transect is not to scale. This might not matter were NRs the only factors affecting land use. However, as suggested above, other factors besides these (e.g. degree of slope, distance from village, capital endowment of target group) also significantly influence land use. As a generic picture the Transect masks the different perspectives on land-use zones held by different categories of individuals as defined by gender, age, occupation and socio-economic status. It can of course be disaggregated (that is a number of transects can be constructed according to these different variables) so that the management/importance of different zones to the different categories of individual and to households of differing wealth can be compared with each other and with that of scientists. The comparison usually reveals differences in scale (as well as of land use in different zones) according to information that the latter think important — in the same way as mapping does. For the respondent the Transect (and Map) is a condensation of a complex of determining factors underlying land-use. It is the researcher's unpicking of this holistic perspective with the assistance of the local people which gives insight into why land use zones are as they are and what opportunities and constraints exist for particular social groups.

Fourthly, just as it is idealised, lacking scale, so the traditional transect is normally atemporal. However, the tabulation can be adjusted to indicate the succession of land use outcomes (e.g. the rotation of crops, or cytamene successions) in each zone over a seasonal or longer period — and again according to how particular social groups exploit NR resources.

Despite the above criticisms, researchers should not ignore the value of transects for obtaining and visualising IK — particularly for natural scientists. Not only do transects summarise information on the NR base and its uses and provide a platform for further investigations with respondents, but it builds rapport with those respondents who have provided information during transect walks. The rider, however, is that researchers — and particularly natural scientists — need to be aware that they approach NR with a particular bias, one which seeks differences between land use zones and has a production focus, rather than one which considers differences between livelihoods of different social strata. This bias is illustrated, for example, by the fact that all transect diagrams in the literature are, as the name suggests, drawn across land use zones — hillside-valley-bottom, forest-field and land-water interfaces — and with good reason since plants are adapted to different micro-environments. A transect within a zone — along a hillside for example — might sound a misnomer to a natural scientist, but if the data is disaggregated by social strata (s)he would readily recognise the complex of socio-economic and biophysical causal factors underlying differences in land use. Shifting the scientific 'gaze' in this way is to shift it towards participative FSR — a concern not with optimising production through the allocation of flora and fauna to their optimum land use zone and improving nutrient flows between them (this can of course still be investigated with NR users), but with investigating identified NR user groups' access to and exploitation of land use zones in terms of the range of socio-economic, technical, and biophysical constraints they face.

Photograph 3.8: View across beel lake and farmland in Bangladesh

Thus one might summarise a typical transect diagram (see below) as a generic summation of land use zones for the community as a whole.

However, the 'picture' needs to be disaggregated by NR user group (or socio-economic strata), and linked to other tools (such as user group livelihood seasonality diagrams, flow charts, resource maps, and so on) to bring out the differences (or not) between groups in their access to NR, as well as the interdependencies there may or may not be between the groups. As with resource mapping, what is captured in the transect diagram is the outcome of NR users' evaluation of the opportunities and constraints of land use zones in terms of their own capacities and the socio-economic context (local and regional) in which they find themselves. The generic transect diagram may

Transect of Pook Paliparan. Dasmarinas, Cavite, Philippines

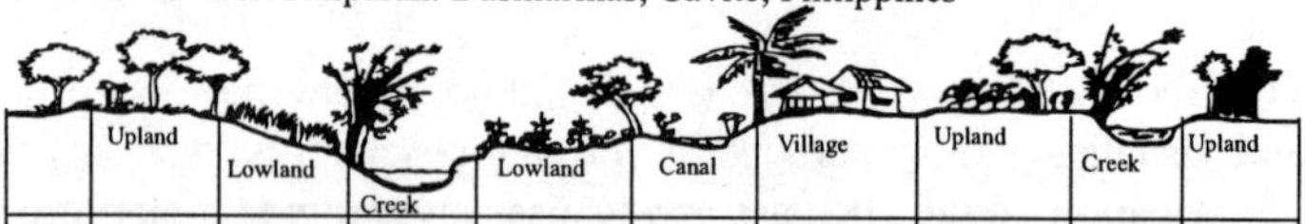

	Upland	Lowland	Creek	Lowland	Canal	Village	Upland	Creek	Upland
Water source	Rain	Rain Irrigation	Rain Runoff/ seepage	Rain Irrigation		Rain Well	Rain	Rain	Rain
Soil	Sandy Loam		Rocky	Clay	Rocky	Sandy Clay Loam	Sandy Clay Loam		Clay
Crops	Rice Sugar-cane Eggplant Beans Corn	Rice Sesbania Pepper Beans Tomato	Bamboo	Rice Sesbania Pepper Garlic Tomato	Bamboo	Okra Horseradish Grapes Beans	Peanuts Cassava Rice Corn Beans	Bamboo	Rice Bean Sugar-cane
Fo-rages	Grass land for grazing	Gliricidia	Grass	Azolla	Grass		Weeds in plots	Guinea grass	Grass land
Trees	Gliricidia Mango Leucaena Guava Banana Tamarind	Gliricidia	Banana Gliricidia Leucaena	Gliricidia Banana Leucaena Acacia Neem	Gliricidia Leucaena	Acacia Mango Guava Coconut Leucaena Jackfruit	Mango		Mango Tamarind Star-apple
Ani-mals	Cow Carabao Goat		Catfish Mudfish Carp Frog Crab	Golden snails Pig Fish Duck Frog	Catfish Frog Snail	Dog Cat Pig Goat Cattle Turkey	Goat Carabao Cattle	Snail Catfish	Cattle Carabao Goat
Prob-lems	Erosion Lack of water	Pest and disease				Lack of cohesiveness among local officials	Erosion Lack of water		Erosion Lack of water
Oppur-tunities						Accessibility to road			

Source: IRRI 1996: 101.

Figure 3.12: Transect from Cavite region, Philippines

indicate where it may be beneficial to improve nutrient flows between land use zones to improve environmental sustainability, but where sustainable livelihoods for the poor are a focus, there is a need to work with them at an intra-community (or in the case of women at an intra-household) level. An example of a more socio-economically nuanced transect linked to a bioresource flow diagram (Figure 3.13) is provided by Lightfoot *et al.* 1993 (in Guijt 1998:7; see Section 3.12 on Flow diagramming).

3.9 Seasonal Calendar/Pattern Chart

Cost	L	Individual/group perspective	I/G
Time	L	Expertise required (social and nat. scientist)	M-H
Data reliability	M-H	Observer bias	L-M
		Control of process (directive)	M-H

Definition: A visual representation of different events over a predetermined time period (such as a year) which the analysts regard as significant to the study being made.

Purpose: To draw out and further explore the timing of a number of significant activities and the potential interrelationships between different biophysical and socio-economic event domains which are cyclical.

In NR research the usual time period represented on a seasonal pattern chart is 18 months, though a shorter or longer period of time could be chosen depending on whether a more detailed analysis of interrelationships is sought (e.g. during a particular season), or whether the human activity system is based on a non-annual cycle (e.g. as among some hunter-gather groups). Some data (e.g. climatic) may be available from official records, but is usually not available at the local scale. Here, unless researchers intend to monitor over an extended period, the only recourse is to IK. As Conway stresses,

Photograph 3.9: Fishing in beel lake: pulling in net

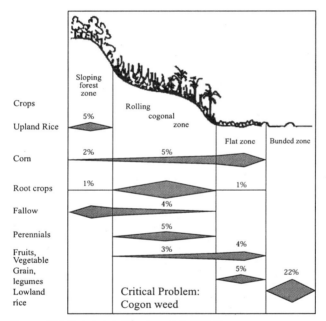

Source: Lightfoot et al. in Chambers et al. 1990:96.

Figure 3.13: Transect of land in Gandara region, Philippines

however, (in Chambers *et al.* 1990:81) local people's own perceptions can be valid, and can indicate their view of conditions on the basis of which they make livelihood (particularly farming) decisions. Conway also notes that a rough guide rather than exact measures (e.g. which are the wettest months, the driest, the hottest, the coldest, and so on) may be all that is possible, but that "relative amounts are adequate for initial diagnostic purposes, showing the pattern into which crops have to fit." The data can be gathered through semi-structured interviews (either with individuals or small groups) using a variety of tools such as ranking (e.g. to sort calendar months on a scale from wettest to driest, hottest to coldest), mapping and diagramming.

3.9.1 Seasonal Impact on Livelihoods

Firstly, it is important to stress the impact that seasonality has on people's livelihoods and well-being — particularly on those of the rural poor with a high reliance on NR- and therefore the need to collect reliable data relating to it. Not only do seasonal climatic fluctuations provide opportunities and constraints to any particular livelihood strategy whether it be herding, fishing, arable farming, horticulture or any mix of these, but they also usually determine a need for livelihood diversification and a range of coping strategies — the building of a 'portfolio' (Ellis 1998) — by most rural production units. These portfolios may consist of both 'on-farm' and 'off-farm' activities of a regular and/or more opportunistic kind, and may vary between different social strata and according to social status (age, gender, ethnicity, religion, etc.). Since seasonal climatic fluctuations are rarely regular in their occurrence from year to year, and climatic conditions are moderated by altitude, topographic features and the like, there can be marked differences in, and the effects of, seasonality within geographical zones. All these factors contribute to the complex, diverse and risk-prone (CDR) environments in which rural people make their living, and to the need for flexibility in natural resource use and in the livelihoods that are built upon them at the local level.

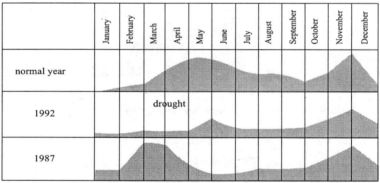

In 1992 the rains came late and were not enougn for the crops. Many people died of hunger. Some moved to the city.

In 1997 the rains came early and were torrential. There were serious floods Many perple in the valley lost their houses. Some crops were washed away.

Source: Action Aid 1996:161.

Figure 3.14: Rainfall calendar for typical and atypical years

(As the Action Aid 1996 authors note (p.160), while a rainfall calendar is one of the most basic calendars and easy to produce, it can be very revealing. First a calendar for a typical year is produced and then respondents are asked to recall those years when the pattern was broken — by floods, droughts, cyclones, etc. — and to recount their coping strategies at those times.)

It is important for researchers to recognise local systems as characterised by uncertainty, complexity and flexibility if they are to understand user perspectives on the NR base and why they act as they do. The way different social units see the opportunities and constraints of the NR base as they unfold through the seasons, and from year to year, and within and beyond their locality, in large measure determines how they allocate resources between livelihood activities. In turn the need to shift resources between different seasonal activities has implications for social organisation, relations between social units, working practices, and so on.

Again the health status of different social strata is strongly influenced by seasonality. For example, a common finding in many tropical rural environments is that the wet season is a difficult and critical time of year when malnutrition, morbidity and mortality peak (see Chambers *et al.* 1981; Longhurst 1986; 1989; Sahn 1989; Gill 1991; Chambers 1993: Chap.4). In consequence the impact of seasonality also has implications for the provision of extension and other public services such as health — though donors and governments have found difficulties with scaling-up from the local in the provision of services.

3.9.2 Social Units and Interdependencies

The social unit to which the data refers may be the whole community, a section of it identified geographically or according to social indices (e.g. occupation, wealth), the individual household, or individuals within the household (e.g. married women, children, or old men). The completed calendars and charts may indicate significant similarities and significant differences in activities between different social units at the same level of scale. For example, seasonal activity charts may be very different for farmers and fishers; daily activity charts may be very different for married women and their husbands; sickness may peak during the same season for women, children and old men; death may be more likely for old people of both sexes during the 'hungry' season, and more likely for very young children at another. This point draws attention to the considerable differences in well-being status and vulnerability that can exist within a population the individuals of which may all be considered poor on formal measures of poverty or well-being (see Section 3.3: Wealth ranking). Seasonal pattern charts, daily activity charts (and even lifecycle charts) assist researchers and respondents to learn about the underlying regularity of certain events and activities, of likely challenges and constraints to target group livelihoods, and provide a platform for further discussion on elements within these using other tools (e.g. Brainstorming, Webbing, Causal analysis and so on).

It is likely that most communities can be stratified according to wealth/poverty/ well-being or vulnerability indices, while the social units within the strata are highly likely to have different portfolios of livelihood strategies. The livelihoods of different social strata may well be interdependent, with complementarities and/or competition between strata at different periods of the year. Thus, while the researcher may collect seasonal pattern data on a specific target group it is well worth collecting data on other user-groups in the community. For example, where the poor do not have access to NR, a significant proportion of their livelihood portfolio may be based on the sale of their labour, while demand for their labour at the local level is met through seasonal migration of labourers — as in Bangladesh (see Gill 1991). However, seasonal pattern charts may reveal that demand for labour in an area peaks at about the same time as labour availability slumps, while labour availability peaks at the same time as demand slumps. A range of measures from regional information exchanges to changing local cropping cycles might then be explored in order to more efficiently match labour supply to demand, and smooth out the working year for the poor. Again, the competition between different groups for scarce CPRs (such as open water fisheries) may be revealed in group-specific seasonal pattern charts, and suggest that the opportunistic, resource-saving, exploitation of this NR by part-time fishers might be reduced (and improve the well-being of both part- and full-time fishers) through the development of micro-enterprise support and credit facilities for alternative livelihood strategies for this group.

Photograph 3.10: Shaking grain from straw

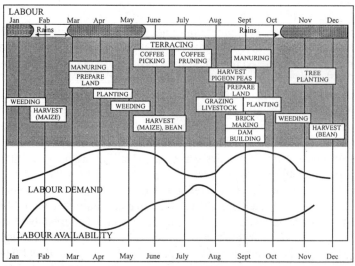

Source: National Environmental Council 1991:38.

Figure 3.15: Seasonal calendar from Mbusyani, Kenya

3.9.3 *Range of Sectors*

The events and activities on which data is sought are likely to include, in the case of groups and communities dependent on natural resources, significant climatic events (e.g. wet and dry, or growing and non-growing seasons), significant animal/fish migration seasons, cropping practice, associated labour allocation and occupational activity (e.g. ploughing, planting, harvesting, cattle-droving, hunting and fishing, labour migration), social activities (e.g. significant festivals or religious periods, seasons for weddings/ second funerals, the school calendar), periods of increased sickness in the population and so on.

Nevertheless calendar charts can be constructed for a very wide range of activities, including market prices, household basic purchases, hunger and abundance calendars, as well as climatic and cropping calendars. We give two examples of this (below) from Action Aid's Reflect Mother Manual.

As the Action Aid authors note (p.154), a market price calendar serves as a tool for further discussion with respondents as to what strategies they might adopt to avoid having to sell crops when prices are low, (usually immediately after the main harvest), and to avoid having to buy the same product back later in the year for their own consumption (usually when it is more expensive). A Hunger and Abundance calendar (see below) involves plotting the availability of food and income through the year to reveal those periods when there is food insecurity, and serves as a platform for further discussions concerning coping strategies. Comparison of the biophysical and socio-economic dimensions of livelihoods captured on seasonal calendars can assist in generating discussion on resource saving and resource enhancing strategies for reducing seasonal and longer term vulnerability.

The Household: Daily Activity Charts
The need to consider interdependencies between social units is also true at the household level where household members have different but interdependent tasks to perform throughout the year and have to make trade-offs between them. This is true however

Photograph 3.11: Fishing in beel lake

	January	February	March	April	May	June	July	August	September	October	November	December
rice	120tk							280tk		x		
maize	60tk				170tk				x			
beans	100tk				160tk						x	x

Source: ActionAid 1996:155 (x = common time to sell).

Figure 3.16: Calendar of market prices

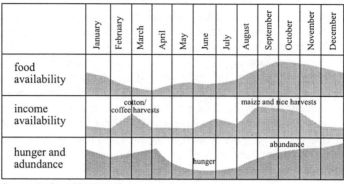

Source: Action Aid 1996:159.

Figure 3.17: Hunger and abundance calendar

the 'household' is defined (see Mikkelsen 1995:157; Guijt 1998:71; Breslin and Delius 1997; Section: 3.3 Wealth ranking) — as is now recognised by international development bodies in their shift from a Women in Development (WID) to a broader gender perspective (see Mikkelsen 1995:155). As feminist writers have highlighted, women have multiple roles — reproductive, productive and managerial. However many household tasks performed by women are not given an economic 'cost' by respondents, are taken for granted as women's work, while decision-making over certain domains they have an interest and input into are made by men. Political-economy theorists have undermined stereotypical assumptions about women's position in society and in the household, and revealed the unequal access to resources and control over them which exists at the household level.

Thus the household can be considered as a 'contested arena' with gender relations being negotiated by household members according to society-wide 'guidelines', and individual livelihood and personal factors. Again, while the household may be treated as a productive and consumptive unit, there is a need to disaggregate it in order to investigate the differing vulnerabilities and also the interdependencies between its members. Finally, the interdependencies between household members differ according to the type of household it is (e.g. male vs. female-headed household), which social strata it belongs to (e.g. wealthy vs. poor), and at which point in its development cycle it has reached (e.g. a newly married couple, couple with young children, couple with older children and other kin, older couple whose children have left home) (see Fortes 1970). (For more on gender and the household see Sections: Gender; Wealth ranking.)

Here again the comparison of the seasonal pattern charts of different household members can indicate where there are opportunities and constraints to improving the well-being of the more vulnerable (women, children, and the old) through improving their access to and control over particular assets.

Seasonal pattern charts can reveal very different activity-loads for different stakeholders. Household studies have also focused on time allocations through the day through the construction of daily routine charts disaggregated by stakeholder. Here again they are invaluable not only for revealing the different activities that household members perform, but also as a learning and empowerment tool for stakeholders (see Action Aid 1996:216).

Photograph 3.12: Dramatic seasonal change in Bangladesh, monsoon flooding

13 Informants	Dec.	Jan.	Feb.	Mar.	April	May	June	July	Aug.	Sept.	Oct.	Nov.	Dec.	Jan.	Feb.
Harvesting (g/mrts, Cotton, Sorief)															
Finding firewood															
Picking G/nuts from harvested fields															
Threshing (millet sorghum maize)															
Pounding (millet sorghum maize)															
Peeling G/nuts															
Watering Animals (calves, Sheep, goots)															
Weeding															
Tethering Sheep / Goat															
Problems															

Firewood Scarce — Too far from village — Watering Sheep, Calves goats — Hunger malaria common Labour obstructed

Source: Action Aid/IIED 1992:14338, in Mikkelsen 1995:78.

Figure 3.18: Seasonal calendar for women's work

Photograph 3.13: A pot seller carrying his wares

Daily Routine Charts

The following daily routine chart can be compared with Figure 3.20. The first is gender specific and compares the differing time allocations that rural and urban women make to the domestic (non-remunerated), income generating and leisure domains. The data suggests the authors took a WID approach. Its strength from a researcher's perspective is that it indicates time allocations (where 'time' is a standard generic measure) which can be easily compared between populations. A weakness is that further information is required concerning the 'quality' of time allocations, and the trade-offs that are made by women in time (e.g. non-remunerated work) against other 'goods' (e.g. longer-term security) in what are very different social contexts. From a WID perspective, young urban women appear to have greater control over their lives and to have greater leisure time because they allocate a considerable proportion of it to income generation, whereas rural women's opportunity for income-generation and leisure are constrained by (non-remunerative) domestic work.

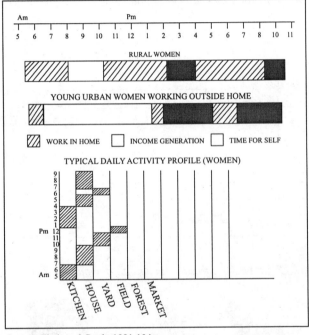

Source: Theis and Grady 1991:104.

Figure 3.19: Daily routine diagram for rural and urban women in Gaza

However, considerably more contextual detail about the social situation of women and men in rural and urban households, and about the relations between them, is required before it is safe to draw conclusions about whether respondents see their allocation to domestic work as a burden or not, what benefits they gain in return for such an allocation, and what they might prefer to do to reduce it (if they see it as a constraint) — that is about their social needs.

A gender approach comparing roles in the same social context (that is seeking 'internal validity' for the data) has largely replaced the WID approach in development. The second chart (below) is a daily routine task for one season of the year. Its strength is that we are able to compare the time allocations of different members of a (typical?) household in an (unspecified) community — though unfortunately no other social data is given concerning the social strata the household belongs to or what stage of the development cycle it is at. Using agreed symbols to represent tasks, it is also more 'user-friendly' than the earlier chart, and is intended for PLA exercises, whereas the above calendar was probably constructed more for researchers' use than for joint learning.

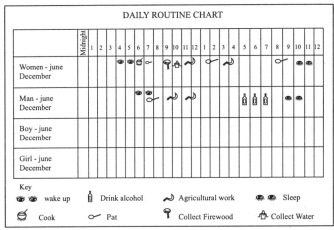

Source: Action Aid 1996:217.

Figure 3.20: Daily routine task chart for one season

From a 'time and motion' perspective (where the emphasis is on efficiency and productivity), seasonal pattern and daily routine charts have been used to identify individual/group time allocation and the opportunities and constraints to any intervention into targeted human activity systems — gaps being seen as an opportunity for introducing additional income generating or well-being enhancing activities. However, they can equally well be used to identify periods of peak labour demand, constraints (such as sickness) to its supply, and how social units meet the challenge and allocate labour to different livelihood strategies accordingly. From this perspective, the intention might be to reduce sickness, increase labour supply and apportion labour demands more equitably between group/household members and more evenly throughout the year.

Photograph 3.14: Daily routine, a woman cutting up rice straw

3.9.4 Ways of Presenting Data

The seasonal calendar below (Figure 3.21) was constructed by researchers ('experts') and presumably intended for researchers' use. Some NR users might have difficulty in interpreting it, which would be a constraint to their participation in further discussions generated by the diagramming. It contains a considerable amount of information on an 18 month calendar. Calendars have long been used in FSR, and as a result tend to detail only those activities and events of significance to the farming system. These have tended to be prioritised by NR researchers. Yet as noted elsewhere, many of the poorest social units in a population may have few NR assets and/or have livelihood portfolios which mix on- and off-farm activities. The shift by researchers to a livelihoods approach requires a target group perspective and purposive sampling. This does not negate the utility of the seasonal calendar, but requires its construction according to the different livelihood strategies undertaken by the target group and a consideration of the interdependencies between stakeholder groups.

The second example (Figure 3.22) from IIRR (1996: 94) was constructed by researchers working with NR users collegiately. Symbols representing climatic conditions, economic and social activities and common illnesses are inserted on a 12-month calendar. The symbols used were developed with respondents drawn from the local community and the calendar was constructed through an exercise with key informants, and validated through a group exercise. The calendar is user-friendly and, as long as the researchers know what the symbols represent, forms a good platform for investigation of the opportunities and constraints that the respondents face in their livelihoods.

A difficulty with this approach is that since the symbols used are relative and location specific, other researchers who are not familiar with what they represent may misunderstand their meaning because they have no means for tying them to more formal measures. For example, while the weather cycle goes from 'sunny/dry' to 'rainy/wet' to 'sunny/dry' again over the course of the year there is no indication of temperature or rainfall range (e.g. whether it is dry and hot or cold; and whether wet and hot or cold) — both of which have significant implications for NR livelihood strategies. Rather this information is assumed to be known by participants and researchers at the local scale and/or can be derived through other methods. However, as Abbot and Guijt point out (1997:28), "the information shared in community-based discussions is now being used for a range of different objectives and must, therefore, meet different standards ... the end users of the information are no longer only local people."

Again 'Common illnesses,' their range and magnitude, are difficult for those unfamiliar with the local context to interpret. That is, the assumption of 'cultural competence' at the micro-scale is a constraint to learning at greater scales. This suggests that combined indicators, where local indices are linked to standard/generic units of value, are required in order to meet the needs of both local participants and of researchers working at a greater scale. Other participative tools can establish combined indicators (e.g. time-lines where local historical events can be linked to national events which local respondents are familiar with; NR evaluation where local non-monetarised NR such as fuelwood, grazing etc. are 'costed' by respondents against a widely circulated monitarised item such as a radio), and the same is possible here.

3.9.5 Other Issues

What seasonal pattern charts are used for is dependent on the objectives of those involved in project design and appraisal. However, it is worth noting a number of issues.

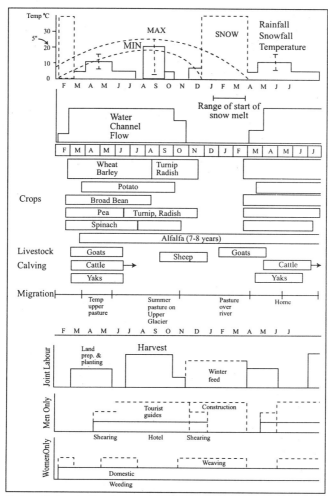

Source: Conway in Chambers *et al.* 1990:80.

Figure 3.21: Seasonal calendar for a village in northern Pakistan

One issue is that there can be an assumption of pre-existing relationships between the different event domains chosen rather than exploration of whether there is any relationship and of what kind between the event domains — for example whether social calendar commitments have already been factored into labour and time allocations for economic activities. (That is seasonal pattern charts start from a reductive perspective and tend to proceed additively rather than holistically.)

Another issue is that the analysis tends to focus on activity gaps (on time periods when other activities may be introduced). This again is an additive approach. This can strengthen a local economy by diversifying individual/household livelihoods, but ignores the opportunity cost aspect of activities — that is some people (e.g. older, disabled, women, the more financially secure) or households may in fact wish to substitute some activities (e.g. laborious, time-consuming, and low paid agricultural work) with immediate/potential higher value activities (e.g. off-farm income generation, education) which reduces labour commitment or allocates it very differently within the household.

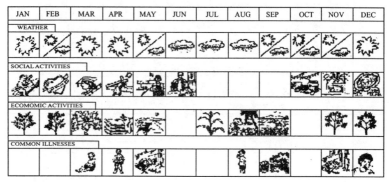

Source: IIRR 1996:94.

Figure 3.22: Sample seasonal calendar matrix

A more holistic approach focusing on individual/ household portfolios of livelihood strategies, and their evaluation of cost and benefit and consequent time and labour allocations, may be more appropriate.

Again there is a danger that such 'time and motion' studies may fail to take proper account of the true nature of human activities and their distribution between household/ group members. For example feminists have argued that earlier studies document men's work but have failed to 'value' the contribution of women's work within the home to overall household income and food security. As feminists have pointed out, while men may have only one job, women frequently have three (raising children, managing the home and household resources, and frequently having a job outside the home as well). The point is to understand how all 'tasks' (economic, social, religious, etc.) are evaluated by and allocated between household/group members over the time period chosen for investigation, and this requires a more holistic approach to the data than is normally associated with seasonal calendar matrices.

There is also a danger that analysis (evaluation) is made by external researchers — even though based on local knowledge (e.g. the prioritisation of 'work' and optimisation of economic value over other activities which is common in European development literature. That is it is analysts who spot ('economic') activity gaps or put activities before people. As such the analysis may lack adequacy at the level of meaning (i.e. internal validity).

In conclusion, we emphasise that seasonal calendar charts can be a useful starting point for discussions with local people about the wide range and social and economic value of the tasks and activity domains they are individually and collectively involved in, but it needs to be approached with caution and used with other tools to give a fuller picture.

3.10 Taxonomies

Cost	L	Individual/group perspective	I/G
Time	L	Expertise required (social and nat. scientist)	M
Data reliability	H	Observer bias	L
		Control of process (directive)	L

Definition: Classifications of objects and ideas by local people. Classifications may be overt with distinct terminology, or may be implicit.

Purpose: To determine how people classify and structure objects and ideas and thus assist understanding of their conceptual universe.

Anthropologists have been investigating local people's understanding of the world — that is how they construct meaning about the world, and the classificatory principles that structure their IK — for over a hundred years. While there is continuing debate about whether individuals in all cultures are motivated by the same innate psychology (instincts/drivers/emotions) or not, anthropologists have shown that different cultures, and different social units (such as women, the old, the poor) within a culture, can have very different 'worldviews' and social psychologies of the self (see Ardener, S. 1978; Heelas and Lock 1981, Carrithers *et al.* 1985). These are embedded in their own distinct taxonomic systems and theoretical schema about how the world works and how people act in the world.

Historically, development has been based on a positivist understanding of the world — that is the world as experienced and understood by reference to western science. Other cultures' taxonomies and theoretical schema have been ignored as 'dated', 'partial', 'misguided' or just plain 'wrong'. Leaving aside the question as to whether western science can give better descriptions of the world and better explanatory theorems about it or whether it just gives different ones (see Kuhn 1962 concerning different 'world-views' in science), the lesson development specialists must draw from anthropology is that it is local people (and not scientists) who ultimately have to manage their natural resources and livelihood systems, and they do so in terms of the current knowledge they have. This knowledge is, like that of science, a dynamic resource and subject to change and development in the light of new knowledge which may be generated through indigenous experimentation or derived from an external source. As with Creole languages (indeed all languages), much of this new knowledge is incorporated into the knowledge base in terms of pre-existing classificatory structures. That is, just as positivist science may extract 'nuggets' of IK from their socio-cultural context and fit them to an extant world-view — but in doing so may change/ misunderstand their meaning — so local NR users may do so too with scientifically-generated knowledge.

This point was understood by Training and Visit (T&V) advocates of extension in their insistence that the introduction of HYV technologies must be accompanied by the whole gamut of cultivation practices developed by scientists 'on-station'. The T&V approach failed not only by reason of its resource intensive nature and the lack of 'fit' between technologies developed on-station and the on-farm context in which they were to be used, but also because of the scope for misunderstanding at every point in the production process (see Section: Participative Technology Development).

As a simple illustration of what can happen, consider the taxa below (Table 3.10). The English grey (as in 'grey mare') translates into Standard Welsh as *gas*, and from here into modern colloquial Welsh as *glas*, but this may later translate back into English as blue — though there are no 'blue mares'! The example may seem facile, but there are plenty of instances of such misunderstanding having more explosive outcomes — as Whorf (1956), who for part of his working life was an insurance assessor, pointed out.

Anthropologists' 'ethnographic' (emic) accounts of how the phenomenological world is ordered in a particular culture are important for understanding why people in that culture act as they do. Natural scientists have neither the time nor resources for studying another cultures' world-view in the depth that anthropologists do, but if they are to build on local peoples' knowledge and skills, they do need to have some understanding of

Table 3.10 Translation confusions

ENGLISH	STANDARD WELSH	MODERN COLLOQUIAL WELSH
green	*gwyrdd*	*gwyrdd*
blue	*gas*	*glas*
grey	*llwyd*	*llwyd*
brown		*brown*
black	*du*	*du*

Source: Ardener, E. 1971: xxi.

how these people (and sub-groups within a population) see the world and act in relation to that 'world'. Understanding local taxonomies, particularly those relating to natural resources and technologies and, most importantly, the values local people attached to items in a taxonomy, is a minimum requirement if there is not to be cultural misunderstanding with 'surprising' consequences for development initiatives (e.g. there is the apocryphal instance in early development literature of prize bulls given to East African peoples to improve their bloodstock being slaughtered in honour of the gift-giver!)

The following example (Figure 3.23), taken from Kersten (1996), indicates how graziers classify rangeland plants in NSW, Australia. As she says (p.23), graziers classify plants according to their value as grazing for their stock and not according to any scientific classification by family and genus. The functions of the classification are quite different, as are the criteria by which plant species are evaluated (see the Table on grazier vs. researcher criteria in Section 3.17 Matrix).

Informants may or may not be able to 'unpack' the principles on which items are classified. However, while some taxonomies are constructed on implicit relations between phenomena, most are not, and there are usually clear linguistic labels identifying phenomena as belonging to the same category. The method for collecting data on the latter taxonomies is therefore fairly straightforward; it is to record all the terms for items in a particular resource 'domain' (for example soils or fish), and then work with local informants — either individually or in small groups — to sort the terms into the categories that they recognise and use.

The last step is to seek an understanding of the grounds on which people classify items as belonging to one category and not another. Items may be classified as belonging to a particular category and not another according to a single criteria (e.g. we distinguish 'bushes' from 'trees' on the criteria of 'the size of the mature plant'), but usually categories are polythetic, while some items may share characteristics of items in different categories and be classified as anomalies, as 'neither fish nor fowl' but a bit of both, and as attracting special dietary, ritual or customary observances (e.g. the Pangolin amongst the Lele of Zambia, the pig amongst Jews and Muslims) (see Douglas 1966, Leach 1976). There may also be 'hollow categories' — essentially a 'pending-tray' which

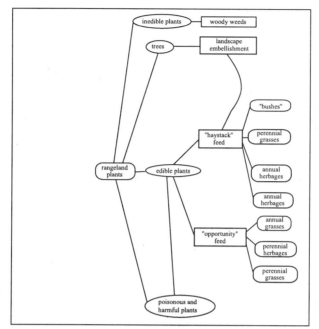

Source: Kersten 1996:23.

Figure 3.23: Grazier classification of rangeland plants

may contain no known item, mythic items, or items waiting to be assigned to other categories once more information becomes available (e.g. The Linnaen classificatory schema originally had the category of 'apeman' to which some modern homo sapiens were initially assigned by science and, while modern science only sees the category as pertinent in evolutionary anthropology, the popular imagination still seeks extant instances — the Yeti, Big-foot etc.). Still other items may seem to an external observer to 'jump around' between domains according to context (e.g. in some cultures large butterflies are classed as 'birds' rather than insects, while their caterpillars and pupae are classed as 'grubs'. Elsewhere tadpoles may be classed as 'small fish', yet the frogs that result may be classed as 'small four-legged animals'. In both cases the developmental relationship between the immature and mature members of a species is either unknown or suppressed in favour of a different principle of classification — such as 'brightly-coloured-flying-things' as opposed to 'dull-coloured-flying-things').

Another method for collecting information on local taxonomies is to write the terms of items in the selected domain on separate cards, mix them up and then get informants to sort the cards into the categories they find important and state what it is that the items in each category have in common and what distinguishes the category from others. Informants are then asked to take the items in each category and sort them into subcategories according to the next principle of discrimination that they find important and to explain what this is. The steps are repeated until the informants state that they cannot subdivide the categories any further and have no reason to do so. The result of this exercise should be a hierarchical classificatory tree detailing the principles by which a particular group discriminate between items in a particular domain (as in Figure 3.23).

Care must be taken to ensure the taxonomies derived are robust and do not lead to later confusions. For validation purposes, in order to explore the generic or group-specific nature of the classificatory system, the sorting and naming exercise should be repeated with different informants from the same social grouping or with informants from different social groupings (e.g. men's groups and women's groups). Rajasekaran 1991 (in IIRR 1996) provides an example of local soil terms and their classification in Tamil Nadu, India which illustrates both the output from the method and the need for care in its construction. It is worth noting that what might appear to us to be inconsistencies in the principles of classification, may not be so for informants. For example, in Tamil Nadu soil (*mann*) is divided into 5 primary types. Three are labelled by colour, two by texture, and one of the latter is divided into three sub-types which are given colour labels that are the same as those for the three primary soil types. Without more information, it is not possible to say whether a confusion was involved, or whether the local language only has three primary colour terms but where additional soil-type labels are required people have adopted 'texture' as an appropriate one, or whether it is the other way round. Whatever the direction of derivation, the example does indicate the potential for confusion between local people and development researchers (akin to misunderstandings when different modes of calibration are not clarified). This may not matter very much to Welsh and English horse-traders, but as NASA recently discovered can be expensive when trying to send a spacecraft to the planets.

It should be remembered that, as with matrix and sorting and ranking exercises, the collection of taxonomies starts from a very reductive perspective. The method seeks information on a small slice of reality, but because it deals with broader knowledge domains than a simple sorting exercise, and with knowledge which is potentially more generic in a population, it is likely to throw up differences between local and scientific classification and thereby stimulate further research as to why this should be (see Sillitoe 2002). That in turn is likely to lead the researcher to a deeper exploration of relations between a taxonomy and other objects/ideas and the criteria of evaluation being used (e.g. Why some Papua New Guinea people say that the Cassowary — a flightless bird — is not a bird.)

3.11 Webbing

Cost	L	Individual/group perspective	I/G
Time	L	Expertise required (social and nat. scientist)	M
Data reliability	M-H	Observer bias	M
		Control of process (directive)	M

Definition: A method for representing relationships between a situation/problem and the causal factors underlying it (see also Participative technology analysis, Section 3.14, and Brainstorming, Section 3.20).

Purpose: To visually represent situations or problems and their causal relationships to other domains with the aim of prioritising constraints and identifying solutions.

This exercise might be undertaken with a number of key informants with experience of the situation or problem, or with a number of different stakeholder groups in group discussions (see Section 3.13 Group discussion/Focus Groups). The main theme (e.g. declining fish yields) is first written or illustrated by means of a sketch in the centre of a large piece of paper or on a chalk-board. Participants are then asked what situations or problems relate to the theme, and what its causes and consequences are. Each situation in turn is further explored with regard to its causal links, and the answers summarised as text-blocks on the paper or board, with each text-block linked by lines to others in causal sequences at primary, secondary and tertiary level. Primary level webs may simply link causal factors around the main theme, but when webs are developed to secondary and tertiary levels it is useful to separate biophysical causes from socio-economic constraints through placing them on different halves of the paper/board. (On all these points see diagrams below).

An example of a three-level causal web drawn by farmers in the Philippines when discussing their Cogon weed problem is provided by Lightfoot *et al.* (in Chambers *et al.* 1990:96) (Figure 3.24). The web indicates the issues and interactions which farmers perceive as involved in the Cogon problem. As Lightfoot notes, the informal participatory survey provided information on biophysical causes and socio-economic constraints associated with the problem. Later the diagram was redrawn as a more formal diagram. Compare transect diagram on the Cogon problem, showing the extent of the problem in the different agro-ecological zones (see Section: Transects).

There may or may not be differences in perceived causal links and consequences between stakeholder groups. A heterogeneous community-wide group is likely to indicate a broad spread of causal links and consequences that pertain to a particular theme, whereas the answers of homogeneous stakeholder groups will most probably be structured by the latters' social characteristics (e.g. age, gender, occupation, etc.). Where the aim of the research is the design of a community-wide intervention to address a community-wide problem, a wide spread of attributed linkages is desirable and a heterogeneous group discussion is probably the best way forward. When an intervention is planned with specific target groups, it is best to work with those groups in order to gain their particular perspectives on the theme under discussion. For example, if the theme is 'access to fuel sources' the causal links are perceived very differently by rich and poor Bangladeshi because the fuel sources on which they depend are very different (see Harvey 1998). By contrast the answers of different stakeholder groups (e.g. fishers and agriculturalists) to the theme 'fish-stock decline' may show some overlap in the perceived causes of decline, but fishers may perceive additional causes which agriculturalists do not, or do not wish to verbalise.

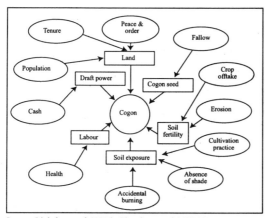

Source: Lightfoot *et al.* 1990 in Chambers *et al.* 1990:96.

Figure 3.24: Web of Cogon weed problem, Philippines

In all cases the information obtained by the method can be compared both with that provided by other groups and with the researchers' expert knowledge. The comparison may indicate that informants' information is either partial or plain wrong (an example would be the belief that HIV infection is spread when those having sexual intercourse have not washed thoroughly, rather than through unprotected sex), and suggest that a public information and awareness campaign as well as technical assistance may be the most appropriate way forward. The comparison will in all probability also reveal stakeholder-perceived causal linkages of which the researchers are unaware and which can be explored further through other methods. An example would be the differential impact on soils of leaf-drip from a variety of tree species identified by Nepalese informants (see Thapa 1994).

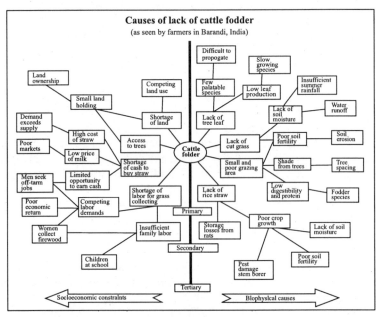

Source: Lightfoot *et al.* 1990; also in IIRR 1996:108.

Figure 3.25: Three-level web indicating biophysical causes and socio-economic constraints

The Webbing method can be developed further through ranking the value or weight that participants give to causal links by drawing thicker (or differently coloured) lines between text-boxes (or by giving proportions to causes/ constraints — as in Lightfoot *et al.*'s formal diagram above). Again it is instructive to compare the results with the weighting and ranking that external experts might give to the causal links. This can assist the identification of potential social constraints to any planned intervention and the possible need for consensus-building and public-awareness campaigns prior to implementation, and the grounds on which external organisations might work with target groups to address needs both hold in common. An example in relation to 'fish-stock decline' would be where experts, but not local people, see deterioration in water quality due to run-off of fertiliser from agricultural land as a major cause of decline, while both experts and informants see deterioration in fish migration due to damaged sluice-gates and poorly designed embankments as another major cause. The first might require a public information and training exercise to achieve more appropriate fertiliser application (and perhaps require justifying to farmers on the grounds of cost-savings rather than fish-habitat improvement which is tangential to or threaten their interests). The second might require local as well as public sector partnership to reduce implementation cost and make an infrastructural intervention feasible, and could be justified to both farmers and fishers in terms of improving land-drainage and fish-habitat.

The method is invaluable not only for revealing local people's understanding of causal links between different domains and the weighting they give to these, but also the factors they consider in their decision-making about a particular theme. It is also useful for raising awareness among participants regarding their problems and identifying those which they, or they and partner-organisations, can do something about and those about which they can do little or nothing. The latter point is of particular importance because it can lead on to the development of action plans where different facets of the problem can be allocated to different 'action-domains' for resolution (i.e. as being the responsibility of individuals, a particular group, the community, a service provider, local government, or requiring a policy initiative at national or even international level).

One caveat that researchers need to bear in mind is that the data collected is participants' understanding of the situation/problem. As such they may not be in possession of the full facts as applying at that time. For example in the case of 'declining fish-stocks' they may attribute decline to deteriorating water quality due to fertiliser run-off, but be unaware that an additional cause is industrial pollution upstream. Or they may not see fish-stock decline as a major issue for their livelihoods, whereas researchers may be aware of international concern about environmental sustainability. Where there is expert knowledge which participants do not have, it would seem appropriate to share it with them so the different primary and secondary stakeholders can form their own opinion as to its value and what trade-offs need to be made to move forward together.

The link between developing participatory data analysis and developing community action plans needs to be stressed. Traditionally development experts have used participatory practice to generate information (IK), but have then developed action plans or policy initiatives with little input from the community. It is good practice to set the generation of new information in the context of participatory learning and action — that is to work collegiately to analyse problems and develop action plans which may or may not require the involvement of external bodies. Such practice can be justified on the basis of good governance, equity and enhanced sustainability of project outcomes.

3.12 Flow Chart/Process Diagram

Cost	L	Individual/group perspective	I/G
Time	L	Expertise required (social and nat. scientist)	M
Data reliability	M	Observer bias	L-M
		Control of process (directive)	H/M

Definition: Chart/Diagram showing a series/cycle/flow of activities, procedures, events or other related factors.

Purpose: To condense long and detailed (production) procedures into easily grasped visual form. A useful 'first step' visual planning tool enabling the disaggregation of a complex whole into discrete sub-units and the relations between them which can be explored further — particularly in order to identify process bottlenecks.

In NR research, a common use would be in recording the series of major activities required to arrive at a determinate outcome such as a crop harvest, or to chart flows of a resource through a system, but it can be used to detail the steps in any production or consumption activity which are inter-related parts of a group's overall livelihood strategy. The charting of the different activity cycles for these can reveal when and where there are competing demands on the resources of individuals and groups, where there are trade-offs, opportunities to diversify or intensify, and/or constraints to doing so.

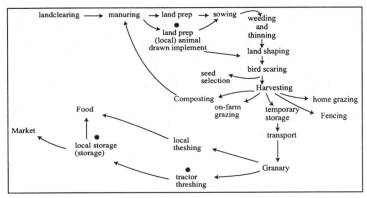

Source: Scheuermeier and Ayuk 1997.

Figure 3.26: Male villagers understanding of the steps in producing crops, Bassenko village, Ougadougou (* = bottlenecks farmers perceive in system)

Each major activity is in turn a determinate outcome which requires a series of activities for it to be successfully achieved. Each activity at the cycle level and at the sub-cycle level has quality, quantity and time (QQT) aspects which vary according to the importance of the strategy in the portfolio of livelihood strategies an individual, household or group constructs. Using other techniques (e.g. discussion, focus group, problem census) the researcher can explore each sub-activity with NR users in order to determine why this part of the process is managed as it is, what trade-offs are involved, and what might be done to remove constraints to its satisfactory completion.

A flow chart may contain different amounts of information depending on its function. Thus it may for example merely detail activities required to derive a cropping outcome (such as site selection, land clearance, soil preparation, planting, weeding, harvesting). Or it may detail what inputs are required (labour, time, finance costs), at what time of year, and whether these fall on the individual (husband, wife), the household or a wider grouping.

A flow chart for a single determinate outcome, such as a crop harvest, makes it easy to grasp the procedures/steps necessary to achieve that outcome. However, it is reductive of the real complexity involved (as exemplified in sector-specific or mono-cropping focused development), and masks the competing demands and trade-offs involved. Systems diagramming (which show a combination of, and the inter-relationships between, different activities/events) can provide a more holistic picture. The bioresource flow diagram below details a before/after integration farming system with indicative inputs.

Scientists may see different opportunities and constraints to local people. The construction of flow charts at different scales (through their disaggregation into sub-units, their aggregation into livelihood portfolios, and their further aggregation into wider

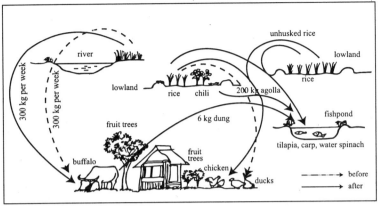

Source: IIRR 1996, p.91.

Figure 3.27: Before and after integration: bioresource flows between natural resources, Philippines

production systems at say the catchment level), and their discussion with local informants, can assist scientists to grasp the NRM thinking of particular groups, and their concepts of value, risk and reward. As a planning tool it can assist in the identification of potential interventions (their costs and benefits) and the likely impacts on different parts of the system being charted.

As indicated above, the flow chart is a useful way into understanding the 'what' and 'how' of local practice and events, but it needs to be supplemented with other methods (for example individual and/or group discussion) to prevent naive outsider (etic) conceptions of NRM reasoning being foisted on the material.

The flow chart has been extensively used in Farming Systems Research (FSR) where the focus has primarily been on the whole farm — that is on the farm as a business (or livelihood). This is useful in that it prioritises people — the farming household — rather than taking a sectoral or commodity focus as government extension services tend to do. Increasingly FSR has gone beyond the farm-gate to consider flows (in labour, capital and kind) between different strategies in households' livelihood portfolios and to consider flows between different user groups and between environmental subsystems. The use of a flow chart in participative FSR is likely to be very different to its use by those coming from a technical or biophysical direction because of FSR's focus on identified client groups and recommendation domains.

Flow charts can usefully be combined with transects to give the latter a greater NR user-oriented 'whole farm' dynamic. Compare the transect diagrams with the two diagrams below by Lightfoot *et al.* (1993). The bioresource flow diagram is that for an individual farm and its multiple NR-based 'Strategies' during one season of the year. (Whether this is for a 'typical' farm or for a particular NR user group is not important here). As with the first diagram in this section (above), system relationships and sustainability may have been improved through advice from researchers. The second diagram (Figure 3.28) is a transect for the same (typical?) farm detailing the resource subsystems — Upland, Alturahin and Salog Lowlands, and Fish pond — the strategies pursued that are taking place there and the inputs into and outputs from each strategies. The flow arrows at the top demonstrate how the system is integrated across land use zones — perhaps suggesting that a sustainable farming enterprise is one which is

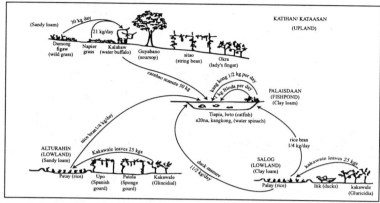

Source: Lightfoot *et al.* 1993 in Guijt 1998:78.

Figure 3.28: Bioresource flow model, wet season, Philippines

Resource System name / Soil type / Enterprise name and area	KATIHAN/KATAASAN (UPLAND) Malabo (Sandy loam)						ALTURAHIN (LOWLAND) Malabo (Sandy loam)			SALOG (LOWLAND) Malagkit (Clay loam)		PALAISDAAN (FISHPOND) Lagkit (Clay)	
	Napier grass 50 m2	Carabao (2)	Soursop trees (10)	Sitao (Stringbean) 400 m2	Okra (Lady's finger) 400 m2	Irrig. Canal (Nat. Irrig. Authority) 0.25 ha.	Kakawate (Gliricidia) 0.25 ha.	Palay (rice) 4000 m2	Upo + patola (bottlegourd + sponge gourd) 200 m2 + 200 m2	Kakawate (Gliricidia) 0.25 ha.	Palay (rice) 6000 m2	Itik (ducks) 16	Tilapia + hito (catfish) 450 m2
External material				Asudin (1 bottle) 0.3L = P90	Pesticide (bottle) 0.3L = P90			Inorg. Fertilizer (80 kg) = P306 Pesticide 0.4L = P120 Seeds (40 kg) = P180			Inorg. Fertilizer (90 kg) = P584 Pesticide 0.4L = P180 Seeds (50 kg) = P270		Inorg. Fertilizer 2kg = P15
Family labor		1 hour/day P50/day	Harvest 3 hrs. = P2625	5.375 person days = P402.50					All activities 4.675 person days = P446.25				Feeding 5.625 person days = P383.75
Hired labor								Planting = P300 (6 Persons) land prep. P280 (contract)			Planting = P450 (6 Persons) land prep. P420 (contract) 6.6 cavans (300kg) = P148	Cleaning/leading 5.625 person days P393.75 60 eggs = P165	
Primary output sold			30 kg P210	204 kg (102 bundles) (p5-P20 per bundle) = 1777	51 bundles = P1600			4.4 cavan (220kg)= P890	Upo 244kg = P1345. Patola 141 pcs = 904		47.4 cavans (2370kg) = P10685 40 eggs = P110		Tilapia 4kg = P120
Primary output other					4 bundles = P44		75 trellis for firewood = P25	31.6 cavans (15800kg) = P7110	Upo 22 pcs. = P110 Patola 40 pcs. P200	75 trellis for firewood = P25			Tilapia 18kg = P440
Bi-products sold													
Bi-products others	3780kg = P1590 Manure 50kg = P25						Gliricidia leaves 25kg = P12 Gliricidia Branches 5kg +P25	Rice bran 90kg = P490		Gliricidia leaves 25kg= P12 Gliricidia Branches 5kg + P25		Duck manure 270kg = P135	
Rents and fees													

Source: Lightfoot *et al.* 1993 in Guijt I. 1998:70

Figure 3.29: Farm transect with wet season monitoring data, Philippines

diversified across these zones. If combined transect-flow diagrams for representative farms of different social strata were to be compared, the different opportunities and constraints to each strata's NR-based livelihoods might become more apparent.

3.13 Historical Comparison/Time Lines

Cost	L	Individual/group perspective	I/G
Time	M	Expertise required (social and nat. scientist)	M/H
Data reliability	H/L	Observer bias	L/M
		Control of process (directive)	M/H

Definition: The comparison of conditions, techniques and practices at different historical points.

Purpose: To evaluate trends and changes over a specified historical period.

Researchers may or may not have reliable baseline data on the biophysical and social context in which they are working. If they do then, once new data on the same variables has been collected, a comparison can be made between conditions at the two historical points. More commonly in the development context there is no baseline data, there is baseline data for only a few of the variables researchers wish to consider, or resource constraints limit the amount of new quantitative data that can be collected. Resource constraints also limit the extent of continuous data collection (e.g. of panel data), and make it extremely difficult to form a firm opinion about whether there are trends and fluctuations over the chosen time period, and about what the causative factors might be. The monitoring of key variables in order to do this is comparatively new.

However, the close questioning of informants about the conditions, techniques and practices that have held over a specific period (e.g. over the last 10 or 20 years, or their lifetime) can give an indication of trends and key changes that have occurred in the region under study. It is even possible to obtain qualitative data about conditions, key events and resulting changes that occurred in the lifetime of informants' parents and grandparents. An interesting use of generational difference in remembering past conditions and practices (essentially collecting 'time-slices' from different generations) is provided by Sadomba (1996) who provides a guide to 'retrospective community mapping' as a tool for community education. We reproduce this below (Box 3.5) without comment as to whether researchers may only be interested in the collection of IK for a specific purpose (such as changing NR use and sustainability) or whether they will be using the maps produced as a platform for wider PLA with a community.

Informants' data needs to be grounded by reference to key calendrical markers (e.g. key events in the lives of informants such as initiation, marriage, the birth of children), and for events that occurred in previous generations to be grounded by reference to markers that are common to both informants and researchers (e.g. the installation of a state president, or the occurrence of a spectacular drought or flood the written records about which serve as benchmarks for unrecorded local events). From these common markers researchers can explore the historical terrain in some detail, and through triangulating what one informant says with that of others, can build a robust picture of events, changes and trends of significance to their informants.

Researchers have previously collected this kind of data to obtain a linear record of what, where, when and how events have unfolded. For example a study by Gujja and Pimbert (1995) on community-based planning for wetland management in Pakistan carried out a Time-line analysis of two RAMSAR site lakes in the Ucchali wetland complex, together with PRA activities to build up a picture of NR endowments, their local management, and the socio-economic composition of communities. As the authors say (p.125), "As the PRA teams interacted with local people living around the lakes, it soon became clear that the management plan for the Ucchali complex would have to address the conflict of interest between internationally defined agendas for wildlife protection and local needs and priorities." A historical reconstruction of wetland history at each site (see Table 3.11) provided a platform for group discussions and semi-structured interviews with representatives from different NR user groups. These showed that groups have different perspectives on the issue and on the relative value of the lakes to their livelihoods, while there is a "profound mismatch between local experience of

Box 3.5: Retrospective community mapping (RCM)

A STEP-BY-STEP GUIDE TO RCM

Step 1. Establish a baseline date and intervals of maps
When the community is gathered, and the procedure outlined, let them decide on the baseline date for their mapping. The basic question at this point is, "How far back do we remember our community?" Usually those who have lived longest in that community will determine the year to begin from. Then the community decides on the intervals of maps. From our experience, maps were easily developed for each decade with 1920 being the base year.

Step 2. Divide the community into mapping age groups
Each community member has to decide at which age she/he was mature enough to understand the pattern of life and the environment of the community. Relevant groups are formed for each mapping period.

Step 3. Drawing of maps
Each group draws a community map for their given period. They can do this on the ground using available resources. It is important that they try by all means to show everything that can be shown on the map e.g. their hunting grounds, rivers that used to flow and fish in them, wildlife, vegetation, settlement pattern, croplands, grazing etc.

Step 4. Presentation of maps
All groups gather and go round to each group to present their map. Question time is given during or at the end of each presentation, whatever is preferred by the community. If the maps are drawn on paper, the groups will take turns to present the maps.

Step 5. Description of socio-economic and cultural conditions
The community goes back into their respective groups and describe the pattern of life in their period. They discuss demographic changes and associated impacts. They recall various institutions for health, education, bringing up children, family, marriage etc. They discuss their cardinal philosophy of life and belief patterns including religion, social cohesion etc. They discuss economic activities, (hunting, tillage, industrial production etc.) They also discuss access to means of production during their period such as land and finished commodities.

Step 6. Presentation of life patterns of the period
The community goes into another plenary session where each group presents the life pattern of their period. The community describes different patterns of life for each mapping period. Other community members can ask any questions and this can lead into any course of discussion. This provides a good background for the communities to choose what themes they will want to discuss and what problems they want to focus on and resolve. This becomes an important step, because this is how people determine themselves what they want to learn and decide the content of their education.

> "We simply cannot go to the workers — urban or peasant — in the banking style, to give them knowledge or to impose upon them the model of the 'good man' contained in a programme whose content we have ourselves organised ... . The starting point for organising a programme content of education ... must be the present, existential, concrete situation, reflecting the aspirations of the people" (Freire, 1972).

Step 7. Focus group discussions
A focus group discussion usually flows naturally from the questions raised. Themes can be chosen without control whatsoever by the facilitator. Community members should ask questions, debate and discuss freely without fear of getting out of topic. The focus group discussions will also show the facilitator what the community is interested in. If the facilitator has other areas he/she feels have to be discussed, then open ended questions and other methods are suggested.

Source: Sadomba 1996: 12.

wetland history and the perceptions of outside professionals who have invariably assumed that Lakes Ucchali and Khabbaki are natural and longstanding features of the landscape" (p.135). The authors conclude (p.134-5) that methodologically, "The quality and depth of information generated on local livelihoods and their relationships with natural resources was much richer than that generated by more conventional survey and questionnaire-based studies. Moreover, this information was obtained in a relatively short period (two weeks) and at a lower financial cost than conventional management plan formulation by outside experts."

Table 3.11 Time-line analysis of Lake Khabbaki, Punjab, Pakistan

1860	First land titles (settlement) of Dhadar village given.
1892-93	Second land titling took place.
1894	Water gathered at the lake site.
1912	Heavy rainfall in the area and lake size increased to about 500 acres; third land titling took place.
1913-14	Third land titling of Dhadar villages completed.
1955	Lake totally dried and farming at the lake site was possible.
1957	Heavy rain in the area and lake site flooded again.
1973	Heavy rain in the area: fourth land titling took place.
1977-78	Fourth land titling completed.
1982	Heavy rain in the area.
1983	More rain: lake size increased considerably, which flooded the old Nushara Jaba.

Source: Gujja and Pimbert 1995:126.

The same kind of data might also be represented in graphic form as trend lines, as was done by researchers in a PRA exercise in Kenya (see Figure 3.30).

However, researchers can go further than this to collect data from informants as to what they think the impact of certain events and changes has been and why they think they occurred and can produce diagrams, charts or maps summarising the main differences between historical periods. Participative problem-tree analysis, systems diagramming and other techniques can be used to explore events and changes in the past as much as

Photograph 3.15: Marketing vegetables on the roadside

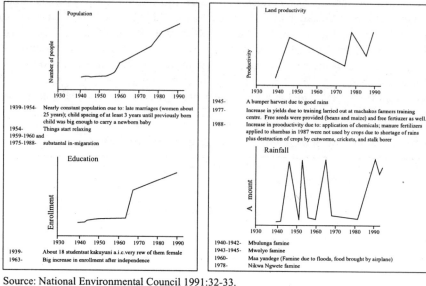

Source: National Environmental Council 1991:32-33.

Figure 3.30: Trend lines from Mbusyani, Kenya

PERIOD SOURCE OF LIVELIHOOD	Until the end of swamp rice > 25 yrs ago	Until the end chinese rice project 15-25 yrs ago	Period of chinese rice project 12-15 yrs ago	End of rice project to fertilizer problem 3-12 yrs ago	PRESENT (past 3 years)
Millet	12	19	7	22	30
Groundnut	8	19	5	24	40
Rice	15	6	19	5	10
Maize	8	17	8	20	32
Findoo Grain	4	4	4	4	5
Gardening	14	18	5	20	40
Tree products	20	20	20	20	45
Cattle	18	20	20	20	20
Sheep and Goats	17	20	20	20	20
Money from Relatives	5	5	10	25	30
Fishing	8	8	10	8	10
Pumpkins	7	7	10	10	20

Source: Schoonmaker Freudenberger 1994 in Guijt 1998:81.

Figure 3.31: Historical matrix comparing coping strategies in times of crisis, Senegal

in the present. Scientists may consider the validity of this data to be somewhat less than robust (since history is — partially — 'in the eye of the beholder' who may have a hidden agenda to promote), but the same is true of most data gathered from respondents — whether qualitative or quantitative. Hence the need for 'triangulation.' If nothing else, different informants' explanations for events and changes can suggest other causal factors in complex and dynamic socio-biophysical systems to those NR researchers might normally consider, while they need to be taken account of for reasons of sound policy-making.

The joint exploration by informants and researchers of historical change in techniques and practices (e.g. cropping practices) can highlight what appears to be appropriate/ inappropriate practice for sustainable development, and can be used to derive key indicators for monitoring positive/negative impact on the system in the future. Scientists may feel more comfortable with these techniques than with the participatory reconstruction of historical time-lines, since they may take the present as their baseline and establish their own (objective) indicators for monitoring future outcomes. However, where respondents report on outcomes, rather than scientists quantitatively measuring them, there is still the potential for bias. Since 'before' and 'after' loom large in monitoring and evaluation studies, we reproduce a few diagrams contained in Guijt's book on *Participatory monitoring and impact assessment of sustainable agricultural initiatives.* This book is very informative and illustrates a wide range of PRA tabulating and diagramming tools.

3.13.1 Historical Matrices

The first example (Figure 3.31) uses matrix scoring, which is frequently used for comparing outcomes or values between different preferences, options, issues, problems and the like, with a repetition of the exercise at different periods. The result is a picture detailing the changes that have taken place in Senegalese livelihood strategies in times of crisis over a 25 year period. While it is not entirely clear from the matrix what the scoring relates to over time, within each time period the relative importance of the individual sources of livelihood is clear, as is the long term trend towards more diversified livelihoods and probably cash cropping and a cash economy (as instanced by the increase in the value allocated to 'Groundnut', 'Maize', 'Gardening', 'Tree products' and 'Money from Relatives').

The second example (Table 3.12) takes a Needs/Problem Census matrix and repeats the exercise five years later in two communities in Kenya. In the period between the census exercises, a new pipeline met the original first priority for water (which in turn may have partially met the second priority — improvements in 'Health' — since in both communities Employment/Lack of Income replaced it in second place, moving up the rank order together with 'Food shortage'). No further details are given as to the reasons for this. Perhaps there had been other social and infrastructural initiatives in the intervening 5 year period which partially met earlier stated needs, since priorities in Kamathatha were more specific in 1996 — e.g. 'police post', 'cattle dip, 'artificial insemination', 'market', 'playground' — than in 1992. Or perhaps, and more likely, it was a failure by a researcher to 'consolidate' respondents' answers to the exercise in 1996 in Kamathatha as opposed to doing so in 1992 and in Nagumu in 1996. This points to a need for caution by researchers in the comparison of and conclusions to be drawn from qualitative data from different historical periods (is like being compared with like?), just as there should be with data from different localities. Nevertheless the example does illustrate the potential for the method, as well as re-emphasising the need for on-going monitoring to ensure that development is meeting stakeholders' current needs.

Table 3.12 Comparison of changing community needs

Shifting Priorities: Comparison of Needs in 1992 and 1996 Nagumu and Kamathatha Zones in Gilgil		
Original Ranked Priorities	Reranked Priorities for Kamathatha: 1996	Reranked Priorities for Nagumu: 1996
1. Water	1. Food Shortage	1. Food Shortage
2. Health	2. Employment	4. Lack of Income
3. Wildlife	3. Hospital	2. Health
4. Technical Services	4. Lack of Income	4. Migrating Livestock
5. Education	5. Police Post	5. Roads
6. Transport	6. Cattle Dip	6. Lack of trees
7. Lack of Income	7. Artificial Insemination	7. Wildlife
8. Food Shortage	8. Market	7. Veterinary Services
Ranking priorities at regular intervals provides indicators of changing priorities within a community. In Gilgil, new pipelines reduced the need for water; however, priority for jobs, income, and food have moved to higher levels.	9. Playground	
	10. Poor Transport Network	
	11. Water	
	12. Schools	
	13. Lack of Woodfuel	
	14. Wildlife Menace	

Source: Ford *et al.* 1996; in Guijt 1998:90.

3.13.2 Historical Transects
It is also possible to do historical transects — essentially combining transect diagrams and timelines — in order to visualise how land use has changed over a specified period. This might be presented in the form of a number of cross-sectional diagrams (similar to a transect disaggregated by NR user group/social strata at one point in time) (see Figure 3.32). It might also be presented in the form of three-dimensional pictures (see Figure 3.33), or even photographs (see Guijt 1998: 63).

3.13.3 Larger Comparative Historical Analysis Scale
The majority of time-line studies are done at the micro level and focus on intra-household/community variation over time. A difficulty (for policy-makers) is what to do with such case studies when policy requirements necessitate working at much larger spatial scales. Unless random sampling procedures have been followed, there must be uncertainty as to whether a case study is typical of a region as a whole, while such normative procedures mask the variation between households/communities which is the likely reality on the ground. Policy-making based on case studies is hazardous because it can have unintended (negative) impacts on different NR user groups' livelihoods, and is made without reference to their particular needs. PRA techniques have been shown to be cost effective at the micro-level, to provide rich data, and to be socially inclusive in accessing variations in NR user group perspectives, and there is no *a priori* reason why the same techniques cannot be used at both a greater spatial and temporal scale to reveal regional variation in trend data.

A good example of what can be achieved is provided by Thomas and Danjaji (1997). Their study explored spatial patterns of change within the Hadejia-Jama'are floodplain

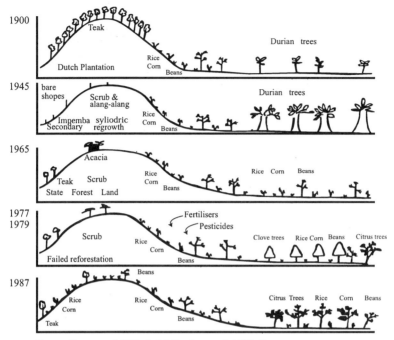

Source: Pretty *et al.* 1988; in McCracken *et al.* 1988:41.

Figure 3.32: Transect through time illustrating land use trends, Eastern Java

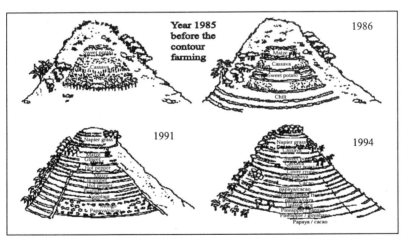

Source: IIRR 1996:81.

Figure 3.33: Changes on a farm in the Philippines through adoption of upland farm management technology

in northern Nigeria over a 20 year period in response to a programme of dam-building and a prolonged drought in the Sahel region (see Figure 3.34). Most previous ecological and economic studies have treated the floodplain as a spatially homogeneous unit and changes caused by the dams as though they were uniform. 'There has also been

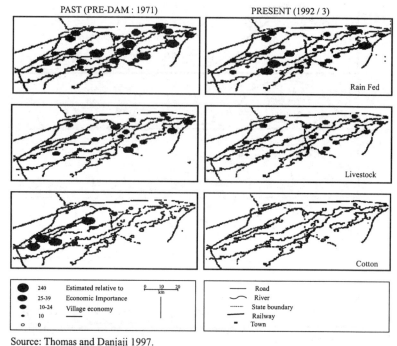

Source: Thomas and Danjaji 1997.

Figure 3.34: Spatial patterns of change in the economic importance of rainfed farming, livestock production and cotton farming in the Hadeija-Jama'are floodplain, Nigeria 1971-1992/3

little attempt to explore temporal dimensions to change ... . Yet floodplains are known to be spatially and temporally highly dynamic systems' (1997:29). The study sought a more nuanced understanding of temporal and spatial variation by collecting data from 27 floodplain villages collected by stratified random sampling and, in the absence of base-line statistical information and written records, relied on the recall of floodplain inhabitants for information on environmental and socio-economic change. The nature and timing of abnormal fluctuations in flooding identified by respondents was linked to a standard scale provided by key events in recent Nigerian history. The study also sought data on changes in the economies of the sample villages over the chosen historical period. This was done through a ranking exercise to determine the relative importance of different economic activities to each village's economy with reference to two periods, and the results then formed a platform for discussions on what and why change had taken place.

The authors emphasise that the sample size is small and therefore the findings must be interpreted with caution, but they also say that, "The results show clearly that suppositions regarding 'the floodplain' as a homogeneous economic unit for planning and development are mistaken" (1997:31). They note, for example, that in the fishing sector environmental changes have interacted with wider economic and technological change to produce complex patterns of development. Thus while the relative contribution of fishing to village economies has decreased in most parts of the floodplain, and fish diversity, size and catch has declined, in some villages the importance of fishing to the local economy has remained constant or has increased. The reason for this is that the price of fish has increased at a greater rate than have the prices of other commodities "fuelled by the scarcity of fish induced by environmental change, and also by expanded markets due to improvements in communications ..." (1997:33).

Besides the specific findings of the study concerning actual micro-level changes, and variations in these over a wider geographical area — which are of value to policy-makers and regional planners — the study demonstrates the potential of PRA techniques to cost-effectively access NR users' IK. As the authors say, choosing the most appropriate scale for study is an important decision to make and is determined by the objective of the study.

Thus "studying the household picks up on socio-economic factors, whereas studying the entire floodplain misses important within-floodplain differences ... that are an important influence on village level economic development." If there is one caveat to the study (from a poverty-reduction and livelihoods perspective) it would be a wish that the authors had also studied inter-household variation and the impact of change on the poorest NR user groups within the sample villages. This may not have been possible for resourcing reasons, but would have been useful for policy-makers, planners and extension services in the targeting of services on those most at risk (for as the authors say, "Understanding variation is essential if development is to be equitable and reach those at the "margins" of society"(1997:29)).

Photograph 3.16: Spreading grain to sun dry

3.13.4 Methodological Issues

Data Reliability

There are two major issues in the use of IK by researchers for historical comparison. The first concerns the reliability of the data. Researchers are right to be cautious as to the veracity of previous events to which respondents attach significance in the present. We have made much of the fact that different observers have different perspectives on NR, and the same is true for the same observer over time. As livelihoods, and the social context in which they occur, change so do individual perspectives on them. That means that the remembered past is a selective past. However, the remembered past is not entirely open to the vagaries of personal whim in the present. It is usually a shared past, and the veracity of facts can be checked against what other people say (and perhaps against written or visual records where they exist). Unless the social group as a whole have a 'hidden agenda', the main NR details that researchers seek can be robust, and is one reason why it is prudent to triangulate individual responses (in interviews, etc.) in group discussion contexts (e.g. focus groups). The interpretation of facts by respondents is of course far more open to change (due to present individual/group circumstance and/or hidden agendas), and researchers should treat indigenous interpretations with the same caution as they would their own.

Interpretation

The second major issue is the validity of the conclusions which are drawn from the data by researchers (and NR users). It is difficult enough to draw conclusions as to what the main causal factors are underlying NRM in any particular context in the present, let alone the past, given the multiple socio-economic and biophysical factors which NR users have to take into account in their livelihoods. The major thrust of the PRA approach has been to improve this causal analysis by drawing on NR users' knowledge. However, as Richards (in Chambers 1990:39-43) has noted, NR users' management practices are frequently more 'performative' in response to the complexity and uncertainties they face than they are 'planned'. Over a longer time period and in retrospect, however, NR users may well rationalise their management practice as underpinned by a 'plan'. It is doubly difficult then to draw conclusions from data which may or may not represent 'snapshots' of a 'moving target' at different time periods (with perhaps no continuous/panel data between the snapshots) together with respondents' explanations for their past NRM practice which may also have 'moved'.

This is not to say that researchers should not seek to identify trends, step changes and the like, and should not seek IK relating to changing management practice. They should, and where there are few written records, NR users' recall of past conditions and their NRM may be all there is to go on. However, it is to say that researchers should be cautious as to the conclusions which they draw from the data. We reproduce a time series chart (below) which perhaps illustrates this.

Table 3.13 Time series analysis of the experiences of Chandavana village, Junagadh, India

Year	1950	1960	1970	1980	1990
Number of wells	7	100	150	200	400
Depth of well where water available (ft.)	30	30	45	100	150
Expenditure per well (Rupees)	3000	5000	10,000	12,000	130,000 (including pump)
Certainty of striking water	100%	100%	100%	80%	50%

Source: Shah 1997.

The drawing of a map of water resources and the location of wells and check dams was the first exercise carried out by villagers (see Section on Mapping for an example). The second exercise was a participatory time series analysis of well development in the village. Respondents were able to indicate the number of wells constructed, the depth where water was found, the cost of sinking a well and the certainty of striking water over a 40 year time period. The author states that, "the table shows a rapid increase in the number of wells constructed from a mere 7 in 1950, to 400 in 1990. Over the same time period, the water has fallen from about 30 feet to more than 100 feet and the cost of irrigation wells has risen significantly. On the other hand the certainty of striking water, which was almost 100% till 1970, has decreased to 50%" (p.76). He concludes that, "the time series analysis revealed the need for ground water to be recharged through the construction of check dams."

Shah may be right in his conclusion, but a note of caution is in order. Time series data are difficult to interpret for a variety of reasons, not least because of the difficulty of comparing like with like over time, and because changes may be due to a number of factors. For instance as regards cost, the author does not say whether these are actual costs (as stated by respondents) or whether they are adjusted for inflation as measured against a base-line year. They appear to be the former. Yet while the cost (in rupees) appears to have increased dramatically over 40 years, the increase may be partially due to the increase in well depth (over 5 times) and the need for a pump, while its cost relative to average household expenditure may actually have fallen. With regards the number of wells sunk over the time period this may be a function of an increasing population (perhaps with in-migration). The population in 1950 may have been concentrated in those areas where water was to be found at the 30 foot mark, but as their wealth and technology permitted they felt able to sink wells in ever more marginal areas (perhaps on hillsides away from the river) — that is where there was a 80% probability of water being found at 100 feet (in 1980) and 50% probability at 150 feet (in 1990).

Put very simply, the time series data that is presented needs to be augmented by a considerable amount of other data (e.g. on changes in population density and location, on people's need for well water, on economic opportunities in the area, on the purchasing power of the rupee, the morphology and hydrography of the area, and so on. Some of this may be available from state records (changes in the value of the rupee, and changes in population densities), while others may be gleaned from discussion, transect walks, participatory mapping and the like with respondents.

Elsewhere we have referred to the need to check data through 'triangulation', but there is an even greater need to check interpretations of the data. Put baldly, without considerably more contextual data of the sort suggested in the last paragraph, the time series analysis cannot be said to reveal "the need for ground water to be recharged through the construction of check dams." One would want to know whether the construction of check dams would have any impact on ground water levels in the marginal areas (where well depth is 150 feet), and whether the wells sunk in the 1950-1970 period needed rehabilitation in this way (i.e. has the water table dropped to the 100 foot mark here or not?).

Lastly, if the goal of the intervention (and its funding) is to make a difference to the livelihoods of the poorest (as is the case with most agency programmes), one would want to know whether check dam rehabilitation and construction is likely to proportionally benefit them or not. For example, they may be living in marginal areas (where well depth is 100-150 feet), but ground water recharge through check dams may never reach these areas, and so never benefit them. Again they may have very different ideas to researchers about what intervention would most benefit them. As repeated elsewhere, there is a need for researchers (and particularly those with a technical or sectoral focus) to take account of client need and perspective, and to recognise that respondents in participatory appraisal exercises may be drawn from particular interest groups unless care is taken to disaggregate the population and seek the views of the different identified groups.

3.14 Group Discussion/Focus Groups

Cost	L	Individual/group perspective	G
Time	L	Expertise required (social and nat. scientist)	M/H
Data reliability	H	Observer bias	L
		Control of process (directive)	L/M

Definition: Discussions with small groups of informants on one or several related topics.

Purpose: To generate new information, clarify further points of detail, validate information derived through other methods, to build consensus between group members.

Groups may be formed to meet on a one-off or on a recurrent ('panel') basis depending on need. As Chambers and Jiggins note (1986:24), "Consultation with groups and panels does not fit normal professionalism. Even FSR methods are concerned with individual farmers and farms. Groups or panels are, to our knowledge, scarcely mentioned." However, the increasing devolvement of responsibility for the management of CPRs to the micro- (community and catchment) level, the shift away from generating recommendation domains for individual sets of farmers, and the growth of participatory practice stimulated by demand-side research and development, has generated a need to consider the interdependencies between social groups. Thus a variety of new techniques for data collection and analysis have emerged and include stakeholder and social impact analysis (see Section: Stakeholder analysis), together with techniques for facilitating PLA — for example the problem census (see Section: Problem Census). PLA goes beyond PRA in seeking to improve livelihoods not only through technical interventions but through socio-economic ones as well (e.g. improving access to natural and social capital through negotiation). While working with individuals is still important, much PLA work is done at the group level.

Group Formation

Group discussions have generally been based on the assumption that the group, community or section of it can reach agreement on the topic(s) under discussion, even though these may be hotly debated by participants. The group discussion method, as illustrated in IIRR's book (1996), notes that, "ideally group members come from various walks of life and socio-economic categories, representing formal and informal community organisations." There can be advantages in having a heterogeneous group, not least in obtaining a variety of views on a topic according to representatives' perspectives, and the quantity of data that is generally provided. Group discussion can also be very useful in developing participation and potentially for moving towards consensus between participants concerning a particular course of action.

However, there are significant drawbacks to the method, not least because those making up the discussion group may not be truly representative of all stakeholder groups in a community, and because the representatives of certain groups (e.g. women, the poor, those of lower caste or class) may not feel able to express their opinions openly in public. Additionally, a group discussion is an oral event, it is not a behavioural event in a natural setting. Thus behaviour may be rationalised in response to the group and the facilitator. The biases implicit in the method may therefore need to be counterbalanced by the use of other methods such as individual interview/discussion, participant-observation (see Section 3.1: Participant Observation) and so on to capture the differences between the groups, even though these methods are more time and resource intensive. Additionally the method implicitly ignores the politico-economic dimension underlying resource allocation within and between communities, social groups and households.

3.14.1 Focus Groups

The Focus Group technique is an extension of the group discussion technique, but is based on the assumption that the community is not homogeneous, that the context is not neutral, and that different stakeholders within it may be unable to express their views freely in open forum. This is a tool for studying ideas (perhaps the perspective of a specific target group) in a group context and is based on the belief that, 'The whole is greater than the sum of its parts' (see Morgan 1988). As Morgan emphasises, social science may use the group interview for convenience, but as a systematic research technique Focus Groups represent the explicit use of the group interaction to produce data and insights that would be less accessible without the interaction found in a group. Meanings emerge over time, and are refined. The method relies on interactions within the group based on topics supplied by the researcher/moderator. However, and most importantly in the development context, the method is a technique for exploring the range of knowledge and opinion on a topic within a social group, but also the diversity of knowledge bases, opinions and perspectives between different stakeholder groups that make up a community.

In consequence the formation of the discussion groups and the management of the discussion process is all-important. The aim is to have a number of homogeneous groups discussing the same topic(s). The different stakeholder groups within a community in relation to a particular topic have therefore to be identified first (for example through a wealth ranking exercise (see Section: Wealth ranking), where the topic concerns livelihoods' enhancement and poverty alleviation). As the prime purpose of the focus group technique is to generate 'rich' data on a topic, there is no need for participants to either agree, disagree or reach any kind of consensus. Only later when the data from different focus group exercises are placed before decision-makers, may there be a need for other consensus-building techniques.

The focus group method can be used at any point in a project, from appraisal, through implementation, to monitoring and summative evaluation. The focus group technique is useful for exploring new avenues for research (i.e. generating questions) as in a social needs assessment — perhaps through a problem census — and for clarifying findings from other data (i.e. generating answers) as in validation workshops. The goal is to get closer to participants' understandings of the topic(s) under discussion. Data can be sought on attitudes/opinions, but is more preferably sought on participants' experiences and perspectives — the reason being that self-reported experiences form better data than opinions with an unknown basis in behaviour, and because discussion of them produces a livelier group dynamic. The stress in discussion is on deriving the manifest content of group discussion rather than on the micro-dynamics of the interaction process — that is on meaning rather than structure. The technique goes beyond summaries of attitudes to reveal the cognitive processes involved and the process of opinion formation (i.e. differences in perspectives and their modification, and group rationale for these). As Morgan notes (1988), "Focus groups are useful when it comes to investigating what participants think, but they excel at uncovering why participants think as they do."

Where the focus group technique is being used as part of a PLA process (e.g. as part of a consensus-building process where there is multiple but conflicting use of natural resources), it is an efficient mechanism for generating data for consideration by primary and secondary stakeholders. The needs, perspectives, and solutions to problems volunteered by the homogeneous groups can be shared with and compared by the other groups to see where there are differences and similarities, and (when linked into a broader PLA framework) with a view to identifying ways forward which are acceptable to or can be negotiated with all groups while benefiting the target group.

It should be remembered that respondents' opinions, explanations and perspectives expressed in a group context are, like those expressed in a one-to-one context to a researcher, partial (or emic). The researcher gains a wider perspective on the topic(s) discussed from a summation and comparison of information from all the groups, and can add his/her 'expert knowledge' (etic knowledge) to this. Discussions on a topic are held separately with each group, but where the intention is a wider process of community consensus-building or systems' learning, the knowledge and perspectives of all groups, together with 'expert knowledge', may be presented in a public forum (see Section: Village Workshop) and may form the basis for further discussion on ways forward as a community. Thus facilitators may carry out their own content analysis on focus group data with a view to identifying whether the causes of conflict between groups are due to interest, value, structural, relationship, or data reasons, and to identifying potential responses to these and place these before decision-makers (see Environment Council 1998:8).

Box 3.6: Advantages and disadvantages of focus groups

Advantages

- an efficient data collection technique (data from a number of people rather than one in interview at the same time) = increase in overall sample size;
- it gives some quality control on data collection (participants provide checks and balance on each other which weeds out false or extreme views);
- group dynamics leads to a focus on the most important topics and issues (see Four Stages of Group Development, Section 3.21: Brainstorming);
- easy to assess the extent to which there is a relatively consistent, shared view by participants.

Disadvantages

- since the amount of response time to any given question is increased considerably by the number of people responding, the number of questions that can be asked is limited;
- facilitation requires considerable group-process skills (it is important to manage the process well, and prevent dominant views, 'sleepers' etc.);
- unexpected diversions can occur, as can conflicts, power struggles etc.;
- it is important to avoid survey-like interpretations (given small size and non representativeness of the sample);
- it is resource intensive.

Points to Remember

- reporting: the unstructured nature of more exploratory observation presents many of the same issues/problems as reporting on participant-observation;
- robustness of the data: it is only a 'slice of life'. The greater the moderator control the more structured answers will be and the tighter the circle of interrelated issues/topics that are likely to be raised; the more unstructured, the greater the likelihood of unforeseen and unexpected relational linkages being made by participants. This is the same issue as occurs with structured vs. open-ended questions in survey questionnaires (see diagram; 'structure-unstructure') and reductive vs. holistic evaluatory methods (see Stufflebeam and Shinkfield 1985).

Patton (1987:135) suggests that the focus group interview is "an interview. It is not a discussion. It is not a problem-solving session. It is not a decision-making group. It is an interview." While one may agree with him (in his role as an evaluator who is interested in the method as a highly efficient qualitative data collection technique), the technique itself does offer opportunities for discussion, problem-solving, and decision-making within PLA and consensus-building frameworks. That is that the qualitative data gleaned through using the technique is not just for the use of outsiders (as is common in managerial-type projects and blueprint evaluation), but is data which can be shared by different stakeholders — and most definitely including primary stakeholders — with an interest in addressing the issues around which the data was generated in the first place.

3.14.2 Using the Method

The Focus Group method has been used in Sociology since the 1950's (see Merton *et al.* 1956, Kirk and Miller 1986) and has been extensively taken up in Market Research. Its use in development has been limited, but more recent interest in the value of IK for development and a focus on client needs and perspectives (as typified by USAID's shift to 'Customer Service Plans') suggests that it might be used more widely in development work in future. Since the method is not generally mentioned in manuals on methods for recording and using IK in development work, the next section gives details of how the method might be used.

Planning for Focus Groups

There are a number of planning issues that need to be resolved before the technique is used.

- Political and ethical constraints. These are the same as for any social research.
- Budgetary and Time constraints. Focus groups are not a quick and easy technique except in the very limited function of preliminary investigation to which they are usually relegated. As always the quality of data derived is dependent on the quality of preparation.
- Number of groups. This is the primary dimension of variability. The more groups, the more research staff or data collection sessions are needed over an extended period — with time/cost implications. (Market Research gives a rough guide — i.e. vary the number of groups according to whether additional discussions are producing new data or not — typically 3-4 groups.) Do only as many as are required to answer the research question. The more homogeneous groups are in background and role-based perspectives, the less groups are required; the more distinct population sub-groups are, the more are needed.

- Group size. There are economies of scale in running larger groups, but the dynamics of discussions are different to small groups. Size is determined by whether researchers' need is to hear an individual or collective perspective. Both small and large groups have biases in their composition ('experts', friendship pairs, uncooperative participants, 'loafing', difficulty of control by moderator). 4 seems to be the smallest size possible, 12 the largest.
- Participant selection. The issue is sample bias (representativeness) and is especially important where learning about other's experiences/perspectives is the aim. Capturing a full range is a fool's errand. A typical solution is to work with theoretically chosen sub-groups, and concentrate on population segments providing the most meaningful information (i.e. in terms of a significant variable such as gender or class). Recruitment has time/cost implications. Pre-screening is necessary to ensure group members have the same characteristics (or discussion can get totally off track). One issue is whether to mix different categories or run separate groups for each category. (Reasonable homogeneity is necessary to foster discussion). The goal is homogeneity in background, rather than attitudes.
- Level of moderator involvement (and potential bias). This can vary from low (non-directive) to high (control of topics and dynamics of discussion) dependent upon the research goals. Exploratory research needs a non-directive approach in order to capture participants' perspectives rather than researcher-imposed agendas. The same is true for full-scale content analysis (perhaps using CAQDAS, see Section 3.22) otherwise it will capture the moderator's interests rather than that of the participants). High control of the discussion process is more appropriate where there is a strong, externally-generated agenda (e.g. comparing the perspectives of a new set of participants with that previously found with others; addressing issues for use in another research setting; providing answers to sharply drawn research questions). The bonus of a non-directive approach is the potential it gives to assess participants' own interests while allowing them space to raise controversial matters. A disadvantage is the disordered nature of content, the difficulty of analysis, and the potential absence of some topics from discussion. But a group can self-manage itself if the moderator cues them on: topics, wanting their experiences and issues, avoiding irrelevant discussion, restarting discussion, expressing individual opinion, obtaining a say from everybody, etc. (n.b. A test of the method is: If it is highly structured, would a survey method be better; if unstructured, would participant-observation be better? The question to ask — as of all methods is 'Why choose this method?').

Conducting and Analysing Focus Groups

Observation

Merton *et al.* (1956) note four operational criteria for effective focus group discussions — Range, Specificity, Depth, and Personal Context, where:

- 'Range' denotes the extent of topics/issues the group raises (and may go beyond those anticipated by researchers).
- 'Specificity' denotes the degree of focus on participants' experiences in relation to the topic under discussion. (These experiences reveal individuals' attitudes/opinions. The intention is to avoid generalities and to derive data as specific to the topic as possible.)

Photograph 3.17: Focus group discussions

- 'Depth' denotes the degree of participants' emotional involvement with material under discussion. (Again avoiding generalities ensures participant involvement.)
- 'Personal Context' refers to participants' personal situation, social role, etc. — their 'standpoint'. (This enables the researcher to grasp the individual's perspective on a topic. The group situation means that individuals have to justify their perspective to others, and in doing so reveal their 'standpoint' on issues — something which is difficult to obtain through other methods.)

Determining Group Discussion Content

- The goal is to construct a discussion which covers the topic while satisfying Merton's four criteria for achieving effective group dynamics. The main body of the discussion may be either unstructured (through self-directed group-work with minimum input from the moderator) or structured (with greater moderator control). However, as there is usually a constraint on time allowable for discussion, content may need to be structured according to a 'topic guide' covering questions researchers would like addressed but not presented as questions (since this limits group interaction with focus being on the questioner, and is too structured) A topic guide facilitates a natural progression in discussion and comparison between groups. However, flexibility is important (see 'Range' above), as is avoiding moderator-dominance (or 'moderator-as-expert').
- Group discussion may be brought to a conclusion either through moderator intervention in self-directed group-work or through individual closing statements in a highly structured group interview (with perhaps informal, but recorded, discussion after closure, or follow-up visits to individuals to collect further/private thoughts).
- Practicalities: The moderator should introduce the discussion topic in an honest but general fashion (to avoid restricting discussion) and stress that researchers wish to learn from participants' greater and specific experiences even though

they might think the researcher is a supposed 'expert'. Ground rules (e.g. only one person speaking at a time, no side conversations, all to participate, etc.) need to be established, and a collective 'icebreaking' activity undertaken while establishing each individual's basic perspective and social location (thereby committing them to their view and deterring 'group-think') before the main discussion is commenced.

Data Collection

- Ideally the location should meet the needs of both participants and researcher. Data collection may be through audio-taping if detailed content analysis is intended later, since transcripts represent the raw data. However, audio-taping requires someone to note who is speaking when and to whom, and this approach is resource intensive. A cheaper option for the development context is for a Recorder to manually note the main gist of the exchanges between the moderator and participants. Supplementary information (clarifying points) may be sought pre- or post-discussion through individual interview/questionnaire — though a disadvantage is that these methods are mutually contaminating. In addition the moderator/researcher should keep field notes of each session (for debriefing later), but it should be borne in mind that these are interpretations/analysis and not raw data.

Analysis

There are two potential approaches to analysis —

- qualitative/ethnographic summary with illustrative quotation from group discussions.
- systematic coding via content analysis to produce numerical descriptions.

There is strength in combining both (e.g. Morgan and Spanish 1985 identified 'asking questions' as a code category to be explored, with quotations used to illustrate this, while developing new code categories such as 'comparisons'. This represents an iterative process where transcripts operate as a source of potential quotations for confirming code categories and as a source of inspiration for new code categories.) Focus group discussions structured by a moderator's topic-guide have a practical structure for organising topic-by-topic analysis, and this facilitates analysis. (Where topics are not predetermined, the process for developing hypotheses and coding schemes is a major issue).

Computer-Assisted Qualitative Data Analysis Systems (CAQDAS) have speeded up content analysis, but this approach is still resource intensive, and in most development situations analysis to achieve a qualitative/ethnographic summary is likely to be preferred. This is far less resource intensive while still capturing the main points and degree of similarity and difference within and between groups (on computerised content analysis see Weber 1985).

As with all data, the content may also be analysed according to criteria which did not inform the original discussion context, though it should be remembered that conclusions drawn from the data will be less robust and will require validation by other methods. An example is analysing data from a problem census and village workshop exercise in terms of DFID's Sustainable Livelihoods Framework (see Barr and Haylor 1999).

Systematic content analysis with focus group data is controversial (see Axelrod 1975) since it violates the assumptions of independence in significance tests. But the mere collection of observations in groups does not violate any statistical laws; it simply requires proper allowances (e.g. 'nested design') for the grouped data (see social-psychology experimental design). However, the quantitative analysis of focus group data remains an open issue.

Reporting
The topic-guide of the more structured group-discussions serves as a report-guide (as in individual interviewing). By comparison the unstructured nature of more exploratory observation presents many of the same issues/problems as reporting on participant-observation.

3.14.3 Additional Possibilities for the Method
There are also a number of other possibilities for the use of the focus group method. Which is chosen will depend upon the objective of the research/intervention. Four are mentioned by Morgan (1985)

- Combining focus groups and other research methods in the same project. This is the most common combination. For example there could be a survey to identify the main socio-economic or occupational subgroups in a community and the proportion of the population belonging to each; Focus group discussion and ranking exercises with representatives of these subgroups to identify and rank the main constraints to their livelihoods; in-depth participant-observation and use of a range of farming systems research methods with subgroup representatives (including interviews to build flow-, transect- and seasonal- pattern charts) and to stand as case-studies of subgroup livelihood strategies; and group discussions for systems learning.
- Varying the composition of groups. This allows for a systematic comparison of the groups according to the variable of difference chosen — which could be age, gender, disability, socio-economic, occupational or religious status, and so on. Our DFID projects in Bangladesh, for example, were concerned with contributing to poverty alleviation through accessing local people's IK in order to under-stand the livelihood strategies and interdependencies of subgroups in floodplain communities, and to explore the potential for consensually-agreed interventions to address the needs of the poorest. The composition of focus groups was therefore varied according to socio-economic status, occupation and gender to capture the differences and similarities in perspectives between groups. (See also, for example, Knodel *et al.* 1987 study with different generations of Thais to compare perspectives on family size/planning).
- A two-step research programme where some sessions mix types of participants (i.e. heterogeneity) (e.g. exploratory), while others use outcomes of these to determine categories and separate by type (i.e. homogeneity). The reverse is also possible, especially if relevant subgroups are known in advance. For example, the LWI project in Bangladesh made use of both in a problem census/village workshop exercise in which there were initial plenary and summative sessions with a mixing of social categories (i.e. heterogeneity) and interdigitated focus group sessions with representatives of previously identified subgroups (i.e. homo-geneity) (see Section 3.19: Problem Census).
- Comparison to observe changes that occur in single groups over time (i.e. of attitudinal change as a result of group interaction). Such an approach is common

in social-psychology and market research (see Lazarsfeld 1952, Axelrod 1975), but less so in development — though participatory action research (PAR) with its roots in Marxism usually seeks to overcome 'false consciousness' (i.e. to achieve attitudinal change) as a necessary condition for development (see Freire 1972, Fals-Borda and Rahman 1991). However, as natural resource problems are increasingly defined as complex, requiring a mix of soft- as well as hard-system methodologies to address them, so there is increasing interest in monitoring attitudinal change in social groups and its contribution to sustainable development — examples might be young people's attitudes to environmental pollution, or of 'at-risk' groups to safe sex. While attitudinal change can be monitored through survey questionnaires, the focus group method may be more cost-effective and a useful adjunct to a panel survey.

- Multistage groups (i.e. comparison between earlier and later sessions with the same participants, or with participants from several different earlier groups (i.e. 'second order groups', or mixing earlier participants with new ones.) The intention here, for example, might be to monitor the changing attitudes of participants to representatives of other groups differentiated on the basis of social characteristics (e.g. gender, caste) as a result of social awareness/education programmes.

3.15 Participatory Technology Analysis

Cost	L	Individual/group perspective	I/G
Time	L	Expertise required (social and nat. scientist)	M
Data reliability	M-H	Observer bias	L-M
		Control of process (directive)	L-M

Definition: A means for the participative learning of and about a given technology and the implications the technology has for social organisation, time allocations and the like for social units.

Purpose: To enable researchers and local stakeholders to explore the different technical aspects of a particular technology and the implications that these have for different social units and their livelihoods.

The method can be used by researchers to participatively explore the socio-economic and technical implications which an *in situ* technology has for the social organisation and working practices of different social units in the field location. It can also be used to explore the potential impact that a proposed technology might have on the socio-economic well-being of these social units, or to evaluate actual impact on them. The data from these analyses can assist in pinpointing opportunities and constraints to the adaptation of technologies and suggest new lines of inquiry.

The technology analysed may be simple or complex — that is it may have few attributes (e.g. a sickle-knife) or it may consist of a bundle of attributes (e.g. a plant cultivar) or consist of a number of discrete technologies/processes within a wider production or consumption process (e.g. rice cultivation). The analysis may have been preceded by a problem census to identify those areas of most concern to identified client groups, and may be succeeded by participative ranking or scoring exercises to focus attention on the preferred areas for technology improvement.

The method consists in breaking up the totality of a technology or process into discrete units and then breaking each of these up into its constituent parts and so on, and discussing each of the steps of the analysis with a view to identifying potential opportunities and constraints for improvements. Both researchers and respondents from different primary stakeholder groups can undertake this exercise since they may have different perspectives on what is significant and why. The data sought is about operational sequences and procedures; the inputs and outputs at each stage of the transformational process; the purpose, advantages and disadvantages of each; and potential substitutions in the process. The information sought is essentially a Strength Weakness Opportunity and Constraint (SWOC) analysis of who does what, with what, when, where, how and why, and with what outcome. In this respect it is little different to the Total Quality Management (TQM) analyses carried out on industrial production processes in the developed world.

To take the example of wet-rice cultivation in South-East Asia. The steps in the production process may be identified as land preparation, sowing, weeding, harvesting, and post-harvest disposal. Each of these may be broken down in turn into discrete input steps. For example land preparation might include building terraces, flooding fields, and ploughing; while ploughing in turn might be broken down as a process into its input elements — draught cattle, plough, ploughman. The transformational process of ploughing has input costs (in time and resources) which can be identified and which have implications for the quality of the product (ploughed land) which in turn has implications for downstream stages of the process (sowing, weeding, crop growth, harvesting and disposal of the crop). For example, a less thorough ploughing of the land may reduce input costs, but may lead to greater weed but poorer crop growth, a lower final crop volume and quality, and a lower final return to the farmer.

Photograph 3.18: Ploughing a paddy

3.15.1 Demand: A Customer Orientation

However, before the researcher recommends that returns can be optimised by improve-ments made at the ploughing stage, he should explore what it is that the farmer wants and what opportunities and constraints there are to his achieving his aims. Thus he may not want to optimise yield because the market for his crop is limited; or while there is a lower yield, the crop ripens earlier and commands a higher price in the market; or because he needs more rice straw which is encouraged by a less thorough ploughing. He may also not be able to afford to hire the ploughing unit for longer, or he may wish to use his own ploughing unit to plough others' land and earn income for seed and fertiliser for his own rice crop. And so on.

Historically, it is at just this stage of the process that technology development has often gone wrong. ToT approaches (such as Training and Visit), with their focus, for example, on national food security through yield optimisation, prioritised supply-side technological solutions of a high-external-input nature. While this approach may have addressed national needs, it did not address the needs of the resource-poor living in complex risk-prone environments where resource-saving strategies (e.g. low external inputs) are as important to people's livelihoods as resource optimising ones. In short, ToT approaches have tended to ignore the socio-economic and biophysical context in which poor people make their living. Participative approaches, as in Farmer First (see Rhoades 1984; Chambers *et al.* 1990), reverse this by seeking to understand the local socio-economic and biophysical context in which poor NR users make a living, the trade-offs that they make, and the multiplex decisions that are involved. Once researchers do that, they can move towards designing (or assisting NR users in the design) of technology which is in large measure demand-driven while incorporating elements originating in their own expertise. Even with a shift to a client focus, there is great potential for failure in the delivery of the appropriate technology due to the many steps between determining what the 'customer' wants (and indeed who the customer is) and the delivery of the product. In Total Quality Management (TQM) terms the 'quality of conformance to design' is the extent to which the product or service achieves the quality of design. As Oakland says (1995:10) "What the customer actually receives should conform to the design. Quality cannot be inspected into products or services; the customer satisfaction must be designed into the whole system ... . It is not sufficient that marketing specifies the product or service 'because that is what the customer wants.' There must be agreement that the operating departments can achieve that requirement." Figure 3.35 sums up the issues nicely.

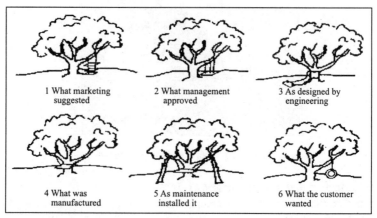

Source: Oakland 1995:10.

Figure 3.35: Quality of design

A participative technology analysis enables a production process such as that given above to be analysed in detail. The researcher could observe the process over the cropping year and could chart a variety of seasonal calendars of work activities and the like. However, the quickest way to find out why people do what they do is to ask them. The important next step is not to prejudge what they are doing and what their intentions are, but to ask them what these are for each stage of the production process, and to explore with them potential opportunities and constraints. The comparison between the IK that primary stakeholders have and the scientific and technological knowledge that researchers have can lead to the identification of appropriate interventions. This is essentially what 'early' FSR did. It analysed the farming system to understand what the process was, what the inputs and outputs were and what the flows were between the various units of the farming system (see 3.11 Flow charts). It then made recommendations based on this information. 'Later' FSR improved on this by incorporating farmers' knowledge and their overall aims for the farming system into their analysis.

3.15.2 Impact Analysis: Stakeholders

However, there are good reasons for going beyond this analysis. A technological analysis is not sufficient in itself. As noted elsewhere technology development lies at the interface between the technical and the social. Technologies have upstream and downstream implications both at the level of the farm and beyond. Changes have impacts on social organisation, and more importantly have different implications for the well-being and livelihoods of different primary stakeholders. A simple example: a researcher might suggest that the rice production system can be improved if a farmer invests in, or hires, a power-tiller rather than the traditional oxen-plough. This is speedier. The farmer can plough less or more thoroughly depending on whether he wants an early or late crop, less or more grain and/or straw and, while a power-tiller costs more to hire, the efficiency gains will offset this. However, there may be downstream social drawbacks to this technology shift. Firstly, while the farmer himself may be willing to forgo the other benefits that draught-animals give him (milk, meat, and manure), his wife may not — particularly in poorer households where expenditure saving is a critical part of livelihood strategies. Secondly, the increased allocation of household resources for the hire of a power tiller may result in a reduction in the availability of natural and capital resources for other household enterprises — say small stock breeding, yoghurt/ cheese-making, dung fuel-stick making and market trading. If these are women's enterprises, while rice farming is men's, the adoption of power tillers may result in a shift of resources from women to men, a reduction in household livelihood diversification and no overall gain in household income or well-being security. Another more obvious example is that a shift to power tillage (perhaps followed by power planting, harvesting, threshing) reduces livelihood opportunities for other, often poorer, stakeholders through their provision of labour and other inputs.

The overall lesson then is that technology development is rarely socially neutral in its impact. Small shifts in materials, combinations and processes can have wider ramifications due to system linkages and feedback. Impacts may be positive, neutral, or negative for different parts of a system and for different stakeholders. These impacts may be unexpected. Changes in technology or system relations may reduce or increase access to natural, social and economic resources for different stakeholders and impact on livelihood security. Researchers therefore need to carry out detailed social impact analysis as well as technical appraisal prior to implementation, and this should include a benefit producing and (as importantly) expenditure saving analysis for different stakeholders which goes beyond a simple economic cost-benefit analysis. Key indicators of social impact on the livelihoods of stakeholders — particularly the poor — should be identified prior to planned changes and used to monitor and evaluate any intervention. These may need to be developed participatively in order to capture effects on a range of different stakeholders at different scales. Contingency planning mechanisms should be put in place with stakeholders to respond to monitoring information and adapt implementation in the light of this. At all times, researchers should ask who the technology is for, whether it is appropriate to their needs, and in the light of the international community's focus on poverty eradication, who is affected by it and how, and consult with stakeholders to obtain their views.

3.16 Strengths and Weaknesses

Cost	L	Individual/group perspective	I/G
Time	L	Expertise required (social and nat. scientist)	L
Data reliability	H	Observer bias	L
		Control of process (directive)	L

Definition: A group exercise to list the strengths and weaknesses of a technology, practice, or event and provide additional information concerning this judgement (see also Participative technology analysis Section 3.15).

Purpose: To access opinions as to the suitability or otherwise of a technology, practice or event, and the reasoning behind this judgement, and with a view to making improvements to it.

The researcher first introduces the topic of discussion to the group, draws a tabular record chart on a blackboard or distributes a tabular record sheet on which participants can enter those characteristics of the technology, practice or event which they think are its strengths and weaknesses, and briefly say why. The standard tabular record consists of five columns, the first details the characteristics, the second and fourth indicate strength (+ or tick) or weakness (- or x) and the third and fifth, the reason for this evaluation (see Table 3.14). The participants can then either individually or collectively fill in the record chart. After the exercise has been completed the researcher can seek further clarification as to the reasoning behind individuals/group evaluations, and explore potential improvements to the technology, practice or event and possible constraints to these.

Table 3.14 A sickle knife

Characteristics	Strengths	For whom	Why	Weaknesses	For whom	Why
Long blade	+++	men	cuts rice stalks well	- -	women	blade too long
Heavy blade	++	men	assists cutting swing	- - -	women	too heavy
Iron blade	++	men	easily sharpened	-	men and women	easily blunted

A strengths and weaknesses analysis may also be merged with an Opportunities and Constraints analysis (as in a SWOC analysis). The tool provides a framework assisting individual or group analysis and/or evaluation of issues. Four categories (Strengths,

Weaknesses, Opportunities and Constraints) are used to examine, define, and record the issues and provide a framework for further discussion around these. The tool is easy to explain, easy to use, and easily understood by respondents. The method can be used with heterogeneous groups (e.g. made up of representatives from different stakeholder groups) or with homogeneous ones (e.g. poor women, or landless labourers). When used in a group context it encourages input from many people, and facilitates discussion of constraints and potential solutions to them, as well as the identification of alternatives ('opportunities') and their potential limitations. It is very useful for assisting participants to recognise that there are usually two different sides (positive and negative) to any given issue or situation and that discussion of both from the perspectives of different stakeholders is required. Thus it can help to set the basis for the identification of trade-offs and for negotiations between stakeholders.

The issue or situation can be broad or narrow. SWOC analysis can handle most issues, as long as they are clear and understandable. The analysis may be carried out in relation to a variety of variables (e.g. social, technical, economic, political, and sustainability) — a STEPS analysis — and from different stakeholder group perspectives.

Box 3.7: A strengths, weaknesses, opportunities and constraints analysis

SWOC Analysis Variables

Strengths: Strengths are those things which have worked well. Strengths are the best aspects of any given situation, issue or persons.

Weaknesses: Weaknesses are those things that have not worked so well, the inferior aspects of any given situation, issue or persons.

Opportunities: Opportunities are the possibilities for positive change, given both the strengths and weaknesses. Opportunities are the chance to change things for the better.

Limitations: Limitations are those things that prevent opportunities from being realised. Limitations stop change from happening. Some limitations can be overcome, others cannot.

It is possible to combine a ranking exercise with a SWOC analysis — that is to put a value on each of the characteristics/properties identified using a simple indicative scale (e.g. on a scale of 1 to 3, 1 to 3 ticks/pluses and 1 to 3 crosses/minuses). Again differences between stakeholders, not only in their perception as to whether something is an opportunity or a constraint, but also in the weighting they give these can be very informative and provide the basis for further investigations as to why this may be so (see Table 3.14).

Further discussion around the above technology, may reveal that it is men who, growing cash crops (e.g. rice), determine what farm implements the household can afford, and that women have to make do with a technology which is designed by men, preferred by men, chosen by men and sold to men by men in the market without too much consideration for the different needs of their household's women. Further discussion may reveal that the technology is inappropriate for women not only because it is too heavy for them to use effectively, but also because it is unsuited to the different crops and tasks that women attend to. As Gass *et al.* (1995) note, while one third of all households globally are headed by women, "the design of much mechanical technology have remained grounded in the misguided assumption of the male-headed household."

Photograph 3.19: A seller of various knives

Since the intention of a SWOC exercise is to seek an improvement in the technology or situation under investigation, discussion after the exercise should seek potential solutions to the identified weaknesses. In the above example, it might be possible to suggest technical improvements which would satisfy both men and women (e.g. a slightly shorter and lighter blade, but made of hardened steel which is less easily blunted), or it might be possible to suggest two separate types of sickle be produced and marketed — one suitable for men and the other for women. In both instances, other considerations (e.g. cost, and control of household finances) will also have to be taken into consideration, with perhaps a range of options (i.e. sickles having different characteristics) being produced for a range of different 'consumer' groups.

There are two ways to approach a SWOC analysis, depending on the specific situation or issue. Either go through all the strengths first, then all the weaknesses, all the opportunities, and all the limitations. Or identify each strength, then each 'matching' weakness, and so on. Some points may be discussed at length before agreement is reached. Each point is written on the framework only after agreement has been reached. Sensitive subjects may arise. The facilitator may wish to change the topic and return to the sensitive point later on. This can reduce the chance of possible problems. As with all data, it is important to note who is saying what and why and in relation to what topic.

The method is a relatively quick means for participants to provide an evaluation of something which a researcher has reason to think may be problematic or can be improved, or an evaluation of something (e.g. a technology) which a researcher feels may be usefully introduced if it were adapted to the particular needs of the target group. The method is client-oriented in seeking their evaluation of a technology, practice or event, and their input into design improvements. For example, with an 'off-the-shelf' technology, the method highlights those problems that need to be overcome for the technology to be adopted by the target group, potential local solutions for overcoming the problems, and what steps should be taken next to take the adoption process forward.

Traditionally, development specialists have prioritised the production side and have put most emphasis on the improvement of farmers' production technologies. Frequently, however, they have regarded farmers as socially undifferentiated and have relied upon a few interested farmers for evaluatory and design purposes. Unfortunately, there is the danger that the results may be skewed towards the needs of a particular social group, or that in forming a heterogeneous group for the exercise, the probable potential for uptake by different client-groups is not clearly identified. In reality most technologies, practices and events are multifaceted. They have multiple characteristics to do with technical features (e.g. size, shape, colour, smell, complexity and so on), which have time, cost, social status and other implications for evaluators. As importantly, different social groups have different needs, likes, predilections, livelihoods and different natural, social, human, financial and other assets with which to carry these livelihoods out. These influence their evaluation of any technology, practice or event; different individuals/groups will evaluate the characteristics of any technology differently dependent upon their social position (according to age, gender, occupation, socio-economic status, and so on). For that reason, and to ensure that technology is tailored to the needs of target groups, it is advisable to identify the latter prior to the Strengths and Weaknesses exercise and work with a homogeneous rather than a heterogeneous social group.

3.17 Sorting and Ranking

Cost	L	Individual/group perspective	G
Time	L	Expertise required (social and nat. scientist)	M/H
Data reliability	H	Observer bias	L
		Control of process (directive)	L/M

Definition: Sorting: The division of objects/ideas into different categories according to single or multiple criteria. Ranking: The arrangement of objects/ideas into a hierarchical rank order according to single or multiple criteria. (n.b. Sorting and Ranking are two separate activities, but the second frequently follows the first in development enquiry.)

Purpose: To assist researchers understand how specified individuals/groups see and classify their world, what their preferences are concerning particular objects, technologies etc., and to enable further dialogue concerning the criteria on which they are making judgements about these.

Main Uses

- for generating data on people's priorities and preferences concerning list items which can be used by researchers, planners and implementors of interventions (including local people themselves).
- for generating discussion and/or awareness among participants regarding people's priorities and the causal relationships between list items and other phenomena.
- for monitoring and evaluatory purposes, by providing baseline and outcome comparisons of list item uptake/disposal, preference, prioritisation.

Anthropologists have devoted much attention to 'sorting'. There is a large anthropological literature on how and why individual cultures classify the elements of their world (ranging from taxa of natural resources to kinship systems), whether other people's statements about similarity/difference should be taken literally or whether they should be treated as metaphoric (e.g. the statement by the Nuer of the Sudan that 'twins are birds'), and what implications for action there are when elements do not 'fit' the classificatory system and are anomalous (e.g. twins among some West African peoples). A prime message coming out of the literature is that different cultures (and different groups within a culture) classify the world very differently — that is they experience and perceive the world very differently — and that since classificatory systems in large measure influence people's behaviour, it is not helpful to insist on our values, goals and means of achieving them. Rather, in a post-positivist world, it is beholden on us to try to see the world from their point of view — even though this can be difficult (see Winch 1958) — and to work with them as joint-stakeholders to achieve improvements in livelihoods and well-being. (Two examples are given in Section 3.10: Taxonomies).

Development anthropologists have taken indigenous classifications as a first step (though not always as seriously as they perhaps should), but because they are concerned with improvements to livelihoods and well-being, have focused more on the ranking of items within the sectors they are dealing with. Previously, ranking of need/preference was done by external experts. For example in the agricultural sector, need amongst many of the poor was identified as being a need for food security, and to be achieved through yield improvements based on grain cultivars developed by scientists. The Green revolution was based on this 'supply-side' mentality. Similarly in the social development sector, needs were identified as primarily basic education and health, and to be achieved through a raft of social measures designed and implemented by external experts. There has been considerable debate in the development literature about the 'success'/'failure' of this brand of development, and about which social strata did best from it, and here is not the place to rehearse the arguments. It need only be mentioned that supply-driven development rarely took into account the preferences of those who were to be the beneficiaries of it. Today, certainly among most development specialists working at the micro-level (if not always those working at the meso- and macro-level), the identification of need and preference are done by those who are stakeholders to a development programme/intervention. Reasons for doing so vary between functionality (achieving better technological 'fit' and therefore uptake) and empowerment (best practice/governance). The process can include primary NR users, intermediate institutions, funding bodies and even representatives of the wider 'community.' In this 'demand-driven' process, the identification of preference — particularly by primary stakeholders — becomes particularly important, and is a reason why participative ranking exercises have grown in importance. It is essentially market-research of client preference.

An example of a ranking technique is provided in Action Aid's Mother Reflect Manual (1996). The example (Figure 3.36) uses pairwise ranking in which each item on the list is ranked vis-à-vis each of the other items when respondents are asked which crop they prefer to plant. The number of times the item occurs in the matrix indicates its preference order (i.e. in Figure 3.36) from least preferred to most preferred: rice does not appear, maize and beans appear twice, groundnuts three, and coffee and sweet potatoes four times).

However, the method can be taken further to create a matrix table to indicate why respondents prefer one crop over another. Thus during the pairwise exercise, respondents can be asked to explain in simple terms why they prefer a particular crop. The explanation can be summated as a short phrase (e.g. 'money from sale goes to women') which form one axis of a table with the crops as the other axis (see Table 3.15). Here each

		Preference ranking of crops (a)					
		1	2	3	4	5	6
		●	(img)	(img)	(img)	(img)	(img)
1	maize		1	1	4	5	6
2	coffee			2	2	2	2
3	rice				4	5	6
4	sweet potatoes					5	6
5	beans						6
6	groundnuts						

coffee is better than maize
groundnuts are better than maize.
I prefer groundnuts to beans.
rice is good for selling not eating

Source: ActionAid 1996:145.

Figure 3.36: Ranking of food crops

Table 3.15 Matrix ranking of crops against reasons for preferences

Preference ranking of crops (b)

space for pictures drawn by participants	Maize	Coffee	Rice	Sweet potatoes	Beans	Groundnuts
Good food for family	5	0	0	2	8	8
Short growing season	5	0	0	8	8	8
Good market price	8	8	4	3	3	3
Money from sale goes to women	0	0	0	6	6	6
Resistant to drought	8	7	0	0	0	0
Not much labour needed	5	9	2	5	5	3
Not much money for seed	5	9	2	7	7	8

Source: Action Aid 1996: 146.

crop is evaluated against each criteria on a scale from zero ('criteria not relevant') to ten ('very good') — though other numeric or verbal labels (poor, moderate, good) could be used. As the authors emphasise (p.142), "The aim is not to attempt to show an overall score but to show the complexity of all decisions in relation to choosing which crops to plant." The complexity is of course increased by the fact that different stakeholder groups (men versus women; richer households with good and extensive land versus poorer families with limited and marginal land) will rank the criteria of different crops differently because of their overall livelihood needs. The method is particularly useful in highlighting the fact that there are socio-economic as well as biophysical aspects to technologies and that a 'client-focus' is necessary. (For another example of plant criteria and respondent evaluation see Kersten 1996, in Section 3.18: Matrix).

It needs to be remembered, therefore, that communities are not homogeneous, but are made up of individuals belonging to different primary stakeholder groups. While members of a community may have knowledge in common and may classify much of

Photograph 3.20: Harvesting rice in dry season

the world according to the same criteria, local specialists tend to have more detailed criteria of discrimination between objects/ideas. Additionally, depending on their social position (gender, age, occupation, etc.) different individuals/groups put very different values on objects/ideas and their characteristics. An example of the latter might be men's evaluation of rice varieties as good, average, or poor on criteria which include stem length (and therefore straw yield), role in crop-succession, and flood tolerance; while women may consider these characteristics as unimportant (to them), but mention colour and size of grain, ease of preparation for cooking and palatability. Neither may consider grain yield as particularly important, even though this may be the characteristic most sought by the plant breeder.

The point here is that all individuals (whether rich man, poor man, woman or researcher) evaluate elements of their livelihood strategies in relation to other elements of these strategies, put different weightings on these relationships and, with the greater majority of elements, in relation to multiple characteristics. That is they evaluate systemically and holistically. Secondly, they do so from their own perspective, which may or may not accord with that of others, but which is usually structured by social position (gender, age, occupation, etc.).

Sorting and ranking exercises assist the researcher in understanding matters from the local (emic) point of view and counterbalance the tendency of researchers to assume that these perspectives will be the same as their own. The exercises provide the researcher with information on the advantages and disadvantages of different objects and ideas for particular NR user groups, and a platform for further discussion as to what properties the informants take into account in evaluating these.

As with Matrices (see Section 3.18: Matrix) and Focus groups (see Section 3.14: Focus Groups), sorting and ranking exercises are best carried out with broadly homo-geneous groups of persons, and these of course need to be identified first (e.g. through a Wealth/Well-being ranking exercise; see Section 3.4 on this). Working with small groups enables cross-checking to arrive at a group consensus and give the data robustness. However, because group exercises are costly in terms of time for informants, prior sorting and ranking exercises might be carried out on a one-to-one basis with individual representatives drawn from identified target groups, with a controlled checking of the main characteristics of objects/ideas and criteria of discrimination and evaluation in a homogeneous group exercise later. For example, while the main constraints to a livelihood may be identified through quizzing informants about them, it makes sense to confirm (or not) the generic nature of the constraints and their importance to that livelihood (and/or others) through a group exercise — such as a problem census (see Section 3.20: Problem Census) using Focus Group techniques.

It should be remembered that, as with Matrices, sorting and ranking exercises start from a very reductive perspective. They seek information on a small slice of reality, and do not in themselves enable the exploration of relations with other objects/ideas and criteria of evaluation of these beyond those included in the exercise. This may be alright if the IK sought is simply of the decision kind — for example about which crop variety is most preferred and why. However, if the intention is a deeper understanding of the reasoning behind a livelihood strategy, then the exercise might have to be repeated many times to tease out the relations between objects/ideas (see Section 3.10: Taxonomies), and merges into the more ongoing participant-observer approach characteristic of anthropology. Such an approach denies reductionism and stresses the holistic nature of knowledge.

3.18 Matrix

Cost	L	Individual/group perspective	G
Time	L	Expertise required (social and nat. scientist)	M/H
Data reliability	H	Observer bias	L
		Control of process (directive)	L/M

Definition: A method for collecting data on the characteristics of a number of specified items such as vegetable or crop types or livestock or fish species either at a one point in time (the present) or over a longer historical period.

Purpose: To assist researchers grasp the characteristics and qualities of different animal and plant species which informants find important to their livelihoods, and assist in identifying opportunities for improvement within the constraint of their overall livelihoods portfolios.

The exercise can be carried out either with individuals (as part of an individual questionnaire) or groups (in discussion sessions) and, if ranking is involved (see Section 3.17: Sort/Rank), it can be repeated at different stages of the project cycle in order to monitor whether there is any change in rank orders of list items (for an example see Section 3.13: Historical Comparison).

Informants are asked to draw up a list, perhaps in order of importance to their livelihoods, of for example rice species. This list is detailed on one axis of the matrix (which can be sketched out on the ground, on a blackboard or on paper). Informants then detail those characteristics for each list item which they consider important to their livelihoods and give an evaluation of each characteristic (e.g. good, average, poor, or on a numerical scale), and these are listed along the other axis of the matrix. An example would be a variety of wetland rice, the characteristics of which local people might list as, water tolerance, rate of stem growth, length of stem growth, early maturation, late maturation, resistance to pests and disease, yield, ease of husking, size of grain, colour, cooking consistency, palatability, taste, smell, storage properties and so on.

An example is provided by Kersten (1996) who conducted a matrix ranking exercise with graziers in the semi-arid rangelands of western NSW, Australia. The exercise was linked to semi-structured interviews and group meetings. Plant species mentioned by 11 graziers were written on cards, and criteria mentioned in discussions were written on other cards (distinguishable from the first). The plants were ordered by graziers from best to worst (the top row of Table 3.16) and ranked for each of the criteria mentioned. These were then combined into values of 'high', 'moderate', 'low'. The combined matrix was presented with the six most frequently mentioned criteria (drought resistance, fattening quality, cattle feed, sheep feed, winter feed, summer feed), with plant species filling the cells of the table (see Table 3.16).

Table 3.16 A way of presenting analysed matrices from different participants

VALUE	CRITERIA			
	GENERAL	CRITERION 1	CRITERION 2	CRITERION 3
HIGH	Plant A Plant E	Plant B	Plant A Plant B	Plant Q
MODERATE	Plant F	Plant D	Plant C	
LOW	Plant B Plant G			

Source: Kersten 1996: 23.

It is essential to allow informants to draw up their own list of items, characteristics and ratings, and not to 'direct' them to characteristics which the researcher may think important. For example, due to a concern with meeting food security needs in the developing world, agricultural scientists and plant breeders have traditionally been most concerned with yield, to the virtual exclusion of many other plant characteristics. That is they have taken a monothetic rather than polythetic approach — the reverse of what most NR users do. Breeders have also usually taken a single species approach, rather than one which considers a plant variety in relation to a farmer's overall farming system or portfolio of livelihoods strategies. Yet maximum yield is not necessarily the most important characteristic of a plant from the perspective of a farmer who has many other management factors to consider. (Remember Rhoades *et al.*'s 1984 surprise at finding that small misshapen potatoes which were considered useless by plant scientists were valued by local growers for a variety of reasons.) That is, a plant (or animal) species/variety is chosen to fit into a complex farming and livelihoods system as managed by a particular farmer/household according to its resources and needs (or indeed by a number of different households). A farmer/household selects a species/variety according to the kinds of characteristics detailed above, together with a host of other factors such as costs of production (finances, labour, time), return on the investment of these, household and market preferences, household need for 'by-products' and so on, and in relation to other food and income generating activities both within and beyond the farm boundary. An obvious example is the multiple use value of tree or forest products (see Figure 3.37). This means that there are inevitable trade-offs, but a farmer/household seeks to achieve a balance between the different parts of the farming system according to overall need.

It is important to bear the last point — that of need — in mind when selecting informants for a matrix exercise. Traditionally scientists and plant/livestock breeders have taken a production' rather than 'client-need' approach, with inevitable failures of technology uptake among the general target population. Yet there are usually distinct

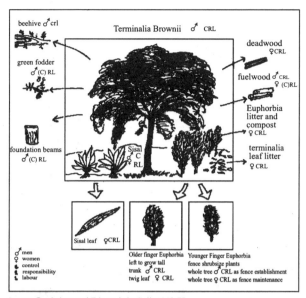

Source: Rocheleau and Edmunds in Guijt 1998:77.

Figure 3.37: Gender division of plants and tree products from joint tree management, Kenya

Photograph 3.21: Women sorting preferences during PRA exercise

differences between individuals (because of gender, age, occupation and other social characteristics) and between households (because of their socio-economic position) which structure their identification and evaluation of list item characteristics. While a matrix exercise can be done with informants drawn randomly from a target population, the outcome can mislead through confusing the preferences and evaluations of different types of individual/ household. This can lead to hidden bias (e.g. in items preferred by better endowed members of the community receiving greater weighting in the matrix over those favoured by the less well-endowed — for example women, those with disabilities, the poor). Just as focus groups (see Section 3.14: Focus Groups) are usually constructed from respondents with similar socio-economic characteristics so that differences between groups can be identified, so a matrix exercise is best done with members of previously identified target groups.

The above example of Australian graziers (Kersten 1996) provides an example. Kersten carried out her matrix exercise with 11 graziers, and then used these as part of a dialogue meeting with graziers collectively (and possibly to come up with a generic ranking of rangeland plants). Kersten correctly notes that the "criteria used by graziers for evaluating plant species were very different from criteria commonly used by researchers for selecting native grasses for domestication. Graziers focus on the value of plants for their stock. Researchers evaluate native grasses on their ability to survive, perenniality and seed production independent of their value as stock feed. These different criteria reflect the differences in perception of rangelands by both groups" (1996: 23) (see Table 3.17). However, Kersten may or may not have recognised that there were probable differences between members of her dialogue group for discussing vegetation, vegetation management and alternative livelihood strategies. As she says, "at one meeting, there was initial reluctance to rank important rangeland plants, because participants presented different land systems" (1996:22). The point being that individual participants are likely to have difficulty determining a single rank order where each values the plants differently because of the different role individual plant species play in their livelihood systems — which differ.

Table 3.17 Criteria for evaluating plant species mentioned by graziers and by researchers (domestication of native grasses)

Criteria Mentioned by Graziers during Matrix Ranking	Criteria Used by Researchers for Selection of Native Grasses for Domestication
Stock Related Criteria	**Morphological Criteria**
• winter feed	• seed head architecture
• summer feed	• type of seed head (easy to harvest)
• flood feed	• non-shattering seed
• drought feed/survival	
• fattening value	Longevity
• palatability	• perennial
• good fodder	• seed longevity and seed bank available
• reliability	• a seed coat that enables the seed to respond
• maintenance value	• to sequences of rainfall and reduces false
• nutritional	• germination
• nutritional for sheep	• potential predation of seed by ants
• nutritional for cattle	
• sheep feed	**Ability to Establish a Species**
• cattle feed	**Practicalities for the Landholder**
• wool growing	
• poisonous	
• scouring	
• nuisance	
Non-Stock Related Criteria	
• winter growth	
• summer growth	
• drought resistance	
• reliability	
• fuel for burning for woody weed control	
• soil binding ability	
• ability to regenerate	
'woody weeds' are unpalatable woody shrubs invading the area	

Source: Kersten 1996:24.

A matrix is useful in visually displaying informants' preferences and priorities and the problems they faced with any particular list item in a simple and easily graspable fashion. Under the earlier RRA approach this tended to be all that happened, with scientists/policy-makers retreating to the experimental station/policy institute to design a technology/policy — usually one with which they were already familiar (e.g. rice) — for later field trials. While a client-needs approach can achieve a better fit between the technology/policy development process and uptake, there are real differences between experimental station/policy institute and on-farm technology development which crucially influence the end product. Taking a systemic perspective, Sustainable Livelihoods approaches recognise list items as interdependent elements which intersect with other non-NR domains in individual/household livelihood strategies. Changes in the characteristics of any one item impact on and beyond the NR subsystem of which it is a part. Off-farm technology/policy development is reductive of the real complexity of the farm/household situation, so that technology/policy developed there can have unexpected impacts when introduced on-farm. Livelihoods approaches (incorporating systems learning through PRA and PLA methodology) recognise that new technology/policy design and development should be with the active participation of client-groups if it is to be tailored to their needs and the chance of unexpected negative impacts minimised.

For these reasons, a matrix approach is a useful step in researchers' learning about the preferences that a client-group has with regards list items. However, the matrix only lists elements in the domain requested (e.g. crops). It does not detail the linkages between items, between list items and others not mentioned (e.g. wild vegetables, domestic animals, fish, the market). These relationships need to be explored in much greater detail, if the wider livelihoods systems of target groups are to be grasped, and potential impacts on them and on those of other groups by any new technology/policy appraised (perhaps using flow diagrams, see Section 3.12: Flowcharts, but particularly through individual and group interview techniques).

Additionally, as Kersten notes (1996:25), it is important not to focus over much on the ranking and the production of a final matrix because this can obscure the importance of the discussion about the ranked objects and their criteria. That is, by linking matrix exercises and (heterogeneous) group discussion we learn not just about plant species, but about plant species in relation to different livelihoods (researchers', environmentalists', and that of different grazier farm-types.) (If Aborigines were present we would also learn some very different valuations of the plants in the semi-arid rangelands!) However, we can go beyond researcher-learning about respondents' classifications and value systems (illuminating but primarily an extractive and only weakly 'participative' process), and use the method as part of an empowering PLA process. Kersten's research was part of a process working with graziers to encourage livelihood diversification through identifying 'alternative industries' such as eco-tourism or kangaroo harvesting. Thus the matrix exercise and dialogue meetings were not primarily being used to identify plant species of most value to graziers and on which researchers should focus their domestication and improvement efforts; rather it was being used to foster discussion, to expose participants to other stakeholders' perspectives on the rangelands and together build 'richer pictures'. Of particular note in this respect is that the process focused not on environmental constraints (which natural scientists seek to relax through, for example, selective breeding programmes), but on the opportunities that the present landscape offered in relation to new consumer interests (e.g. environmentalism and eco-tourism).

3.18.1 Pairwise Ranking Matrices

Pairwise ranking is an accepted method for arriving at a rank order for the items listed. It is frequently used in development as a means of achieving unbiased ranking lists prepared by respondents. It may be used to establish the preferences of a particular client group within a community or of the community as a whole, and is particularly important when valuable or scarce resources are involved. The intention is to enable all respondents to have a say in the process, rather than just the most powerful or forceful.

Table 3.18 Pairwise ranking of development problems in Miputu, Ndola District, Zambia

Problem	1	2	3	4	5	6	7	8	Score	Rank
1. Lack of fertilizer and seed		1	3	1	1	6	7	1	4	4
2. Lack of transport			3	2	2	6	7	2	3	5
3. Poor roads and bridges				3	3	6	7	4	6	2
4. Lack of work oxen and tools					4	6	7	4	2	6
5. No consumer shops						6	7	5	1	7
6. Lack of clinic							6	7	7	2
7. Lack of classrooms and houses								5	5	3
8. Lack of market									0	8

Source: Russell 1997.

Russell (1997) gives an example of pairwise ranking of development problems (see Table 3.18). Each problem is compared with each of the others in turn and if preferred its number is put in the appropriate box. Each problem's score is determined by the number of times its number appears in the matrix. Scores are then compared to derive a rank order.

As Russell notes (p.26), a difficulty of the method is that the construction of the matrix can become very tedious and 'is also difficult for all but the most numerate to understand.' Russell has proposed another method which is quicker to execute and easier to understand, and which involves placing a stone/seed next to the more important problem when each is compared in turn with the others. The problems are then ranked according to the number of stones/seeds each has beside it (see Table 3.19).

The method is useful for prioritising one (or more) problems for attention when used with a community as a whole. However, where the focus is on achieving an improvement in well-being for a specific group (such as the poor, most vulnerable or socially excluded), a community-wide ranking exercise will mask the needs of this group. Here members of the target group need to be identified and a ranking exercise carried out solely with members drawn from their ranks. Ranking exercises might also be carried out with other identified primary stakeholder groups in order to assess the degree of overlap between the different groups' needs (and which may serve to build strategic support within a community for a particular intervention).

The same note of caution in the use of pairwise Matrices as for other ranking exercises (see Section 3.17: Sort/Rank) needs to be entered. They are best treated as a platform for further dialogue with respondents, and when treated as 'stand alones' the conclusions emerging from them should be treated with caution. Firstly matrices are most commonly

Table 3.19 Problem ranking matrix using stone counters

Problem	Score (in stones/seeds)	Score	Rank
1. Lack of wells	□ □ □ □ □ □ □ □ □ □ □	12	2
2. Broken bridges	□ □ □ □ □ □ □ □ □	9	4
3. Clinic not big enough	□ □ □ □ □ □	6	7
4. Hunger	□ □ □ □ □ □ □ □ □ □ □ □	13	1
5. No market for honey	□	1	13
6. Lack of transport	□ □ □ □ □	5	10
7. Theft		0	14
8. Dam broken	□ □	2	12
9. No hammer mill		6	7
10. Few oxen for ploughing	□ □ □ □ □ □ □ □	8	6
11. No timber for coffins	□ □ □	3	11
12. Poor cooperation between people	□ □ □ □ □ □ □ □	9	4
13. School not big enough	□ □ □ □ □ □ □ □ □ □	11	3
14. Roads need repairing	□ □ □ □ □ □	6	7

Source: Russell 1997.

used to identify constraints/problems rather than opportunities, and while giving points of entry for scientists, may prioritise external over indigenous expertise in technology development, (which might be seen as a continuation of the ToT approach under another name).

Secondly the categories used tend to be summative rather than specific. For example in the ranking matrix from Kenya (Figure 3.38), 'climate', 'pests', 'weeds', 'cost of inputs' may be researcher-determined categories of individually-specific items mentioned in a problem census. 'Cost of inputs' is ranked as the number one problem, but without 'unpacking' the category into its constituent items it is impossible to know whether answers may have been skewed by the cost of a particular input or whether this is a general problem across a range of inputs (including labour, finance, raw materials and technology). A further ranking exercise might clarify this, and show that if the problem of the high cost of seed is addressed, the rank order of 'Cost of inputs' falls to the bottom. Again this suggests that the matrix is best treated as a platform for further dialogue rather than a decision tool in its own right.

Thirdly, as noted in relation to ranking in general (see Section 3.17: Sort/Rank), matrix exercises may mask the preferences of those people whom development practitioners are most concerned to assist — the poorest of the poor — if their representation in the exercise is small. This suggests that researchers need to identify which NR user group is their target group or, if working at the community level, to ensure that the different stakeholders have equal representation in the exercise prior to its administration.

3.18.2 Historical Matrices

It is also possible to develop historical matrices with list items or activities on one axis and dates (e.g. of introduction, significant development, discontinuation) on the other. Historical matrices are useful for revealing changes in the significance or use of list items over time, and give a point of entry for exploring why change has taken place,

Problems	Climate	Pests	Weeds	Cost of inputs	Lack of land	Lack of Irrig.	Lack of Tech k
Climate		Climate	Climate	Cost of inputs	Climate	Climate	Climate
Pests			Pests	Cost of inputs	Lack of land	Lack of Irrig.	Pests
Weeds				Cost of inputs	Lack of land	Lack of Irrig.	Weeds
Cost of inputs					Cost of inputs	Cost of inputs	Cost of inputs
Lack of land						Lack of land	Lack of land
Lack of irrigation							Lack of Irrig.
Lack of tech know-how							

Problems	Number of times preferred	Rank
Climate	5	2
Pests	2	5
Weeds	1	6
Cost of inputs	6	1
Lack of land	4	3
Lack of irrigation	3	4
Lack of technical knowledge	0	7

Source: National Environmental Council 1991: 64.

Figure 3.38: Pairwise ranking matrix, Kenya

whether significant underlying trends are occurring, and how a client-group is adapting to the new situation (An example is given from Ford *et al.* 1996 'Shifting priorities of needs in Gilgil, Kenya' in Section 3.13: Historical Comparison). As Guijt (1998:79) says, "Although the results are recorded as numbers, the greatest value of matrix scoring comes from the discussions that are provoked as the group or individual comes to a decision about the final score of each option." As Guijt also notes, the method can be useful for identifying key indicators which can then be monitored by other methods, although there is always a danger that what may be key indicators (e.g. of community need/household well-being) at one point in time may change.

3.19 Five Questions

Cost	L	Individual/group perspective	I
Time	L	Expertise required (social and nat. scientist)	M
Data reliability	M	Observer bias	H
		Control of process (directive)	H

Definition: A method for assessing causal impacts.
Purpose: To assist in the assessment of local beliefs and/or practices in order to determine whether, according to science, they have a positive negative, or neutral impact.

The technique consists of the researcher identifying a particular local practice or belief, its causal relationship to a believed outcome, and that outcome. The researcher then evaluates the causal relationship for scientific validity or its absence, before suggesting an appropriate course of action. It is called 'five questions' because the elements of the method consist of five steps (practice/belief, cause/effect, research findings, impact, action).

Some writers (e.g. Gonzaga and Fortuna, in IIRR 1996) suggest that the value of the tool lies in its help in discerning "whether a particular belief has any basis in scientific fact," is useful for determining the difference between local and scientific views, and may assist in suggesting an intervention based on local experience and belief.

However, a caveat might be entered here, and the method should be used with great caution. This can be illustrated with reference to the example the above authors give. The practice/belief they give is that (they do not say where) a pregnant woman should not eat squash or else she will have a baby with a bald head. The authors state that scientific evidence is that squash is a rich source of vitamin A and that not eating squash may have a negative impact by depriving the mother of this vitamin. Further that the action which might be taken may be to offer pregnant women alternative vegetables rich in vitamin A.

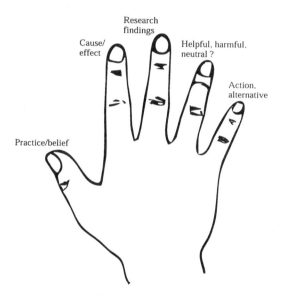

Source: IIRR 1996:58.

Figure 3.39: Using the fingers to enumerate the five questions

This all sounds laudable, but there are some difficulties with this line of reasoning. Firstly the cause-effect that is judged for scientific validity is not that between eating squash and baldness in babies at birth, but between not eating squash and a vitamin A deficiency in pregnancy — that is a side-effect identified by the scientist not by the local believer. But what one scientist (with an interest in health) may judge as poor practice, another may judge as having little or no health impact (since pregnant women may already eat sufficient other vegetables containing vitamin A), and a third may judge as good practice (for instance because squashes in this area, while rich in vitamin A, also contain a fungus which may cause the hair of new born babies to fall out if their mother should eat squash during pregnancy — or worse may cause abortion!) Validity here is a slippery concept indeed.

The lesson that should be taken from this is that it is not sufficient, and is judgemental, to take beliefs and practices in isolation. Knowledge, whether it be science or local knowledge, is systemic. Individual elements are embedded in, and understood, in relation to other elements of the system and other beliefs and practices. While we measure the world all the time according to different scales of value, we need to recognise that meaning is internal to a system, and that its measurement according to external criteria changes that meaning or fails to capture sufficient meaning. This after all is the criticism that qualitative researchers directed early on at the quantitative survey approach, and why qualitative research looks to more 'open' questioning techniques. Thus from a local knowledge perspective, it is more appropriate to first explore why people hold a particular belief and whether they know that it may have the unintended side-effects the scientist has noted, whether they have compensated for this, whether they know but regard vitamin A deficiency and its consequences as a lesser risk than having a baby with a bald head if a woman should eat squash during pregnancy, what the social consequences of having such a baby are, whether the causal statement is to be taken literally or metaphorically (e.g. squash perhaps standing for sexual intercourse), and so on. Against this wider context, it may then be appropriate to determine a course of action which will satisfy the concerns of the different parties (or stakeholders) to what is not just a technical issue as the scientist has framed it, but one which has social ramifications as well. And that is to incorporate local knowledge into scientific research on other cultures.

Having entered this caveat, the five question tool can nevertheless be useful in assisting researchers to explore causal chains identified in respondents' statements, the nature of the statements and the contexts in which they are made. If this is a way into a deeper understanding (a more holistic grasp) of the knowledge system (or world-view) of those being studied, then it serves a useful purpose. If it is used in a reductive fashion, with priority being given to science and the technical, it stands as a barrier and not a bridge to the incorporation of local knowledge into development practice.

3.20 Problem/Option Census

Cost	L	Individual/group perspective	I/G
Time	L	Expertise required (social and nat. scientist)	L-M
Data reliability	H	Observer bias	L
		Control of process (directive)	L-M

Definition: A method for collecting data on the problems/options that a target population (or target individuals and NR user groups) face in particular sectors or in their overall livelihoods, and the ranking of these according to respondents' preference.

Purpose: To assist researchers grasp the variety of constraints and/or opportunities that respondents face to their livelihoods and how they prioritise these.

The Problem Census is a particular case of Matrix scoring. Matrix scoring (see Section 3.18: Matrix) is primarily a method for evaluating different list items (whatever these may be), by scoring and ranking the items. The Problem Census also does this, but is primarily used to identify problems/options as a precursor to further discussion of these.

The Problem/Option Census can be carried out within the context of either the individual or group interview. The individual context is obviously more resource intensive than the group one, and for this reason the method is usually undertaken with groups. It can also be carried out at various stages of the project cycle. For example it is particularly useful as a first step for identifying the constraints that members of a target group face to their livelihoods or well-being, and how they prioritise them, prior to further discussion about the different problems raised and about what options there are for addressing these. However, it could be used at various stages of implementation as a monitoring and management tool for measuring changes in the prioritisation of problems/options and consequent changes in project implementation.

Box (1990: 64-65) questions the whole rational for the problem census because his experience has been that respondents, "give standard answers when asked for problems: low prices, exploitation by middlemen, poor roads or no access to credit. All these may be real, but are always mentioned and do not provide much new knowledge on which agricultural researchers can base their priorities." Box and his team, therefore, did not ask individuals about their problems (and presumably did not hold a problem census), but based their research on biographical analysis (of cassava cultivation in the Dominican Republic) with individual respondents, and "deduced problems from the synthesis made towards the end of the interview." Problem identifications were then fed back to group meetings, while further verification was derived from a random sample survey amongst farmers and a survey amongst researchers, extensionists and others. Box's argument is persuasive but he appears to have had considerable time (5 years) in which to carry out in-depth studies and could allow farmer's perceptions of problems to emerge over the longer term. Others may not have that luxury. Researchers must make their own minds up in the light of resource and other constraints as to whether the problem census allied to other techniques (such as the extended interview, participant-observation) is the best way to proceed. Certainly a problem census is only one step, and other techniques (such as causal diagramming, concept mapping) will be needed to 'unpack' the issues for both researchers and respondents (see Sections 3.11 and 3.21: Webbing and Brainstorming). Additionally, it may also be advisable to focus on 'opportunities' as well as 'problems', since the latter may be deep-seated and not easily resoluble (see Jones 1996, see also Roos and Mohatle 1998).

3.20.1 Group Formation

As with all group exercises, focus groups for a problem census exercise may be formed according to criteria that create heterogeneous or homogeneous groups. As noted elsewhere (e.g. see Section 3.18: Matrix) data from heterogeneous groups may contain biases due to over-/under-representation of participants from certain social categories (e.g. women, children, those with disabilities, the aged, the poor). Individuals across the social spectrum may or may not face the same constraints to their livelihoods and well-being, and have different needs (see Table 3.20), and it seems preferable to first carry out a separate problem census exercise with members drawn from the target social strata or, if a community initiative is envisaged, all primary stakeholder groups. There may or may not be commonalities between the groups in the livelihood constraints they identify. The social strata/stakeholder groups, of course, have first to be identified (see Section 3.4: Wealth/Well-being Ranking for an example from Bangladesh based on national land-holding categories and a participative wealth-ranking exercise).

Table 3.20 A comparison of the needs of different primary stakeholder groups

Young men	Old men	Young women	Old women
Lack of credit	Lack of work	Water supply	Ill health
Low wages	No credit	Low productivity	Low income
Low prices	Ill health	Lack of education	Drought
Pests	Lack of respect	Large families	
Drought	Poor soils	Overwork	
Erosion	Climate	Health of children	
AIDS	Poor roads	Deforestation	
Lack of training		Pests	
Health		Poor storage	

Source: Action Aid 1996:51.

Photograph 3.22: Conducting a problem census

An (unconsolidated) example from Bangladesh undertaken by the authors and colleagues again indicates the different problems that different stakeholder groups face in their livelihoods (see Table 3.21). It also indicates some of the commonalities that exist between individual groups. For example while the main concern of landless/ near-landless men and rich farmers is with constraints to agricultural production (in the fields), the main concern of women is with lack of capital and the domestic/homestead domain, while the main concern of fishermen is with threats to fish stocks and access to water bodies. Yet there are also jointly held concerns about the problems to production in land and water NR caused by embankments and poorly maintained sluice gates (stagnant water, interruptions to fish migration). The group-specific exercises identify areas where there could be interventions to improve targeted user group well-being. The identification of commonalities between groups, however, can provide a platform for more integrated development in which growth in the local economy is supported while poorer groups proportionately benefit more (i.e. through pro-poor growth policies and interventions on the ground).

3.20.2 Focus
Problem census exercises can be broadly or narrowly focused. A broadly-based exercise would not specify a particular sector when asking representatives of NR user

Table 3.21 Problem census results according to stakeholder groups, Bangladesh

Landless sharecroppers and other labourers

1. Local control over NR distribution
2. Low crop prices early in season
3. Access to irrigation water
4. Access to capital for cropping
5. Water depth in *beels* for fish and irrigation
6. Poor local support structures (*samities*)
7. Early flooding of *beel* lands damaging crops
8. Scarcity of sharecropping land
9. No training in rice-fish production techniques
10. No water regulator for crop/fish cultivation
11. No jobs during lean period (the rainy season)
12. Low wage rates for agriculture labour
13. Low fish stocks in open waterbodies
14. Poor quality fertilizer, pesticides, seeds
15. No training for poultry/cattle raising
16. No efficient drainage system for irrigation

Rich farmers

1. Stagnant flood water in *beel* delaying planting
2. Scarcity of quality agricultural inputs
3. Lack of agricultural training
4. Lack of local control in villages
5. Lack of capital
6. Low crop prices early in season
7. Scarcity of irrigation water
8. Lack of training in fish culture
9. No improved livestock and veterinary facility
10. Problem of poor fruiting of fruit trees
11. Disease of fish and over fishing

Fishermen

1. Shortage of capital
2. Sluice gates blocking fish migration
3. Decline of open water fish species
4. Use of fish poison to kill indigenous fish
5. Decline of young fishes due to fine-mesh net
6. Crabs killing fish and cutting nets
7. Rich farmers leasing government water bodies
8. Decline of *beel* fish species
9. Heavy work load
10. Rich landowners restricting fishing near *kua* pits
11. Fishing by non-fishers in the water bodies leased by the fishermen

Women from poor families

1. Landlessness, no land even for homesteads
2. Extreme poverty; lack of capital
3. No room for stock rearing
4. No land for sharecropping
5. Fuel crisis; difficult to gather biomass fuel
6. No CPR for stock needs
7. Pay discrimination; half wage of male workers
8. Fish and mollusc/snail/crab very scarce; wild vegetable, fruits, seeds from village trees scarce
9. High prices of fertilisers, insecticides, seeds
10. No medical facility, treatment expensive
11. Too high a work load
12. No veterinary service for stock
13. Difficulty in accessing draught animals
14. BRAC not buying growing chicks
15. Lack of sanitary latrine, poor hygiene
16. Joblessness of manual rickshaw pullers
17. Husband's negligence and torture

Women from non-poor families

1. Lack of capital and cash
2. Lack of homestead land
3. Lack of veterinary facilities for small stock
4. Disease of vegetables, fruit and garden plants
5. Scarcity of domestic servant during harvest
6. Scarcity of crop land
7. No access roads to the homesteads
8. Insects destroying the fruits on trees
9. Scarcity of domestic fuel
10. Lack of earning members in the family
11. Problems with sharecropping
12. Lack of drinking water during the dry season
13. Lack of opportunities of female education
14. Lack of training in small stock raising

Source: Barr *et al.,* 2000.

groups about the constraints they face to their livelihoods. Since individuals view the world from their own perspective and may have a variety of strategies in their liveli-hood portfolio (e.g. some men may mix farming, fishing, trading, construction, while some women may mix household/family duties, petty trading, small stock rearing, prostitution), stakeholders are likely to identify a wide range of constraints. Thus lack of credit, health and educational facilities may rank higher than NR constraints — which can be disconcerting for NR researchers. A livelihoods approach, however, seeks to meet client identification of need, rather than to identify and prioritise one sector (e.g. the NR domain) according to external experts' determination of need; this is one reason for working in interdisciplinary teams with clients. Other (intermediate) stakeholders of course have an interest in outcomes and their impacts, and their interests should be represented in the process.

Problem census exercises can also be narrowly focused. Here a sector (such as the NR sector) may be specified and constraints to its role in user groups' livelihoods may be sought. Again respondents from different user groups will identify constraints from their own livelihoods' perspective. In the Bangladesh example (see Table 3.21), the problems farmers, fishers, and women identify are very different. Researchers and exten-sion services with an agricultural remit could focus just on agricultural improvements through better drainage, improved access to inputs (seed, fertiliser, pesticides), and improved infrastructure (roads). Such a sectoral approach may lead to considerable improvements in agricultural output and potentially improve national food security, but researchers should also be aware that it could also have negative impacts on the livelihoods of landless/near-landless and fishing households and lead to greater food insecurity and vulnerability at the micro-level for poorer people (as appears to have happened in Bangladesh) (see Dixon *et al.* 2000). The lesson for researchers with a sectoral bias is that they need to be aware that they are dealing with a limited 'slice' of reality, that improvements in one sector may have unintended impacts in others for stakeholders with whom they are not working, and that social and environmental impact assessments are necessary prior to implementation.

Thus, on the basis of a comparison of problems different stakeholder groups face, and after further discussion of the problems/options and the issues that they raise, researchers may wish either to explore the potential for 'community-based' solutions to one or a number of the problems or to suggest sectoral interventions by extension agencies for targeted social units. That is the Problem Census may be used to identify 'entry-points' for extension agencies with particular remits and capacities (e.g. rice research, fisheries management, micro-credit), and achieve incremental well-being enhancement for their target groups. As an 'entry-point' approach is reductive of the complex whole, extension agencies would need to guard against unintended implementation bias in the distribu-tion of benefits to different social units, and against unintended consequences for non-target groups and in other sectors. Multi-agency partnerships and pan-agency steering committees might be a way forward here. By contrast 'community-based' approaches may be more considerate of the interdependencies between social units, and enable different social units to participate in designing and implementing interventions, but may have difficulty in achieving well-being changes for target groups because of the inclusiveness of the management process.

3.20.3 Analysis/Interpretation
What is presented here is one possible 'evaluation' according to the purpose underlying the data collection (i.e. the research question which gave focus to data collection).

Given the above comments, it is clear that much hangs on the analysis/interpretation of the data derived from a problem census exercise. If the exercise is part of a participatory-learning process with a community, the data could just be presented to its members so that they can see the complexity involved where there are social units with different goals, needs and capacities. As with other ranking exercises (see Section 3.17: Sort/Rank) the aim may not be "to attempt to show an overall score but to show the complexity of all decisions in relation to choosing" which options to take (Action Aid 1996: 145). However, development requires decisions to be made concerning priorities in a context of limited resources. This requires guidelines in order to 'filter' the data.

In the Bangladesh example (see Table 3.21) the problem census exercises held with different stakeholder groups reached no generic conclusions, while it was not straightforward to identify a single priority problem that all stakeholder groups could agree to address through an intervention. An intermediate stage was therefore developed by which the heterogeneity of problems could be distilled and also passed through external filters as appropriate. This stage of the process served to reduce the number of key problems to a workable level (since each of the 8 groups at each field site identified 10-15 priority problems, leading to potentially 80-120 problems to be dealt with).

The process reported here was developed as part of a research project, but stands in its own right as part of a development process at the study sites (see Barr *et al.,* 2000). This, and other associated development activities are likely to involve external agents — donors, government bodies, NGOs, etc. — each having their own agenda and a series of goals they are trying to achieve. For example, DFID's goals are set out in its White Paper on International Development (DFID, 1997), in which elimination of poverty is given as the goal, to be achieved through the creation of sustainable livelihoods for poor people, the promotion of human development and conservation of the environment. These external agents are also stakeholders (secondary rather than primary) and are representative of wider interests in the livelihood strategies of floodplain dwellers and their actual or potential impact on wider socio-economic and environmental systems. Their goals and activities therefore need to be taken into account.

Additionally, each member of an interdisciplinary research or appraisal team generally has a number of different capabilities and areas of expertise. In this project the research team's skills were in crop production, soil management, aquaculture, fisheries management, farming systems, social development and indigenous knowledge methodologies. These capabilities structured the filtering of the constraints identified by groups in the problem census exercise. However, other agencies with different comparative advantages could assist in respect of other constraints (e.g. credit, health, etc.) arising from the problem census exercise which the research team did not feel competent to address.

In the Bangladesh research project, in order to limit the range of problems that arose from the problem census, a filtering or distillation process was introduced between the problem census and the systems-based workshop which followed. This involved an analysis of the problem census results by research team members to identify the problems which they thought were:

1. coherent with DFID's goals for poverty elimination (helping the poorest of the poor) and environmental soundness.
2. technically feasible (according to the team's capabilities).
3. possible in the given time and resource limits of the project.

A drawback of this approach is that the prioritisation of the constraints to be addressed is determined by external experts and there is little space for community members to determine what is the best way forward. However, there is the attendant danger that if the process is left solely to the community, then the more powerful may determine the outcome to their benefit and the detriment of the less powerful — usually the poorest — while being socially and environmentally unsound.

Alternative approaches that were considered include:

- Prioritising the most impoverished/disadvantaged groups (women and landless people) and working on their highest ranked problems.
- Taking the highest priority problem from every group and working on what was preponderantly the most important common issue.

As can be seen from the Bangladesh data above, (Table 3.21) the drawback of these latter approaches are that many of the highest ranked problems of each group relate to problems that an NR research project could not directly address — for example lack of capital. Nonetheless these are important problems which can be directed to other agencies for their attention. Additionally other problems (e.g. 'Low crop prices early in season') may only be tractable at the macro- rather than micro-level. Thus the filtering and distillation step is a recognition that participatory development is a partnership between internal and external parties, or primary and secondary stakeholders (or even 'client' and 'contractor'), and that each has a view, an agenda, and something to offer to the process. This step provides an entry point for secondary stakeholders to influence outcomes. It does, however, make the assumption of benign intent, and may thus not be an universally appropriate model for all secondary stakeholder involvement.

In the Bangladesh exercise the research team's distillation of the problem census results led to the narrowing down of the problems identified by stakeholder groups to a maximum of three which could be considered in greater detail at a later date in systems-based workshops, and which the research team felt they were competent to address. There was a commonality in the identification of the problems across the majority of stakeholder groups, but greater weighting was given to their prioritisation by resource-poor groups and womens' and fishers' groups to meet the proportionality required by DFID guidelines on poverty alleviation, sustainable rural livelihoods and environmental soundness. Interestingly, however, the number of opportunities identified by respondents to relax the constraints they had mentioned in the problem census exercise was quite limited. The reason for this may have to do with many NR users taking a 'performative' (or reactive) rather than 'planned' (proactive) approach to their livelihood strategies (see Richards 1990:39-42), and suggests a need for participatory learning with stakeholders (and including problem/causal analysis exercises and the like) in order to draw out innovative solutions to constraints which they are undoubtedly capable of making.

The overall lesson emerging from the Bangladesh analytic exercise was that the identification of options for further exploration with primary stakeholders or for progressing to an intervention phase is not easy. Multiple criteria need to be considered and include social equity and sustainability issues (both environmental and economic); the interests of primary and secondary stakeholders; the political, social, economic and technical feasibility of options from the perspective of the community, target stakeholder groups, extension agencies, and the research team; their 'ownership' by primary stakeholders and whether interventions should be progressed through the community or through targeted stakeholder groups. This suggests the need to use a number of other participatory learning tools (social and environmental impact analysis, stakeholder and institutional analysis, STEP analysis, and so on) even at this preliminary stage and before any work can be done to generate Community Development Plans (or Village Resource Management Plans) or Recommendation Domains. In the light of Box's concerns about problem identification it also suggests a need for verification of problems, their extent, and who they are problems for, through other methods. (For further development of the problem census/ village workshop methodology in relation to NR management see DFID 2001.)

3.21 Brainstorming

Cost	L	Individual/group perspective	I/G
Time	L	Expertise required (social and nat. scientist)	L-M
Data reliability	H	Observer bias	L
		Control of process (directive)	L-M

Definition: Group discussion where all participants contribute to discussion and the generation of ideas (data) on a specified topic in a largely unstructured and non-directive way.

Purpose: To collect a large amount of IK on a specified topic from a group the members of which 'spark' off each other.

The facilitator outlines what the topic is and explains that members of the group (which should not be so large as to be unmanageable) should contribute ideas as and when they think they have a contribution to make, and that the ideas can be directly or tangentially relevant to the topic under discussion. Each idea may be recorded as it is contributed as a single word, phrase or symbol summary on a card and attached to a chalk-board or large sheet of paper or placed on the ground. Once there are no further ideas coming from participants the different ideas may be sorted into separate themes or categories, the results recorded as a 'concept map', and the themes emerging from the exercise discussed.

For example Maxwell *et al.* (1997) were concerned with gaining respondents' perceptions on the problems of food insecurity, malnutrition and its causes. They note that, "the link between poverty" and food insecurity was clear in people's perceptions of the problem of malnutrition and for some people this was the standard answer. However, they determined to unpack the issue further through a participatory concept-mapping exercise which relied on brainstorming with focus groups made up of women sharing a single characteristic (e.g. lactating mothers, working mothers) but who otherwise represented a broad cross-section of the community.

The sorting of ideas into themes may or may not be an issue, depending upon whether this is primarily done by the facilitator, or by the participants, or is a joint exercise. If the former, then the data may be being passed through the conceptual grid of someone who is external to the culture or community with misleading conclusions being drawn from the data; if the latter then it may be true to the taxonomic reckoning of the participants but be less readily usable by the analyst (see Section 3.10: Taxonomies). Researchers need to keep this in mind at all times since this step is critical in the construction of knowledge, and there are dangers in the external 'expert' too readily assuming linkages between concepts. In the above example (see Figure 3.40), Maxwell *et al.* (1997) were concerned with whether they had biased the results of the exercise through the kinds of questions they asked in the week prior to the concept mapping exercise, but their conclusion was that, "the concept map was truly that of the groups, even though some of the concepts may have been gleaned from the study team" (p.15). Importantly the construction of the concept map was done by the participants and not by the research

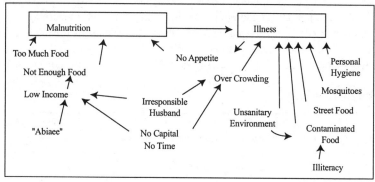

Source: Maxwell *et al.* 1997:14.

Figure 3.40: Concept map of malnutrition: lactating mothers' group, Accra, Ghana

team. Thus each concept was written down on a piece of card (or given a symbol), and the group was then asked to discuss the concepts and arrange them "in such a way as to show how they thought the various concepts were related to the central issue of malnutrition," using lines, arrows etc. to "indicate the kind of relationship they believed to exist between two or more of the concepts brainstormed" (p.12-13). This part of the exercise involved minimal input from researchers, other than posing questions such as 'what is related to what?' and 'what leads to what?' when a group showed signs of difficulty.

Photograph 3.23: Listing issues on flipchart during workshop

A brainstorming session may be used as a stand-alone activity, as an 'icebreaker' to another activity — as in group development (see Box 3.8) — or to get participants to think laterally, or as part of a process for generating ideas and topics which may be considered in greater detail and in a more structured fashion through other methods (e.g. individual interview, problem census, problem-tree analysis). As Maxwell *et al.* stress (1997:13) the use of a group brainstorming session (to construct a concept map) made it much easier to move beyond the simplistic poverty-malnutrition nexus presented by some respondents. It provided a platform for discussion and analysis by participants of the multiplex causes of malnutrition, and naturally led into further discussions about what might be done to address these. The great value of brainstorming is that it can generate a considerable amount of information in a short space of time, which can

---

Box 3.8: Four stages of group development

Forming-Storming-Norming-Performing: The Four Stages of Group Development

In Business Studies and Change Management emphasis is put on group- or team-working as an efficient and effective way to address issues. If the team bonds effectively (i.e. focuses on the issue to hand rather than on interpersonal 'politics'), members are able to bring their individual perspectives, knowledge and expertise to the analysis and solution of the 'problem'. Group dynamics in this 'interdisciplinary' context — which increasingly consists of researchers and NR users working together as equals — is all important. Theorists suggest that groups go through a number of stages before they establish a shared vision and begin to perform effectively.

In the early forming stage, the group is a collection of individuals, each with her/his own agenda and expertise and little or no shared experience.

As these individuals become more familiar with one another, they will almost certainly enter a storming phase where personal values and principles are challenged, roles and responsibilities are taken on and/or rejected, and the group's objectives and way of working together are defined.

At the norming stage, the group settles down and develops a clear identity. The members begin to understand their roles in relation to one another and establish a shared vision or goal.

Once these norms have been established, the group will be ready to focus on output and will enter the performing phase. It is in this phase that they will work most effectively as a team. The confidence level of the team will have reached the point where they are willing to take significant risks and try out new ideas on their own.

Source: After Handy 1985.

provide a quick overview of the topic under discussion from the perspective of members of the group.

As with other methods, the information derived is dependent on the make-up of the group. A group formed on heterogeneous principles may provide a wider range of data than one formed on homogeneous ones. This may be suitable where community-wide interventions are envisaged, but may be of limited use where targeted ones are. (Also the information derived is of a rough and ready nature which may be suitable for some purposes, but is likely to require validation through other 'triangulation' methods if it is to be used with any confidence in more far-reaching development work.)

One of the advantages of purposive sampling with homogeneous groups is that it can reveal how knowledge is socially structured, and where some causal relationships are of more significance to the livelihoods of some social units than to others. For example, brainstorming the problem 'Fish-stock decline,' participants may mention causal factors such as overfishing, use of illegal nets, damaged sluice gates, bunds interfering with fish-migration, more people fishing, fewer fish reaching maturity, overuse of insecticides and fertilisers by agriculturalists, use of water for irrigation, improved drainage system emptying water bodies too quickly after annual floods, the high price of fish encouraging more to fish, lack of alternative employment during the wet season encouraging more to fish, and so on. The facilitator may place some order on this to ease further discussion by, for example, grouping the issues — fish habitat issues (migration, sluices, water quality), fishing issues (overfishing, fish not reaching maturity, more people fishing, use of illegal nets), with the latter subdivided into fishing issues for f/t fishers (high market price encouraging overfishing, use of illegal nets), fishing issues for p/t fishers (high market price, lack of alternative livelihood strategies during the wet season), economic issues. Each of these groupings can then be discussed in greater detail with respondents and in a multi-disciplinary way with researchers. However, researchers need to bear in mind that the grouping is theirs and not respondents, and that they may unconsciously prioritise one grouping over another because of their own technical skills (e.g. economics) rather than exploring issues more holistically from respondents' perspectives and evaluations of importance.

Importantly such exercises can also reveal knowledge gaps either at the level of the community or of target groups. This in turn provides opportunities for researchers to bring their disciplinary expertise to bear on the issues to hand. Researchers will need to cross-check that 'knowledge gaps' in respondents' answers/maps are real and not just idiosyncrasies of the method (for example people just 'forgetting' to mention some facets). A group exercise, rather than individual interview, can reduce the likelihood of this to some extent, but the 'structuring' of both exercises (i.e. topic-led discussion, semi-structured interviewing) is probably necessary, as is triangulation through other methods. That is group sessions need to be as non-directive as possible while ensuring that participants move beyond standard answers (e.g. 'malnutrition is due solely to poverty') to reveal what they know and what they do not know about a particular topic. It is where there appear to be real knowledge-gaps that scientists may be able to assist, while stakeholders will be able to evaluate in terms of their own livelihood strategies whether the new knowledge scientists bring is relevant to their particular circumstances.

Brainstorming sessions may lead to causal diagramming (see Section 3.11: Webbing) for example sorting respondents' statements into one-, two-, three- or more levels. Normally, due to their holistic perspectives on issues, the causal factors that respondents mention will span both the biophysical, technical and socio-economic domains. An important point that emerges from such an analysis is that problems are usually multidimensional — they have socio-economic as well as bio-physical dimensions. However, these impact on NR users in different ways depending on their socio-economic status, capacities and livelihood strategies. It is now well accepted that researchers and NR users have different perspectives on NR opportunities and constraints, but less readily recognised that target populations are made up of different 'stake-holder groups' with distinct needs, capacities, perspectives and livelihood goals. For this reason, researchers need to be aware that the information gleaned in brainstorming sessions (as in all social encounters) is structured by the make-up of the group. Thought therefore needs to be given to the purpose of the brainstorming session, how the information is generated and how it will be used. Too often data gained in one context is extrapolated from to support initiatives in other contexts where it may not hold. For example, a brainstorming session with Bangladesh farmers, or with a heterogeneous group with a preponderance of farmers (or even with a minority of farmers who are influential in their community) may identify flooding as a major constraint to agricultural production, and lead researchers to identify flood-control measures as a potential way forward. However, action to reduce flooding may harm the livelihoods of non-farmers — who are likely to be the poor and fishers — who depend upon the flood and its benefits for a part of their livelihoods. A similar brainstorming session with non-farmers may make no mention of flooding as a 'problem', but instead mention sluice-gates, pesticides, and road building as constraints to their livelihood. This confirms the social 'character' of opportunities and constraints associated with a natural event such as flooding. That is flooding is not just a technical problem but a 'social issue' and a matter for debate and negotiation when it comes to considering interventions (see Section 3.20: Problem Census).

3.22 Assessment Workshops/Envisioning

Cost	L	Individual/group perspective	I/G
Time	L	Expertise required (social and nat. scientist)	M-H
Data reliability	M-H	Observer bias	L-M
		Control of process (directive)	M-H

Definition: Workshop with respondents for the consideration of information, and movement towards a specific output.

Purpose: To produce a specific output after the joint consideration by participants of background information, and the voicing of participants' views on the issues under discussion.

Workshops can vary considerably depending on their purpose, the data that is presented at them, and the range of participants that are present at them. A workshop may serve as an introduction to a project (as in a planning workshop), at which the purpose, goals and activities of a project, or of a specific phase of a project, may be presented, discussed and clarified by the participants. A workshop may also serve as an informal and on-going IK data-generation and discussion forum — as an intermittent brainstorming session on the one hand with participants randomly or purposively chosen to take part, or as an informal 'steering committee' on the other with representatives of stakeholder groups meeting on a regular basis. Here both planning and monitoring project activities and outputs may occur. A workshop may serve as a vehicle at which PLA training is given (see Jones 1996), or as the final activity of a project at which participants appraise the project, evaluate the process, project activities and outputs, and look forward to a new cycle of activities.

The participants attending workshops may consist of individuals who express an interest in attending, or individuals purposively chosen to represent different stakeholder interests, or individuals drawn from a specific target group. Whether workshop participants represent a homogeneous or heterogeneous group will depend upon the purpose of the workshop. A homogeneous group (essentially a focus group, see Section 3.14: Group discussions) may be necessary if the intention is to enable those whose voices are not normally heard (e.g. women, children, the aged, disabled, the poor) to express an opinion and move towards some determinate outcome or plan of action which may conflict with the interests of other community members. A heterogeneous group, consisting of representatives of different stakeholder groups may be necessary where the intention is to seek the views of different stakeholders on issues (courses of action) which have implications for the livelihoods of all groups. It should be remembered that in open-forum settings the voices of some representatives may not be heard (because they are politically weak, or custom demands they remain silent in public), and that 'community' decisions may be biased as a result. Public collective decision-making must be treated with caution, and it is preferable to cross-check the wishes of minority groups (or majority but politically-weak groups) prior to moving towards more binding community decisions.

Democracy (one voice one vote) does not work very well in this context. Where the needs of the poor are a priority of the project, it is necessary to enable their concerns and views to be expressed and, as importantly, for decisions taken at (community) workshops to be focused on those needs — that is to be seen as activities leading to the purpose of poverty alleviation. Historically researchers (and participants), in the contexts to which development has traditionally been targeted, have held to the 'myth of community' and failed to disaggregate it into its constituent stakeholder/livelihood groups (see Section 3.4: Wealth ranking). This has had the effect of 'hiding' the poorest and most vulnerable members of communities and of allowing the less vulnerable/more wealthy to co-opt the development process to their own interests. While it is recognised that whole populations may be poor in absolute terms, and that in-country government departments may have a duty to provide extension services for all, international aid is targeted on the needs of the poorest and researchers funded under this have a duty to ensure that scarce resources and the activities they fund are used for the purpose they are intended - the alleviation of poverty.

This means that researchers need to be clear who their target groups are, and develop strategies to promote their interests (see Section 3.4: Wealth ranking). A prime requirement here then is not only the clarification of the technical or policy purposes of workshops (e.g. agricultural improvements, linkages to extension services), but also their social development purposes — that is improvement in the livelihoods of the poorest. To put this message over, and to achieve it in practice without generating opposition from better-off members of the community (who may very well feel their interests are threatened) is a difficult task. The process involves getting community members to accept that 'pro-poor growth' at the local level (just as at the national level) can provide opportunities for livelihood and well-being enhancement for all — that there can be 'win-win' solutions rather than zero-sum ones. Traditionally, and given the short-termism of many NR users in complex risk-prone environments, persuading them that such solutions are possible is no mean feat, but researchers need to give some thought to how technologies will be taken up, their potential impacts, the different agendas that stakeholder groups have, and therefore to how they can facilitate the process to achieve the desired outcomes. (A variety of tools have been developed to assist here and are listed under Section 3.4: Wealth ranking).

Poor preparation of data gathering exercises (e.g. interviewing) can lead to poor data. This is also true too where workshops are used for generating IK and can lead to unsound policy at a higher level, but where workshops are used as an instrument for collective decision-making it can lead to unsound community action plans. With the greater focus on good governance and subsidiarity in development today, workshops as mechanisms for accessing local-level needs and concerns have grown in importance. Forward planning for them is therefore of considerable importance.

An approach to running a workshop is to be found in IIRR's Manual (1996), so only the major points will be given here (see also Jones 1996). The emphasis will be on workshops as decision-making bodies, though it should be remembered that communities will have a range of pre-existent 'traditional' and local government institutions. Whether these are likely to be a constraint to achieving donors' and national governments' poverty-alleviation goals or whether they can be built upon to facilitate them, they need to be taken into account. The same is true for local extension services and NGO bodies, and this is a prime reason for carrying out institutional analyses at the local level (see Section 3.6: Venn diagrams). Bottom-up community 'self-help' initiatives, as promoted by many NGOs, have tended to ignore/avoid traditional and local government institutions as inefficient, as representing vested interests and as barriers to achieving livelihood enhancements for the poor. However, donors and national governments are working to make these institutions more responsive to the needs of their constituents. These bodies have their own expertise, may have invaluable inputs to make to the development process and may be able to leverage resources which local communities on their own are not able to do (see National Environmental Council *et al.* 1991:69). 'Joined-up' development, through partnerships with other bodies which have credibility and longer-term existence at the local level, is more likely to lead to sustainable livelihood enhancement for the poor than time-bound projects.

Objectives: Researchers need to be clear in their own minds about what they hope to achieve from a workshop and how they might move towards this in the workshop, while retaining the necessary flexibility to allow the process to be 'owned by' the participants and for the latter's input to be at the fore in the decision process. The objectives for the workshop need to be clarified with participants together with a provisional programme for achieving outcomes. These may usefully be circulated prior to the workshop in order to get feedback and improve the event.

Participants: Workshop managers need to be clear about who needs to attend (whether a homogeneous or heterogeneous group and whether representatives of all primary and secondary stakeholder groups are required).

Location and Agenda: Managers need to ensure that participants are given back-ground information and agenda prior to the workshop, to ensure that the location and time are suitable for participants and that materials appropriate to context (paper, chalk-boards, overheads) are available. For example, women may find it difficult to attend at certain times of day due to pressure of domestic work, while the poor may have migrated for work during certain seasons). Chalk, stones, paper, colouring pens and so on may be the best materials to use with poor people 'on the ground' since they promote greater participation by reason of being less inhibiting and are flexible, but if greater permanence to the data is sought (for future analysis) then any diagrams made will need to be trans-ferred to paper, film, or computer (via digital camera) (see Jones 1996:29, after Chambers).

Activities:

a. At a first meeting of participants, there may be general introductions by the chair, or individuals may be asked to introduce themselves to the others. There may be an 'ice-breaking' game at this point, or after (b), to put everyone at their ease and improve 'ownership' of the process by participants (see Photograph 3.24).

b. The Chairperson briefly explains the purpose of the workshop, the likely activities that will take place, and the hoped for outputs. Participants then have an oppor-tunity to clarify any points they are unsure about.

c. The planned activities are carried out by participants with the assistance of facilitators where the purpose is the generation of primary data, and as round-table discussions where views are sought from different stakeholders on courses for future action. For data collection purposes the workshop may split into smaller groups for discussions/brainstorming (buzz groups), or for matrix ranking, causal diagramming, problem census purposes, and so on. Where the workshop splits into small groups (which may or may not be homogeneous, but usually the former), each group should present their work/findings at a plenary session. This is usually very instructive when groups are formed according to livelihood since they are likely to have very different perspectives on the opportunities and constraints that they face and put different values on the same NRs (see e.g. Barr *et al.* 2000).

Photograph 3.24: Ice-breaking exercise

d. Where the workshop is primarily for data collection purposes by researchers, the participants should be given a provisional evaluation/analysis of the outputs by researchers and some indication of what the workshop is likely to lead on to (e.g. more in-depth work with individuals or focus group sessions), and to explore questions, problems, issues which have come up during the workshop. Participants should also be given some indication as to whether workshops are likely to be a regular occurrence as part of an iterative PLA sequence leading to Action Plans to bring about change.

Post-workshop: Researchers should consolidate and analyse the data outputs and review the process with a view to learning from it. In particular they should ask 'did the workshop go as planned', 'did it produce the planned outputs', 'did everyone contribute', 'were domineering individuals handled firmly but diplomatically', were 'the shy' (women and children) encouraged to contribute, were there enough facilitators, were facilitators effective, and so on? There also needs to be feedback from the workshop organisers to participants with regard to the outputs, both in order to give external perspectives on the issues under discussion to validate the findings and, where workshops are part of a wider training programme, in order to discuss the process and hand it over to those who will carry it forward after the training team has left.

A timeline of a series of PRA workshops held by INTRAC in Central Asia is given (see Table 3.22) as an example of a possible programme (see Jones 1996:73).

3.22.1 Future/Envisioning Workshops

These are workshops which go beyond data collection and PRA to Participatory Learning and Action (PLA), with the emphasis being on bringing about change at the local level by the primary stakeholders themselves. Essentially it consists of an iterative cycle of workshops in which participants identify the problems they face in their livelihoods and explore the opportunities they have for relaxing these. The problems may be individual, specific to a particular livelihood group, or be common to all in a community. Frequently, individual and NR user group problems are 'issues', where different groups have different perspectives on their nature, extent and possible solution (see for example the problem census/village workshop exercise carried out in Bangladesh

Table 3.22 Workshop timeline for INTRAC NGO PRA training in Central Asia

OSH	
4/8:	Introductions/orientation, philosophy and principles of PRA, behaviour and attitudes, Case Studies from Scotland and Mongolia
5/8:	Mapping and materials, planning and team contracts, Village visit (1) — orientation and mapping
6/8:	Analysis of village visits, matrices, seasonal calendars and institutional analysis, well-being ranking, planning for the second village visit
7/8:	Village visit (2) — local appraisal, use of a greater range of methods, wider understanding of local issues
8/8:	Analysis of village visit, feedback on the village visits, transects, farm profiles, action planning diagrams, planning for next field exercise
9/8:	Village visit (3) — further use of a range of methods, overnight stay in villages
10/8:	Village visit (4) — developing plans/analysing action
11/8:	Free morning, analysis of village visits, preparation of reports
12/8:	Feedback on the village visits, review of expectations, poverty analysis, preparation for BISHKEK presentation
BISHKEK	
13/8:	Travel to BISHKEK Preparation for BISHKEK presentation
14/8:	Workshop for local NGOs on PRA and lessons learned from OSH, introduction, PRA talk, display of photos, video, village presentations, presentation to government officials and donors, introduction, speeches, PRA talk, village presentations, video, issues around poverty, policy recommendations, poverty assessments
15/8:	Preparation of materials for source-book, writing reports
16/8:	Discussion of training materials, watching videos, consolidation, country planning for follow-up, individual action plans and commitments, Evaluation, Party

Source: Jones 1996:73.

by Barr *et al.* (2000)). As Mikkelsen notes (1995:81), "participants, who preferably represent different experiences, contribute their ideas to change and improve the situation." In these and the similar 'scenario workshops' at which participants develop future scenarios before opting to plan along the lines of one of them, there may or may not be an attempt to bring about consensus (see DFID 2001). However, whether the process is taken forward at the individual, household, stakeholder/livelihood group or community level, the focus is on developing an Action Plan to address the problems and improve livelihoods and well-being.

An example of a Community Action Plan is given in the National Environmental Council *et al.*'s Handbook (1991) for Kenya. As the authors note (p.69) the plan covers the development priorities agreed upon by the community, proposed actions and requirements, duties and responsibilities for individuals and groups, work schedules, and the identification of areas where the community needs outside assistance. Importantly the community takes the lead in developing this Village Resource Management Plan (VRMP), supported by the research team, external NGOs and extension agencies. The plan can be very detailed and cover a number of sectors (as is the case with the VRMP), but is based on a participatory appraisal of the problems and opportunities a community faces, causal analyses of these, and various ranking and option assessment exercises to prioritise the problems the Action Plan should address (see Tables 3.23 and 3.24).

The Options Assessment Chart (Table 3.24) takes a 'scenario' approach and evaluates the various options (Boreholes, Roof Catchment, etc.) against a number of key variables including Impact (Productivity, Stability, Sustainability, Equitability), Time

Table 3.23 Problems and opportunities chart, Mbusyani, Kenya

The PRA team and Mbusyani residents identified the following problems and opportunities while gathering data during the PRA exercise. Water resource development was consistently identified as the priority problem.

Problems	Opportunities
1. Water	- Boreholes
	- Roof catchment
- quality	- Natural springs
	- Rehabilitate dams
	- Shallow wells
	- Develop new surface dams
2. Tools	- Seek outside funding to purchase tools
	- *Harambee* (Kenyan word meaning community action) to purchase tools
3. Income Generation	- *Posho* mill
	- Drought-tolerant crop like sunflower (growing and processing for oil)
	- Improve marketing of baskets (Nthungi)
	- Poultry keeping
	- Goat keeping
	- Vegetable growing instead of flower growing
	- Fruit growing
	- Fish farming
4. Marketing	- Seek external assistance in finding a market for baskets
- baskets	
- other goods	
5. Soil Erosion	- Continue Mwethya group conservation efforts
	- Dig cut-off drains at the top of hills
6. Food Availability	- Diversify food production to other crops
	- Introduce dry land crops
	- Emphasise food crop production over cash crop production
	- Intercropping of food crops with coffee
	- Irrigated vegetable growing

Source: National Environment Council 1991:59.

Table 3.24 Options assessment chart, Mbusyani, Kenya

Best Bet or Innovation	Productivity	Stability	Sustainability	Equitability	Time to benefit	Cost	Technical social feasibility	Priority
Boreholes	?	0	–	0	3	3	3	6
Roof Catchment	+	+	++	+	1	1	2	3
Natural Springs	+	+	+	++	1	2	2	
Rehabilitate Dams	++	+	++	++	1	2	2	
Shallow Wells	+	+	++	0	2	1	2	
New Surface Dams	++	+	++	++	1	2	2	

KEY

?	Unknown
–	Negative impact
0	No impact
+	Positive impact
++	Very positive impact

	Time	Cost	Feasibility
3	Long	High	Low
2	Medium	Medium	Medium
1	Short	Low	High

Source: National Environmental Council *et al.*, 1991:59.

to Benefit, Cost, Feasibility, and Priority. It is not clear whether the scoring was done by participants or by experts, but the diagram illustrates the method well enough. Given today's concern with enhancing livelihoods for the poorest, a community approach may or may not be the most appropriate way forward, while Equitability and Sustainability might be given a higher priority besides Time to Benefit, Cost and Feasibility. From the chart 'Rehabilitate Dams' and 'New Surface Dams' may look the 'best bet' in terms of Productivity, Sustainability, and Time to Benefit, at medium Cost and requiring only medium Feasibility. From a livelihoods perspective, however, these may be inappropriate to the needs of the poor who may require far less water than is likely to be stored in dams. It may be that for the poor, Natural Springs and Roof Catchment are the best bet, or that scarce resources are better devoted to non-hydrological interventions such as improved access to micro-credit and extension services and small business development.

This suggests that other analytic steps are needed prior to moving to community level Action Plans in order to evaluate the particular needs of different livelihood groups unless there is an issue which unites them against a higher-order stakeholder (for example a National Parks Authority) (see Warner *et al.* 1996; Gujja and Pimbert 1995). This is recognised by Barr *et al.* (2000) in their disaggregation of local populations in Bangladesh for data gathering and PLA exercise purposes. However, while this report documents the priorities of a variety of problems to different social strata, it does not contain much data on the livelihood portfolios of these groups or the relative 'value' of NR (and other 'capitals') to the strategies which make up any single portfolio. Two approaches are suggested here.

3.22.2 Evaluating Livelihood Strategies: Pie Diagramming

Pie diagrams are simple and visually effective means of illustrating proportionality where there are a number of criteria or elements. Pie diagrams have been used by the INTRAC training team in Central Asia to illustrate the strategies making up livelihood portfolios (see Jones 1996:53) (see Figure 3.41). As the author says, "... various aspects of livelihoods can be shown ... . One pie can be taken to represent the total income of a household, and the slices of the pie show the relative importance of different income sources. The same process can be carried out for expenditure" (p.49). (As the author also notes (p.49) pie diagrams can be used in a multitude of contexts to show proportions. E.g. "... land under different crops can be indicated, with a series of pie charts either illustrating historical changes, or comparing different areas of land." See Section 3.13: Historical Comparison.)

Another way to represent proportionality in the importance of livelihood strategies would be to use an 'evaluation wheel' (see under Section 3.6: Venn diagramming/ Institutional analysis).

3.22.3 Evaluating Livelihood Strategies: Standard Measures of Value

One difficulty of this method, however, is that it relies upon livelihood strategies being evaluated in terms of a common standard — such as money (in the Central Asian example). However, in many of the contexts in which the poor live, many strategies of the poor are resource-saving. Thus livelihood strategies are not costed in monetary terms, or there is a mix of monetised and non-monetised strategies. We therefore need valuation techniques which can allow people to define the value of livelihood strategies within the context of their own perceptions, needs and priorities rather than according to external measures.

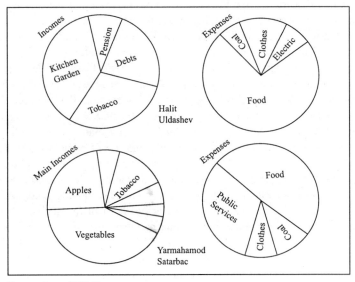

Source: Jones 1996:53.

Figure 3.41: Pie-diagram for livelihood analysis, Central Asia

Emerton and Mogaka (1996), for example, have made a useful contribution here. As part of a community consultation exercise to plan for a shift by the Kenyan Forest Department from traditional forest protection measures to one integrating local communities into forest conservation, the authors generated new knowledge on how and why people use forests in Kenya, and attempted to gauge the value of subsistence forest use in the Aberdares Forest. They had "to find a numeraire for valuation which forms part of the local socio-economy, has wide significance as an item of value, and can be translated into a monetary amount" A number of items were proposed, but in the example below a radio was chosen. This allowed a valuation of different forest resources to respondents (see Figure 3.42), while other scoring exercises and discussion around them enabled a picture of the importance of different forest resources to the household to be built up. Using counters and the radio as the 'standard of value', it was possible to translate forest products into an annual forest use value (see Figure 3.43), and this allowed for a comparison of the value of forest use against alternative land-use options, and an assessment of its value in poor people's livelihoods. Conclusions from the research were that, "Quantifying forest values highlights the heavy costs forest protection has incurred on local communities by removing vital sources of subsistence. It also demonstrates the benefits of a conservation system based on sustainable forest use according to local needs and priorities rather than on protection and exclusion," while a range of customary management systems linked to local forestry knowledge and practice provide valuable building blocks for participatory forest conservation.

3.23 Data Analysis Tools (Computer Software in IK Projects)

Cost	H	Individual/group perspective	I/G
Time	H	Expertise required (social and nat. scientist)	H
Data reliability	H	Observer bias	L
		Control of process (directive)	H

Definition: Use of computer software in the analysis of IK data.

Purpose: To facilitate the storage and manipulation of large amounts of qualitative data such as collected in IK research.

Forest Values for Mama Njoroge: A Case Study

Mama Njoroge chose a radio as the numerate for valuation. Although she does not own one herself, she often listen to her neighbour's radio while she is working on her farm, and aware of how much it costs to buy. This is how she valued forest resources:

1. Fuelwood	2. Grazing	3. Construction

4. Honey hives	5. Medicines	6. Wild foods

7. Hunting	8. Timber	9. Radio

Forest use is worth nearly KSh 9000 a year to Mama Njoroge, over half as much as the annual net value of food production on her *shamba* (garden). Like most households in the area Mama Njoroge relies on the forest for a range of subsistence items because they are unavailable elsewhere. She collects fuelwood everyday with a group of women from the village. Although she does not hold a license she knows that the Forest Guards will not arrest her it she pays a small bribe (e.g. maize flour). While she is gathering fuelwood, she may also gather herbs or plants which she uses in her role as midwife. She values these medicines but thinks they are not as important as forest products, such as fuelwood, that directly sustain the household.

Because her farm is small most local land is under cultivation, there is no space for pasture. Glades in the forest provide the only local source of grazing. They are highly valued because livestock are an important part of household security and wealth. Mama Njoroga's grandson takes her cattle into the forest everyday and cuts grass for zero-grazing. He stays at some distance from the herd because he is afraid of being caught and beaten by the Forest Guards. While he is in the forest, he sets traps for antelopes and hunts birds with his catapult. He roasts the meat and shares it with the other boys who herd nearly. Like the wild fruits and vegetables that the children gather, these foods are never brought back to the homestead. They are not considered 'proper foods' because they are not central to the family's diet. They are not valued highly by Mama Njoroge.

Mama Njoroge lives in a mud and thatch house. The poles and roof come from the forest because there are no trees on farm and she cannot afford to buy timber frames. Construction materials are highly valued because they are difficult to get elsewhere and shelter is critical. Mama Njoroge's son owns 16 beehives in the forest. He works in Nairobi and hires them to a relative, who pays for their use with a proportion of the honey harvest. Mama Njoroge uses the honey for brewing *uki*, a traditional beer, with which she pays her neighbour to plough her farm each season.

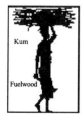

Source: Emerton and Mogaka 1996:7.

Figure 3.42: Participatory environmental evaluation of forest resources, Kenya

Steps in Valuing Forest Use for Aberdares Households

i. Scoring forest uses by allocating counters.

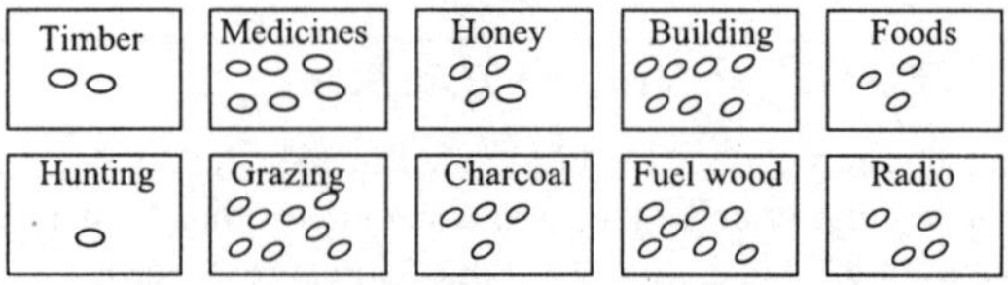

Timber	Medicines	Honey	Building	Foods
○○	○○○ ○ ○○ ○	○○ ○○	○○○○ ○ ○○ ○	○ ○ ○ ○

Hunting	Grazing	Charcoal	Fuel wood	Radio
○	○○○○ ○○ ○	○○○ ○	○○○ ○○○	○ ○ ○○

ii. Translating forest products into wealth item equivalents and overall values.

Picture card	Points allocated	Points in radio equivalents	Overall value (KSh)
Timber	2	2/4 = 0.5	0.5 × 10000 = 5000
Medicines	6	6/4 = 1.5	1.5 × 10000 = 15000
Honey	4	4/4 = 1	1 × 10000 = 10000
Building materials	7	7/4 = 1.75	1.75 × 10000 = 17500
Wild foods	3	3/4 = 0.75	0.75 × 10000 = 7500
Hunting	1	1/4 = 0.25	0.25 × 10000 = 2500
Grazing	8	8/4 = 2	2 × 10000 = 20000
Charcoal	4	4/4 = 1	1 × 10000 = 10000
Fuelwood	7	7/4 = 1.75	1.75 × 10000 = 17500
Radio	4	–	10000

iii. Dividing lifetime values to give annual values using the formula:

$$\frac{1}{T}\sum_{t-1}^{T}\frac{V}{T}1+r^{(T-t)}$$

where T is the total lifetime of the wealth item (10 years), V is the lifetime value of the forest activity, r is the discount rate (10%) and t the year.

Forest product	Overall value (KSh)	Average annual value (KSh)
Timber	5000	877
Medicines	15000	2630
Honey	10000	1753
Building materials	17500	3068
Wild foods	7500	1315
Hunting	2500	438
Grazing	20000	3506
Charcoal	10000	1753
Fuelwood	17500	3068
Total	**105000**	**18408**

Source: Emerton and Mogaka 1996:7.

Figure 3.43: Calculating values of forest resources, Kenya

The use of computers to handle qualitative data is increasing in ethnographic research and they are becoming an important methodological aid (Coffey *et al.* 1996). The types of data which can be dealt with using computer-based tools is increasing following our inexorable progress towards a digital world. Such software facilitates the storage,

Photograph 3.25: A problem census

selective retrieval and manipulation of numerical, textual and graphical data. Increasingly IK, be it in the form of word processed documents, audio tapes, or video tapes, is also being stored in computers. The software provides tools to code IK and assist in its analysis. IK data, being largely qualitative, demand interpretation to draw out evident trends and patterns. The computer is useful for storing, rapidly retrieving, comparing and contrasting data fragments, and can aid in the analysis of complicated patterns (Padilla, 1991). A database is a sophisticated technological aid to long established methodology. In his discussion of ethnographic methodology, Malinowski (1944:17), for example, recommended that "results ought to be tabulated into some sort of synoptic chart, both to be used as an instrument of study, and to be presented as an ethnological document".

Two principal forms of computer-based analysis of IK exist:

- packages which permit coding and querying of data, often raw transcript data, to assist the analyst in building an understanding of the indigenous perceptions and views on the subject in hand (e.g. NRM).
- packages which extract and condense raw data to basic semantic building blocks, as a foundation of an 'expert system' — a type of IK artificial intelligence engine or model of IK that can be questioned and will give predictions about IK responses.

The former type of software has been given the collective name of Computer-Aided Qualitative Data Analysis Software (CAQDAS). The latter, the knowledge modelling or artificial intelligence approach has no such umbrella acronym. The use of database tools, especially CAQDAS, in NR-IK research is described and critiqued at greater length in Barr & Sillitoe (2000).

3.23.1 Computer-Aided Qualitative Data Analysis Software (CAQDAS)[1]

CAQDAS, a tool developed and used largely by sociologists, is described in some detail here because it has not been widely used in IK studies, which have tended to

---

[1] This is accelerating further with the availability of digital audio and digital video devices (Appendix 1). For further information see the ESRC-funded CAQDAS Networking Project at the University of Surrey. http://www.caqdas.soc.surrey.ac.uk/

bifurcate into those that have used more traditional ethnographic methods and those that have used PRA approaches. The expert system approach is a third, and less common one.

Initially, CAQDAS was limited to plain, 80 column, ASCII text. It has now progressed to be better integrated with word processing packages, and can deal with the major word processing formats (Word, WordPerfect, etc.), as well as HTML documents. Recent upgrades of the major CAQDAS packages also allow them to deal with digital audio and digital video. There is growing interest in the presentation of audio data via the computer and the conversion of interview recordings into text formats. Traditionally interviews have been recorded with an analogue tape recorder, and the researcher or a professional stenographer has transcribed these recordings, previously on a typewriter and now largely using a word processor. It remains a slow, laborious, and expensive process. We shall increasingly be able to use voice recognition software to undertake this transcription work. Voice recognition packages are 'trained' to accept a particular voice, so cannot currently cope with many different interviewees. However, the stenographer could listen to tape recording and repeat it into a voice recognition package to generate a transcript. Alternatively the researcher can read his/her written interview notes into the package. Digital tape/mini disc recorders are being used to create sound files (.wav, .au, etc.) that can be imported direct into CAQDAS. The technology does not yet exist whereby digital audio of field interviews can be passed through a voice recognition package to create transcript.

Software Packages

A number of different CAQDAS products exist, probably the best known and most widely used are QDR NUD*IST (which has been extensively revised as QSR Nvivo), and Atlas-ti. Other products include WinMax, Kwalitan, HyperResearch, Ethnograph, Code-A-Text and the free software EZ-Text. We worked with QSR NUD*IST (Figure 3.44) on our Bangladesh projects. We note that some criticisms of this package have been addressed in Nvivo.

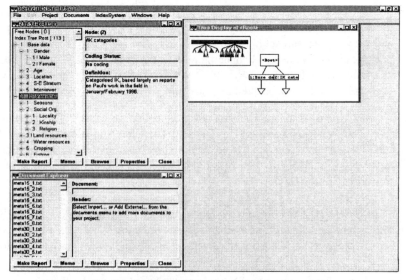

*Figure 3.44: Screen shot of QSR NUD*IST showing code list, documentation list and code tree*

The CAQDAS Process

In the context of IK and NR research, the CAQDAS process essentially involves:

- interviewing farmers[2]
- transcribing their responses
- coding their responses according to various facets of the natural environment and the respondents' views on these
- querying the resulting database of coded interviews to test the researchers' emerging theories about local knowledge of natural resources, and to develop an understanding or a 'model' of local NR knowledge that is supported by the data (Figure 3.45).

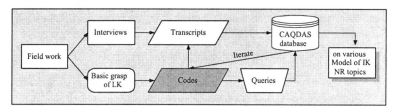

Figure 3.45: The process of using CAQDAS for making IK accessible to scientists

The researcher may use codes that are based on a priori assumptions about IK, or more likely codes that are based on knowledge collected by the researcher during the interviewing process. The coding and querying processes should be iterative. Ideally there should be the opportunity to return back to the field to collect further, more targeted interviews to explore the model, but this is not always possible.

3.23.2 How CAQDAS Operates

In summary, one can use CAQDAS to code qualitative data and then sort, cluster and structure them.

The *data types* which can be handled include word processed text, such as MS Word and .html documents, audio clips (e.g. .wav files) and video clips (e.g. .mpeg files). Additionally non-electronic data, such as hard-copy reports, can be referenced as 'external documents'. For the purposes of IK research the normal type of data will be textual — responses to semi-structured interviews, notes on and transcripts of open-ended interviews, records of focus group discussions, etc.

Responses to questionnaires are quantitative data that are best analysed with a suitable statistical package such as SPSS or SAS. Graphical data generated through PRA, such as participatory maps or cropping cycle diagrams, can be referenced as external 'documents', but the packages do not generally deal with this type of data as well as they do text. It should be noted that a number of attempts have been made to analyse participatory maps using GIS packages in order to combine local and scientific knowledge.[3] Issues such as different spatial frames and non-linear scales have tended to make spatial integration of maps from different knowledge traditions difficult.

When the IK data comprises text, coding is applied to 'text units'. Text units may range from individual words, through lines and sentences to paragraphs and

---

[2] Or any other natural resource user whose IK is of interest.

[3] For a review, see DFID NRSP project R7055, "Issues and methods in the joint application of GIS and participatory enquiry in natural resources research," undertaken by NRI.

document sections to whole documents. Generally two types of coding are recognised (Figure 3.48):

- Factual coding
- Referential coding

Factual coding usually relates to factual information about the interviewee, such as their age, gender, village, occupation, wealth group, stakeholder group (if relevant), etc. This can be applied to the whole document (interview), so that all the references to the information in the document are tagged with this information about its source (e.g. that a wealthy, middle-aged man for village X said this). This process of factual coding is straight-forward for word processed interview transcripts. CAQDAS can cope with group situations, such as focus groups, but it is best to identify who makes each comment in the discussion, as this makes the factual coding more useful. Factual coding is an important strength in CAQDAS as it helps to maintain the socio-cultural context of the IK.

Referential coding refers to 'what the text is about', and involves assigning a selected code to text units. The extent to which referential coding might be applied depends largely on the type of IK data that is being coded and the depth of enquiry that the interviewer managed to reach with the respondent. Thus, as in Figure 3.46, where an interview has largely involved a local person describing the natural environment in their own (emic) terms, referential coding will be based on natural resources features (e.g. one line is coded to 'sandy soil', then two lines are coded to 'soil erosion').

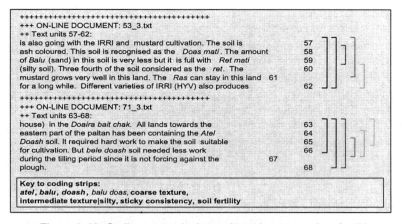

Figure 3.46: Coding text units in two interview transcripts for IK on soil properties (especially texture)

One can achieve a deeper appreciation of local understanding of processes and causality, and indigenous views on natural resources management with a more probing interrogation of the database. Thus, for example, if investigating soil and water conservation, text could be coded to 'contour hedges', and then further coded to attitudinal codes such as 'positive', 'neutral' and 'negative').

Referential coding may be done in two ways. Firstly, any number of interviews can be coded automatically using a batch process than runs a macro command. The macro will search and code for particular terms or phrases. Depending on the protocols used for transcribing the interviews, these search terms may be in English or the local language. The QSR NUD*IST search process has a very sophisticated set of wild-cards which assist here. Secondly, manual interpretative coding can be done on the same interviews. The text is read and coded line-by-line using simple mouse clicks. This approach requires the analyst to think more deeply about the interview, and start theorising about the subject matter. The best coding strategy is to make an initial batch coding, and to supplement this with manual coding. This is a time-consuming exercise.

Coding Structure
QSR NUD*IST allows the analyst to organise codes into either hierarchical structures or free unstructured associations. The package functions best where the codes are structured into trees (Figure 3.47), though objections have been raised about forcing a structure on to IK, particularly where the structure is organised according to researcher-dominated concepts (e.g. IK about crop pests could be organised according to Linnean taxa and genera of pest species). In the newer Nvivo package this device is absent as it codes to non-exclusive 'sets' of codes rather than hierarchical trees, similarly for Atlas.ti.

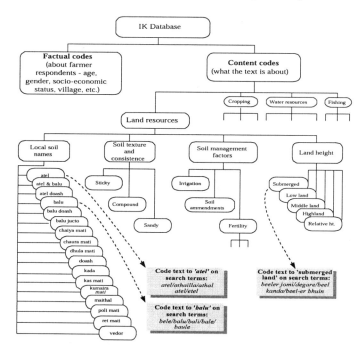

Figure 3.47: Partial coding structure for referential content of transcripts, with examples of search Bengali terms for land and soil

Querying the Data
Once the data are coded they can be easily searched and queried using a range of Boolean-type query tools. The power of QSR NUD*IST comes from these. Iterative querying, testing and building up an in-depth understanding of how all or some local people conceive of different aspects of the natural environment, is the 'analysis' in the CAQDAS acronym. This iterative exploration of the data is the key to the process[4],

---

[4] This iterative process of data exploration is discussed well by Ethnograph author John Seidel in Qualitative Data Analysis (1998). http://www.qualisresearch.com/qda.htm.

and is often obscured by the 'whistles and bells' of the software and academic discussions about coding strategies. Though the query tools function well, 'analysis' is far from an automatic process. At the end of the day, the software makes it easier, quicker and more systematic for the human brain to see patterns in the data.

A query searches all the interview transcripts and displays the text units from any interview that meet the search criteria. Examples of the query tools include:

- 'Intersect'   where two codes exactly coincide, e.g. those text units where the respondent mentions 'cattle' and 'soil erosion' in the same unit. The text units coded to the two search terms (i.e. the 'hits') are displayed along with the header information from that document.
- 'Inside'   where one code occurs within another, (e.g. where a block of transcript is coded to 'fishing', and a text unit coded to 'water hyacinth' falls within that block).
- 'Followed-by'   where a coded text unit is followed within a specified number of text units by a text unit coded to a different specified code (e.g. a text unit coded to 'manure' is followed within 2 lines by another coded to 'soil fertility'). This can be used to explore local concepts of causality.
- 'Matrix'   where two higher level code 'nodes' are used to form a matrix. The lower-level codes are plotted as a series of intersections in each cell of the matrix. For example, respondent's gender in a matrix with tree types (male × acacia, female × acacia, male × mango, female × mango, male × neem, etc.). Similarly, water body types could be plotted in a matrix against fish types, or IK soil categories in a matrix with soil physical properties (Figure 3.48). In each cell of the matrix, the output of the co-incident 'hits' are presented as for the 'intersect' query. This tool is useful to examine what types of knowledge are specific to certain groups in the community, or further examine local categories of IK, as in Figure 3.48.

3.23.3 Evaluation of CAQDAS for IK projects

How useful is CAQDAS for IK-NR projects? It has several attractive features for an IK-NR project. Its supporters talk of its 'systematicity, objectivity and rigour' (Kelle 1997), but it is debatable whether these benefits are achievable. There are three key questions:

- Does CAQDAS offer an improvement on traditional ethnographic data analysis methods?
- Does CAQDAS make IK more accessible to NR scientists?
- Should CAQDAS be recommended, and if so, in what situations?

CAQDAS can offer an improved method of handling and querying qualitative data. This is widely accepted, to the extent that CAQDAS may even be viewed as a new orthodoxy in sociological research (Coffey *et al.* 1996). It obliges researchers to present their data clearly, to be more explicit about the procedures they followed in gathering them and their interpretations of them, something that has long hindered rigorous ethnographic enquiry (Sillitoe 1996; Hesse-Biber 1995).

CAQDAS has the potential to make IK more accessible to non-specialists, but experience from research in Bangladesh was that it did not. The CAQDAS analysis was not available at a time when the NR team members required it. This occurred

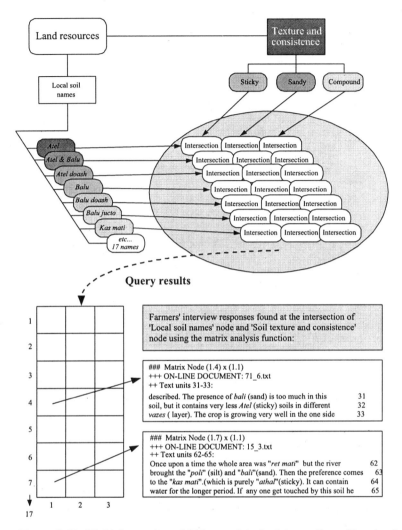

Figure 3.48: 'Matrix' querying of IK transcripts for intersection of local soil names and soil properties

partly because the IK and NR research started simultaneously, the IK analysis could never catch up (as discussed in Chapter 2 under the project wave). The process also proved time-consuming and any project planning to use this software needs to budget adequately for staff to undertake the work or else they have no chance of delivering outputs in a timely fashion. Evidence is that the NR scientists gained as much insight from reading the raw interview transcripts and chapters of the research associates' theses as they did from QSR NUD*IST. The advantage of CAQDAS over interview transcripts, thesis chapters or even the conventional ethnographic monograph is that it is interactive. Reading a report or a monograph is a one-way learning process, the reader cannot (normally) interact with the raw data or the author to ask further questions of interest. This iteration is possible with CAQDAS.

CAQDAS may also assist in the promotion of disciplinary equity in interdisciplinary research. Computer storage and 'analysis' may serve a strategic function in interdisciplinary research in legitimising 'soft' qualitative data in the eyes of those working in the 'hard' natural sciences by giving an impression of 'scientific' rigour. Where an interdisciplinary team shares information formally through the exchange of reports, CAQDAS can provide IK researchers with outputs that offer parity and reciprocity (and possibly even a common language) with outputs from the natural sciences (Crow *et al.* 1992).

The factors which limit its wide use are:

- It requires time to learn to use the software.
- It requires at least an intermediate level of computer literacy.
- The learning curve is steep, the package is not intuitive.
- It is time consuming to transcribe all the interviews and input them into the database, and to code them.
- Coding is a skilled task that demands a lot of experienced researcher time focused on the data.
- It is a comparatively costly tool because of the expert time it demands.

CAQDAS has some potential, but its applicability to IK-NR projects is limited to certain types of investigation. It is best suited to:

- projects with abundant time and resources (Chapter 2, Section 2.5: Cube 3 and Cube 4);
- post-graduate/post-doctorate type IK investigation.

Table 3.25 indicates how useful CAQDAS may be for a range of researchers. This table is based upon typical levels of computer literacy, familiarity with concepts such as grounded truth and ethnographic analysis, and time that can be dedicated to the study, including learning the package and coding the data. This last criterion reduces the suitability of CAQDAS for use by most senior researchers, unless they already have experience of the software.

Its use by a post-graduate researcher, who would collect his/her own raw data, enter them, code them and query them, maximises the researcher's ownership of the process and the outputs. CAQDAS can be used in teams, whereby one or more researchers collect the data, and another/others code it. This was the position in the Bangladesh project, but it resulted in a lack of ownership of the CAQDAS data by the field researchers. However, CAQDAS is used highly successfully in teams, for example in well funded medical research.

The key strengths and weaknesses of CAQDAS for IK-NR projects are:

Strengths of CAQDAS:

- It can lead to IK reports that are more accessible, useful and acceptable to NR scientists than the traditional field report or anthropological monograph.
- It encourages effective data organisation.
- It is supposedly systematic, objective, rigorous, and thus puts IK data on a par with quantitative NR data.
- It facilitates data exchange between researchers.
- It permits NR scientists to question the data for themselves.
- It gives the perception of 'scientific' analysis — NR scientists are comfortable with databases.
- It makes methods more transparent and repeatable, including rural appraisal methods and ethnographic investigation.

Table 3.25 Suitability of CAQDAS for use by different types of researcher

No.	Type of Researcher	Suitability of CAQDAS
1	Village enumerators — trained in IK work by local ethnographer	Very low
2	Local ethnographer	Low
3	Senior national NGO workers with social science training/experience	Low
4	Junior national NGO workers with social science training/experience	Low
5	Undergraduate sociologist — national	Low
6	Undergraduate anthropologist — foreigner	Low
7	National graduate NR scientist with interest in IK work	Low
8	Foreign graduate NR scientist with interest in IK work (might be a VSO-type volunteer or an APO)	Medium-low
9	Graduate sociologist — national	Medium-low
10	Graduate anthropologist — foreigner (might be a VSO-type volunteer or an APO)	Medium
11	National postgraduate NR scientist with interest in IK work	Medium-low
12	Foreign postgraduate NR scientist with interest in IK work	Medium-low
13	Postgraduate sociologist — national	Medium-high
14	Postgraduate anthropologist — foreigner	High
15	Experienced national NR scientist with interest in IK work	Medium-low
16	Experienced foreign NR scientist with interest in IK work	Medium-low
17	Experienced national social scientist with NR science background too	Medium-low
18	Experienced foreign anthropologist with NR science background too	Medium-low
19	Experienced sociologist — national	Medium-low
20	Experienced anthropologist — foreigner	Medium-low

- It supports a culturally diverse knowledge base and supplies information on the informants (IK remains tagged to its origin, and this is explicit through matrix analysis).
- The factual coding can be used as a monitoring device to ensure that interviews cover a representative range of stakeholders (Table 3.26).

Table 3.26 The use of factual codes to monitor the distribution of interviews

Total interviews	n =								
Site 1 (%)	89								
Site 2 (%)	103								
Gender	**Male**	**Female**	**n.r.**						
Site 1	94	–	6						
Site 2	83	17	1						
Age	**5-14**	**15-24**	**25-34**	**35-49**	**50-64**	**65+**	**n.r.**		
Site 1	7	7	18	37	10	15	7		
Site2	–	2	13	21	13	–	51		
Socio-economic group	**Fishers**	**1 poorest**	**2**	**3**	**4**	**5**	**6**	**7**	**n.r.**
Site 1	27	–	–	–	–	–	–	–	73
Site 2	–	9	12	12	19	17	9	7	16

Weaknesses of CAQDAS:

- It requires some familiarity with computer databases.
- It may be seen as a 'computer-task' and be treated as a clerical rather than an analytical responsibility.
- It requires a technological gatekeeper. This is a potentially very powerful position, with significant political implications.
- It can distance researchers from their data.
- It is time consuming to transcribe and code the raw data, and the returns may not warrant the investment.
- It is resource 'hungry'.
- It makes it difficult to maintain farmers' and fishers' access and control over their knowledge.
- It leads to analysis away from the field, in a linear collection-analysis sequence. This reduces the possibility of action research or empowerment.
- It captures a snapshot of IK. It is difficult to cope with the dynamic nature of IK once in a database. Database tools may reify IK (Agrawal, 1995). Machine representations of knowledge systems as 'testable, comprehensive and coherent model of current knowledge on a domain' (Walker & Sinclair 1998) may only be true for a brief period without repeated up-dating.
- It applies 'the logic of survey research' to IK, possibly dismissing the in-depth investigation of single cases.
- The data collection process needs to be tightly defined to start with, so that data are collected in a certain format that is easily inputted into CAQDAS with minimal re-formatting of data.
- A glossary of local terms needs to be created and used, and a standard spelling of local words needs to established early on, otherwise CAQDAS' search functions do not perform well.
- A danger where researchers untrained in anthropological approaches code and structure the data is that they may impose their theoretical views on the data, rather than allowing hypotheses to emerge from interviewees' responses. There is a risk for example, that natural scientists will impose their own disciplinary categories (for example that a soil scientist will code for soil colour, texture, water content, horizon depth, parent material and so on or a botanist code local flora according to Linnean genera, which may not parallel local perceptions). They cannot however violate the integrity of the raw ethnographic data — the transcripts.
- The principal problem is that many users expect that CAQDAS software will 'do the analysis' at the 'push of a button'. In this regard the 'Analysis' in the CAQDAS acronym is a misnomer. It is now widely recognised that CAQDAS is a data management tool more than an analytical one (Kelle, 1999). Rather, it facilitates human analysis by structuring data and enabling him/her to examine patterns and test theories. However, much of this may be more readily and cheaply done through using PRA tools.

3.23.4 IK Expert Systems —Artificial Intelligence & Modelling IK

This type of tool involves computer packages that create 'expert systems' of IK based upon extracting the elemental building blocks of IK from interviews. The most widely reported package is the Agroforestry Knowledge Toolkit or AKT, now available as WinAKT (Box 3.9), developed at the School of Agriculture and Forest Sciences

---

Box 3.9: The main features of WinAKT

The 'Agroforestry Knowledge Toolkit for Windows' (WinAKT) software provides the user with an environment in which to create knowledge bases about a user-selected topic by collating knowledge from a range of sources. It facilitates the synthesis of that knowledge and its valuation, and thereby facilitates its use in planning agroforestry research and extension. This gives a powerful alternative to existing, less formal approaches to evaluating the current state of knowledge.

The WinAKT software provides:
1. A knowledge base structure for strong ecological statements of fact in both natural language and formal representations.
2. A choice of text based diagrammatic input for entering facts into the knowledge base.
3. A set of interfaces for the on-line access to the contents of the knowledge base.
4. A set of mechanisms for reasoning with the contents of the knowledge base.
5. A 'toolkit' which allows the user to specify his own set of functions for accessing and manipulating the knowledge base.
6. A set of mechanisms for producing printed output from the knowledge base in both diagrammatic and text based forms.

---

at Bangor, University of Wales. Research relating to the development and use of the AKT has been reported in *inter alia* Sinclair & Walker (1998), Walker & Sinclair (1998), Walker *et al.* (1994) and Walker *et al.* (1995). Other examples of expert systems in anthropology exist (Fischer *et al.* 1996; Furbee, 1989; Guillet, 1989; Read & Behrens, 1989) but these have generally not been developed with the aim of creating a more utilitarian tool in the way that WinAKT has — see Box 3.9[5].

IK expert systems differ from CAQDAS in that they tend to be developed with specific topics as the focus. Furbee (1889) and Guillet (1989) developed soil-oriented knowledge bases, WinAKT is agroforestry focused, though does have a wider utility, and the APFT code content system (Fischer *et al.* 1996) is forestry focused.

WinAKT with its particular focus on NR-IK, especially agroforestry, is associated with a stage knowledge elicitation process:

- a scoping stage
- a definition stage
- a compilation stage
- a generalisation stage

WinAKT is used in the compilation stage — the stage when information is collected from a stratified sample of key informants. No such clear knowledge elicitation model exists for CAQDAS because of it utilitarian nature. For example it has been used in research into aging by medical teams and by a PhD student studying the perceptions of people whose village was open-cast mined for coal.

The number of informants selected at each stage of the WinAKT knowledge elicitation process depends on the nature of the source communities, the time available and the desired quality of the resulting knowledge base. However, the number of informants will grow at each stage from the definition stage onwards. In practice, in Nepal, the WinAKT team found that 6-10 key informants was sufficient at the definition stage, then five for each identified stratum in the compilation stage, and 100 for the generalisation stage. The very process of feeding the first interview's unitary statements

---

[5] From WinAKT website: http://www.bangor.ac.uk/~afs40c/afforum/winakt/winaktframe.html.

into the WinAKT programme will generate more IK questions. Thus the knowledge elicitation process, forces the researcher to return to their informants two or three times to clarify or to expand upon the information collected. This is a strength of WinAKT as a process rather than a computer package.

Strengths of the expert system approach, with particular reference to WinAKT, are:

- it is subject-matter focused from the outset;
- it emphasises the IK of natural processes (such as erosion), avoiding the risk of over-focusing on description;
- it does not require field notes of interviews to be transcribed into an electronic format for importing into the package;
- it breaks the collected knowledge down into its individual component parts, a process by which misunderstandings and ambiguities can be uncovered during the compilation process, before the knowledge base is completed;
- relying less on the interpretation process inherent in referential coding, WinAKT has been found to be amenable to use by NR scientists (although see below);
- it permits creation of diagrammatic representations of causal flows of ecological knowledge.

Strengths and other features which are shared by WinAKT and QSR NUD*IST include:

- Both systems have the facility to record the definition of all terms used, to record all synonyms, to record information about the informants. They have general memo functions that can be used to include other information, such as domain investigated and sampling strategy used.
- Each has Boolean search facilities that allow searching the knowledge base and collate subsets of knowledge.
- Both systems have other tools to permit more sophisticated interrogations of the knowledge base.
- Both systems allow, or even encourage the creation of object hierarchies, to reflect the hierarchies within local taxonomies.
- If the raw data have been properly coded/made into unitary statement, and sound knowledge bases created (and this is a function of the thoroughness of the researcher, rather than a reflection on the programs), they can be understood, used and interrogated by those who have had nothing to do with their creation.

The expert system approach suffers from many of the same weaknesses as CAQDAS:

- it is very time consuming to enter the data into the system, obliging the researcher to scrutinize what has been said to him/her so minutely, it will enable him/her to uncover ambiguity of meaning, or contradictions in the information given him.
- it is extractive, analysing data away from the field.
- it requires a technological 'gate-keeper'.
- it requires a reasonable level of computer literacy.
- it is thus a rather slow and costly tool to use, and best suited to longer IK studies undertaken by experienced post-graduate or post-doctorate researchers.

However, there are weaknesses specific to the expert system approach, such as:

- it is still necessary for the user to interpret IK statements, in this case for trans-formation into a basic syntax, rather than coding. This step is open to subjectivity by the user.

In the case of WinAKT, entering data into the system involves taking interview scripts and breaking them down into their most basic elements — unambiguous 'unitary statements' e.g. "sandy textured soils are prone to erosion" and building up a 'knowledge base' of such statements (Figure 3.49). These statements can then be combined using Boolean-type statements to give a representation of the IK of more complex phenomena. For example —

"sandy textured soil are prone to erosion"
AND "steep slopes increase erosion risk"
AND "vegetation cover reduces erosion"
THEN ... .

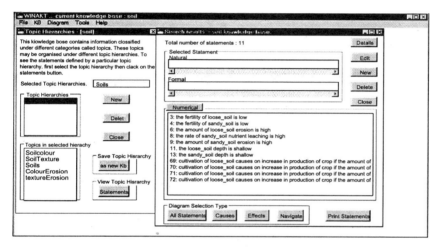

Figure 3.49: Screen shot of WinAKT showing basic statements about soil texture

Identifying and then being able to combine 'unitary statements of factual IK' is the key to WinAKT. This is its strength and weakness. It strength lies in the creation of an interrogatable knowledge base that can provide NR scientists with NR focused IK, by applying artificial reasoning tools to the knowledge base. Its weakness lies in the time taken to extract unitary statements.

Therefore, like CAQDAS, WinAKT is best suited for use by researchers who have plenty of time to conduct their studies — probably post-graduates.

3.24 Others Tools

An approach to IK, like that to sustainable livelihoods, can be socially neutral (see Ashley and Carney 1999; Carney 1998). However, international bodies' commitment to poverty elimination, suggests a tighter focus for the development effort (see the White Paper, DFID 1997). The need is therefore for IK leading to interventions which will have a beneficial impact on the livelihoods of the poor. Participatory approaches have shifted the development community from a supply-side focus on discrete technologies to a concern with 'listening to the poor' and with developing demand-led technical and social interventions in partnership with them and with other stakeholders. As Participatory Poverty Assessments have shown, the constraints poor people face are invariably specific to the local context in which their livelihoods are set, while the poor are able to identify specific and realistic improvements to their situation. Such specificities reinforce the need for policy makers and extension agencies to listen to the poor. Listening to the poor (and to those with whom they have livelihood interdependencies) means accessing their technical (ITK), managerial and wider social knowledge relating to the local and wider 'business environments' in which their livelihoods are set (i.e. interdependencies at the meso and macro scale). The tools detailed above can assist with this. For example, social mapping (using Venn diagramming) is designed to capture these linkages and their relative importance to the livelihoods of different individuals and groups. However, the latter tool also indicates the need for a number of other development tools if IK is to be constructively integrated into the development effort to eliminate poverty. A number of key tools are therefore referenced below.

CRDT. 1998. *Icitrap: training exercise for examining participatory approaches to project management.* Centre for Rural Development and Training: University of Wolverhampton, UK.

DFID. 1998. *The Social Appraisal Annex for a Project Submission*, Social Development Division, Dec. 1998 London: DFID.

——, n.d. Sustainable livelihoods guidance sheets. http://www. dfid.gov.uk.

FAO, n.d. SEAGA Field Handbook. FAO. www.fao.org/sd/seaga/SEfhoool.html.

Gosling, L. 1995. *Toolkits: A Practical Guide to Assessment, Monitoring and Evaluation.* London: Save the Children Fund.

Grimble, R. 1998. *Stakeholder Methodologies in Natural Resource Management. Socio- economic Guidelines.* London: NRI.

Guijt, I. 1998. *Participatory monitoring and impact assessment of sustainable agricultural initiatives.* SARL discussion paper 1. London: IIED.

Howes, M. 1979. 'Stratifying a rural population: trade-offs between accuracy and time', *RRA 2.*

Jobes, K. 1997. *Participatory Monitoring and Evaluation Guidelines: Experiences in the Field. St. Vincent and the Grenadines.* Social Development Division, Dissemination Note No.1, July 1997 London: DFID.

Legum, M. and Field, S. 1995. *Gender Planning* Gender and Planning Associates (GAPA).

Longhurst, R. 1979. 'Assessing economic stratification in rural communities', *RRA 2.*

Marsden, D., Oakley, P. and Pratt, B. 1994. *Evaluating Social Development: Measuring the Process*, Oxford: INTRAC.

ODA. 1993. *Social Development Handbook: A Guide to Social Issues in ODA Projects and Programme.* London: DFID.

—— 1995. *Guidance Note on how to do Stakeholder Analysis of Aid Projects and Programmes.* Social Development Division, London: DFID.

Pretty, J.N., Guijt, I., Thompson, J. and Scoones, I. 1995. *Participatory Learning and Action: A Trainer's Guide.* London: IIED.

4 Further Sources and References for Indigenous Knowledge Projects

4.1 Some Key References

CAQDAS. Networking Project at University of Surrey, Department of Sociology: http://www.caqdas.soc.surrey.ac.uk.

Emery, A.R. 2000. *Integrating indigenous knowledge in project planning and implementation.* Nepean (Ontario): Partnership Publication with Kivu Nature Inc., The International Labour Organization, The World Bank and Canadian International Development Agency.

Grenier, L. 1998. *Working with indigenous knowledge.* A guide for researchers. Ottawa: IDRC.

IIRR. 1996. *Recording and Using Indigenous Knowledge: A Manual.* Silang, Cavite, Philippines: REPPIKA, International Institute of Rural Reconstruction. [Also available through Pact Publications, 777 United Nations Plaza, New York, NY 10017 USA.]

Sillitoe, P. 2000 (ed.). *Indigenous Knowledge Development in Bangladesh. Present and Future.* London: Intermediate Technology Publications, and Dhaka: University Press Ltd.

Sillitoe, P., Bicker, A. and Pottier, J. (eds.). 2002. *Participating in development: Approaches to indigenous knowledge.* London: Routledge.

Warren, D. Michael, L. Jan Slikkerveer, and David W. Brokensha (eds.). 1995. *The Cultural Dimension of Development: Indigenous Knowledge Systems.* London: Intermediate Technology Publications.

4.2 Some Indigenous Knowledge Newsletters

COMPAS Newsletter for Endogenous Development. ETC, P.O. Box 64, Leusden, Netherlands.

Grassroots Voice & Trinamul Uddyog. BARCIK, Lalmatia, Dhaka, Bangladesh.

Honey Bee. Indian Institute of Management, Vastrapur, Ahmedabad 380 015, India.

IK Notes. World Bank, 1818 H Street NW, Washington DC 20433, U.S.A.

IK Worldwide. Linking global and indigenous knowledge. Nuffic P.O. Box 29777, The Hague, Netherlands.

Indigenous Food Plants Programme Newsletter. IFPP P.O. Box 48108, Nairobi, Kenya.

Indigenous Knowledge and Development Monitor. CIRAN P.O. Box 90734, The Hague, Netherlands.

International Work Group for Indigenous Affairs Newsletter. IWGIA, Fiolstraede 10, DK-1171 Copenhagen, Denmark.

Peoples & Plants Handbook. UNESCO, WWF and Royal Botanical Gardens Kew, 7 Place de Fontenoy, 75352 Paris, France.

4.3 Some Indigenous Knowledge Websites

Organisation	Web Address
Centre for Indigenous Environmental Resources	http://www.cier.mb.ca
Centre for Indigenous Knowledge for Agriculture and Rural Development (CIKARD)	http://www.iitap.iastate.edu/cikard/cikard.html

(Contd.)

(Continued)

Organisation	Web Address
Centre for World Indigenous Studies	http://www.halcyon.com
Comparing and Supporting Endogenous Development (ETC)	http://www.etcint.org/compas-news.html
Dene Cultural Institute	http://www.deneculture.org
Honey Bee: Newsletter of Grassroots Creativity and Innovation	http://www.csf.colorado.edu/sristi
IK Worldwide	http://www.nuffic.nl/ik-pages/ikww
ILO (INDISCO — Interregional Programme to Support Self-Reliance of Indigenous and Tribal Communities through Co-operatives and Self-help Organisations)	http://www.ilo.org/public/english/65entrep/coop/indisco.htm
Indian World	http://www.indianworld.org
Indigenous Environmental Network	http://www.alphacdc.com
Indigenous Keepers Programme	http://www.web.net
Indigenous Knowledge and Development Monitor	http://www.nuffic.nl/ciran/ikdm
Indigenous Peoples Biodiversity Information Network	http://www.ibin.org
International Alliance of Indigenous Tribal Peoples of the Tropical Rainforests	http://www.fern.org
National Native Information Centre	http://www.w.innic.com
Native Americans and the Environment	http://www.indians.org
Native Net	http://www.nativenet.uthscsa.edu
Native Web Resources for Indigenous Cultures Around the World	http://www.nativeweb.org
Survival for Tribal Peoples	http://www.survival-international.org
UNESCO	http://www.unesco.org/most/bpindi.htm
World Bank	http://www.worldbank.org/afr/ik/default.htm
World Conservation Union (IUCN)	http://www.iucn.org/icons
World Intellectual Property Organisation	http://www.wipo.org/eng/newindex.index.htm

4.4 Some Participation Websites and Handbooks

Participation

ELDIS gateway: http://nt1.ids.ac.uk/eldis/pra/pra.htm links to practical manuals, e.g. World Bank's *Participation Source Book*; IADB's *Resource Book on Participation*; UNDP's *Empowering People: A Guide to Participation)*. Also links to many research institutes and others, and to PRA library resource. See too *Participation Source Book* http://www.worldbank.org/wbi/sourcebook/sbhome.htm, *Resource Book on Participation* http://www.iadb.org/exr/english/POLICIES/participate/index.htm and *Empowering People: A Guide to Participation* http://www.undp.org/csopp/paguide.htm.

FAO: SDD Home page: http://www.fao.org/sd/. See following FAO manuals *Why People's Participation?* http://www.fao.org/sd/PPdirect/PPan0001.htm. *Participation in Practice: Lessons from the FAO People's Participation Programme* http://www.fao.org/sd/

PPdirect/PPre0044.htm and *SD Dimensions: People's Participation* (An Inter-agency Initiative to Better Understand Sustainable Livelihoods Approaches (SLA) and their Usefulness for our Work — A Note) http://www.fao.org/waicent/FaoInfo/sustdev/PPdirect/default.html.

IDS: http://www.ids.ac.uk/ids/publicat/briefs/brief7.html. *The Power of Participation: IDS Policy Briefing Issue* (7 August 1996) Synopsis of PRA, and notes on PRA information packs available from IDS, and Stewart, S., 1995 *PRA, abstracts of source: an annotated bibliography.* IDS Brighton. Also consult DFID *Sustainable livelihoods guidance sheets.* http://www.ids.ac.uk/livelihoods/.

IIED: *Participatory Learning & Action (PLA) Database* 1998. CD Rom. IIED a Database of over 2,200 bibliographic references on participatory methods and approaches, including a whole index of PLA Notes with abstracts.

IUCN: hhtp://www.iucn.org/themes/spg/beyond_fences/bf_section4_1.html#4.1. See *Beyond Fences: Seeking Social Sustainability in Conservation* 4.1. Social actors and stake-holders and 4.2 Indigenous resource management systems.

The IIED Bookshop: Participation/Training http://www.iied.org/bookshop/tdpart.html. See the following Guijt, I., 1995 *Questions of Difference: PRA, Gender and Environment. A Training Video*, IIED. Sustainable Agriculture and Rural Livelihoods. Language: English (PAL & NTSC formats); Grimble, R., Chan, M., Aglionby, J., and Quan, J., 1995 *Trees and Trade-offs: A Stakeholder Approach to Natural Resource Management.* IIED: Sustainable Agriculture and Rural Livelihoods, Gatekeeper Series SA 52; IIED 1997 *Valuing the Hidden Harvest: Methodological Approaches for Local-Level Economic Analysis of Wild resources.* IIED. Sustainable Agriculture and Rural Livelihoods: Hidden Harvest Research Series 3, 4; IIED 1998 *Participatory Valuation of Wild Resources: An Overview of the Hidden Harvest Methodology Series: Hidden Harvest.* IIED. Sustainable Agriculture and Rural Livelihood and Pretty, J.N., I. Guijt, J. Thompson, I. Scoones 1995 *A Trainer's Guide for Participatory Learning and Action.* IIED Sustainable Agriculture and Rural Livelihoods.

Monitoring and Evaluation

IDRC: http://www.idrc.ca/cbnrm/documents/karenpap.wpd. McAllister K., 1999. *Understanding Participation: Monitoring and evaluating process, outputs and outcomes.* IDRC, Ottawa, Canada. http://www.idrc.ca/cbnrm/documents/karenguide.wpd. McAllister, K., and Vernooy, R., 1999 *Action and reflection: A guide for monitoring and evaluating participatory research.* Item No. 71. IDRC, Ottawa, Canada.

SSC: (Reading Univ Biometrics Advisory & Support Service to DFID) http://www.reading.ac.uk/ssc/.

4.5 Bibliography (Inc. references cited in test)

Abbot, J., Guijt, I. 1977. Creativity and Compromise. *PLA Notes*: No. 28. London: IIED.

Abbot, J. Chambers, R., Dunn, C., Harris, T., de Morode, E., Porter, G., Townsend J., and Weiner, D. 1998. Participatory GIS: opportunity or oxymoron? *PLA Notes*, 33 October.

Aboyade. Ojetunji. 1991. *Some Missing Policy Links in Nigerian Agricultural Development.* Ibadan: International Institute of Tropical Agriculture.

Action Aid. 1996. *The Reflect Mother Manual: Regenerated Freirean Literacy through Empowering Community Techniques.* Chard: Action Aid.

Action Aid/IIED. 1992. *From input to impact: participatory rural appraisal for ActionAid the Gambia* March. Action Aid/IIED.

Adams, A.M., Evans, T.G., Mohammed, R., and Farnsworth, J. 1997. Socio-economic stratification by wealth ranking: is it valid? *World Development*, 25 (7), 1165-1172.

Adams, William M. and L. Jan Slikkerveer (eds.). 1997. *Indigenous Knowledge and Change in African Agriculture.* Studies in Technology and Social Change, No. 26. Ames: CIKARD, Iowa State University.

Adegboye, Rufus O. and J. A. Akinwumi. 1990. Cassava Processing Innovations in Nigeria, pp. 64-79 (In *Tinker, Tiller, Technical Change*, Matthew S. Gamser, Helen Appleton, and Nicola Carter (eds.). London: Intermediate Technology Publications.

Agar, M.H. 1986. *Speaking of Ethnography*. Sage Publication, Beverley Hills.

Agrawal, A. & Gibson, C.C. 1999. Enchantment and Disenchantment: The Role of Community in Natural Resource Conservation. *World Development*, 27 (4), 629-649.

Agrawal, A. 1995a. Dismantling the Divide Between Indigenous and Scientific Knowledge. *Development and Change* 26, 413-439.

——. 1995b. Indigenous and scientific knowledge: some critical comments *Indigenous Knowledge and Development Monitor*, vol. 3 (3), pp. 3-6.

Ahmed, Z.U. 2000. When a Bangladeshi Native is not a Bangladeshi Native, pp. 203-209. In: Sillitoe, P. (ed.). *Indigenous Knowledge Development in Bangladesh: Present and Future*. London: Intermediate Technology Publications and Dhaka: University Press Limited.

Ahmed. A. and C. Shore (eds.). 1996. *The Future of Anthropology: Its Relevance to the Contemporary World*. London: Athlone Press.

Ahmed, Medani Mohamed M. (ed.). 1994. *Indigenous Farming Systems, Knowledge and Practices in the Sudan*. Khartoum: Institute of African and Asian Studies, University of Khartoum.

Allan, W. 1967. *The African husbandman*. London: Oliver and Boyd.

Altieri, M. (ed.) 1987. *Agro-ecology: the Scientific Basis of Alternative Agriculture*. Boulder: Westview Press & London: Intermediate Technology Publications.

Altieri, M. and L. Merrick. 1997. In-situ conservation of crop genetic resources through maintenance of traditional farming systems. *Economic Botany* 41: 86-96.

Altieri, M.A. 1988. The impact, uses and ecological role of weeds in agro-ecosystems. In M.A. Altieri & M. Lieman (eds.). *Weed management in agro-ecosystems: ecological approaches*. CRC Press, Boca Raton, Florida, USA.

Amanor, K. 1991. Managing the fallow: weeding technology and environmental knowledge in the Krobo District of Ghana. *Agriculture and Human Values* 8 (1 & 2).

Anbalagan, K., Karthikeyan, G., and Narayanasamy, N. 1997. Assessing pollution from tannery effluents in a South Indian village. *PLA Notes* 30 October.

Anjaria, Jayvir. 1996. Ethnoveterinary Pharmacology in India: Past, Present and Future, pp. 137-147. In *Ethnoveterinary Research and Development*. Constance M. McCorkle, Evelyn Mathias, and Tjaart W. Schillhorn van Veen (eds.). London: Intermediate Technology Publications.

Antweiler, C. 1998. Local knowledge and local knowing: an anthropological analysis of contested cultural products in the context of development. *Anthropos* 93: 469-494.

Apffell-Marglin, F. and Marglin, S.A. 1990. *Dominating Knowledge: Development, Culture and Resistance*. Oxford: Oxford University Press.

Appleton, Helen E. and Catherine L.M. Hill. 1994. Gender and Indigenous Knowledge in Various Organizations. *Indigenous Knowledge and Development Monitor* 2 (3): 8-11.

Arce, A., Villarreal, M. & de Vries, P. 1994. The Social Construction of Rural Development, in Booth, D. (ed.) *Rethinking Rural Development: Theory, Research and Practice*, Harlow: Longman, pp. 152-171.

Arce, A. & Long, N. 1993. Bridging Two Worlds: An Ethnography of Bureaucrat-Peasant Relations in Western Mexico. In Hobart, M. (ed.) *An Anthropological Critique of Development: The Growth of Ignorance*, London: Routledge, pp. 179-208.

Ardener, E. 1971. *Social anthropology and language*. London: Tavistock.

Ardener, S. (ed.) *Defining females: the nature of women in society*. London: Croom Helm.

Arnstein, S.R. 1969. A ladder of citizen participation. *Am. Inst. Planners. J.*, 35, 216-224.

Ashby, J.A. 1990. *Evaluating technology with farmers: a handbook*. IPRA projects, CIAT, Colombia.

——. 1991. *Farmer evaluations of technology: methodology for open-ended evaluation: instructional unit no. 1*. CIAT, Colombia.

——. 1993. Identifying beneficiaries and participants in client-driven on-farm research. AFSRE Newsletter 4(1) pp.1-3.

Ashby, Jacqueline A., Carlos A. Quiros, and Yolanda M. Rivers. 1989. Farmer Participation in Technology Development: Work with Crop Varieties, pp. 115-122. In *Farmer First: Farmer Innovation and Agricultural Research*. Robert Chambers, Arnold Pacey, and Lori Ann Thrupp (eds.). London: Intermediate Technology Publications.

Ashby, Jacqueline A., Teresa Gracia, Maria del Pilar Guerrero, Carlos Arturo Quiros, Jose Ignacio Roa, and Jorge Alonso Beltran. 1996. Innovation in the Organization of Participatory Plant Breeding, pp. 77-97. In *Participatory Plant Breeding*, Pablo Eyzaguirre and Masa Iwanaga (eds.), Rome: IPGRI.

Ashley, C. and Carney, D. 1999. *Sustainable livelihoods: lessons from early experience*. London: DFID.

Atran, S. 1990. *Cognitive Foundations of Natural History: Towards an Anthropology of Science*. Cambridge: Cambridge University Press.

Atte, Oluwayomi David. 1992. *Indigenous Local Knowledge as a Key to Local Level Development: Possibilities, Constraints, and Planning Issues*. Studies in Technology and Social Change, No. 20. Ames: CIKARD, Iowa State University.

Aumeeruddy, Yildiz. 1995. Phytopractices: Indigenous Horticultural Approaches to Plant Cultivation and Improvement in Tropical Regions, pp. 308-322. In *The Cultural Dimension of Development: Indigenous Knowledge Systems*, D.M. Warren, L. Jan Slikkerveer, and David Brokensha. (eds.) London: Intermediate Technology Publications.

Axelrod, M.D. 1975. Ten essentials for good qualitative research. *Marketing News 8*, pp.10-11.

Babu, Suresh Chandra, D. Michael Warren and Bhakthavatsalam Rajasekaran. 1995. "Expert Systems for Indigenous Knowledge in Crop Varietal Selection," pp. 211-217. In *The Cultural Dimension of Development: Indigenous Knowledge Systems*, D. Michael Warren, L. Jan Slikkerveer, and David Brokensha (eds.). London: Intermediate Technology Publications.

Bain, G. 1989. Conclusion: issues in the application of traditional knowledge of environmental science. I. Johannes R.E. (ed.) *Traditional ecological knowledge: a collection of essays*. Cambridge: IUCN, The World Conservation Union.

Barker, D. 1977. *Some methodological issues in the measurement, analysis and evaluation of peasant farmer's knowledge of their environment*. MARC Report No. 9, Monitoring and Assessment Research Centre of the Scientific Committee on Problems of the Environment, Chelsea College, University of London.

——. 1980. Appropriate methodology: using a traditional African board game in measuring farmers' attitudes and environmental images. In Brokensha, D., Warren, D.M., and Werner. (eds.) *Indigenous knowledge systems and development*. University Press of America.

Barnes, B. and D. Bloor. 1982. Relativism, rationalism and the sociology of knowledge. In M. Hollis and S. Lukes. (eds.) *Rationality and Relativism*, pp. 1-20. Oxford: Basil Blackwell.

Barnes, J.A. 1969. Networks and political process. In M.J. Swartz (ed.). *Local-level politics* London: University of London Press (pp. 107-130).

Barr J.J.F., and Haylor, G. (in press). Experiences of applying the sustainable livelihoods framework on Bangladesh floodplains (submitted to *World Development*).

Barr, J.J.F. and Sillitoe P. 2000. Databases, indigenous knowledge and interdisciplinary research. In P. Sillitoe (ed.) *Indigenous knowledge development in Bangladesh: Present and future* (pp. 179-195). London: Intermediate Technology Publications & Dhaka: University Press Limited.

Barr, J.J.F., Dixon, P-J., and Rose, D. 2000. *Mache, Bhate, Bangali: understanding rural livelihoods on the Bangladesh floodplains*. Video for NRSP, DFID, London.

Barr, J.J.F., Dixon, P-J., Rahman, M.M., Islam, A., Zuberi, M.I., McGlynn, A.A., and Ghosh G.P. 2000. *Report on a participatory, systems-based, process for identification of improved natural resources management for better floodplain livelihoods. Project Report for NRSP project R 6756*. London: DFID, NRSP.

Barreiro, Jose (ed.). 1992. Indigenous Economics: Toward a Natural World Order. Special Issue of *Akwe kon Journal*, vol. 9, no. 2.

Barrow, E.G.C. 1992. Building on local knowledge: The challenge of agroforestry for pastoral areas. *Agroforestry Today*, 3 (4): 4-7.

Basant, Rakesh. 1990. Farmers, Fabricators, and Formal R&D — The Pipe Frame Multipurpose Tool Bar in Gujarat, India, pp. 103-120. In *Tinker, Tiller, Technical Change*, Matthew S. Gamser, Helen Appleton, and Nicola Carter (eds.). London: Intermediate Technology Publications.

Bates, R. (ed.) 1988. *Toward a political economy of development: a rational choice perspective*. Berkeley: University of California Press.

Baumann, M., Bell, J., Koechlin, F. and Pimbert, M. 1996. *The Life Industry: Biodiversity, People and Profits*. London: Intermediate Technology Publications.

Bebbington, A. 1994. Theory and Relevance in Indigenous Agriculture: Knowledge, Agency and Organization, in Booth, D. (ed.) *Rethinking Social Development: Theory, Research and Practice*, pp. 202-225. Harlow: Longman.

Bebbington, A.J., Carrasco, H., Peralbo, L., Ramon, G., Trujillo, J. and Torres, V. 1993. *Rural peoples' knowledge, farmer organisations and regional development: Implications for agricultural research and extension*. ODI Agricultural Administration Unit (Research and Extension) Network Paper No. 41. London: Overseas Development Institute.

Belbin, M. 1981. *Management Teams — why they succeed or fail*. Butterworth Heinemann. Belbin Associates homepage: http://www.belbin.com/home.html.

Bell, M. 1979. The exploitation of indigenous knowledge or the indigenous exploitation of knowledge: whose use of what for what? In *Rural Development: Whose knowledge counts? IDS Bulletin*, vol.10 (2): 44-50.

Belshaw, D. 1979. Taking indigenous knowledge seriously: the case of intercropping techniques in East Africa. *IDS Bulletin* 10 (2) 24-27.

——. 1980. Taking Indigenous Technology Seriously: The Case of Inter-Cropping Techniques in East Africa, pp. 197-203. In *Indigenous Knowledge Systems and Development*, David W. Brokensha, D. Michael Warren, and Oswald Werner, (eds.) Lanham, MD: University Press of America.

Bentley, J. 1989. What farmers don't know can't help them: the strengths and weaknesses of indigenous technical knowledge in Honduras. *Agriculture and Human Values* 3: 25-31.

——. 1992. Alternatives to pesticides in Central America: applied studies of local knowledge. *Culture and Agriculture*, part 44, pp. 10-13.

——. 1992. *The epistemology of plant protection: Honduran campesino knowledge of pests and natural enemies*. In Gibson R.W. and Sweetmore, A. (eds.), Proc. Seminar Crop Protection Resource-Poor Farms, pp. 107-118.

Bentley, J.W. and Andrews, K.L. 1991. Pests, Peasants, and Publications: Anthropological and Entomological Views of an Integrated Pest Management Program for Small-Scale Honduran Farmers. *Human Organization*, 50 (2): 113-124.

Berg, Trygve. 1996. The Compatibility of Grassroots Breeding and Modern Farming, pp. 31-36. In *Participatory Plant Breeding*, Pablo Eyzaguirre and Masa Iwanaga. (eds.) Rome: IPGRI.

Berkes, Fikret and Carl Folke. 1992. A Systems Perspective on the Interrelations between Natural, Human-Made and Cultural Capital. *Ecological Economics* 5: 1-8.

Berlin, B. 1992. *Ethnobiological classification: principles of categorization of plants and animals in traditional societies.* Princeton University Press.

Berlin, B., Breedlove, D.E. & Raven, P.H. 1974. *Principles of Tzeltal plant classification: an introduction to the botanical ethnography of a Mayan-speaking people of highland Chiapas.* New York: Academic Press.

Bernard, H.R. 1995. *Research methods in anthropology.* London: Sage.

Berry, S. 1993. Coping With Confusion: African Farmers' Responses to Economic Instability in the 1970's and 1980's, in Callaghy, T.M. & Ravenhill, J. (eds.) *Hemmed In: Responses to Africa's Economic Decline*, pp. 249-278. New York: Colombia University Press.

Bicker, A., Sillitoe, P. and Pottier, J. (eds.) in press *Development and local Knowledge: New approaches to issues in natural resources Management, conservation and agriculture.* London: Routledge.

—— in press *Investigating local knowledge: new directions, new approaches.* Aldershot: Ashgate.

Biggs, S.D. 1989. Resource-poor farmer participation in research: a synthesis of experiences from nine agricultural research systems. *OFCOR Comparative Study Paper No. 3.* The Hague: ISNAR.

Binsbergen, W. van 1988. The land as body: an essay on the interpretation of ritual among the Manjaks of Guinea Bissau. *Medical Anthropology Quarterly*, pp. 386-401.

Biot, Y., Blaikie, P.M., Jackson, C. and Palmer-Jones, R. 1995. *Rethinking research on land degradation in developing countries.* World Bank Discussion Paper 289, Washington DC, World Bank.

Bjønness, I. 1986. Mountain hazard perception and risk-avoiding strategies among the Sherpa of Khumbu Himal, Nepal. *Mountain Research and Development* 6:4 277-292.

Blaikie, P. and H. Brookfield (eds.). 1987. *Land degradation and society.* London: Methuen.

Blaikie, P. 1985. *The political economy of soil erosion in developing countries.* London: Longman Development Series.

Blaikie, P. Brown, K. Dixon, P. Sillitoe, P., Stocking, M. and Tang, L. 1996. Understanding local knowledge and the dynamics of technical change in developing countries. Paper presented at ODA Natural Resources Systems Programme Socio-economic Methodologies Workshop.

Blaikie, P. Cameron, J. and Sneddon, D. 1980. *Nepal in crisis: Growth and stagnation at the periphery.* Oxford University Press.

Blaxter, M., 1990. *Health and Lifestyles.* London: Tavistock/Routledge.

Blum, E. 1993. Making biodiversity profitable: a case study of the Merck-INBio agreement. *Environment* 35 (4): 17-45.

Blunt, P. and M. Warren (eds.). 1996. *Indigenous organizations and development.* London: Intermediate Technology Publications.

Booth, D. 1992. Why Tanzanian Society is not Experiencing Structural Adjustment: The Case of Iringa. In Maghimbi, S & Foster, P. (eds.) *The Tanzanian Peasantry: Economy in Crisis*, Aldershot: Avebury, pp. 250-271.

——. 1994. Rethinking Social Development: An Overview. In Booth, D. (ed) *Rethinking Social Development: Theory, Research and Practice*, pp. 3-34. Harlow: Longman.

Booth, D., Lugangira, F., Masanja, P., Mvungi, A., Mwaipopo, R., Mwami, J., Redmayne, A. 1993. *Social, economic and cultural change in contemporary Tanzania: A people-oriented focus.* Stockholm: SIDA.

Bouma, J. and Hoosbeek, M.R. 1996. The Contribution and Importance of Soil Scientists in Interdisciplinary Studies Dealing with Land, pp. 1-15 in Wagenet, R.J. and Bouma, J. (eds.).

The Role of Soil Science in Interdisciplinary Research. SSSA Special Publication No. 45. Soil Science Society of America and American Society of Agronomy, Madison.

Box, L. 1987. *Experimenting cultivators: a methodology for adaptive agricultural research*, ODI Agricultural Administration Network Discussion Paper 23.

——. 1990. Virgilio's theorem: a method for adaptive agricultural research. (In Chambers, R. *et al.* 1989, pp. 61-67). Farmer First London: IT Publishers.

Boyer, P. 1990. *Tradition as Truth and Communication: A Cognitive Description of Traditional Discourse*, Cambridge: Cambridge University Press.

Brammer, H. 1980. Some innovations don't wait for experts. A report on applied research by Bangladeshi peasants. *Ceres* 13(2): 24-28.

Breemer, J.P.M. van den 1992. Farmers' perception of society and environment, and their land use: the case of the Aouan in Ivory Coast. In Croll, E. and D. (eds.) *Bush base, forest farm: culture environment and development*. London: Routledge.

Breslin, E.D., and Delius, P. 1997. A Proper Household — exploring household and community dynamics in South Africa. *PLA Notes* 28 February.

Brislin, R.W. 1980. Cross cultural research methods. In Altman, I., Rappaport, R.A. and Wohlwill, J.F. (eds.) *Human behaviour and environment: Advances in theory and research*, pp. 47-82. New York: Plenum Press.

Brocklesby, M.A., and Holland, J. 1998. *Participatory poverty assessments and public services: key messages from the poor*. London: DFID.

Brokensha, David W., D. M. Warren, and Oswald Werner. (eds.) 1980. *Indigenous Knowledge Systems and Development*. Lanham, MD: University Press of America.

Brookfield, H. and Padoch, C. 1994. Appreciating agrodiversity: a look at the dynamism and diversity of indigenous farming practice. *Environment* 35 (5): 7-11.

Brookfield, M. 1996. Indigenous knowledge: a long history and an uncertain future. *People, Land Management and Environmental Change News and Views* 6 March: 23-29.

Brosius, J.P., Lovelace, G.W. and Marten, G.G. 1986. Ethnoecology: An approach to understanding traditional agricultural knowledge. In Martin, G.G. (ed.), *Traditional agriculture in South-East Asia: A human ecology perspective*, pp. 187-197. Boulder: Westview Press.

Brown, C.H. 1984. *Language and living things: uniformities in folk classification and naming*. New Brunswick: Rutgers University Press.

——. 1995. Lexical acculturation and ethnobiology: utilitarianism versus intellectualism. *Journal of Linguistic Anthropology* 5(1): 51-64.

Brown, K. 1994. Approaches to valuing plant medicines: the economics of culture or the culture of economics? *Biodiversity and Conservation* 3: 734-750.

Brush, Stephen B. and Doreen Stabinsky. (eds.) 1996. *Valuing Local Knowledge: Indigenous People and Intellectual Property Rights*. Washington D.C.: Island Press.

Bryant, R.L. 1992. Political ecology: an emerging research agenda in Third-World studies *Political Ecology* 11:1 12-36.

Bulmer, R.N.H. 1967. Why is the cassowary not a bird? A problem of zoological taxonomy among the Karam of the New Guinea Highlands. *Man* 2:5-25.

Bunders, Joske, Bertus Haverkort, and Wim Hiemstra. (eds.) 1997. *Biotechnology: Building on Farmers' Knowledge*. Basingstoke, UK: Macmillan Education.

Burkey, S. 1994. *People first: a guide to self-reliant participatory rural development*. London: Zed Books.

Burnett, R.M. 1963. Some cultural practices observed in the Simbai Administrative Area, Madang District, Papua New Guinea. *Papua New Guinea Agriculture Journal* 16:79-85.

Caplan, P. 1992. Socialism from Above: The View From Below. In Maghimbi, S. & Foster, P. (eds.) *The Tanzanian Peasantry: Economy in Crisis*, Aldershot, Avebury, pp. 103-123.

Carney, D. 1998. *Sustainable rural livelihoods. What contribution can we make?* London: DFID.

Carney, Judith. 1991. Indigenous Soil and Water Management in Senegambian Rice Farming Systems. *Agriculture and Human Values* 8 (1&2): 37-48.

Carrithers, M., Collins, S., and Lukes, S. (eds.) 1985. *The category of the person: anthropology, philosophy, history*. Cambridge: Cambridge University Press.

Carvalho, S., and White, H. 1997. Combining the quantitative and qualitative approaches to poverty measurement and analysis: the practice and the potential. *World Bank Technical Paper* No. 366. Washington D.C.: The World Bank.

Cashman, K. 1991. Systems of knowledge as systems of domination: the limitations of established meaning. *Agriculture and Human Values* 8 (1&2).

——. 1989. Agricultural Research Centres and Indigenous Knowledge Systems in a Worldwide Perspective: Where Do We Go from Here? pp. 10-20. In *Indigenous Knowledge Systems: Implications for Agriculture and International Development*, D. Michael Warren, L. Jan Slikkerveer, and S.O. Titilola. (eds.) Studies in Technology and Social Change, No. 11. Ames: CIKARD, Iowa State University.

Castro, Peter. 1995. *Facing Kirinyaga: A Social History of Forest Commons in Southern Mount Kenya*. London: Intermediate Technology Publications.

Center for Integrated Agricultural Development (CIAD). 1994. *Indigenous Knowledge Systems and Rural Development in China: Proceedings of the Workshop*. Beijing: Beijing Agricultural University.

Center for Traditional Knowledge. 1977. *Guidelines for Environmental Assessments and Traditional Knowledge*. Ottawa: Centre for Traditional Knowledge (2nd Draft Prototype for Field Testing).

Cernea, M. 1991. *Putting People First: sociological variables in rural development*. Oxford: Oxford University Press for World Bank.

CGIAR. 1993. Indigenous Knowledge. In *People and Plants: The Development Agenda*, p. 8 Rome: Consultative Group on International Agricultural Research.

Chadwick, D.J. and Marsh, J. (eds.) 1994. *Ethnobotany and the Search for New Drugs*. CIBA Foundation Symposium 185 John Wiley and Sons, Chichester.

Chambers, R. 1979. Rural Development: Whose Knowledge Counts? Special issue of *IDS Bulletin* (Institute of Development Studies, University of Sussex), vol. 10, no. 2.

——. 1980. Understanding professionals: small farmers and scientists. IADS Occasional Paper. New York: International Agricultural Development Service.

——. 1983. *Rural Development: Putting the Last First*, London: Longman.

——. 1986. Normal professionalism, new paradigms and development. *Institute of Development Studies (Sussex Univ.) Discussion Paper* 227.

——. 1987. Shortcut methods in social science information gathering for rural development projects. In *Proceedings of the 1985 International Conference on Rapid Rural Appraisal*. Rural Systems Research Project and Farming systems Research Project, Kohn Kahn University, Thailand, pp. 33-46.

——. 1992. Rural appraisal: rapid, relaxed and participatory. *IDS Discussion Papers* 311: 1-90.

——. 1993. *Challenging the professions: Frontiers for rural development*. London: Intermediate Technology Publications.

——. 1993. Health, Agriculture, and Rural Poverty — Why Seasons Matter In Chambers, R. *Challenging the professions: frontiers for rural development*. London: IT Publications.

——. 1994. The Origins and Practice of Participatory Rural Appraisal. *World Development* 22 (7): 953-969.

——. 1995. Making the Best of Going to Scale, *PLA Notes*, pp. 57-61, 24 October 1995.

——. 1995. Poverty and rural livelihoods: whose reality counts? *Environment and Urbanization*, vol.7, no.1, pp. 172-204.

Chambers, R., and Conway, G.R. 1992. Sustainable rural livelihoods: practical concepts for the 21st century. *IDS Discussion paper 296*. Brighton: IDS.

Chambers, R., and Ghildyal, B.P. 1985. Agricultural research for resource-poor farmers: the Farmer-First-and-Last model. *IDS Discussion Paper 203*. Brighton: Institute of Development Studies.

Chambers, R., and Jiggins, J. 1986. Agricultural research for resource poor farmers: a parsimonious paradigm. *IDS Discussion Paper 220*. Brighton: Institute of Development Studies.

Chambers, R., Longhurst, R., Pacey A. (ed.) 1981. *Seasonal dimensions to rural poverty*. London: Frances Pinter.

Chambers, R., Pacey, A. and Thrupp, L.A. (eds.) 1989. *Farmer First: Farmer innovation and agricultural research*. London: Intermediate Technology Publications.

Checkland, P.B. and Scholes, J. 1990. *Soft systems methodology in action*. New York: Wiley.

Chin, S.C. 1985. *Agriculture and resource utilization in a lowland rainforest Kenyah community* Special Monograph No.4. The Sarawak Museum Journal, vol. XXXV No.56 (New Series).

Chubin, D.E., Porter, A.L. and Rossini, F.A. 1986. *Interdisciplinary Analysis and Research. Theory and Practice of Problem Focused Research and Development*. Lomond, Mt. Airy.

CIRAN. 1993a. Background to the International Symposium on Indigenous Knowledge and Sustainable Development. *Indigenous Knowledge and Development Monitor* 1 (2): 2-5.

——. 1993b. Recommendations and Action Plan. *Indigenous Knowledge and Development Monitor* 1 (2): 24-29.

Clifford, J. 1988. *The predicament of culture: twentieth century ethnography, literature and art*. Cambridge, Mass: Harvard University Press.

——. 1992. Travelling cultures. In L. Grossberg, C. Nelson and P. Treichler. (eds.) *Cultural studies*. New York: Routledge.

Cochrane, G. (ed) 1976. *What We Can Do for Each Other. An Interdisciplinary Approach to Development Anthropology*. Amsterdam: B.R. Grüner Publishing Co.

Coffey, A., Holbrook, B. and Atkinson, P. 1996. Qualitative Data Analysis: Technologies and Representations. *Sociological Research Online*, 1 (1): http://www.socresonline.org.uk/socresonline/1/1/4.html.

Colby, B. 1966. The analysis of culture content and the patterning of narrative concern in texts. *American Anthropologist*, 68: 366-75.

Colchester, M. 1994. *Salvaging Nature: Indigenous Peoples, Protected Areas and Biodiversity Conservation*. Discussion Paper DP55. UNRISD Geneva and WWF, Gland.

——. Towards indigenous intellectual property rights. *Seedling* 11: (4) 2-6.

Collinson, Michael. 1985. Farming Systems Research: Diagnosing the Problems, pp. 71-86. In *Research-Extension-Farmer: A Two-Way Continuum for Agricultural Development*. Michael M. Cernea, John K. Coulter, and John F. A. Russell. (eds.) Washington D.C.: The World Bank.

Compton, J. 1989. The integration of research and extension. In J. Lin Compton (ed.). *The transformation of international agricultural research and development*, pp. 113-36. Boulder, CO: Lynne Rienner.

Compton, J.L. 1989. Strategies and Methods for the access, integration and utilization of indigenous knowledge in agricultural and rural development. In Warren, D.M., Slikkerveer, L.J. and Titilola, S.O. (eds.) *Indigenous knowledge systems: Implications for agriculture and international development*. Studies in Technology and Social Change No.11, Iowa State University, Ames.

Conklin, H.C. 1957. Hanunoo agriculture: a report on an integral system of shifting cultivation in the Philippines. *F.A.O. Forestry Development Paper* No. 12. Rome: FAO.

Cornwall, A. & Fleming, S. 1995. Context and Complexity: Anthropological Reflections on PRA, *PLA Notes*, pp. 8-12, 24 October 1995.

Cornwall, A., Guijt, I., Welbourn, A. 1993. Acknowledging process: challenges for the agricultural research and extension methodology, *IDS Discussion Paper* 333. Brighton: Institute of Development Studies.

Cox, P.G., Shulman, A.D., Ridge, P.E., Foale, M.A. and Garside, A.L. 1995. An integrative approach to system diagnosis: an invitation to the dance *Journal for Farming Systems Research-Extension*, vol.5, no.2, pp. 67-83.

Critchley, W.R.S. 1992. *Indigenous Soil and Water Conservation — Prospects for Building on Traditions*. Overseas Division Report OD/92/12. Silsoe, UK: Silsoe Research Institute.

Critchley, W.R.S., Chris Reij, and T.J. Willcocks. 1994. Indigenous Soil and Water Conservation: A Review of the State of Knowledge and Prospects for Building on Traditions. *Land Degradation and Rehabilitation* 5: 293-314.

Croll, E. and Parkin, D. (eds.) 1992. *Bush base, forest farm: culture environment and development*. London: Routledge.

Crow, G.M., Levine, L., and Nager, N. 1992. Are Three Heads Better Than One? Reflections on Doing Collaborative Interdisciplinary Research. *Am. Educ. Res. J.*, 29(4): 737-753.

Curtis, D. 1995. Power to the People: Rethinking Community Development, in Nelson, N. and Wright, S. (eds.), *Power and Participatory Development*, pp. 115-124. London: Intermediate Technology Publications.

Cusworth, J.W. and Franks, T.R. (eds.) 1993. *Managing Projects in Developing Countries*. Harlow: Addison Wesley Longman Ltd.

Cvetkovich, A. and Kellner, D. (eds.) 1996. *Articulating the global and the local: globalization and cultural studies*. Westview Press.

Davis, Diana K. 1995. Gender-based Differences in the Ethnoveterinary Knowledge of Afghan Nomadic Pastoralists. *Indigenous Knowledge and Development Monitor* 3(1): 3-4.

Davis, Shelton H. (ed.) 1993. *Indigenous Views of Land and the Environment*. World Bank Discussion Papers, No. 188. Washington D.C.: The World Bank.

Davis, Shelton H. and K. Ebbe. (eds.) 1995. *Traditional Knowledge and Sustainable Development*. Environmentally Sustainable Development Proceedings series, No. 4. Washington D.C.: The World Bank.

de Boef, Walter, Kojo Amanor, and Kate Wellard, with Anthony Bebbington. 1993. *Cultivating Knowledge: Genetic Diversity, Farmer Experimentation and Crop Research*. London: Intermediate Technology Publications.

de Campos, P. 1991. Etudes sociolinguistiques et projets de developpement. In O. de Sardan, J-P and E. Paquot *D'un savoir a l'autre: les agents de developpment comme mediateurs*. Groupe de Recherche et d'Echanges Technologiques, Paris: Min. de la Coop. et du Develop.

de Haan, A. 1999. Social exclusion: towards a holistic understanding of deprivation. Paper for World Development Report 2001 Forum (presented Berlin Feb. 1999).

de Koning, K. 1995. Participatory Appraisal and Education For Empowerment? *PLA Notes*, pp. 34-37, 24 October 1995.

de Queiroz, J.S. and Norton, B.E. 1992. An assessment of an indigenous soil classification used in the Caatinga region of Ceara State, Northeast Brazil. *Agricultural Systems* 39: 289-305.

de Schlippe, P. 1956. *Shifting Cultivation in Africa*. London: Routledge and Kegan Paul.

den Biggelaar, Christoffel and N. Hart. 1996. *Farmer Experimentation and Innovation: A Case Study of Knowledge Generation Processes in Agroforestry Systems in Rwanda*. Rome: FAO.

den Biggelaar, Christoffel. 1991. Farming Systems Development: Synthesizing Indigenous and Scientific Knowledge Systems. *Agriculture and Human Values* 8 (1&2): 25-36.

Dennis, C. 1993. Current Issues in Development Management. pp. 217- 229. In Cusworth, J.W. and Franks, T.R. (eds.) *Managing Projects in Developing Countries*. Harlow: Longman.

Denzin, N.K., and Lincoln, Y.S. 1994. *Handbook of qualitative research*. Chapter 1. London: Sage.

DeWalt, B.R. 1994. Using indigenous knowledge to improve agriculture and natural resource management. *Human Organisation* 53(2): 123-131.

DFID, n.d. *Sustainable livelihoods guidance sheets*. http://www.dfid.gov.uk; or http:// www.ids. ac.uk.

——. 1997. *Eliminating world poverty: a challenge for the 21st century*. London: DFID.

——. 1998. *The Social Appraisal Annex for a Project Submission*. Social Development Division, London: DFID.

——. 2000. Strategies for achieving the international development target: poverty eradication and the empowerment of women (Consultation document). London: DFID.

——. 2001. Methods for consensus-building for management of common property resources. Final Technical Report. NRSP project R7562. London: DFID.

Dialla, Basga E. 1994. "The Adoption of Soil Conservation Practices in Burkina Faso". *Indigenous Knowledge and Development Monitor* 2 (1): 10-12.

Dixon P.J., Barr, J.J.F. & Sillitoe, P. 2000. Actors and rural livelihoods: integrating interdisciplinary research and local knowledge. In P. Sillitoe (ed.), *Indigenous knowledge development in Bangladesh: Present and future*, pp. 161-177. London: Intermediate Technology Publications and Dhaka: University Press Limited.

Dohrenwend, B.S., and Richardson, S.A. 1965. 'Directiveness and nondirectiveness in research interviewing: a reformulation of the problem. *Psychological Bulletin*, 63:475-485.

Douglas, M. (ed.) 1982. *Essays in the sociology of perception*. London: Routledge and Kegan Paul.

——. 1966. *Purity and danger: an analysis of concepts of pollution and taboo*. London: Routledge and Kegan Paul.

——. 1975. 'Deciphering a meal.' In Douglas, M. *Implicit meaning: essays in anthropology*. London: Routledge and Kegan Paul.

Dove, M.R. 1981. Swidden systems and their potential role in agricultural development: a case study from Kalimantan. *Prisma, Indonesia* 21: 81-100.

——. 1985. *Swidden agriculture in Indonesia: the subsistence strategies of the Kalimantan Kantu*. Berlin: Mouton.

Dupre, Georges. (ed.) 1991. *Savoirs Paysans et Developpement*. Paris: Karthala/ORSTOM.

Durkheim, E. and Mauss, M. 1963. *Primitive Classification* (trans. R. Needham). London: Cohen and West.

Dyson-Hudson, R. and N. 1969. Subsistence herding in Uganda. *Scient. Am.* 220, pp. 76-89.

Eckholm, E. 1976. *Losing ground: Environmental stress and food problems*. New York: W.W. Norton.

Edwards, M. 1994. Rethinking Social Development: The Search for Relevance. In Booth, D. (ed.) *Rethinking Social Development: Theory, Research and Practice*, pp. 279-297. Harlow: Longman.

Ellen, R., Parkes, P. and Bicker, A. (eds.) 2000. *Indigenous environmental knowledge and its transformations*. Amsterdam: Harwood.

Ellen, R.F. 1984. *Ethnographic research: A guide to general conduct.* London: Academic Press.

———. 1993. *The cultural relations of classification: an analysis of Nuaulu animal categories from Central Seram.* Cambridge: Cambridge University Press.

Ellis, F. 1998. Household strategies and rural livelihood diversification. *Journal of Development Studies*, vol.35, no.1, pp. 1-29.

Emerton, L., and Mogaka, H. 1996. Participatory environmental evaluation of forest resources in the Aberdares, Kenya. *PLA Notes*, pp. 6-10, 26 June.

Environment Council. 1998. *Working with your stakeholders: Resolving conflict and building consensus on environmental issues.* Workbook: School of Policy Studies, Bristol.

Epstein, A.L. 1961. The network and urban social organisation. *Rhodes-Livingstone Journal* 29:29-62.

Epton, S.R., Payne, R.L. and Pearson, A.W. (eds.) 1983. *Managing Interdisciplinary Research.* Wiley & Sons, Chichester.

Escobar, A. 1995. *Encountering Development. The Making and Unmaking of the Third World.* Princeton: Princeton University Press.

Evans-Pritchard, E.E. 1962. Anthropology and history. In *Essays in social anthropology.* London: Faber.

Everett, Yvonne. 1995. Forest Gardens of Highland Sri Lanka — An Indigenous System for Reclaiming Deforested Land, pp. 174-184. In *The Cultural Dimension of Development: Indigenous Knowledge Systems*, D. M. Warren, L. Jan Slikkerveer, and David Brokensha. (eds.) London: Intermediate Technology Publications.

Eyben, R. and Ladbury, S. 1995. Popular Participation in Aid-Assisted Projects: Why More in Theory than Practice? In Nelson, N. and Wright, S. (eds.) *Power and Participatory Development*, pp. 192-200. London: Intermediate Technology Publications.

Eyzaguirre, Pablo and Masa Iwanaga (eds.) 1996. *Participatory Plant Breeding.* Proceedings of a Workshop on Participatory Plant Breeding, 26-29 July 1995. Wageningen, the Netherlands. Rome: International Plant Genetic Resources Institute (IPGRI).

Fairhead, J. 1993. Representing Knowledge. The New Farmer in Research Fashions, in Pottier, J. (ed.) *Practising Development: Social Science Perspectives*, pp. 186-204. London: Routledge.

———. n.d. Indigenous technical knowledge and natural resources management in Sub-Saharan Africa: A critical overview. Natural Resources Institute, Chatham Maritime, Kent, UK.

Fairhead, J. and Leach, M. 1996. *Misreading the African landscape: society and ecology in a forest-savanna mosaic.* Cambridge: CUP.

Fals-Borda, O. and Rahman, M.A. (ed.) 1991. *Action and knowledge: breaking the monopoly with participatory action research.* London: IT Publishing.

FAO. 1989. *Farming Systems Development.* Rome: FAO.

Farrington, J. 1996. Farmers participation in research and extension: lessons from the last decade. *Tropical Agriculture Association Newsletter* 16(2): 9-15.

Farrington, J. and Martin, A. 1988. *Farmer participation in agricultural research: A review of concepts and practices.* ODA Agricultural Administration Unit Occasional Paper No. 9. London: Overseas Development Institute.

Farrington, J., Thirtle, C., and Henderson, S. 1997. Methodologies for monitoring and evaluating agricultural and natural resources research. *Agricultural systems*, vol. 55, No.2.

Fedra, K. 1995. Decision Support for Natural Resources Management: Models, GIS, and Expert Systems. *AI Applications*, 9, (3), 3-19.

Feierman, S. 1990. *Peasant Intellectuals. Anthropology and History in Tanzania.* Madison: University of Wisconsin Press.

Fergusson, J. 1994. *The anti-politics machine: 'development', depoliticization and bureaucratic power in Lesotho*. Cambridge: Cambridge University Press.

Fernandez, Maria E. 1994. Gender and Indigenous Knowledge. *Indigenous Knowledge and Development Monitor* 2 (3): 6-7.

Feyerabend, P. 1975. *Against method: outline of an anarchistic theory of knowledge*. London: Verso.

Fischer, M., Kortendick, O. and Zeitlyn, D. 1996. *The Avenir des Peoples des Fôrets Tropicales (APFT) Content Code System*. CSAC Monograph 13. Centre for Social Anthropology and Computing, University of Kent at Canterbury.

Flavier, Juan M., Antonio De Jesus and Conrado S. Navarro. 1995. The Regional Program for the Promotion of Indigenous Knowledge in Asia (REPPIKA), pp. 479-487. In *The Cultural Dimension of Development: Indigenous Knowledge Systems*. D. Michael Warren, L. Jan Slikkerveer, and David Brokensha (eds.). London: Intermediate Technology Publications.

Floyd, C.N., Lefroy, R.D.B. and D'Souza, E.J. 1988. Soil fertility and sweet potato production on volcanic ash soils in the highlands of Papua New Guinea. *Field Crops Research* 19:1-25.

Ford, R.B., Thomas-Slayter, F., Leo, C., Kabutha, N., Mageto, N., Muhia, S., Muthoka, C., Katunge. 1996. Conserving resources and increasing production: using participatory tools to monitor and evaluate community-based resource management practices. Draft Report. Clark University, Worcester and Egerton University, Kenya.

Forde, C.D. 1934. *Habitat, economy and society: a geographical introduction to ethnology*. London: Methuen.

Forsyth, T. 1996. Science, myth and knowledge: testing Himalayan environmental degradation in Thailand *Geoforum 27 (3):375-392*.

Fortes, M. 1970. The development cycle of the domestic group. In Fortes, M. *Time and social structure and other essays*. London School of Economics monographs on social anthropology No. 40. London: Athlone.

Foster, Lance M., Samuel A. Osunwole, and Bolanle W. Wahab. 1996. Imototo: Indigenous Yoruba Sanitation Knowledge Systems and their Implications for Nigerian Health Policy, pp. 26-38. In *Alaafia: Studies of Yoruba Concepts of Health and Well-Being in Nigeria* Frank Fairfax III, Bolanle Wahab, Layi Egunjobi, and D.M. Warren, (eds.) Studies in Technology and Social Change No. 25. Ames: CIKARD, Iowa State University.

Foucault, M. 1972. *The archaeology of knowledge*. London: Tavistock.

Freeman, J.D. 1955. *Iban Agriculture*. London: Stationery Office.

Freire, P. 1972. *Pedagogy of the Oppressed*. London: Sheed and Ward.

Friedman, J. 1992. *Empowerment: The Politics of Alternative Development*. Oxford: Clarendon.

Fujisaka, S. 1986. Pioneer shifting cultivation, farmer knowledge and an upland ecosystem: Co-evolution and systems sustainability in Calminoe, Philippines. *Philippine Quarterly of Culture and Society* 14: 137-164.

——. 1992. Farmer knowledge and sustainability in rice-farming systems: blending science and indigenous innovation. In J. Moock and R. Rhoades (eds.) *Diversity, farmer knowledge and sustainability*, pp. 69-83. Ithaca: Cornell University Press.

——. 1991. What Does 'Build Research on Farmer Practice' Mean? Rice Crop Establishment (*Beusani*) in Eastern India as an Illustration. *Agriculture and Human Values* 8 (1&2): 93-98.

——. 1995. Taking Farmers' Knowledge and Technology Seriously: Upland Rice Production in the Philippines, pp. 354-370. In *The Cultural Dimension of Development: Indigenous Knowledge Systems*, D. Michael Warren, L. Jan Slikkerveer, and David Brokensha. (eds.) London: Intermediate Technology Publications.

Furbee, L. 1989. A Folk Expert System: Soils Classification in the Colca Valley, Peru. *Anthropological Q.*, 62 (2), 83-102.

Gadgil, Madhav, Fikret Berkes and Carl Folke. 1993. Indigenous Knowledge for Biodiversity Conservation. *Ambio* 22 (2&3): 151-156.

Gamser, Matthew S., Helen Appleton, and Nicola Carter (eds.). 1990. *Tinker, Tiller, Technical Change*. London: Intermediate Technology Publications.

Gardner, K. & Lewis, D. 1996. *Anthropology, Development and the Post-Modern Challenge*. London: Pluto Press.

Gass, G.M., Biggs, S., and Kelly, A.P. 1995. Criteria for poverty focused rural mechanisation research and development (R&D). In Mullen, J., (ed.) *Rural Poverty Alleviation: International Development Perspectives*. Aldershot: Avebury.

Gatter, P. 1993. Anthropology in Farming Systems Research. A Participant Observer in Zambia, in Pottier, J. (ed.) *Practising Development: Social Science Perspectives*, pp. 152-186. London: Routledge.

Gell, A. 1975. *Metamorphosis of the cassowaries: Umeda society, language and ritual*. London: Athlone Press.

——. 1992. *The anthropology of time: cultural constructions of temporal maps and images*. Oxford: Providence.

Gherardi, S., and Turner, B. 1987. *Real men don't collect soft data*. Quarderno 13. Dipartimento di Politica Sociale, Universita di Trento: Italy.

Gianotten, Vera and Winfried Rijssenbeek (eds.). 1995. *Peasant Demands: Manual for Participatory Analysis*. The Hague: Ministry of Foreign Affairs.

Gill, G.J. 1991. *Seasonality and agriculture in the developing world: a problem of the poor and powerless*. Cambridge: CUP.

Giri, A. 1997. Transcending disciplinary boundaries: creative experiments and the critiques of modernity. *Madras Institute of Development Studies Working Paper* No. 150.

Gladwin, C. 1989. Indigenous knowledge systems, the cognitive revolution, and agricultural decision making. *Agriculture and Human Values* 3: 25-32.

Glaser, B.G., and Strauss, A.L. 1968. *The discovery of grounded theory: strategies for qualitative research*. Chicago: Aldine.

Gliessman, S. 1981. The ecological basis for the application of traditional technology in the management of tropical agroecosystems. *Agro-ecosystems* 7: 173-85.

Goldey, P., Martin, A., Marcus, R., and Le Breton, S. 1997. Approaches to address specific gender needs in relation to access to technological change. *Agricultural systems*, vol. 55, No.2.

Goody, J. 1995. *The expensive moment: anthropology in Britain and Africa 1918-1970*. Cambridge: Cambridge University Press.

——. 1977. *The domestication of the savage mind*. Cambridge: Cambridge University Press.

Goonatilake, S. 1999. *Toward a global science: mining civilizational knowledge*. New Delhi: Vistaar.

Gordon, A. 1997. Needs assessment: strengths, weaknesses and barriers to uptake. *Agricultural systems*, vol. 55, No.2.

Gosling, L. 1995. *Toolkits: A Practical Guide to Assessment, Monitoring and Evaluation*. London: Save the Children Fund.

Gottlieb, A. 1982. Sex, fertility and menstruation among the Beng of the Ivory Coast: a symbolic analysis. *Africa* 52 (4): 34-47.

Goulet, D. 1989. Participation in Development: New Avenues. *World Development* 17(2): 165-178.

Grandin, B.E. 1983. 'The importance of wealth effects on pastoral production: a rapid method of wealth ranking,' pp. 237-254. In *Pastoral systems research in sub-Saharan Africa*, Proceedings of the workshop held at ILCA, Addis Ababa, Ethiopia, August 1983.

Grandin, B.E. 1988. *Wealth ranking in smallholder communities: a field manual*. London: IT Publications.

Green, Edward C. 1994. *AIDS and STDs in Africa: Bridging the Gap between Traditional Healing and Modern Medicine*. Boulder: Westview Press.

——. 1996. *Indigenous Healers and the African State*. New York: Pact Publications.

——. 1997a. Is There a Basis for Modern-Traditional Cooperation in African Health Promotion? *Journal of Alternative and Complementary Medicine*, vol. 3.

——. 1997b. The Participation of African Traditional Healers in AIDS/STD Prevention Programmes. *Tropical Doctor* 27 (1): 56-59.

——. 1998. *African Theories of Contagious Disease*. Newbury Park, CA: Altamira/Sage Press.

Green, Edward C., Bonnie Pedersen, and D. Michael Warren. 1989. *Strategies for the Establishment of Cooperative Programs Involving African Traditional Healers in the Control of Diarrheal Diseases of Children*. Report for WHO. Washington D.C.: WHO *ad hoc* Working Group on Traditional Medicine and Diarrheal Disease.

Greenbaum, T.L. 1987. *The practical handbook and guide to focus group research*. Lexington MA: Lexington.

Greenland, D.J., Bowen, G., Eswaran, H., Rhoades, R. and Valentin, C. 1994. *Soil, Water and Nutrient Management Research: A New Agenda*. International Board for Soil Research and Management, Bangkok.

Grenier, L. 1998. *Working with indigenous knowledge: A guide for researchers*. Ottawa: IDRC.

Grillo, R.D. and Stirrat, R.L. (eds.) 1997. *Discourses of development: anthropological perspectives*. Oxford: Berg.

Grimble, R. 1998. *Stakeholder Methodologies in Natural Resource Management*. Socio-economic Guidelines. London: NRI.

Grimble, R. and Wellard, K. 1997. Stakeholder methodologies in natural resource management: a review of principles, contexts, experiences and opportunities. *Agricultural systems*, vol. 55, No.2.

——. n.d. Stakeholder methodologies in natural resource management: a review of principles, contexts, experiences and opportunities. Paper presented at ODA Natural Resources Systems Programme Socio-economic Methodologies Workshop.

Groenfeldt, David. 1991. Building on Tradition: Indigenous Irrigation Knowledge and Sustainable Development in Asia. *Agriculture and Human Values* 8 (1&2): 114-120.

Guarino, L. 1995. Secondary Sources on Cultures and Indigenous Knowledge Systems, pp. 195-228. In *Collecting Plant Genetic Diversity: Technical Guidelines*, L. Guarino, V. Ramanatha Rao, and R. Reid, (eds.) Wallingford, Oxon UK: CAB International on behalf of the International Plant Genetic Resources Institute in association with the FAO, IUCN, and UNEP.

Guba, E.G. 1989. *Fourth generation evaluation*. Chapters 3, 5, 6. London: Sage.

Guijt, I. 1992. The elusive poor: a wealth of ways to find them. *RRA Notes*. 15 May.

——. 1998. *Participatory monitoring and impact assessment of sustainable agricultural initiatives*. SARL discussion paper 1. London: IIED.

Guijt, I. and Cornwall, A. 1995. Editorial: Critical Reflections on the Practice of PRA. *PLA Notes* 24, pp. 2-7, October 1995.

Guijt, I. and Shah, M.K. (eds.) 1998. *The myth of community: gender issues in participatory development*. London: IT.

Guillet, D. 1989. A Knowledge-Based-Systems Model of Native Soil Management. *Anthropological Quarterly*, 62(2): 59-67.

Gujja, B., and Pimbert, M.P. 1995. Community-based planning for Wetland Management: Lessons from the Ucchali Complex in Pakistan. In *Community-based wetland management in Pakistan*. Proceedings of Workshop 3: Wetlands, Local People and Development, of the International Conference on Wetlands and Development held in Kuala Lumpur, Malaysia, 9-13 October 1995, Wetland International, pp.121-138.

Gulliver, P.H. 1955. *Social Control in an African Society*. London: Routledge and Kegan Paul.

Gunn, Anne, Goo Arlooktoo and David Kaomayok. 1988. The Contribution of the Ecological Knowledge of Inuit to Wildlife Management in the Northwest Territories, pp. 22-30. In *Traditional Knowledge and Renewable Resource Management*, Milton M.R. Freeman and Ludwig N. Carbyn (eds.). Edmonton: Boreal Institute for Northern Studies.

Gupta, A. 1992. Building upon people's ecological knowledge: framework for studying culturally embedded CPR institutions, p. 28. Ahmedabad: Centre for Management in Agriculture, Indian Institute of Management (mimeo).

——. 1995. Survival under Stress: Socioecological Perspectives on Farmers' Innovations and Risk Adjustments, pp. 407-418. In *The Cultural Dimension of Development: Indigenous Knowledge Systems*, D. Michael Warren, L. Jan Slikkerveer, and David Brokensha (eds.). London: Intermediate Technology Publications.

Gupter, A. Peasant knowledge. Who has rights to use it? In Haverkort, B., J. van der Kamp and A. Waters-Bayer (eds.) *Joining farmers' experiments. Experiences in participatory technology development*. London: Intermediate Technology Publications.

Gurung, S.M. 1989. Human perceptions of mountain hazards in the Kakani-Kathmandu area: experiences from the Middle Mountains of Nepal. *Mountain Research and Development* 9:4, pp. 353-364.

Gustafsson, Roald. 1995. *The Way We Work with Indigenous and Tribal Peoples*. INDISCO Guidelines for Extension Workers, No. 1. Geneva: Cooperative Branch, International Labour Office.

Haggart, K. (ed.) 1994. *Rivers of life*. London: PANOS.

Haile, J. 1996. Umbilical *Anthropology in Action Journal for Applied Anthropology in Theory and Practice*, vol.3, no.2, pp. 52-55.

Hailu, Z. and Runge-Metzger. 1993. *Sustainability of land use systems: The potential of indigenous measures for the maintenance of soil productivity in Sub-Saharan African agriculture*. Tropical Agroecology No. 7 Verlag Josef Margraf Scientific Books, Weikersheim, Germany.

Hall, B.L. 1981. Participatory research, popular knowledge and power: a personal reflection. *Convergence* 14 (3): 6-17.

Hall, N. (ed.) 1992. *The New Scientist guide to chaos*. London: Penguin.

Handy, C. 1985. *Understanding Organisations*. Harmondsworth: Penguin.

Hanmer, L., Pyatt, G., and White, H. 1996. *Poverty in sub-Saharan Africa: what can we learn from the World Bank's Poverty Assessments*? The Hague: Institute of Social Studies.

Hansen, A. 1988. Correcting the underestimated frequency of the head-of-household experience for women farmers. In Poats, S.V., Schmink, M., and Spring, A. (eds.) *Gender issues in farming systems research and extension*, pp. 111-26. Boulder, Colarado: Westview.

Harris, T. and Weiner, D. n.d. Community-Integrated GIS for Land Reform in Mpumalanga Province, South Africa.

Harvey, D. 1998. *Fuel use, biomass cycling and sustainability issues in a Bengali village*. MSc. thesis, Department of Agricultural and Environmental Science, University of Newcastle, UK.

Hausler, S. 1995. Listening to the people: the use of indigenous knowledge to curb environmental degradation. In Stiles, D. (ed.) *Social aspects of sustainable dryland management*. Chichester: Wiley, pp. 179-188.

Haverkort, B. and Hiemstra, W. (eds.) 1999. *Food for thought: ancient Visions and new experiments of rural People*. London: Zed.

Haverkort, B., van der Kamp, J. and Waters-Bayer, A. 1991. *Joining Farmers' Experiments*. London: Intermediate Technology Publications.

Hays, T.E. 1991. Interest, use, and interest in uses in folk biology. In A. Pawley (ed.) *Man and a half: essays in Pacific anthropology and ethnobiology in honour of Ralph Bulmer*. Auckland: Polynesian Society Memoir No. 48, pp. 109-114.

Hecht, S.B. 1989. Indigenous soil management in the Amazon Basin. Some implications for development. In Browder, J. (ed.) *Fragile Lands of Latin America Westview*, pp. 166-181. USA: Boulder Colarado.

Hecht, Susanna B. and Darrell A. Posey. 1989. Preliminary Results on Soil Management Techniques of the Kayapo Indians. *Advances in Economic Botany* 7: 174-188.

Heelas, P. and Lock, A. (ed.) 1981. *Indigenous psychologies: the anthropology of the self*. London: Academic Press.

Herbert, John. 1993. A Mail-Order Catalog of Indigenous Knowledge. *Ceres: The FAO Review* 25(5): 33-37.

Hesse-Biber, S. 1995. Unleashing Frankenstein's Monster? The use of computers in qualitative research, pp. 25-41. In Burgess, R.G. (ed.) *Computers and Qualitative Research. Studies in Qualitative Methodology*, vol. 5. London: JAI Press.

Hill, P. 1972. *Rural Hausa: a village and setting*. Cambridge: CUP.

——. 1986. *Development economics on trial: the anthropology case for the prosecution*. Cambridge: Cambridge University Press.

Himestra, Wim with Coen Reijntjes and Erik van der Werf. 1992. *Let Farmers Judge — Experiences in Assessing Agriculture Innovations*. London: Intermediate Technology Publications.

Hobart, M. (ed.). 1993. *An anthropological critique of development: the growth of ignorance*. London: Routledge.

——. 1993. Introduction: The Growth of Ignorance, in his (ed.). *An Anthropological Critique of Development: The Growth of Ignorance*, pp. 1-30. London: Routledge.

Howes, M. 1980. The use of indigenous technical knowledge in development. In Brokensha, D., Warren, D.M. and Werner, O. (eds.) *Indigenous knowledge systems and development*, pp. 323-334. Lanham: University Press of America.

Howes, M. and Chambers, R. 1980. Indigenous technical knowledge: Analysis implications and issues. In Brokensha, D., Warren, D.M. and Werner, O. (eds.) *Indigenous knowledge systems and development*, pp. 225-252. Lanham: University Press of America.

Howes, M., and Jabbar, M.A. 1986. Rural fuel histories in Bangladesh: the evidence from four villages. *IDS Discussion Paper* 213: 1-44.

Hughes, J. 1990. *The philosophy of social research*. London: Longman.

Hughes, R., Adnan, S. and Dalal-Clayton, B. 1994. *Floodplains or flood plans? A review of approaches to water management in Bangladesh*. London: IIED.

Hughes, R., and Dalal-Clayton, B. 1997. *Participation in Environmental Impact Assessment: A review of issues*. IIED Environmental Planning Issues Series No. 11.

Hunter, Phoebe R. 1994. *Language Extinction and the Status of North American Indian Languages*. Studies in Technology and Social Change, No. 23. Ames: CIKARD, Iowa State University.

Hussein, K. 1995. Participatory Ideology and Practical Development: Agency Control in a Fisheries Project, Kariba Lake. In Nelson, N & Wright, S. (eds.) *Power and Participatory Development*, pp. 170-180. London: Intermediate Technology Publications.

Hviding, Edvard and Graham B.K. Baines. 1992. *Fisheries Management in the Pacific: Tradition and the Challenges of Development in Marovo, Solomon Islands*. Discussion Paper No. 32. Geneva: United Nations Research Institute for Social Development.

ICAF. n.d. *Strategic Leadership and Decision Making*. Industrial College of the Armed Forces, National Defense University, Washington D.C. http://www.ndu.edu/ndu/inss/books/strategic/cont.html.

IDS Workshop. 1989. Interactive research, pp. 100-105. In Chambers. R., Pacey, A. and Thrupp, L.A. (eds.). Farmer First. *Farmer innovation and agricultural research*. London: Intermediate Technology Publications.

International Institute for Environment and Development (IIED). (ed.) 1993. *Rural Peoples' Knowledge, Agricultural Research and Extension Practice: Overview Papers*. IIED Research Series, vol.1, no.1. London: IIED.

——. 1995. *PLA Notes: Notes on Participatory Learning and Action* No. 22. [Formerly *RRA Notes* — Rapid Rural Appraisal.] London: IIED.

IIRR. 1996. *Recording and Using Indigenous Knowledge: A Manual*. Silang, Cavite, Philippines: REPPIKA, International Institute of Rural Reconstruction and Pact Publications, 777 United Nations Plaza, New York, NY 10017 USA.

Iliffe, J. 1979. A Modern History of Tanganyika. Cambridge: Cambridge University Press.

ILO/INDISCO. 1995. *We Evaluate ... INDISCO Partner Indigenous and Tribal Communities Evaluate their own Development Projects in India and the Philippines*. Geneva: Cooperative Branch, International Labour Office.

Indigenous Knowledge and Development Monitor 1995-2000.

Inglis, Julian T. (ed.) 1993. *Traditional Ecological Knowledge: Concepts and Cases*. Ottawa: International Program on Traditional Ecological Knowledge and International Development Research Centre.

Innis, Donald Q. 1997. *Intercropping and the Scientific Basis of Traditional Agriculture*. London: Intermediate Technology Publications.

International Board for Plant Genetic Resources. 1993. Rural Development and Local Knowledge: The Case of Rice in Sierra Leone. *Geneflow*: 12-13.

International Development Research Centre. 1993. Special Issue on Indigenous and Traditional Knowledge. *IDRC Reports* 21(1).

INTRAC. 1999. *The Participatory Approaches Learning Study*. Overview Report. London: DFID.

Ison, R.L., Maiteny, P.T. and Carr, S. 1997. Systems methodologies for sustainable natural resources research and development. *Agricultural Systems*, 55(2), pp. 257-272.

Jackson, M. 1989. *Paths towards a clearing: radical empiricism and ethnographic enquiry*. Bloomington and Indianapolis. Indiana University Press.

Jameson, F. and Miyoshi, M. (eds.) 1998. *The cultures of globalization*. Durham: Duke University Press.

Janssen, W. and Goldsworthy, P. 1996. Multidisciplinary research for natural resource management: conceptual and practical implications. *Agricultural Systems*, 51, pp. 259-279.

Jobes, K. 1997. *Participatory Monitoring and Evaluation Guidelines: Experiences in the Field. St. Vincent and the Grenadines*. Social Development Division, Dissemination Note No. 1, July. London: DFID.

Johannes, Robert E. (ed.) 1989. *Traditional Ecological Knowledge: A Collection of Essays*. Gland, Switzerland: International Union for the Conservation of Nature (IUCN).

Johnson, A.W. 1972. Individuality and Experimentation in Traditional Agriculture. *Human Ecology* 1: 149-159.

Jones, C. 1996. *PRA in Central Asia: coping with change*. Oxford: INTRAC.

Jones, S. 1994. *Agricultural Marketing Reform in Africa: Privatisation and Policy Reform* (Report to Overseas Development Administration), Oxford: Food Studies Group.

Juggins, J. 1986. Problems of understanding and communication at the interface of knowledge systems. In Poats, S., Sptring, A. and Schmink, M. (eds.) *Gender issues in farming systems research and extension*. Westview, Boulder, Colarado.

Kadappuram, John. 1990. Artificial Fishing Reef and Bait Technologies by Artisanal Fishermen of South-west India, pp. 150-176. In *Tinker, Tiller, Technical Change*, Matthew S. Gamser, Helen Appleton, and Nicola Carter, (eds.) London: Intermediate Technology Publications.

Kahn, R.L., and Cannell, C.F. 1957. *The dynamics of interviewing*. New York: Wiley.

Keat, R., and Urry, J. 1982. *Social theory as science*. London: Routledge and Kegan Paul.

Kelle, U. 1997. Theory Building in Qualitative Research and Computer Programs for the Management of Textual Data. *Sociological Research Online*, 2 (2): http://www.socresonline.org.uk/socresonline/2/2/1.html.

——. 1999. The Impact of QSR NUD*IST on research and researchers. Keynote speech at the conference: *Strategies in Qualitative Research: QSR NUD*IST software and methodological issues* held at Institute of Education, University of London on 24th February 1999.

Keller, Bonnie B. Elizabeth Chola Phiri, and Mabel C. Milimo. 1990. "Women and Agricultural Development," pp. 241-262. In *The Dynamics of Agricultural Policy and Reform in Zambia*, Adrian P. Wood, Stuart A. Kean, John T. Milimo, and D. Michael Warren, eds. Ames: Iowa State University Press.

Kennedy, A. 1985. *The Buddhist vision: an introduction to the theory and practice*. London: Rider & Co.

Kersten, S. 1996. 'Matrix ranking: a means to discussion.' *PLA Notes*, 26 June, pp. 21-25.

Khan, N.A. and Sen, S. (eds.) 2000. *Of Popular Wisdom: indigenous knowledge and practices in Bangladesh*. Dhaka: BARCIK.

Kiely, R. and Marfleet, P. 1998. *Globalisation and the third world*. London: Routledge.

Kirk, J., and Miller, M.L. 1986. *Reliability and validity of qualitative research*. Sage, Qualitative research methods series, vol.1. London: Sage Publishing.

Knorr-Cetina, K.D. 1981. *The manufacture of knowledge: an essay on the constructivist and contextual nature of science*. Oxford: Pergamon.

Kohler-Rollefson, Ilse. 1996. Traditional Management of Camel Health and Disease in North Africa and India, pp. 129-147. In *Ethnoveterinary Research and Development*, Constance M. McCorkle, Evelyn Mathias, and Tjaart W. Schillhorn van Veen. (eds.) London: Intermediate Technology Publications.

Kothari, Brij. 1995. From Oral to Written: The Documentation of Knowledge in Ecuador. *Indigenous Knowledge and Development Monitor* 3(2): 9-12.

Kothari, R. 1988. *Rethinking development: in search of humane alternatives*. Delhi: Ajanta.

Kreisler, Ann and Ladi Semali. 1997. Towards Indigenous Literacy: Science Teachers Learn to Use IK Resources. *Indigenous Knowledge and Development Monitor* 5(1): 13-15.

Kroma, Siaka. 1995. Popularizing Science Education in Developing Countries through Indigenous Knowledge. *Indigenous Knowledge and Development Monitor* 3(3): 13-15.

Krueger, R.A. 1988. *Focus groups: a practical guide for applied researchers*. Newbury Park: Sage.

Kuhn, T.S. 1962. *The structure of scientific revolutions*. Chicago: University of Chicago Press.

Kumar, K. 1987. *Rapid low cost data collection methods for A.I.D.* A.I.D. Program Design and Evaluation Methodology Report No. 10, Agency for International Development, Washington D.C., USA.

Kumar, Yogesh. 1996. Building on the *Panchayat*: Using *Jal Samitis* in Uttar Pradesh, pp. 123-131. In *Indigenous Organizations and Development*, Peter Blunt and D. Michael Warren (eds.). London: Intermediate Technology Publications.

Lambert, J.D.H. and Arnason, J.T. 1989. Role of weeds in nutrient cycling in the cropping phase of milpa agriculture in Belize, Central America. In J. proctor (ed.), Mineral nutrients in tropical forest and savanna ecosystems, pp. 301-13. Oxford: Blackwell.

Lamers, J.P.A. and Feil, P.R. 1995. Farmers' Knowledge and Management of Spatial Soil and Crop Growth Variability in Niger, West Africa. *Netherlands J. Agric. Sci.*, 43, 375-389.

Lansing, J. Stephen and James N. Kremer. 1995. A Socioecological Analysis of Balinese Water Temples, pp. 258-268. In *The Cultural Dimension of Development: Indigenous Knowledge Systems*, D.M. Warren, L. Jan Slikkerveer, and David Brokensha, eds. London: Intermediate Technology Publications.

Larson, L.E. 1976. *A History of the Mahenge (Ulanga District), 1860-1957*, Ph.D Thesis, University of dar es Salaam.

Latour, B. 1993. *We have never been modern* (trans. C. Porter). London: Harvester Wheatsheaf.

Latour, B. and S. Woolgar. 1979. *Laboratory life: the social construction of scientific facts.* Beverly Hills: Sage.

Lazarsfeld, P.F. 1972. *Qualitative analysis: historical and critical essays.* Boston: Allyn and Bacon.

Le Thanh, Nghiep. 1986. The land rotation farming system in Northern Brazil: conditions for its continuation and transition to the sedentary cultivation system. *IDCJ Working Paper Series, International Development Centre of Japan* No 34.

Leach, E. 1976. *Culture & communication: the logic by which symbols are connected: an introduction to the use of structuralist analysis in social anthropology.* Cambridge: CUP.

Lee, R.B. 1969. Kung Bushman subsistence: an input-output analysis. In A.P. Vayda (ed.). *Environment and Cultural Behavior.* Austin: University of Texas Press.

Legum, M. and Field, S. 1995. *Gender Planning.* Gender and Planning Associates (GAPA).

Leonard, D.K. 1977. *Reaching the peasant farmer: organisation theory and practice in Kenya.* Chicago: University Press.

Lévi-Strauss, C. 1966. *The savage mind.* London: Weidenfeld and Nicholson.

——. 1968. Introduction: history and anthropology. In his *Structural anthropology*, pp. 1-27. London: Allen Lane.

——. 1968. *Structural anthropology.* London: Allen Lane.

Lieberson, S. 1985. *Making it count: the improvement of social research and theory.* Berkeley: University of California Press.

Lightfoot, C., Singh, V.P., Pris, T., Mishra, P. and Salman, A. 1990. *Training resource book for farming systems diagnosis.* Manila: IRRI.

Lightfoot, C., Dalsgaard, J.P., Bimbao, M., and Fermin, F. 1993. Participatory procedures for managing and monitoring sustainable farming milestones. Journal of Asian Farming Systems Association, 2: 67-87.

Lindberg, C., Loiske, V-M., Mung'ong'o, C., and Ostberg, W. 1993. Handle with care! — rapid studies and the poor. Working paper No. 24 EDSU, School of Geography, Stockholm University, Stockholm.

Lipton, M. and R. Longhurst. 1989. *New seeds and poor people.* London: Unwin Hyman.

Lipton, M. and Maxwell, S. 1992. The new poverty agenda: an overview. *IDS Discussion Paper 306*. Brighton: IDS.

Lofchie, M. 1993. Trading Places: Economic Policy in Kenya and Tanzania. In Callaghy, T.M. and Ravenhill, J. (eds.). *Hemmed In: Responses to Africa's Economic Decline*, pp. 398-462. New York: Colombia University Press.

Lofland, J. 1971. *Analysing social settings: A guide to qualitative observation and analysis.* Belmont, CA: Wadsworth.

Long, M. and Vilareal, M. 1994. The interweaving of knowledge and power in development interfaces. In Scoones, I., Thompson, J. and Chambers, R. (eds.). *Beyond Farmer First*, pp. 41-52. London: Intermediate Technology Publications.

Long, N. and van der Ploeg, J. 1994. Heterogeneity, Actor and Structure: Towards a Reconstitution of the Concept of Structure, in Booth, D. (ed). *Rethinking Social Development: Theory, Research and Practice*, pp. 62-89. Harlow: Longman.

Long, N. (ed.). 1989. *Encounters at the interface: a perspective on social discontinuities in rural development*. Wageningse Sociologische Studies 27: Wageningen.

Long, N. and Long, A. (eds.). *Battlefields of knowledge: the interlocking of theory and practice in social research and development*. London: Routledge.

Long, N., and van der Ploeg, J.D. 1994. Heterogeneity, actor and structure: towards a reconstitution of the concept of structure. [In Booth, D. (ed.). *Rethinking social development: theory, research and practice*]. London: Longman.

Longhurst, R. (ed.). 1986. Seasonality and Poverty. *IDS Bulletin*, vol. 17, No.3, July.

Lutz, E., S. Pagiola, and C. Reiche. 1994. The Costs and Benefits of Soil Conservation: The Farmers' Viewpoint. *The World Bank Research*. Observer 9 (2): 273-295.

Maghimbi, S. 1992. The Abolition of Peasant Cooperatives and the Crisis in the Rural Economy in Tanzania. In Maghimbi, S. and Foster, P. (eds.) *The Tanzanian Peasantry: Economy in Crisis*, pp. 216-235. Harlow: Avebury.

Malik, Jitendra K., Aswin M. Thaker and Allauddin Ahmad. 1996. Ethnoveterinary Pharmacology in India: Past, Present and Future, pp. 148-157. In *Ethnoveterinary Research and Development*, Constance M. McCorkle, Evelyn Mathias, and Tjaart W. Schillhorn van Veen (eds.). London: Intermediate Technology Publications.

Malinowski, B. 1944. *A scientific theory of culture*. Chapel Hill: University of North Carolina Press.

Manikutty, S. 1997. Community Participation: So What? Evidence from a Comparative Study of Two Rural Water Supply and Sanitation Projects in India, pp. 115-140. *Development Policy Review* 15.

Mapolu, H. 1986. The State and the Peasantry, in Shivji, I. (ed.) *The State and the Working People in Tanzania*. Dakar: CODESRIA.

Margolis, M. 1988. *Mothers and such*. Berkeley: University of California Press.

Marsden, D. 1994a. Indigenous Management: Introduction, in Wright, S. (ed.) *Anthropology of Organizations*, pp. 35-40. London: Routledge.

——. 1994b. Indigenous Management and the Management of Indigenous Knowledge. In Wright, S. (ed.) *Anthropology of Organizations*, pp. 41-55. London: Routledge.

Marsden, D., Oakley, P. and Pratt, B. 1994. *Evaluating Social Development: Measuring the Process*. Oxford: INTRAC.

Martin, A. and Sherington, J. 1996. Participatory research methods: implementation, effectiveness and institutional linkages. Paper presented at ODA Natural Resources Systems Programme Socio-economic Methodologies Workshop.

——. 1997. Participatory research methods — implementation, effectiveness and institutional linkages. *Agricultural systems*, vol. 55, No.2.

Martin, Gary J. 1995. *Ethnobotany: A Methods Manual*. London: Chapman and Hall.

Mason, A. and Khandker, S. 1996. *Measuring the Opportunity Costs of Children's Time in a Developing Country. Implications for Education Sector Analysis and Interventions*. Washington: World Bank, Human Capital Development Working Papers 72.

Mathias, Evelyn. 1995. Framework for Enhancing the Use of Indigenous Knowledge. *Indigenous Knowledge and Development Monitor* 3 (2): 17-18.

——. 1996. How Can Ethnoveterinary Medicine be Used in Field Projects? *Indigenous Knowledge and Development Monitor* 4(2): 6-7.

Mathias-Mundy, Evelyn and Constance M. McCorkle. 1989. *Ethnoveterinary Medicine: An Annotated Bibliography*. Bibliographies in Technology and Social Change, No. 6. Ames: CIKARD, Iowa State University.

Mathias-Mundy, Evelyn, Olivia Muchena, Gerard McKiernan and Paul Mundy. 1992. *Indigenous Technical Knowledge of Private Tree Management: A Bibliographic Report*. Bibliographies in Technology and Social Change, No. 7. Ames: CIKARD, Iowa State University.

Maunda, Patrick. 1995. Methodology for Collecting and Sharing Indigenous Knowledge: A Case Study. *Indigenous Knowledge and Development Monitor* 3(2): 35.

Maxwell, D., Armar-Klemesu, M., Brakohapia, L., Annorbah-Sarpeil, J. 1997. Participatory concept mapping to understand perceptions of urban malnutrition *PLA Notes*. 30 October.

Maxwell, S. 1999. The meaning and measurement of poverty. *ODI poverty briefing*. London: ODI.

Mazzucato, Valentina. 1997. Indigenous Economies: Bridging the Gap between Economics and Anthropology. *Indigenous Knowledge and Development Monitor* 5(1): 3-6.

McCall, M. 1988. The implications of Eastern African rural social structure for local-level development: the case for participatory development based on indigenous knowledge systems, pp. 41-72. *Regional Rural Dialog* 9:2.

McCall, M.K. ITK in East African farming systems. *Indigenous Knowledge and Development Monitor*, vol. 4(1), pp. 20-22.

——. 1995. *Indigenous Technical Knowledge in Farming Systems of Eastern Africa: A Bibliography*. Bibliographies in Technology and Social Change, No. 9. Revised edition. Ames: CIKARD, Iowa State University.

McCorkle, C.M. 1989. Toward a knowledge of local knowledge and its importance for agricultural R.D. & E. *Agriculture and Human Values* 4, 3, 4-13.

——. 1994. *Farmer Innovation in Niger*. Studies in Technology and Social Change, No. 21. Ames, Iowa: CIKARD, Iowa State University.

McCorkle, Constance M. and Gail McClure. 1995. Farmer Know-how and Communication for Technology Transfer: CTTA in Niger, pp. 323-332. In *The Cultural Dimension of Development: Indigenous Knowledge Systems*, D. Michael Warren, L. Jan Slikkerveer, and David Brokensha (eds.). London: Intermediate Technology Publications.

McCorkle, Constance M., Evelyn Mathias, and Tjaart W. Schillhorn van Veen (eds.). 1996. *Ethnoveterinary Research and Development*. London: Intermediate Technology Publications.

McCracken, J.A., Pretty, J. and Conway, G.R. 1988. *An introduction to rapid rural appraisal for agricultural development*. London: IIED.

McGraw. K.L. 1989. *Knowledge acquisition: principles and guidelines*. Englewood Cliffs: Prentice Hall International.

McGreal, I.P. (ed.). 1995. *Great thinkers of the Eastern World: the major thinkers and philosophical and religious classics of China, India, Japan, Korea and the world of Islam*. New York: Harper Collins.

McGregor, Elizabeth (ed.). 1994. *Indigenous and Local Community Knowledge in Animal Health and Production Systems — Gender Perspectives: A Working Guide to Issues, Networks and Initiatives.* Ottawa: World Women's Veterinary Association.

Meehan, P. 1980. Science, ethnoscience and agricultural knowledge utilization. In D. Brokensha, D. Warren and O. Werner (eds.). *Indigenous knowledge systems and development*, pp. 383-92. Lanham, MD: University of Chicago Press.

Menon, Geeta. 1997. *Nature and Us: Indigenous and Tribal Peoples Guidelines on Natural Resource Management in India.* INDISCO Guidelines for Extension Workers, No. 3. Geneva: Cooperative Branch, International Labour Office.

Merton, R.K., Fiske, M., Kendall, P.L. 1956. *The focused interview.* Glencoe: Free Press.

Messerschmidt, Donald A. 1995. Local Traditions and Community Forestry Management: A View from Nepal, pp. 231-244. In *The Cultural Dimension of Development: Indigenous Knowledge Systems*, D.M. Warren, L. Jan Slikkerveer, and David Brokensha (eds.). London: Intermediate Technology Publications.

Mettrick, H. 1993. *Mobilising indigenous knowledge: development oriented research in agriculture.* The Netherlands: ICRA.

Mikkelsen, B. 1993. *Methods for development work and research: a guide for practitioners.* London: Sage.

Miles, M.B., and Huberman, A.M. 1994. *Qualitative data analysis.* Newbury Park: Sage.

Ministry of Agriculture, Water and Rural Development: Namibia. 1998. Understanding Farmers Circumstances. Method report No. 4, Proceedings of the workshop held at Oshakati. 17 September, Farming Systems Research and Extension Unit, North Central District.

Mitchell, J.C. (ed.). 1969. *Social networks in urban situations.* Manchester: Manchester University Press.

Montgomery, R.F. 1988. Some characteristics of moist savanna soils and constraints on development with particular reference to Brazil and Nigeria. *Journal of Biogeography* 15.1 11-18.

Moock, Joyce Lewinger and Robert E. Rhoades (eds.). 1992. *Diversity, Farmer Knowledge, and Sustainability.* Ithaca: Cornell University Press.

Moore, G.T. and Golledge, R.G. (eds.). 1976. *Environmental Knowing: Theories, Research and Methods.* Dowden: Hutchinson and Ross Inc. Stroudsburg, Pennsylvania.

Moore, H. and Vaughan, M. 1994. *Cutting Down Trees. Gender, Nutrition and Agricultural Change in the Northern Province of Zambia, 1890-1990.* London: James Currey.

Moore, H.L. (ed.) 1996. *The future of anthropological knowledge.* A.S.A. decennial conference series. London: Routledge.

Morgan, D.L. 1988. *Focus groups as qualitative research.* Qualitative research methods series 16. London: Sage Publications.

Morgan, D.L., and Spanish, M.T. 1984. Focus groups: a new tool for qualitative research. *Qualitative Sociology* 7, pp. 256-270.

Moris, J.R. and C.R. Hatfield a new reality: Western technology faces pastoralism in the Maasai Project. In I.R.R.I./U.N.D.P. (eds.) *The role of anthropologists and other social scientists in interdisciplinary teams developing improved food production technology.* Los Banos, Philippines.

Moris, Jon. 1991. *Extension Alternatives in Tropical Africa.* Agricultural Administration Unit, Occasional Paper 7. London: Overseas Development Institute.

Morren, G.E.B. 1986. *The Miyanmin: human ecology of a Papua New Guinea society.* Ann Arbor: UMI Research Press.

Morrison, John, Paul Geraghty, and Linda Crowl (eds.). 1994. *Science of Pacific Island Peoples*, 4 vols. Suva, Fiji: Institute of Pacific Studies, The University of the South Pacific.

Moser, C. 1989. Gender planning in the Third World: meeting practical and strategic gender needs. *World Development*, vol. 17, No. 11.

———. 1993. *Gender planning and development: theory, practice, and training.* London: Routledge.

Mosse, D. 1994. Authority, Gender and Knowledge: Theoretical Reflections on the Practice of Participatory Rural Appraisal, *Development and Change* 25, pp. 497-526.

———. 1994. Authority, gender and knowledge: theoretical reflections on the practice of participatory rural development. *PLA Notes*, 24: 27-33.

Mosse, D. *et al.* 1995. Social Analysis in Participatory Rural Development, *PLA Notes.* 24 October 1995, pp. 27-33.

Mukherjee, A. (ed.). 1995. *PRA: Methods and Applications in Rural Planning.* Vikas: New Delhi.

Muller-Boker, U. 1991. Knowledge and evaluation of environment in traditional societies of Nepal. *Mountain Research and Development* 11(2): 101-114.

Mundy, Paul A. and J. Lin Compton. 1995. Indigenous Communication and Indigenous Knowledge, pp. 112-123. In *The Cultural Dimension of Development: Indigenous Knowledge Systems*, D.M. Warren, L. Jan Slikkerveer, and David Brokensha (eds.). London: Intermediate Technology Publications.

Murdoch, J. and Clark, J. 1994. Sustainable knowledge. *Geoforum* 25:2, pp. 115-132.

Nader, L. 1996. *Anthropological Inquiry into Boundaries, Power and Knowledge.* London: Routledge.

Narayan, D. and Srinivasan, L. 1994. *Participatory Development Tool Kit: Materials to Facilitate Community Empowerment.* Washington D.C.: World Bank.

Narayanasamy, N., Dwaraka, B.R., Tamilmani, B., Ramesh, R. 1996. Whither childrens' hour? An experimental PRA among labouring rural children. *PLA Notes.* 25 February.

National Environmental Council. 1991. *Participatory rural appraisal handbook: conducting PRAs in Kenya.* Edgerton University, Clark University, CIDE of the World Resources Institute.

National Research Council. 1991. *Toward Sustainability: A Plan for Collaborative Research on Agriculture and Natural Resource Management.* Washington D.C.: National Academy Press.

———. 1992a. *Conserving Biodiversity: A Research Agenda for Development Agencies.* Washington D.C.: National Academy Press.

———. 1992b. *Neem: A Tree for Solving Global Problems.* Washington D.C.: National Academy Press.

———. 1993. *Vetiver Grass: A Thin Green Line Against Erosion.* Washington D.C.: National Academy Press.

Needham, R. 1979. *Symbolic classification.* Santa Monica, Calif.: Goodyear Publishing Company.

Nelson, N., and Wright, S. (eds.). 1995. *Power and participatory development: Theory and practice.* London: IT.

Niemeijer, David. 1996. The Dynamics of African Agricultural History: Is It Time for a New Development Paradigm? *Development and Change* 27 (1): 87-110.

Norgaard, R. 1984. Traditional agricultural knowledge: past performance, future prospects and institutional implications. *American Journal of Agricultural Economics*, 66.

Normann, Hans, Ina Snyman, and Morris Cohen (eds.). 1996. *Indigenous Knowledge and Its Uses in Southern Africa.* Pretoria: Human Sciences Research Council.

Norton, A., and Bird, B. 1998. *Social Development Crises in Sector-wide Approaches.* DFID Social Development Paper No. 1. London: DFID.

Oakland, J.S. 1995. *Total quality management.* Boston: Butterworth-Heinemann.

Oakley, P. *et al.* 1991. *Projects with People: The Practice of Participation in Rural Development.* Geneva: International Labour Office.

ODA. 1992. *Poverty reduction in developing countries.* Report of a joint ODA/IDS Workshop. London.

——. 1993. *Social Development Handbook: A Guide to Social Issues in ODA Projects and Programmes.* London.

——. 1995. *Guidance Note on how to do Stakeholder Analysis of Aid Projects and Programmes,* Social Development Division, London.

Okali, C., Sumberg, J. and Farrington, J. 1994. *Farmer participatory research.* London: Intermediate Technology Publications.

Oldfield, M.L. and Alcorn, J.B. 1987. Conservation of traditional agroecosystems: Can age-old farming practices effectively conserve crop genetic resources? *Bioscience* 37(3): 199-208.

Orlove, B.S. 1980. Ecological Anthropology. *Annual Review of Anthropology* 9: 235-273.

Ostberg, W. 1995. *Land is coming up: The Burunge of Central Tanzania and their environments.* Stockholm: Almqvist and Wiksell International.

——. 1996. Looking to the future: map drawing in Madah, central Tanzania. *PLA Notes*, pp.26-28, 26 June.

Paglau, M. 1982. Conservation of soil, water and forest in Upper Simbu valley (trans. A. Goie). In L. Morauta, J. Pernetta & W. Heaney (eds.). *Traditional conservation in Papua New Guinea: implications for today*, pp. 115-119. Waigani: IASER.

Papastergiadis, N. 1995. Restless hybrids. *Third Text* 32, pp. 9-18.

Patten, B.C. 1994. Ecological systems engineering: towards integrated management of natural and human complexity in the ecosphere. *Ecological Modelling*, 75/76, 653-665.

Patton, M.Q. 1986. *Utilisation-focused evaluation.* Beverly Hills: Sage.

——. 1990. *Qualitative research methods.* Newbury Park: Sage.

Pauly, D., M. L. D. Palomares, and R. Froese. 1993. Some Prose on a Database of Indigenous Knowledge on Fish. *Indigenous Knowledge and Development Monitor* 1 (1): 26-27.

Pawluk, Roman R., Jonathan A. Sandor, and Joseph A. Tabor. 1992. The Role of Indigenous Soil Knowledge in Agricultural Development. *Journal of Soil and Water Conservation* 47 (4): 298-302.

Peil, M. 1982. *Social science research methods: an African handbook.* London: Hodder and Stoughton.

Pelto, P.J. and Pelto, G.H. 1978. *Anthropological research: The structure of inquiry.* London Cambridge University Press.

Peters, T.J. 1982. *In search of excellence: lessons from America's best-run companies.* London: Harper & Row.

Phillips, Adedotun O. 1989. Indigenous Agricultural Knowledge Systems for Nigeria's Development: The Case of Grain Storage, pp. 31-40. In *Indigenous Knowledge Systems for Agriculture and Rural Development: The CIKARD Inaugural Lectures*, Paul Richards, L. Jan Slikkerveer, and Adedotun O. Phillips (eds.) Studies in Technology and Social Change, No. 13. Ames: CIKARD, Iowa State University.

Pickering, A. (ed.) 1992. *Science as practice and culture.* Chicago: Chicago University Press.

Pinkerton, Evelyn (ed.). 1989. *Co-operative Management of Local Fisheries: New Directions for Improved Management and Community Development.* Vancouver: University of British Columbia Press.

Pitt, D.C. 1976. *Development from below: anthropologists and development studies.* The Hague and Paris: Mouton.

Pokhrel, Durga and Anthony B.J. Willet. 1996. History of an Indigenous Community Management Organization in Nepal, pp. 109-122. In *Indigenous Organizations and Development*, Peter Blunt and D. Michael Warren (eds.). London: Intermediate Technology Publications.

Polat, Huseyin and Manuela Tomei. 1996. *The Philippines: Participatory Development Framework for Indigenous Peoples.* TSS1 Report, 2nd edition. Geneva: Cooperative Branch, International Labour Office.

Posey, D. 1990. Intellectual property rights and a just compensation for indigenous knowledge. *Anthropology Today* 6(4): 13-16.

Posey, D.A. 1983. Indigenous ecological knowledge and development of the Amazon. In Moran, E.F. (ed.) *The dilemma of Amazonian development.* Westview Press, Boulder, pp. 225-250.

——. 1983. Indigenous knowledge and development: An ideological bridge to the future. *Cienca e cultura* 35 (7): 877-894.

——. 1984. Ethnoecology as applied anthropology in Amazonian development. *Human organisation* 43(2): 95-107.

——. 1985. Management of Tropical Forest Ecosystems: The Case of the Kayapo Indians of the Brazilian Amazon. *Agroforestry Systems* 3(2): 139-158.

Posey, D.A., Dutfield, G. and Plenderleith, K. 1995. Collaborative research and intellectual property rights. *Biodiversity Conservation* 4: 892-902.

Posey, Darrell A. and Graham Dutfield. 1996. *Beyond Intellectual Property: Toward Traditional Resource Rights for Indigenous Peoples and Local Communities.* Ottawa: IDRC Books.

Pottier, J. 1993a. Introduction: Development in Practice. Assessing Social Science Perspectives, in his (ed.) *Practising Development: Social Science Perspectives*, pp. 1-12. London: Routledge.

——. 1993b. The Role of Ethnography in Project Appraisal, in his (ed.) *Practising Development: Social Science Perspectives*, pp. 13-33. London: Routledge.

Pottier, J., Bicker, A. and Sillitoe, P. (eds.) 2003. *Negotiating local knowledge: identity, power and situated practice in development intervention.* London: Pluto.

Prain, Gordon and C.P. Bagalanon (eds.). 1994. *Local Knowledge, Global Science and Plant Genetic Resources: Towards a Partnership.* Los Banos: UPWARD.

Prain, Gordon, Sam Fujisaka, and D.M. Warren (eds.). 1998. *Biological and Cultural Diversity: The Role of Indigenous Agricultural Experimentation in Development.* London: Intermediate Technology Publications.

Pretty, J., and Chamber, R. 1993. Towards a learning paradigm: new professionalism and institutions for agriculture. *IDS Paper 334.* Brighton: IDS.

Pretty, J.N. 1995. *Regenerating Agriculture: Policies and practice for sustainability and self-reliance.* London: Earthscan.

——. 1994. Participatory Learning for Sustainable Agriculture. *World Development*, 23, (8), pp. 1247-1263.

——. 1991. Farmers' Extension Practice and Technology Adaptation: Agricultural Revolution in 17th-19th Century Britain. *Agriculture and Human Values* 8 (1&2): 132-148.

Pretty, J.N., Guijt, I., Thompson, J. and Scoones, I. 1995. *Participatory Learning and Action: A Trainer's Guide.* IIED Participatory Methodology Series. Sustainable Agriculture Programme, International Institute for Environment and Development, London.

Pretty, J.N., McCracken, J.A., McCauley, D.S., and MacKie, C. 1988. *Agroecosystem analysis training in central and eastern Java, Indonesia.* London: IIED.

Pretty, J.N., Subramanian, S., Ananthakrishnan, D., Jayanthi, C., Muralikrishnasamy, S., and Renganayaki, K. 1992. Finding the poorest in a Tamil Nadu village: a sequence of mapping and wealth ranking, pp. 39-42. *RRA Notes 15.*

Price, Thomas L. 1995. Use of Local Knowledge in Managing the Niger River Fisheries Project, pp. 286-295. In *The Cultural Dimension of Development: Indigenous Knowledge Systems,*

D.M. Warren, L. Jan Slikkerveer, and David Brokensha (eds.). London: Intermediate Technology Publications.

Purcell, T.W. 1998. Indigenous knowledge and applied anthropology: questions of definition and direction. *Human Organization* 57 (3): 258-272.

Quintana, Jorge. 1992. American Indian Systems for Natural Resource Management. *Akwe kon Journal* 9 (2): 92-97.

Quiros, C. 1996. Local knowledge systems contribute to sustainable development. *Indigenous Knowledge and Development Monitor*, vol. 4(1), pp. 3-5.

Radcliffe-Brown, A.R. 1952. *Structure and function in primitive society*. London: Cohen and West.

Rahman, A.A., Haider, R., Huq, S., and Jamsen, E.G. (eds.) 1994. *Environment and development in Bangladesh*. Dhaka: The University Press Limited.

Rahnema, M. 1992 Participation, in Sachs, W. (ed.). *The Development Dictionary: A Guide to Knowledge as Power*, pp. 116-131. London: Zed.

Rajaram, G., D.C. Erbach, and D.M. Warren. 1991. "The Role of Indigenous Tillage Systems in Sustainable Food Production". *Agriculture and Human, vols.* 8 (1&2): 149-155.

Rajasekaran, B. 1991. Local soil terms and their classification in Tamil Nadu, India. Draft paper, CIKARD, Iowa State University, Ames, Iowa, USA.

Rajasekaran, B. and D. Michael Warren. 1994. IK for Socioeconomic Development and Biodiversity Conservation: The Kolli Hills. *Indigenous Knowledge and Development Monitor* 2 (2): 13-17.

——. 1995a. Indigenous Taxonomies and Decision-making Systems of Rice Farmers in South India, pp. 202-210. In *The Cultural Dimension of Development: Indigenous Knowledge Systems*, D. Michael Warren, L. Jan Slikkerveer, and David Brokensha (eds.). London: Intermediate Technology Publications.

——. 1995b. Role of Indigenous Soil Health Care Practices in Improving Soil Fertility: Evidence from South India. *Journal of Soil and Water Conservation* 50 (2): 146-149.

Rajasekaran, B. and Michael B. Whiteford. 1993. Rice-Crab Production: The Role of Indigenous Knowledge in Designing Food Security Politics. *Food Policy* 18 (3): 237-247.

Rajasekaran, B., D. Warren and S. Babu. 1991. Indigenous natural resource management systems for sustainable agricultural development — a global perspective. *Journal of International Development* 3 (1): 1-15.

——. 1991. Indigenous Natural-Resource Management Systems for Sustainable Agricultural Development — A Global Perspective. *Journal of International Development* 3 (4): 387-401.

Rajasekaran, B., Robert Martin, and D.M. Warren. 1994. A Framework for Incorporating Indigenous Knowledge Systems into Agricultural Extension Organizations for Sustainable Agricultural Development in India. *Journal of International Agricultural and Extension Education* 1(1): 25-31.

Rajasekaran, Bhakthavatsalam. 1994. *A Framework for Incorporating Indigenous Knowledge Systems into Agricultural Research, Extension and NGOs for Sustainable Agricultural Development*. Studies in Technology and Social Change, No. 22. Ames: CIKARD, Iowa State University.

Ravallion, M. 1992. *Poverty comparisons: a guide to concepts and methods*. World Bank LMS working paper No. 88. Washington: World Bank.

Ravnborg, H.M. 1990. Peasants' production systems and their knowledge of soil fertility and its maintenance: the case of Iringa District, Tanzania. *CDR Working Paper* 90/1. Copenhagen, Denmark: Centre for Development Research.

——. 1992. Resource-poor farmers: finding them and diagnosing their problems and opportunities. Proceedings of the 12th Annual Farming Systems Symposium, September pp.13-18, Michigan State University, USA.

Ravnborg, H.M. and Sano, H.O. 1994. Operationalisation of the poverty objective in development assistance. Centre for Development Working Paper, Stockholm University.

Read, D.W. and Behrens, C. 1989. Modeling Folk Knowledge as Expert Systems. *Anthropological Quarterly*, 62(2): 107-120.

Redford, K. and Padoch, C. (eds.) 1992. *Conservation of neo-tropical forests*. New York: Columbia University Press.

Reid, W.V., Laird, S.A., Meyer, C.A., Gamez, R., Sittenfeld, A., Janzen, D., Gollin, M. and Juma, C. 1993. *Biodiversity prospecting: using genetic resources for sustainable development*. Washington D.C.: World Resources Institute.

Reij, Chris. 1993. Improving Indigenous Soil and Water Conservation Techniques: Does It Work? *Indigenous Knowledge and Development Monitor* 1(1): 11-13.

Reijntjes, Coen, Bertus Haverkort and Ann Waters-Bayer. 1992. *Farming for the Future: An Introduction to Low-External-Input and Sustainable Agriculture*. Leusden: ILEIA.

Rew, A. 1992. The consolidation of British development anthropology. *Development Anthropology Network* 10, 1: 23-26.

——. 1996. *The Incorporation of Social and Cultural Factors in the Planning and Evaluation of Development Projects* papers in International Development No. 21. Centre for Development Studies Swansea University of Wales.

Reyna, S.P. 1994. Literary anthropology and the case against science. Man 29: 3, pp. 555-581.

Rhoades, R. and R. Booth. 1982. Farmer-back-to-farmer: a model for generating acceptable agricultural technology. *Agricultural Administration* 11: 127-37.

Rhoades, R., Booth, R., Shaw, R. and R. Werge. 1982. The involvement and interaction of anthropological and biological scientists in the development and transfer of post-harvest technology at CIP. In *The Role of Anthropologists and Other Social Scientists in Interdisciplinary Teams Developing Improved Food Production Technology*, pp. 1-8. Los Banos, Philippines: IRRI.

Rhoades, R.E. 1984. *Breaking new ground: Agricultural anthropology*. Lima International Potato Centre, Lima, Peru.

——. 1987. *Farmers and experimentation*. ODI Agricultural Administration (Research and Extension) Network Discussion Paper No. 21, Overseas Development Institute, London.

——. (ed.) 2001. *Bridging human and ecological landscapes: Participatory research and sustainable development in an Andean agricultural frontier*. Dubuque: Kendall/Must.

Rhoades, R.E., Horton, D.E. and Booth, R.H. 1986. Anthropologist, Biological Scientist and Economist: the Three Musketeers or Three Stooges of Farming Systems Research? pp. 21-40 in Jones, J.R. and Wallace, B.J. (eds.). *Social Sciences and Farming Systems Research: Methodological Perspectives on Agricultural Development*. Boulder: Westview Press.

Rhoades, Robert E. and Anthony Bebbington. 1995. Farmers Who Experiment: An Untapped Resource for Agricultural Research and Development, pp. 296-307. In *The Cultural Dimension of Development: Indigenous Knowledge Systems*, D. Michael Warren, L. Jan Slikkerveer and David Brokensha (eds.). London: Intermediate Technology Publications.

Richards, Paul. 1985. *Indigenous agricultural revolution*. London: Hutchinson.

——. 1986. *Coping with Hunger: Hazard and Experiment in an African Rice-farming System*. London: Allen and Unwin.

——. 1989. Doing what comes naturally: ecological inventiveness in African rice farming. In R.E. Johannes (ed.) *Traditional ecological knowledge: a collection of essays*. Cambridge: IUCN, The World Conservation Union.

——. 1989. Farmers also experiment: a neglected intellectual resource in African science. *Discovery and Innovation* 1989 1 (1): 19-25.

——. 1990. Agriculture as performance. In Chambers, R., Pacey, A. and Thrupp, L.A. (ed.). *Farmer First; farmer innovation and agricultural research*, pp. 39-42. London: IT Pubs.

——. 1993. Cultivation: Knowledge or Performance? In Hobart, M. (ed.) *An Anthropological Critique of Development: The Growth of Ignorance*, pp. 60-78. London: Routledge.

——. 1995. Participatory Rural Appraisal: a quick and dirty critique. *PLA Notes* 24: 13-16.

Riches, C.R., Shaxon, L.J., Logan, J.W.M. and Munthali, D.C. 1993. Insect and Parasite weed problems in Southern Malawi and the use of farmer knowledge in the design of control measures. In *Agric Admin Network Paper*, Vol./Part 42A, pp. 1-17.

Riley, B.W. and Brokensha, D. 1988. *The Mbeere in Kenya, vol. II. Botanical identities and uses.* Lanham: University Press of America.

Roach, Steven A. 1997. *Land Degradation and Indigenous Knowledge in a Swazi Community.* MA thesis. Ames: Department of Anthropology, Iowa State University.

Röling, N. 1988 *Extension science: information systems in agricultural development.* Cambridge: Cambridge University Press.

Röling, Niels and A. Wagemakers (eds.). 1998. *Facilitating Sustainable Agriculture: Participatory Learning and Adaptive Management in Times of Environmental Uncertainty.* Cambridge: Cambridge University Press.

Röling, Niels and Paul Engel. 1989. IKS and Knowledge Management: Utilizing Indigenous Knowledge in Institutional Knowledge Systems, pp. 101-115. In *Indigenous Knowledge Systems: Implications for Agriculture and International Development*, D.M. Warren, L. Jan Slikkerveer, and S.O. Titilola (eds.) Studies in Technology and Social Change, No. 11. Ames: CIKARD, Iowa State University.

——. 1991. The Development and Concept of Agricultural Knowledge Information Systems (AKIS): Implications for Extension, pp. 125-138. In *Agricultural Extension: Worldwide Institutional Evolution and Forces for Change*, W.M. Rivera and D.J. Gustafson (eds.). New York: Elsevier Science Publishing Company.

Roos, M., and Mohatle, M. 1998. Investigating local markets using PRA. *PLA Notes* 33 October.

Rosenthal, R., and Rubin, D.B. 1978. Interpersonal expectancy effects: The first 345 studies. *The Behavioural and Brain Sciences* 3, pp. 377-415.

Rothman, T. and Sudarshan, G. 1998. *Doubt and certainty.* London: Perseus.

RRA Notes. 1992. Special Issue on applications of wealth ranking, *RRA Notes* No.15, May.

Ruddle, Kenneth. 1994. *A Guide to the Literature on Traditional Community-Based Fishery Management in the Asia-Pacific Tropics.* FAO Fisheries Circular, No. 869. Rome: FAO.

Rundstrum, R. 1995. GIS, indigenous peoples, and epistemological diversity. *Cartography and Geographic Information Systems* 22 (1): 45-57.

Rural Advancement Fund International. 1994. *Conserving Indigenous Knowledge: Integrating Two Systems of Innovation.* New York: United Nations Development Programme.

Russell, T. 1997. Pairwise soaking made easy. *PLA Notes.* 28 February.

Rusten, E.P. and Gold, M.A. 1991. Understanding an indigenous knowledge system for tree fodder via a multi-method on-farm research approach. *Agroforestry Systems* 15: 139-165.

——. 1995. Indigenous Knowledge Systems and Agroforestry Projects in the Central Hills of Nepal, pp. 88-111. In *The Cultural Dimension of Development: Indigenous Knowledge Systems*, D.M. Warren, L. Jan Slikkerveer, and David Brokensha (eds.). London: Intermediate Technology Publications.

Sadomba, W.Z. 1996. Retrospective community mapping. *PLA Notes*, 25 February.

Sahn, D.E. (ed.). 1989. *Seasonal variability in Third World agriculture: the consequences for food security.* Baltimore: Johns Hopkins U.P.

Sands, R.G. 1993. Can You Overlap Here?: A Question for an Interdisciplinary Team. *Discourse Processes*, 16, 545-564.

Saouma, Edouard. 1993. Indigenous Knowledge and Biodiversity, pp. 4-6. In *Harvesting Nature's Diversity*. Rome: FAO.

Sardan, O. de, J-P. & E. Paquot. 1991. *D'un savoir a l'autre: les agents de development comme mediateurs*. Groupe de Recherche et d'Echanges Technologiques, Paris: Min. de la Coop. et du Develop.

Schafer, J. 1989. Utilizing indigenous agricultural knowledge in the planning of agricultural research projects designed to aid small scale farmers. In Warren D.M., Slikkerveer, L.J. and Titilola, S.O. (eds.) 1989. *Indigenous knowledge systems: Implications for agriculture and international development*. Studies in Technology and Social Change No.11, Iowa State University, Ames.

Scheuermeier, U., and Ayuk, E.T. 1997. Visualisation as a platform for entry into dialogue with farmers. *PLA Notes* 30, pp. 16-20.

Schneider, J. (ed.) 1995. *Indigenous knowledge in conservation of crop genetic resources*. International Potato Center, Indonesia.

Schoffeleers, J.M. 1979. Introduction. In J.M. Schoffeleers (ed.) *Guardians of the land: essays on central African territorial cults*. Gwelo: Zimbabwe.

Schoonmaker, Freudenberger, K. and M. 1994. Livelihoods, livestock and change: the versatility and richness of historical matrices. *RRA Notes 20*, pp. 144-148.

Schuman, H., and Presser, S. 1979. The open and closed question. *American Sociological Review*, 44: 692-712.

Scoones, I. 1995. *Investigating Difference: Applications of Wealth Ranking and Household Survey Approaches among Farming Household in Southern Zimbabwe*.

——. 1998. *Sustainable Rural Livelihoods: A Framework for Analysis*. Working Paper 72. Institute of Development Studies, University of Sussex, Brighton.

Scoones, I. and Thompson, J. 1994. Knowledge, power and agriculture: towards a theoretical understanding. In Scoones, I. and Thompson J. (eds.) *Beyond farmer first: rural people's knowledge, agricultural research and extension practice*, pp. 16-32. London: Intermediate Technology Publications.

——. 1993. Challenging the populist perspective: rural people's knowledge, agricultural research and extension practice. *IDS Discussion Paper 332*. IDS/IIED.

—— (eds.). 1994. *Beyond Farmer First: Rural People's Knowledge, Agricultural Research and Extension Practice*. London: Intermediate Technology Publications.

Scott, C.A. and Walter, M.F. 1993. Local knowledge and conventional soil science approaches to erosional processes in the Shivalik Himalaya. *Mountain Research and Development* 13:1 61-72.

Seeley J., Nabaitu, J., Taylor, L., Kajura, E., Bukenya, T., Kabunga, E., Ssembajja, F. 1996. Revealing gender differences through well-being ranking in Uganda. *PLA Notes*, 25 February.

Selener, D. 1997. *Participatory action research and social change*. Ithaca, USA: Cornell U.P.

Selener, Daniel with C. Purdy and G. Zapata. 1996. *Documenting, Evaluating and Learning from Our Development Projects: A Systematization Workbook*. New York: International Institute of Rural Reconstruction.

Sellers, T., and Westerby, M. 1996. Teenage facilitators: barriers to improving adolescent sexual health. *PLA Notes* 25, pp. 77-80. February.

Semali, L.M. & Kincheloe, J.L. 1999. *What is indigenous knowledge?: Voices from the academy*. New York: Falmer Press.

Semali, Ladislaus. 1997. Cultural Identity in African Context: Indigenous Education and Curriculum in East Africa. *Folklore Forum* 28: 3-27.

Sen, G. 1992. *Indigenous vision: peoples of India, attitudes to environment*. New Delhi: Sage.

Senge, P.M. 1993. *The fifth discipline: the art and practice of the learning organisation*. London: Century Business Press.

Serrano, Rogelio C., Romeo V. Labios, and Ly Tung. 1993. Establishing a National IK Resource Centre: The Case of PHIRCSDIK. *Indigenous Knowledge and Development Monitor* 1 (1): 5-6.

Shah, Tushaar and Michael Johnson. 1996. Informal Institutions of Financial Intermediation: Social Value of Vishis, Chit Funds and Self-Help Groups, pp. 132-142. In *Indigenous Organizations and Development*, Peter Blunt and D. Michael Warren (eds.). London: Intermediate Technology Publications.

Sharland, R.W. 1989. *Indigenous knowledge and technical change in a subsistence society: Lesson from the Moru of Sudan*. ODI Agricultural Administration (Research and Extension) Network Discussion Paper No. 9, London: Overseas Development Institute.

——. 1995. Using Indigenous Knowledge in a Subsistence Society of Sudan, pp. 385-395. In *The Cultural Dimension of Development: Indigenous Knowledge Systems*, D. Michael Warren, L. Jan Slikkerveer, and David Brokensha (eds.). London: Intermediate Technology Publications.

Shaxson, L. and Riches, C. 1998. Where there was grain to burn: a farming system in crisis in eastern Malawi. *Outlook Agr.* 27(2): 101-5.

Shiva, V. 1991. *The violence of the Green Revolution: Third World agriculture, ecology and politics*. London and New Jersey: Zed Books; Penang, Malaysia: Third World Network.

——. 1993. *Monocultures of the Mind: Perspectives on Biodiversity and Biotechnology*. London: Zed Books.

SHOGORIP. 1992. *PRA Guidelines: a manual to support PRA activities in Bangladesh*. Bangladesh: Dhaka.

Shyamsundar, P. and Lanier, G.K. 1994. Biodiversity prospecting: an effective conservation tool? *Tropical Biodiversity* 2 (3): 441-446.

Siedel, J. 1998. *Qualitative Data Analysis*. Qualis Research. (Explanation of the iterative process of qualitative data exploration in CAQDAS). http://www.qualisresearch.com/QDA.htm.

Sikana, P. 1993. Mismatched models: how farmers and scientists see soils. *ILEA Newsletter* 9 (1): 15-16.

Sillitoe, P. 1983. *Roots of the earth: crops in the highlands of Papua New Guinea*. Manchester: Manchester University Press.

——. 1994. Cultural perspectives on agricultural development: an advocacy of anthropology. *Tropical Agriculture Association Newsletter* 14:2.

——. 1996. *A place against time: land and environment in the Papua New Guinea highlands*. Amsterdam: Harwood Academic.

——. 1998. Defining Indigenous Knowledge. Paper presented at National Workshop on *The State of Indigenous Knowledge in Bangladesh*. Held by BARCIK; Dhaka, 6th-7th May 1998.

——. 1998a. The development of indigenous knowledge: a new applied anthropology. *Current Anthropology* 39 (2): 223-252.

——. 1998b. Defining indigenous knowledge: the knowledge continuum. *Indigenous Knowledge and Development Monitor* 6 (3): 14-15.

——. 1998c. Knowing the land: soil and land resource evaluation and indigenous knowledge. *Soil Use and Management* 14 (4): 188-193.

——. 2000. Introduction: the state of indigenous knowledge in Bangladesh. In P. Sillitoe (ed.) *Indigenous knowledge development in Bangladesh: Present and future*, pp. 3-20. London: Intermediate Technology Publications and Dhaka: University Press Limited.

——. 2002. Contested knowledge, contingent classification: animals in the highlands of Papua New Guinea. American Anthropologist 104 (4): 1162-1171.

Simpson, B.M. 1997. Towards a conceptual framework for understanding the structure and internal dynamics of local knowledge systems. Paper presented at Creativity and Innovation at the Grassroots Conference, Ahmedabad, January 1997.

——. 1994. Gender and the Social Differentiation of Local Knowledge. *Indigenous Knowledge and Development Monitor* 2 (3): 21-23.

Sinclair F.L. and Walker, D.H. 1998. Acquiring qualitative knowledge about complex agroecosystems Part 1 Representation as natural language. *Agricultural systems* 56 (3): 341-363.

Sinclair, F.L., Muetzelfeldt, R., Robertson, D., Haggith, M., Walker, D.H. Kendon, G. and Randell, D. 1995. *Formal Representation and Use of Indigenous Ecological Knowledge about Agroforestry*. Final Report of ODA Forestry Research Programme Project R4731.

Slaybaugh-Mitchell, Tracy L. 1995. *Indigenous Livestock Production and Husbandry: An Annotated Bibliography*. Bibliographies in Technology and Social Change, No. 8. Ames: CIKARD, Iowa State University.

Slikkerveer L. Jan and Mady K.L. Slikkerveer. 1995. Taman Obat Keluarga (TOGA): Indigenous Indonesian Medicine for Self-reliance, pp. 13-34. In *The Cultural Dimension of Development: Indigenous Knowledge Systems*, D.M. Warren, L. Jan Slikkerveer and David Brokensha (eds.). London: Intermediate Technology Publications.

Slikkerveer, L. Jan 1995. INDAKS: A Bibliography and Database on Indigenous Agricultural Knowledge Systems and Sustainable Development in the Tropics, pp. 512-516. In *The Cultural Dimension of Development: Indigenous Knowledge Systems*, D. Michael Warren, L. Jan Slikkerveer, and David Brokensha (eds.). London: Intermediate Technology Publications.

Slocum, R., Wichart, L., Rocheleau, D., Thomas-Slayter, B. 1995. *Power, Process and Participation: Tools for change*. London: Intermediate Technology Publications.

Smith, L.T. 1999. *Decolonising methodologies: research and indigenous peoples*. London: Zed Books.

Sombroek, W.G. 1979. Soils of the Amazon region and their ecological stability. *Annual Report International Soil Museum*, Wageningen, Netherlands, pp. 14-27.

Spradley, J.P. 1980. *Participant observation*. London: Holt, Reinhart and Winston.

Springle, S. 1986. Measuring social values. *Journal of consumer research*, 13, pp. 110-13.

Srinivas, Nidhi. 1996. Taking Count of the Depth of the Ditches: Understanding Local Organization Forms, Their Problems and Strategic Responses, pp. 143-157. In *Indigenous Organizations and Development*, Peter Blunt and D. Michael Warren (eds.). London: Intermediate Technology Publications.

Srinivasan, L. 1990. *Tools for Community Participation: A Manual for Gaining Gainers*. UNDP.

Stevenson, M.G. 1996. Indigenous knowledge in environmental assessment. *Arctic*, vol. 49, no.3, pp. 278-291.

Stewart, S., *et al.* 1995. *PRA: Abstracts of sources: an annotated bibliography*. Brighton: IDS.

Stirrat, R.L. 1996. Participation as a millennial movement. Paper presented in Development, Ecology and Environment session at Edinburgh University Anthropology Department's demi-centenary conference 'Boundaries and Identities'.

Sumberg, James and Christine Okali. 1997. *Farmers' Experiments: Creating Local Knowledge*. Boulder: Lynne Rienner Publishers.

Sutherland, A. 1998. *Participatory Research in Natural Resources.* DFID Socio-Economic Methodologies Best Practice Guidelines. Natural Resources Institute, University of Greenwich, Chatham Maritime.

Sutherland, A. and Martin, A.M. 1999. Institutionalising Farmer Participatory Research — Key Decisions Based on Lessons from Africa, pp. 46-65. In: Grant, I.F. and Sear, C. (eds.). *Decision Tools for Sustainable Development.* Natural Resources Institute, University of Greenwich, Chatham Maritime.

Swift, J. 1979. Notes on traditional knowledge, modern knowledge and rural development. *IDS Bulletin*, vol. 10 (2), pp. 41-43.

Syers, J.K. and Bouma, J. (eds.). 1998. *Proceeding of the Conference on Resource Management Domains.* Kuala Lumpur, 26-29 August 1996. IBSRAM Proceedings no 16. IBSRAM, Bangkok.

Systemwide Programme on Participatory Research and Gender Analysis. 1997. *A Global Programme on Participatory Research and Gender Analysis for Technology Development and Organisational Innovation.* AGREN Network Paper No. 72. London: Agricultural Research and Extension Network, UK Overseas Development Administration (ODA).

Thapa, B. 1994. Farmers' ecological knowledge about the management and use of farmland tree fodder resources in the mid-hills of Eastern Nepal. Ph.D thesis University of Wales.

Thapa, B., Sinclair, F.L. and Walker, D.H. 1995. Incorporation of indigenous knowledge and perspectives in agroforestry development, part 2. *Agroforestry Systems* 30: 249-261.

Theis, J., and Grady, H.M. 1991. *Participatory rapid appraisal for community development: A training manual based on experiences in the Middle East and North Africa.* London: IIED and Save the Children.

Thomas, D., and Danjaji M.M. 1997. Mapping change in time and space: floodplain fishing communities in Nigeria. *PLA Notes.* 30 October, pp. 29-33.

Thompson, J., Abbot, J., and Hichcliffe, F. 1996. Participation, policy and institutionalisation: an overview. *PLA Notes.* 27 October.

Thorne, P.J., Sinclair, F.L., & Walker, D.H. 1997. Using local knowledge of the feeding value of tree fodder to predict the outcomes of different supplementation strategies. *Agroforestry Forum* 8 (2), pp. 45-49.

Thrupp, L.A. 1989. Legitimizing local knowledge: 'scientized packages' or empowerment for Third World people. In Warren, D.M., Slikkerveer, L.J. and Titilola, S.O. (eds.) 1989. *Indigenous knowledge systems: Implications for agriculture and international development.* Studies in Technology and Social Change No.11, Iowa State University, Ames.

——. 1989. Legitimizing local knowledge: from displacement to empowerment for Third World people. *Agriculture and Human Values* 3: 13-25.

Thurston, H. David. 1992. *Sustainable Practices for Plant Disease Management in Traditional Farming Systems.* Boulder: Westview Press.

——. 1997. *Slash/Mulch Systems: Sustainable Methods for Tropical Agriculture.* Boulder: Westview Press and London: Intermediate Technology Publications.

Tibbetts, P. 1977. Feyerabend's Against Method: the case for methodological pluralism. *Philosophy of the Social Sciences* 7: 265-75.

Tierney, A. 1998. Studies in the anthropology of development: their relevance for social policy. *Poverty Research Unit at Sussex Working Paper*, No. 5.

Titilola, S.O. 1990. *The Economics of Incorporating Indigenous Knowledge Systems into Agricultural Development: A Model and Analytical Framework.* Studies in Technology and Social Change, No. 17. Ames: CIKARD, Iowa State University.

Tripp, R. 1985. Anthropology and On-Farm Research. *Human Organization*, vol. 44, no. 2, pp.114-124.

Ulluwishewa, R. 1993. Indigenous knowledge, National IK Resource Centers and sustainable development. *Indigenous Knowledge and Development Monitor* 1 (3): 11-13.

——. 1994. Women's Indigenous Knowledge of Water Management in Sri Lanka. *Indigenous Knowledge and Development Monitor* 2 (3): 17-19.

Ulluwishewa, Rohana and Hemanthi Ranasinghe (eds.). 1996. *Indigenous Knowledge and Sustainable Development: Proceedings of the First National Symposium on Indigenous Knowledge and Sustainable Development, Colombo, March 19-20, 1994.* Nugegoda, Sri Lanka Resource Centre for Indigenous Knowledge, University of Sri Jayewardenapura.

UNDP. 1994. *Conserving Indigenous Knowledge: Integrating two systems of innovation.* UNDP.

——. 1996. *Report on human development in Bangladesh: a pro-poor agenda. Poor people's perspectives.* Dhaka, Bangladesh: UNDP.

——. 1997. *Human Development Report.* New York: OUP.

UNESCO. 1994a. Special Issue — Traditional Knowledge in Tropical Environments. *Nature and Resources*, vol. 30, no. 1.

——. 1994b. Special Issue — Traditional Knowledge into the Twenty-First Century. *Nature and Resources*, vol. 30, no. 2.

Uphoff, N. 1992. *Learning from Gal Oya; possibilities for participatory development and post-Newtonian social science.* Ithaca, NY: Cornell University Press.

——. 1996. Understanding the world as a heterogeneous whole: insights into systems from work on irrigation. *Systems research*, vol.13, No.1, pp. 3-12.

van der Ploeg, J.D. 1989. Knowledge systems, metaphor and interface: the case of potatoes in the Peruvian Highlands. In *Encounters at the interface: A perspective on social discontinuities in rural development* (ed. N. Long) Wageningse-Sociologische-Studies-Landbouwuniversiteit-Wageningen No 27: 145-163.

van Maanen, J., Miller, M., and Johnson, J. 1982. An occupation in transition: traditional and modern forms of commercial fishing. *Work and Occupations*, 9 (2), pp. 193-216.

van Ufford, P.Q. 1988. The Hidden Crisis in Development: Development Bureaucracies in Between Intentions and Outcomes, in van Ufford, P.Q. Kruijt, D. and Downing. T. (eds.) *The Hidden Crisis in Development: Development Bureaucracies*, Amsterdam, Free University Press, pp. 9-38.

van Veldhuizen, Laurens, Ann Waters-Bayer, Ricardo Ramirez, Deb Johnson, and John Thompson (eds.). 1997. *Farmers' Experimentation in Practice: Lessons from the Field.* London: Intermediate Technology Publications.

Vayda, A.P. 1996. *Methods and explanations in the study of human actions and their environmental effects.* Jakarta: Center for International Forestry Research and World Wide Fund for Nature.

Von Liebenstein, Guus and Akke W. Tick. 1994. Indigenous Knowledge: Towards an Effective Strategy. Paper for the National Symposium on Indigenous Knowledge and Sustainable Development, Sri Lanka Indigenous Knowledge Resource Centre (SLARCIK), Colombo, 19-20 March 1994.

Von Liebenstein, Guus, L. Jan Slikkerveer, and D. Michael Warren. 1995. CIRAN: Networking for Indigenous Knowledge, pp. 441-444. In *The Cultural Dimension of Development: Indigenous Knowledge Systems*, D. Michael Warren, L. Jan Slikkerveer, and David Brokensha (eds.). London: Intermediate Technology Publications.

Wahab, Waheed Bolanle. 1997. *The Traditional Compound and Sustainable Housing in Yorubaland, Nigeria: A Case Study of Iseyin.* Ph.D dissertation. Edinburgh: Department of Architecture, Heriot-Watt University.

Walker, D.H. and Sinclair, F.L. 1998. Acquiring Qualitative Knowledge about Complex Agroeco-systems. Part 2: Formal Representation. Agricultural Systems, 56 (3), 365-386.

Walker, D.H., Sinclair, F.L. and Kendon, G. 1995. A knowledge-based systems approach to agroforestry research and extension. AI Applications, 9 (3), 61-72.

Walker, D.H., Sinclair, F.L. and Thapa, B. 1995. Incorporation of indigenous knowledge and perspectives in agroforestry development, Part 1. *Agroforestry Systems* 30: 235-248.

Walker, D.H., Sinclair, F.L., Joshi, L. and Ambrose, B. 1997. Prospects for the use of corporate knowledge bases in the generation, management and communication of knowledge at a frontline agricultural research centre. *Agricultural Systems* 54 (3), 291-312.

Walker, D.H., Sinclair, F.L., Kendon, G., Robertson, D., Muetzelfeldt, R.I., Haggith, M. and Turner, G.S. 1994. Agroforestry knowledge toolkit: methodological guidelines, computer software and manual for AKT1 and AKT2, supporting the use of a knowledge-based systems approach in agroforestry research and extension. School of Agricultural and Forest Science, University of Wales, Bangor.

Walker, Peter J.C. 1995. Indigenous Knowledge and Famine Relief in the Horn of Africa, pp. 147-154. In *The Cultural Dimension of Development: Indigenous Knowledge Systems*, D.M. Warren, L. Jan Slikkerveer, and David Brokensha (eds.). London: Intermediate Technology Publications.

Wallman, S. (ed.). 1992. *Contemporary futures: perspectives from social anthropology*. A.S.A. Monograph 30. London: Routledge.

Wamalwa, B.N. 1989. Indigenous knowledge and natural resources Kiriro, A., C. Juma (eds.) *Gaining ground: institutional innovations in land-use management in Kenya*. Nairobi: Acts Press.

Warner, K. 1991. Shifting cultivators: local technical knowledge and natural resources management in the humid tropics. *FAO Community Forestry Note* 8. Rome: FAO.

Warner, M. and Jones, P. 1998. Assessing the need to manage conflict in community-based natural resources projects. *ODI Natural Resources perspectives*. No.35.

Warner, M., Robb, C., Mackay, A., and Brocklesby, M. 1996. Linking PRA to policy: the Conflict Analysis Framework. *PLA Notes*. 27 October, pp.42-47.

Warren, D., Slikkerveer, L. and Brokensha, D. 1995. 'Introduction' to their (eds.) *The Cultural Dimension of Development. Indigenous Knowledge Systems*. London: Intermediate Technology Publications.

Warren, D. Michael and B. Rajasekaran. 1993. Indigenous Knowledge: Putting Local Knowledge to Good Use. *International Agricultural Development* 13 (4): 8-10.

——. 1994. Using Indigenous Knowledge for Sustainable Dryland Management: A Global Perspective, pp. 193-209. In *Social Aspects of Sustainable Dryland Management*, Daniel Stiles (ed.). New York: John Wiley.

Warren, D. Michael and Jennifer Pinkston. 1997. Indigenous African Resource Management of a Tropical Rainforest Ecosystem: A Case Study of the Yoruba of Ara, Nigeria, pp. 158-189. In *Linking Social and Ecological Systems*, Fikret Berkes and Carl Folke (eds.). Cambridge: Cambridge University Press.

Warren, D. Michael and Joe D. Issachar. 1983. Strategies for Understanding and Changing Local Revenue Policies and Practices in Ghana's Decentralization Programme. *World Development* 11 (9): 835-844.

Warren, D. Michael, L. Jan Slikkerveer, and David W. Brokensha (eds.). 1995. *The Cultural Dimension of Development: Indigenous Knowledge Systems*. London: IT Publications.

Warren, D. Michael, Layi Egunjobi, and Bolanle Wahab (eds.). 1996. *Indigenous Knowledge in Education: Proceedings of a Regional Workshop on Integration of Indigenous Knowledge into Nigerian Education Curriculum*. Ibadan: Indigenous Knowledge Study Group, University of Ibadan.

——. 1997. *Studies of the Yoruba Therapeutic System in Nigeria*. Studies in Technology and Social Change, No. 28. Ames: CIKARD, Iowa State University.

Warren, D. Michael, Remi Adedokun and Akintola Omolaoye. 1996. Indigenous Organizations and Development: The Case of Ara, Nigeria, pp. 43-49. In *Indigenous Organizations and Development*, Peter Blunt and D. Michael Warren (ed.). London: Intermediate Technology Publications.

Warren, D. Michael. 1989a. Linking Scientific and Indigenous Agricultural Systems, pp. 153-170. In *The Transformation of International Agricultural Research and Development*, J. Lin Compton (ed.). Boulder: Lynne Rienner Publishers.

——. 1989b. Utilizing Indigenous Healers in National Health Delivery Systems: The Ghanaian Experiment, pp. 159-178. In *Making Our Research Useful*, John van Willigen, Barbara Rylko-Bauer, and Ann McElroy (eds.). Boulder: Westview Press.

——. 1990. *Akan Arts and Aesthetics: Elements of Change in a Ghanaian Indigenous Knowledge System*. Studies in Technology and Social Change, No. 16. Ames: CIKARD, Iowa State University.

——. 1991a. The Role of Indigenous Knowledge in Facilitating a Participatory Approach to Agricultural Extension, pp. 161-177. In *Proceedings of the International Workshop on Agricultural Knowledge Systems and the Role of Extension*, Hermann J. Tillmann, Hartmut Albrecht, Maria A. Salas, Mohan Dhamotharah, and Elke Gottschalk (eds.). Stuttgart: University of Hohenheim.

——. 1991b. *Using Indigenous Knowledge in Agricultural Development*. World Bank Discussion Papers, No. 127. Washington, D.C.: The World Bank.

——. 1992. *A Preliminary Analysis of Indigenous Soil Classification and Management Systems in Four Ecozones of Nigeria*. Ibadan: African Resource Centre for Indigenous Knowledge and the International Institute of Tropical Agriculture.

——. 1994. Indigenous Agricultural Knowledge, Technology, and Social Change, pp. 35-53. In *Sustainable Agriculture in the American Midwest*, Gregory McIsaac and William R. Edwards (eds.). Urbana: University of Illinois Press.

——. 1995a. Indigenous Knowledge, Biodiversity Conservation and Development, pp. 93-108. In *Conservation of Biodiversity in Africa: Local Initiatives and Institutional Roles*, L.A. Bennun, R.A. Aman, and S.A. Crafter (eds.). Nairobi: Centre for Biodiversity, National Museums of Kenya.

——. 1995b. Indigenous Knowledge and Sustainable Agricultural and Rural Development: Policy Issues and Strategies for the INDISCO Programme of the ILO, pp. 107-122. In *Proceedings of the INDISCO Technical Review Meeting*. Geneva: Cooperative Branch, International Labour Office.

——. 1995c. Indigenous Knowledge for Agricultural Development: A Keynote Speech. Workshop on Traditional and Modern Approaches to Natural Resource Management in Latin America, The World Bank, April 25-26, 1995.

——. 1996b. The Role of Indigenous Knowledge and Biotechnology in Sustainable Agricultural Development, pp. 6-15. In *Indigenous Knowledge and Biotechnology*. Ile-Ife, Nigeria: Indigenous Knowledge Study Group, Obafemi Awolowo University.

——. 1997. *Studies of the Yoruba Therapeutic System in Nigeria*. Studies in Technology and Social Change, No. 28. Ames: CIKARD, Iowa State University.

——. 1998. The Role of the Global Network of Indigenous Knowledge Resource Centers in the Conservation of Cultural and Biological Diversity. In Luisa Maffi (ed.) *Language, Knowledge and the Environment: The Interdependence of Cultural and Biological Diversity*.

Warren, D.M. 1989. Linking scientific and indigenous agricultural systems. In J. Lin Compton (ed.) *The transformation of international agricultural research and development*, pp. 153-70. Boulder, CO: Lynne Rienner.

Warren, D.M. and Cashman, K. 1988. *Indigenous knowledge for sustainable agriculture and rural development*. Gatekeeper Series No. SA10, Sustainable Agriculture programme, International Institute for Environment and Development, London.

Warren, D.M., G. Von Liebenstein and L. Slikkerveer. 1993. Networking for indigenous knowledge. *Indigenous Knowledge and Development Monitor* 1 (1): 2-4.

Warren, D.M., Slikkerveer, L.J. and Titilola, S.O. (eds.). 1989. *Indigenous knowledge systems: Implications for agriculture and international development*. Studies in Technology and Social Change No.11, Iowa State University, Ames.

Watters, R.F. 1971. *Shifting cultivation in Latin America*. Rome: FAO Forestry Development Paper No. 17.

Weber, R. 1985. *Basic content analysis*. Sage, Quantitative research methods series, vol. 49.

Werner, O. and Schoepfle, G.M. 1987a. *Systematic fieldwork: Foundation of ethnography and interviewing*, vol. 1. Sage Publication.

Werner, O. and Schoepfle, G.M. 1987b. *Systematic fieldwork: Ethnographic analysis and data management*, vol. 2. Sage Publication.

Whickam, T.W. 1993. Farmers ain't no fools: exploring the role of Participatory Rural Appraisal to access indigenous knowledge and enhance sustainable development research and planning: a case study, Dusun Pausan, Bali, Indonesia. M.A. thesis University of Waterloo. Ann Arbor: U.M.I., 1996.

White, H. 1995. Import Support Aid: Experiences from Tanzania and Zambia, *Development Policy Review* 13 (41-63).

Whorf, B.L., 1956. *Language, thought, and reality: selected writings of Benjamin Lee Whorf*. Edited by John B. Carroll. Institute of Technology; Wiley, Chapman & Hall.

Wignaraja, P. 1990. *Women, poverty and resources*. New Delhi: Sage.

Wilken, G.C., 1989. Transferring traditional technology: a bottom-up approach for fragile lands. In J.O. Brouder (ed.) *Fragile lands of Latin America*. Westview, Boulder, Colarado, pp 44-57. USA.

Willcocks, Theo. J. and Francis N. Gichuki (eds.). 1996. *Conserve Water to Save Soil and the Environment: Proceedings of an East African Workshop on the Evaluation of Indigenous water and Soil Conservation Technologies and the Participatory Development and Implementation of an Innovative Research and Development Methodology for the Provision of Adoptable and Sustainable Improvements*. SRI Report No. IDG/96/15. Bedford. UK: Silsoe Research Institute.

Williams, G. and McAlpine, M. 1995. The gender lens: management development for women in "developing countries". (Chapter 14 of Itzin, C., and Newman, J., *Gender, culture and organisational change*). London: Routledge.

Willmer, A. and Ketzis, J. 1998. Participatory gender resource mapping: a case study in a rural community in Honduras. *PLA Notes*. October.

Wiltgen, Beverly and Bolanle Wahab. 1997. The Influence of Alaafia on the Design and Development of Yoruba Housing: A Case Study of Ibadan and Iseyin, pp. 98-116. In *Studies of the Yoruba Therapeutic System in Nigeria*, D.M. Warren, Layi Egunjobi, and Bolanle Wahab (eds.) Studies in Technology and Social Change, No. 28. Ames: CIKARD, Iowa State University.

Winch, P. 1958. *The idea of a social science and its relation to philosophy*. London: Routledge.

Winslow, Donna. 1996. *An Annotated Bibliography of Naturalized Knowledge Systems in Canada*. Bibliographies in Technology and Social Change, No. 10. Ames: CIKARD, Iowa State University.

Wolfe, J., Bechard, C., Cizek, P. and Cole, D. 1992. Indigenous and western knowledge and resource management systems *Rural Reportings, Native Canadian Issues Series 1*. University of Guelph, Canada.

Wolff, Norma H. and Bolanle Wahab. 1995. Learning from Craft Taxonomies: Development and a Yoruba Textile Tradition. *Indigenous Knowledge and Development Monitor* 3 (3): 10-12.

Wood, A.W. and Humphreys, G.S. 1982. Traditional soil conservation in Papua New Guinea. In L. Morauta, J. Pernetta & W. Heaney (eds.). *Traditional conservation in Papua New Guinea: implications for today*, pp. 93-114. Waigani: IASER.

Wood, G.D. 1994. *Bangladesh: whose ideas, whose interests?* Dhaka: University Press Limited.

World Bank, The. 1990. *Vetiver Grass: The Hedge Against Erosion.* 3rd edition. Washington, D.C.: The World Bank.

——. 1992. *Poverty reduction handbook and operational directives.* Washington D.C.: The World Bank.

Wright, S. and Nelson, N. 1995. Participatory Research and Participant Observation: Two Incompatible Approaches, in Nelson, N. and Wright, S. (eds.) *Power and Participatory Development*, pp. 43-59. London: Intermediate Technology Publications.

——. (eds.). 1995. *Power and participatory development: theory and practice*, pp 192-200. London: Intermediate Technology Publications.

WWF. 1996. *Who holds the stick? Behaviour and attitudes in PRA.* Video. World Wide Fund for Nature: Gland, Switzerland.

Zimmerer, K.S. 1994. Local Soils Knowledge: Answering Basic Questions in Highland Bolivia, pp. 29-34, *J. Soil & Water Conservation*, January-February.

Zurick, D.N. 1990. Traditional knowledge and conservation as a basis for development in a west Nepal village. *Mountain Research and Development* 10(1): 23-33.

Index

Abbot, J., 86, 89, 128-9, 152, 241, 272

Aboyade, Ojetunji, 241

Action Aid, 144, 147-8, 192-3, 206, 209, 241

Adams, A.M., 241

Adams, William M., 241

Adedokun, Remi, 275

Adegboye, Rufus O., 242

Adnan, S., 256

adoption of interventions, 17

advance hegemonies, 8

African community, 119

Agar, M.H., 24, 26, 242

Agrawal, A., 5, 47, 234, 242

agricultural
economists, 9, 12; improvements, 208, 216; issues, 116; practices, 128; production, 121, 206, 214

agriculture, 116, 128, 207, 245-6, 248-50, 253, 255, 259, 262, 265, 268-70, 272, 276

agro-ecological
science, 15, 23; zones, 159

agro-environmental phenomena, 15

Agroforestry Knowledge Toolkit for Windows (WinAKT)
knowledge toolkit, 234-5; software, 235; type deconstruction, 67; type expert system, 65

agroforestry, 57, 235, 244, 272, 274

agronomists, 9

Ahmad, Allauddin, 260

Ahmed, Medani Mohamed M., 242

Ahmed, Z.U., 36, 43, 61, 242

Ahmed. A., 242

aid organisations, 117

Aids, 119

Akinwumi, J.A., 242

Alcorn, J.B., 264

Allan, W., 242

Altieri, M.A., 242

altruism, 34

Amanor, Kojo, 242, 249

Ambrose, B., 274

analysis tools, 28-9, 49, 67, 222

Ananthakrishnan, D., 265

Anbalagan, K., 127, 242

Andrews, K.L., 244

animal husbandry, 138

Anjaria, Jayvir, 242

Annorbah-Sarpeil, J., 261

anthropological
research, 4, 25; writing, 20

anthropologist(s), 6, 22, 24, 35-6, 39, 41-3, 45, 64-6, 68-9, 71, 88, 95-7, 110, 112, 155, 192, 233, 262, 264 academic, 110; development of, 92, 110

anthropology, 7, 12, 20-2, 33, 36-8, 42-4, 58, 63, 67, 72, 88, 92, 96, 110, 155, 157, 195, 235, 242, 245, 247, 250-3, 256, 259, 265-7, 270, 272, 274

Antweiler, C., 242

Apffell-Marglin, F., 242

Appleton, Helen E., 242, 244, 253, 258

appropriate
alternative, 18; methodologies, 18, 26

Arce, A., 242

Ardener, E., 156, 242

Ardener, S., 155, 242

Arlooktoo, Goo, 255

Armar-Klemesu, M., 261

Arnason, J.T., 259

Arnstein, S.R., 11, 16, 242

Ashby, Jacqueline A., 243

Ashley, C., 85, 237, 243

Atkinson, P., 248

Atran, S., 243

Atte, Oluwayomi David, 243

Aumeeruddy, Yildiz, 243

Axelrod, M.D., 182, 184, 243

Ayuk, E.T., 269

Babu, S., 266

Babu, Suresh Chandra, 243

Bagalanon, C.P., 265

Bain, G., 243

Baines, Graham B.K., 257

Bangladesh Resource Centre for Indigenous Knowledge (BARCIK), 239, 258, 270

Bangladesh, 1, 19, 36, 40, 44-5, 105, 107, 117, 121, 132-3, 136, 141, 145, 149, 205-10, 214,

218, 221, 226, 230, 232, 239, 242-4, 250, 256, 258, 266, 270-1, 273, 277; LWI project in, 183

Barker, D., 243

Barnes, B., 243

Barnes, J.A., 243

Barr, J.J.F., 120-1, 133, 182, 207, 209, 217, 219, 221, 225, 243-4, 250

Barreiro, Jose, 244

Barrow, E.G.C., 244

Basant, Rakesh, 244

Bates, R., 244

Baumann, M., 244

Bebbington, Anthony, 244, 249, 267

Bechard, C., 276

Behrens, C., 235, 267

Belbin, Meredith, 74-6, 244

Bell, J., 244

Bell, M., 244

Belshaw, D., 244

Beltran, Jorge Alonso, 243

Bentley, J., 57, 244

Berg, Trygve, 244, 254

Berkes, Fikret, 245, 253, 274

Berlin, B., 245, 249-50

Bernard, H.R., 24, 26, 98, 101, 103-4, 106-8, 245

Berry, S., 245

Bicker, A., 16, 239, 245, 250, 265

Biggs, S.D., 10-2, 17, 85, 245, 253

bioresource flow, 125, 142, 162-4

Biot, Y., 245

Bird, B., 86, 263

Bjønness, I., 245

Blaikie, P.M., 109, 245

Blaxter, M., 105, 118, 245

Bloor, D., 243

Blum, E., 245

Blunt, Peter, 245, 259, 264, 270-1, 275

Boolean-type query tools, 229

Booth, D., 114, 242, 244-5, 250, 260

Booth, R.H., 267

Boreholes, 219-20

boro season, 19

Bouma, J., 72, 76, 245, 272

Bowen, G., 254

Box, L., 246

Boyer, P., 246

brainstorming, 49, 145, 158, 178, 205, 211, 214

Brakohapia, L., 261

Brammer, H., 246

Breedlove, D.E., 245

Breslin, E.D., 115-6, 139, 148, 246

Brislin, R.W., 246

Brocklesby, M.A., 111, 117-9, 246, 274

Brokensha, David W., 3, 239, 243-4, 246, 251-2, 255-6, 259, 261-3, 266-8, 270-1, 273-4

Brookfield, H., 245-6

Brookfield, M., 246

Brosius, J.P., 246

Brown, C.H., 246

Brown, K., 245-6

Brush, Stephen B., 246

Bryant, R.L., 246

budgets
    basic, 50; pilot scale, 69

Bukenya, T., 269

Bulmer, R.N.H., 246, 256

Bunders, Joske, 246

Burkey, S., 246

Burnett, R.M., 246

Burunge, 125, 264

Cameron, J., 245

Cannell, C.F., 101, 258

Caplan, P., 247

Carney, D., 85, 237, 243, 247

Carney, Judith, 247

Carr, S., 257

Carrasco, H., 244

Carrithers, M., 155, 247

Carroll, John B., 276

Carter, Nicola, 242, 244, 253, 258

Carvalho, S., 118, 247

Cashman, K., 247, 276

Cassowary, 158

Castro, Peter, 247

cattle-droving, 146

Central Research Fund (CRF), 30

Centre for International research and Advisory Networks (CIRAN), 239, 248, 273

Centre for Rural Development and Training (CRDT), 238

Cernea, M., 247-8

Chadwick, D.J., 247

challenges to management, 72

Chamber, R., 16, 265

Chambers, Robert, 10, 39-40, 46, 48, 89-90, 99, 101, 103, 112-4, 116, 138, 143, 145, 159, 174, 176, 186, 217, 241, 243, 246-8, 256-7, 260, 268

Checkland, P.B., 110, 248

Chin, S.C., 248

Chubin, D.E., 72, 248

Cizek, P., 276

Clark, J., 252, 263

classificatory systems, 158, 192

classificatory tree, 157

Clifford, J., 248

Cochrane, G., 45, 248

coding structure, 229

Coffey, A., 224, 230, 248

Cohen, Morris, 263

Colby, B., 108, 248

Colchester, M., 248

Cole, D., 276

collective decision-making, 215-6

Collins, S., 247, 261

Collinson, Michael, 248

common
group learning, 77; illnesses, 152; pool resources, 53, 62

communication
pathways, 84; strategy, 65-6, 81, 84

community decisions, 215

Community Development Plans, 211

Comparing and Supporting Indigenous Agricultural Systems (COMPAS), 239

Compton, J. Lin, 248, 263, 275

Computer Aided Qualitative Data Analysis Software (CAQDAS), 2, 46, 52, 55, 57, 61, 63, 65, 67, 71, 81, 108, 180, 182, 225-32, 234-7, 239, 270; evaluation of, 63, 230; packages, 226; process, 227; strengths of, 232; suitability of, 232-3; weaknesses of, 232, 234

confidential interviewing techniques, 102

Conklin, H.C., 249

Conlin, Sean, 110

consultancy, 34, 69-71

consultants, 33, 43, 54, 77

Consultative Group on International Agricultural Research (CGIAR), 73-4, 247

Conway, G.R., 138, 142-3, 248, 261

coping strategies, 115-7, 144, 147, 168

Cornwall, A., 92, 100, 249, 254

cosmologies, 3

Coulter, John K., 248

Cox, P.G., 249

Critchley, W.R.S., 249

Croll, E., 246, 249

crop(s), 2, 9, 36, 39, 49, 57, 103, 114, 116, 121, 127, 137-41, 143, 147, 162, 185, 187, 189, 192-5, 199, 207, 209-10, 220-1, 229, 242, 264, 269-70

cross-cultural
epistemological problems, 19; study, 15

Crow, G.M., 232, 249

Crowl, Linda, 262

cube
axes, 59; device, 59; scenario, 60, 62-3, 65, 68-70; sub-cube, 60, 62, 69

cultural
constraints, 18; context, 14, 17, 19, 23, 33, 39-40, 47, 61-2, 64, 66-7, 130, 155, 228; environment, 14, 44; repertoire, 4, 24; tradition, 3, 4, 6, 44

Curtis, D., 249

Cusworth, J.W., 1, 249-50

Cvetkovich, A., 249

cybernetics, 95

cyclones, 144

Dalal-Clayton, B., 256

Danjaji, M.M., 170, 272

data analysis tool, 47, 67

data collection, 2, 42-3, 50, 57, 62, 65, 67-70, 85, 92, 97, 102, 111, 113, 117, 120, 122-3, 136, 165, 176, 178-9, 208, 217-8, 234, 259

Davis, Diana K., 249

Davis, Shelton H., 249

de Boef, Walter, 249

de Campos, P., 249

de Haan, A., 249

de Jesus, Antonio, 252

de Koning, K., 249

de Morode, E., 241

de Queiroz, J.S., 249

de Schlippe, P., 250

de Vries, P., 242

de, J-P., 269

deep tubewell, 121

Delius, P., 115-6, 139, 148, 246

demand-led r&d, 90

democracy, 215

den Biggelaar, Christoffel, 45, 250

Dennis, C., 31, 250

Denzin, N.K., 250

Department for International Development (DFID), 1, 20, 28, 30, 74, 108, 117, 122, 182-3, 209-11, 219, 227, 238, 241, 243-4, 246-7, 250, 257, 263, 272; guidelines, 210; projects in Bangladesh, 183; White Paper (on International Development), 85, 209, 237

Descartes, 95

development
agencies, 14, 111; barrier, 15; notion of, 7; paradigms, 8; practice, 10, 204; research, 2, 26, 158, 276; subsidiarity in, 216; two-way process, 15

DeWalt, B.R., 250

Dialla, Basga E., 250

disaster, 75, 115

Dixon, P.J., 89, 120, 208, 244-5, 250

Dohrenwend, B.S., 98, 250

Douglas, M., 88, 92, 156, 250

Dove, M.R., 250

drought(s), 144, 165, 171, 193, 196, 198

Dunn, C., 241

Dupre, Georges, 250

Durkheim, E., 250

Dutfield, Graham, 257, 265

Dwaraka, B.R., 263

Dyson-Hudson, R., 250

Ebbe, K., 249

Eckholm, E., 250

economic capital, 119

eco-systems, 22

educational facilities, 208

Edwards, M., 250, 275

Edwards, William R., 275

Egunjobi, Layi, 252, 274, 276

Electronic Development Information System (ELDIS), 240

Ellen, R.F., 250-1

Ellis, F., 139, 144, 251

Emerton, L., 222-4, 251

Emery, A.R., 239

empowerment, 8, 15, 17, 35, 86, 92, 148, 192, 234, 250, 272; debate, 15, 17; tool, 148

Engel, Paul, 268

enumerators, 35, 41, 61-2, 66, 233

Environment Council, 178, 220, 251

environmental
    constraint, 14, 199; interactions, 14; issues, 31, 57, 251; knowledge, 3, 22-3, 60, 242, 250; pollution, 15, 184; science, 6, 36, 42, 243; sustainable adaptations, 13

Epstein, A.L., 251

Epton, S.R., 71-2, 251

Erbach, D.C., 266

Escobar, A., 251

Eswaran, H., 254

ethical dilemmas, 25

ethnographic
    archive, 22; documentation, 20; enquiries, 19, 24, 230, 257; findings, 13, 20; information, 20, 108; reporting, 20; tools, 71

ethno-science investigations, 57

European development literature, 154

Evans, T.G., 241

Evans-Pritchard, E.E., 251

Everett, Yvonne, 251

exploitation, 15, 63, 113, 139, 141, 145, 205, 244; of land, 141

extension
    services, 95, 131, 133, 163, 173, 208, 216, 221; strategies, 14

Eyben, R., 251

Eyzaguirre, Pablo, 243-4, 251

factual coding, 228, 233

Fairhead, J., 97, 251

Fals-Borda, O., 184, 251

family planning, 132

famines in Africa, 115

farm walk, 47, 49, 61-2, 64, 66, 68, 70-1, 135-7

Farmer Firsts and Last (FFL), 89-90

farmer(s), 4-5, 8-12, 14, 16-8, 21, 43, 47, 50, 56, 58, 65, 79, 83, 85, 89-90, 92, 99, 103, 112, 114, 116-7, 121, 124, 135, 137, 145, 159, 161-2, 176, 185, 187, 191, 196, 205-8, 214, 227, 234, 243-4, 247, 252, 255, 259, 267-70

farmer-first, 5, 89, 92, 99, 186, 243, 246, 248, 257, 260, 268-9; approaches, 100; practitioners, 100

Farming Systems Research (FSR), 72-3, 85, 92, 94, 120, 141, 152, 163, 176, 187, 248-9, 253, 262, 267

farming
    practices, 21, 246, 264; strategies, 10; systems, 9-10, 12, 25, 50, 104, 128, 152, 162, 183, 187, 196, 209, 242, 252, 255, 258-9, 261, 270

Farnsworth, J., 241

Farrington, J., 85, 251, 264

fauna, 141

Fedra, K., 79, 251

Feierman, S., 251

Feil, P.R., 57, 259

feminism, 89

Fergusson, J., 252

Fernandez, Maria E., 252

fertiliser, 160-1, 186, 208

Feyerabend, P., 92, 252, 272

Field, S., 238, 259

financial reward, 34

Fischer, M., 235, 252

fisherman, 2, 100

fishing, 13, 35, 43, 57, 83, 100, 106, 135, 139-40, 144, 146, 172, 207-8, 213, 230, 272-3

Fiske, M., 262

Flavier, Juan M., 252

Fleming, S., 249

flood(s), 117, 144, 165, 194, 198, 207, 213-4, 256
flooding, 32, 149, 172, 185, 207, 214
floodplain, 1, 170-3, 183, 209, 244, 272
flora, 141, 234
Floyd, C.N., 252
Foale, M.A., 249
focus group(s), 49, 52, 61, 63-4, 66, 68, 70, 87, 102, 122, 127, 131, 137, 158, 162, 166, 174, 176-84, 194, 198, 205, 211, 215, 218, 227-8, 254, 258, 262; discussions, 52, 61, 63-4, 66, 68, 70, 127, 166, 180, 227
Folke, Carl, 245, 253, 274
food
  insecurity, 115, 147, 208, 211; security, 115, 154, 186, 192, 196, 208, 268
Food and Agriculture Organisation (FAO), 20, 238, 240, 249-51, 254, 256, 268-9, 274, 276
Ford, R.B., 135, 170, 202, 252
Forde, C.D., 252
forest
  products, 196, 222-4; resources, 222-4, 251
foresters, 12, 20, 139
forestry, 13, 39, 222, 235
formal
  education, 6; interview, 95, 101; schooling, 6
Forsyth, T., 252
Fortes, M., 148, 252
Foster, Lance M., 245, 247, 252, 260
Foucault, M., 92, 252
Franks, T.R., 1, 249-50
Freeman, J.D., 252, 255
Freire, P., 166, 184, 252
Friedman, J., 252
Froese, R., 264
fuel, 19, 53, 140, 159, 187, 198, 207, 256
Fujisaka, Sam, 252, 265
funding agencies, 15, 28
Furbee, L., 235, 253

Gadgil, Madhav, 253
Gamez, R., 267
Gamser, Matthew S., 242, 244, 253, 258
Gardner, K., 253
Garside, A.L., 249
Gass, G.M., 189, 253
Gatter, P., 253
Gell, A., 126, 253
generic analytical edge, 22
Geographic Information System (GIS), 127-30, 227, 251, 255, 268; approach to, 130; construction of, 130; critique of, 129; maps, 128; packages, 227; participatory, 128, 241

Geraghty, Paul, 262
Ghana, 212, 242, 274
Gherardi, S., 253
Ghildyal, B.P., 248
Ghosh, G.P., 244
Gianotten, Vera, 253
Gibson, C.C., 47, 242, 244
Gichuki, Francis N., 276
Gill, G.J., 119, 145, 253
Giri, A., 253
Gladwin, C., 253
Glaser, B.G., 94, 110, 253
Gliessman, S., 253
globalisation, 4, 21
Gold, M.A., 268
Goldey, P., 253
Goldsworthy, P., 72, 74, 76, 257
Golledge, R.G., 262
Gollin, M., 267
good governance, 161, 216
Goody, J., 253
Goonatilake, S., 253
Gordon, A., 253
Gosling, L., 238, 253
Gottlieb, A., 253
Goulet, D., 253
Gracia, Teresa, 243
Grady, H.M., 272
Grandin, B.E., 112-4, 119-23, 125, 254
graziers, 198
green revolution, 192, 270
Green, Edward C., 254
Greenbaum, T.L., 254
Greenland, D.J., 72, 254
Grenier, L., 3, 239, 254
Grillo, R.D., 254
Grimble, R., 238, 241, 254
Groenfeldt, David, 254
group discussion technique, 136, 177
group interviewing, 102
Guarino, L., 254
Guba, E.G., 254
Guerrero, Maria del Pilar, 243, 275
Guijt, I., 86, 89, 123, 135, 142, 148, 152, 169-70, 202, 238, 241, 249, 254, 265
Guillet, D., 235, 255
Gujja, B., 165, 167, 221, 255
Gulliver, P.H., 255
Gunn, Anne, 255

Gupta, A., 255
Gupter, A., 255
Gurung, S.M., 255
Gustafsson, Roald, 255

Haggart, K., 255
Haggith, M., 271, 274
Haider, R., 266
Haile, J., 255
Hailu, Z., 255
Hall, B.L., 255, 261, 276
Handy, Charles, 76, 213, 255
Hanmer, L., 118, 255
Hansen, A., 104, 255
Harding, P., 30
Harris, T., 129-30, 241, 255
Hart, N., 250
harvesting, 136, 146, 162, 185, 187, 199
Harvey, D., 140, 159, 255
Hatfield, C.R., 262
Hausler, S., 256
Haverkort, Bertus, 246, 255-6, 267
Haylor, G., 182, 243
Hays, T.E., 256
health, 1, 13, 24, 100, 105, 113, 117-8, 127, 132, 145, 166, 192, 203, 206, 208-9, 269
Hecht, Susanna B., 256
Heelas, P., 155, 256
Heisenberg Uncertainty Principle, 91
Henderson, S., 251
Herbert, John, 256
Hesse-Biber, S., 230, 256
Hichcliffe, F., 272
Hiemstra, Wim, 246, 256
Hill, Catherine L.M., 242
Hill, P., 112, 256, 260
Himestra, Wim, 256
historical tradition, 4
historical transect, 170
HIV, 119, 160
Hobart, M., 110, 242, 256, 268
Holbrook, B., 248
Holland, J., 111, 117-9, 246
Honduras, 125, 244, 276
Honey Bee, The, 239-40
honey, 224
Hoosbeek, M.R., 76, 245
Horton, D.E., 267
household
    dynamics, 115; farm-household, 9; female-headed, 104, 148

Howes, M., 238, 256
Huberman, A.M., 103, 262
Hughes, J., 89, 256
Hughes, R., 256
human behaviour, 22, 88, 104
Human Development Report, 111, 273
Humphreys, G.S., 277
hunger and abundance calendar, 147
Hunter, Phoebe R., 256
hunting, 146, 166
Huq, S., 266
Hussein, K., 257
Hviding, Edvard, 257
hybridisation, 4
HYV technologies, 155

identity issues, 44
idioms, 4, 14, 22-3, 58
Iliffe, J., 257
immigrants, 44, 124-5
income generating activities, 196
India, 127, 158, 174, 239, 242, 244, 252, 257-8, 260-2, 266, 270
Indigenous Knowledge (IK)
    component, 1, 24, 27, 29, 31-3, 46, 51-3, 59, 64-5, 68-70, 72-4, 77, 79; data collection, 49, 85; history of, 7; intelligence, 19; investigation, 1, 30-1, 73, 232; literature, 3; meaning of, 2; methodology, 1-2, 5, 7-8, 12-3, 16, 18-21, 24-5, 87, 90, 95-6, 104, 199, 211, 225, 243, 246, 248-9; methods, 33; project design, 2, 25, 48, 52-3, 58-60; projects, 2, 25, 30-1, 42, 44-5, 48, 52-4, 56, 58-60, 63, 66-9, 72, 76-7, 81, 230; research, 1, 4, 6, 12-3, 15, 18, 20-2, 24, 26; research methods, 2; studies, 2, 28-9, 31-2, 34, 36, 53, 56-8, 60-1, 64-71, 80, 84, 225, 236
Indigenous Technical Knowledge (ITK), 3, 52, 55-7, 60-1, 63-5, 67-70, 238, 244, 256, 261; descriptions, 61, 64, 68, 70; report, 52, 61, 67; research, 57; scope, 61, 68-9
INDISCO, 257
Industrial College of the Armed Forces (ICAF), 75, 257
information flow(s), 14, 66, 73, 83
Inglis, Julian T., 257
Innis, Donald Q., 257
Institute of Development Studies (IDS), 74, 76, 241, 244, 247-9, 256-7, 260, 264-5, 269, 271-2; workshop, 74, 76, 257, 264
intellectual
    cultures, 5; property rights, 20, 25, 63, 248, 265; tradition, 22
intercropping pattern, 23
Interdisciplinary Research (IDR), 6, 16, 21, 45, 71-2, 74, 78-9, 209, 231, 243, 250

International Development Research Centre (IDRC), 239, 241, 254, 257, 265

International Institute for Environment and Development (IIED), 92, 238, 241, 254, 256-7, 261, 265, 269, 272, 276

International Institute of Rural Reconstruction (IIRR), 3, 98, 152, 158, 176, 203, 216, 239, 257

International Labour Organisation (ILO), 257

International NGO Training and Research Centre (INTRAC), 1, 28, 218-9, 221, 238, 257-8, 260

International Plant Genetic Resources Institute (IPGRI), 243-4, 251, 254

International Union for the Conservation of Nature (IUCN), 240-1, 243, 254, 257, 267

interpreters, 61, 63, 94, 98

interviewing techniques, 71

irrigation, 19, 25, 175, 202, 207, 213, 273

Islam, A., 244, 261

Ison, R.L., 72, 257

Issachar, Joe D., 274

Iwanaga, Masa, 243-4, 251

Jackson, C., 245

Jackson, M., 257

Jameson, F., 257

Jamsen, E.G., 266

Janssen, W., 72, 74, 76, 257

Janzen, D., 267

Java, 90, 113, 171, 265

Jayanthi, C., 265

Jiggins, J., 103, 114, 116, 176, 248

Jobes, K., 238, 257

Johannes, Robert E., 243, 257, 267

Johnson, A.W., 258

Johnson, Deb, 273

Johnson, J., 273

Johnson, Michael, 270

Jones, C., 205, 215-9, 221, 258

Jones, J.R., 267

Jones, P., 274

Jones, S., 258

Joshi, L., 274

Juggins, J., 258

Juma, C., 267, 274

Kabunga, E., 269

Kabutha, N., 252

Kadappuram, John, 258

Kadappuram, John, 258

Kahn, R.L., 101, 247, 258

Kajura, E., 269

Kaomayok, David, 255

Karthikeyan, G., 242

Katunge, C., 252

Keat, R., 89, 258

Kelle, U., 230, 234, 258

Keller, Bonnie B., 258

Kellner, D., 249

Kendall, P.L., 262, 267

Kendon, G., 271, 274

Kennedy, A., 258

Kenya, 125, 146, 167-9, 197, 201-2, 219-20, 222-4, 239, 247, 251-2, 259-60, 263, 268, 274-5

Kenyan Forest Department, 222

Kersten, S., 156, 193, 196, 198-9, 258

Ketzis, J., 125, 276

key informants, 61, 93, 101, 124, 137-8, 152, 158, 235

Khan, N.A., 258

Khandker, S., 261

Kiely, R., 258

Kincheloe, J.L., 269

kinship, 88, 131, 191

Kirk, J., 91, 109, 179, 258

Knorr-Cetina, K.D., 92, 258

knowledge
    continuum, 6, 18, 270; foreign derived, 6; global, 5; holistic, 7; interface, 14; locally derived, 6; specialised scientific, 3; syncretic, 6; systems, 3-4, 21, 55, 67, 70, 204, 234, 243, 248, 253, 256, 258, 261-2, 266, 268-9, 271-2, 276; traditions, 4-5, 7, 14-5, 22, 227; western scientific, 4, 57

Koechlin, F., 244

Kohler-Rollefson, Ilse, 258

Kothari, Brij, 258

Kothari, R., 258

Kreisler, Ann, 258

Kremer, James N., 259, 262

Kroma, Siaka, 258

Krueger, R.A., 258

Kuhn, T.S., 92, 155, 258

Kumar, K., 259

Kumar, Yogesh, 259

Labios, Romeo V., 270

labour
    allocation, 125, 146, 154; availability, 145; commitment, 153; demands, 151; migration, 146; supply, 145, 151

lactating mothers, 211-2

Ladbury, S., 251

Laird, S.A., 267

Lambert, J.D.H., 259

Lamers, J.P.A., 57, 259

land use, 138-40
    patterns, 124, 128; zones, 140

landowners, 19, 207

language ability, 33

Lanier, G.K., 270

Lansing, J. Stephen, 259

Larson, L.E., 259

Latour, B., 92, 259

layered staffing strategy, 70

Lazarsfeld, P.F., 184, 259

Le Breton, S., 253

Le Thanh, Nghiep, 259

Leach, E., 88, 156, 259

Leach, M., 97, 251

leadership qualities, 74

Lee, R.B., 259, 276

Lefroy, R.D.B., 252

Legum, M., 238, 259

Leo, C., 252

Leonard, D.K., 114, 259

Levine, L., 249

Lévi-Strauss, C., 259

Lewis, D., 253

Liebenstein, G. Von, 276

Lieberson, S., 89, 259

Lieman, M., 242

Lightfoot, C., 138, 142, 159-60, 163, 259

Lincoln, Y.S., 250

Lindberg, C., 114, 259

linguistic
    heritage, 17; labels, 156

Lipton, M., 111, 116, 259-60

livelihood(s)
    in Kenya, 135; mapping, 133-4; portfolios, 139,
    145, 152, 162-3, 208, 221; strategies, 86-7, 94,
    104, 106-7, 112, 124-7, 133, 137, 140, 144-5,
    151-2, 154, 162, 169, 183, 187, 194-5, 198-9,
    209-10, 214, 221; sustainable, 33, 36, 58, 72, 85,
    87, 107, 142, 182, 199, 209, 217, 237, 241, 243;
    systems, 139, 196, 199

livestock, 49, 94, 121, 123, 125, 127, 172, 195-6,
    207, 223, 269

local
    economy, 6, 153, 172, 206; institutions, 36;
    knowledge issues, 8; perceptions and practices,
    6, 13; politics, 35, 61, 130; resource managers,
    7; taxonomies, 156-7, 236

Lock, A., 155, 256

Lofchie, M., 260

Lofland, J., 101, 260

Logan, J.W.M., 268

logical positivism, 95

Loiske, V-M., 259

Long, A., 85, 260

Long, M., 260

Long, N., 85, 92, 242, 260, 273

Longhurst, R., 145, 238, 248, 259-60

Lovelace, G.W., 246

Lugangira, F., 245

Lukes, S., 243, 247

Lutz, E., 260

Mackay, A., 274

MacKie, C., 265

Mageto, N., 252

Maghimbi, S., 245, 247, 260

Maiteny, P.T., 257

Malik, Jitendra K., 260

Malinowski, B., 225, 260

malnutrition, 145, 211-2, 214, 261

managers, 1, 24, 26-7, 36, 217

Manikutty, S., 260

Mapolu, H., 260

Marcus, R., 253

Marfleet, P., 258

Marglin, S.A., 242

Margolis, M., 108, 260

Marsden, D., 238, 260

Marsh, J., 247

Marten, G.G., 246

Martin, A., 251, 253, 260, 272

Martin, A.M., 74, 76, 81, 272

Martin, G.G., 246,

Martin, Gary J., 24, 261

Martin, Robert, 266

Marxism, 89, 184

Masanja, P., 245

Mason, A., 261

Mathias-Mundy, Evelyn, 242, 258, 260-1

Maunda, Patrick, 261

Mauss, M., 250

Maxwell, D., 211-2, 261

Maxwell, S., 111, 113, 116, 260-1

Mazzucato, Valentina, 261

McAlpine, M., 276

McCall, M.K., 261

McCauley, D.S., 265

McClure, Gail, 261

McCorkle, Constance M., 242, 258, 260-1

McCracken, J.A., 90, 103, 113, 261, 265

McElroy, Ann, 275

McGlynn, A.A., 244

McGraw. K.L., 261

McGreal, I.P., 261

McGregor, Elizabeth, 262

McKiernan, Gerard, 261

Meehan, P., 262

Menon, Geeta, 262

Merrick, L., 242

Merton, R.K., 101, 179-81, 262

Messerschmidt, Donald A., 262

Mettrick, H., 262

Metzger, Runge, 255

Meyer, C.A., 267

micro-credit schemes, 117

Mikkelsen, B., 98, 112, 115, 148, 219, 262

Miles, M.B., 103, 262

Milimo, Mabel C., 258

Miller, M.L., 91, 109, 179, 258, 273

Ministry of Agriculture, 140, 262

Mishra, P., 259

Mitchell, J.C., 262

Miyoshi, M., 257

modernisation, 8, 20

Mogaka, H., 222-4, 251

Mohammed, R., 241

Mohatle, M., 134, 205, 268

mono-cropping, 162

Montgomery, R.F., 262

Moock, Joyce Lewinger, 252, 262

Moore, G.T., 262

Moore, H.L., 262

Morgan, D.L., 177-8, 182-3, 262

Moris, J.R., 262

Morren, G.E.B., 262

Morrison, John, 262

mortality, 145

Moser, C., 115, 263

Mosse, D., 263

Muchena, Olivia, 261

Muetzelfeldt, R.I., 271, 274

Muhia, S., 252

Muller-Boker, U., 263

multistage groups, 184

Mundy, Paul A., 261, 263

Munthali, D.C., 268

Muralikrishnasamy, S., 265

Murdoch, J., 263

Muslim-Bengali culture, 44

Muthoka, C., 252

mutual learning, 75, 83

Mvungi, A., 245

Mwaipopo, R., 245

Mwami, J., 245

Nabaitu, J., 269

Nader, L., 263

Nager, N., 249

Narayan, D., 263

Narayanasamy, N., 112, 242, 263

National Agricultural Research (NARS), 54, 73-4; research assistants, 54

National Environmental Council, 217, 219-20, 263

Natural Resources (NR), 1, 7, 9-10, 13-5, 17, 19, 21-3, 25, 28-39, 41-3, 45-53, 56-9, 61-74, 76-81, 85, 87, 89-90, 92-3, 97-100, 102-3, 106, 108-12, 115-6, 119-21, 124-8, 133, 138-42, 144-6, 152, 155-6, 162-5, 167, 169-70, 173-4, 178, 186, 191-2, 194, 196, 199, 201, 204, 206-8, 210-1, 213-4, 216, 218, 221, 225, 227-8, 230-3, 235-7, 244-5, 251, 254, 257, 260, 272, 274; development, 10, 29, 31, 92; project, 28, 31-4, 36, 45, 56-9, 64, 68-71, 73-4, 120, 230, 232; research, 9, 17, 29-33, 36, 43, 48, 50-3, 57-8, 67-72, 74, 80, 85, 87, 92, 97, 103, 106, 108, 110, 116, 142, 152, 162, 169, 208, 210, 227, 231; scientists, 31, 33, 35, 43, 45, 47-8, 57-8, 61, 63-4, 66-7, 79, 98, 138-9, 230-3, 236-7; staff, 43, 45-6, 65; TORs, 32; users, 17, 89-90, 93, 99-100, 108-9, 111-2, 121, 124, 126, 128, 139, 141, 152, 155, 162-3, 165, 170, 173-4, 186, 192, 194, 196, 201, 204, 206, 210, 213-4, 216, 218

Natural Resources Management (NRM), 3, 6, 9, 13, 37-9, 42-3, 57, 60, 72, 128, 163, 174, 225, 228, 244, 250-1, 254, 257, 266, 274; practice, 174; reasoning, 128, 163; thinking, 163

natural adaptive, 94; development, 136, 220; resource exploitation, 22; science, 13, 20, 24, 29, 42-3, 45, 47, 72-3, 76-7, 87, 95-6, 104, 232; scientists, 7-8, 13, 16, 20-1, 25, 45, 47, 89, 94, 98, 100, 140-1, 199, 234; springs, 220-1; squandering, 15

Natutal Resources Systems Programme-Socio-Economic Methodologies (NRSP-SEM), 1

Navarro, Conrado S., 252

Needham, R., 250, 263

Nelson, N., 248-9, 251, 257, 263, 277

Nepal, 62, 235, 245, 255, 262-4, 268, 272, 277

Niemeijer, David, 263

Nigeria, 171-2, 242, 252, 262, 264, 272-6

Non-Governmental Organisation (NGO) bodies, 216; staff, 33, 62, 66; work, 20, 35, 62, 64, 233

Norgaard, R., 263

Normann, Hans, 263
Norton, B.E., 86, 249-50, 263

Oakland, J.S., 186, 263
Oakley, P., 238, 260, 263
Objectively Verifiable Indicators (OVIs), 52-3
Okali, Christine, 264, 271
Oldfield, M.L., 264
Omolaoye, Akintola, 275
options assessment chart, 219
organic matter, 19
Orlove, B.S., 264
Ostberg, W., 124, 259, 264
Osunwole, Samuel A., 252
Overseas Development Administration (ODA), 111, 238, 245, 251, 254, 260, 264, 271-2

Pacey, A., 243, 248, 257, 268
Padoch, C., 246, 267
Pagiola, S., 260
Paglau, M., 264
Pakistan, 153, 165, 167, 255
Palmer-Jones, R., 245
Palomares, M.L.D., 264
Papastergiadis, N., 264
Papua New Guinea, 158, 246, 252, 262, 264, 270-1, 277
Paquot, E., 249, 269
Parkes, P., 250
Parkin, D., 249
Participatory Approaches Learning Study (PALS), 28-9, 257
Participatory Learning and Action (PLA), 86, 110, 151, 161, 165, 176, 178-9, 199, 215, 218, 221, 238, 241-2, 246, 248-9, 251, 254, 257-8, 261, 263-5, 268-9, 272, 274, 276
Participatory Poverty Assessments (PPAs), 115-8, 140; operation hunger, 116
Participatory Rural Appraisal (PRA), 24, 39-40, 46-8, 50, 52, 62-3, 66, 69, 71, 76, 81, 92, 94-5, 99, 101, 103, 110, 119, 122, 128, 133, 165, 167, 169-70, 173-4, 176, 197, 199, 218-20, 226-7, 234, 240-1, 247, 249, 254, 258, 263, 268, 270-1, 274, 276-7; methods, 39, 48, 52, 95; report, 52, 63; toolbox, 48, 62
participatory
    approaches, 10, 12, 20, 28, 238; collegiate methodologies, 19; methods, 10-1, 33, 63, 100, 241; video, 63, 67
Patten, B.C., 79, 264
Patton, M.Q., 94, 98, 105, 179, 264
Pauly, D., 264
Pawluk, Roman R., 264

Payne, R.L., 251
Pearson, A.W., 251
Pedersen, Bonnie, 254
Peil, M., 103, 264
Pelto, G.H., 101, 264
Pelto, P.J., 264
Peralbo, L., 244
pest(s), 2, 19, 57, 137, 195, 201, 229, 244; control, 67; management, 23
Peters, T.J., 110, 264
Philippine(s), 91, 142-3, 159, 163-4, 171, 239, 249, 252, 257, 262, 265, 267
Phillips, Adedotun O., 264
Phiri, Elizabeth Chola, 258
photographic records, 61, 68, 70
Pickering, A., 264
Pimbert, M.P., 165, 167, 221, 244, 255
Pinkerton, Evelyn, 264
Pinkston, Jennifer, 274
Pitt, D.C., 264
plant
    breeder, 194, 196; breeding, 25; rangeland plants, 156-7, 198
planting, 146, 162, 187, 207
Plenderleith, K., 265
ploughing, 146, 185, 201
Pokhrel, Durga, 264
Polat, Huseyin, 265
policymakers, 7, 12, 26, 86, 128, 173, 191
political
    constraints, 87; groupings, 124; left, 8; right, 8; socio-political issues, 8, 17
politicians, 12
poor
    farmers, 5, 8, 245, 248, 266; learning about, 87; poorest of, 111, 114, 116, 120, 123, 201, 209; pro-poor growth, 206, 216; resource-poor farmers, 10, 89, 248; very poor, 11, 48, 121
population, 3, 15, 19, 24, 48-50, 79, 85, 91, 104-6, 111-3, 115-6, 118-22, 128, 139, 145-6, 152, 156, 158, 175-6, 179-80, 183, 196-7, 204, 238; density, 175; of Bangladesh, 116
Porter, A.L., 248
Porter, C., 259
Porter, G., 241
Posey, Darrell A., 256, 265
Pottier, J., 16, 239, 245, 251, 253, 265
Poverty Reduction Strategy Papers (PRSPs), 86
poverty
    absolute poverty, 111, 115; alleviation of, 117; classifications of, 115; criteria for, 114; dynamics of, 85-6; elimination of, 209; indicators of, 117; malnutrition, 212; measure

of, 113; new agenda, 123, 260; poverty line, 113; reduction, 111, 118, 120; studies, 115

power
  brokers, 61; tiller, 187

Prain, Gordon, 265

Pratt, B., 238, 260

Presser, S., 105, 269

Pretty, J.N., 47, 75, 114, 238, 241, 261, 265

Price, Thomas L., 265

Principal Investigator (PI), 61, 77

Pris, T., 259

professionals, 9, 11, 20, 34, 72, 74, 76, 86, 90, 115, 167, 226, 247

Project Cycle Management (PCM), 1, 28-9, 31-2, 56-7, 69

project
  communication, 80; cycle, 1, 24, 28-32, 56-7, 69, 85, 195, 205; design, 3, 17, 27-8, 31, 33, 36, 52-3, 58-9, 67, 73, 152; leaders, 1, 27, 61, 77; management, 1, 19, 31, 60, 238; managers, 27, 30, 34, 52-3, 57, 59-60, 69-71, 76-8; managing projects, 27; time-bound projects, 97, 217

property regimes, 124

Purcell, T.W., 266

purdah, 44

Purdy, C., 269

Pyatt, G., 255

Quintana, Jorge, 266

Quiros, Carlos Arturo, 243, 266

Radcliffe-Brown, A.R., 266

Rahman, A.A., 266

Rahman, M.A., 184, 251

Rahman, M.M., 244

Rahnema, M., 266

Rajaram, G., 266

Rajasekaran, Bhakthavatsalam, 158, 243, 266, 274

Ramesh, R., 263

Ramirez, Ricardo, 273

Ramon, G., 244

Ranasinghe, Hemanthi, 273

Randell, D., 271

Rapid Rural Appraisal (RRA), 24, 46-7, 52, 92, 95, 99, 102, 110, 199, 238, 247, 254, 257, 261, 265, 268-9

Ravallion, M., 113, 266

Raven, P.H., 245

Ravnborg, H.M., 85, 111, 113-4, 266-7

Read, D.W., 235, 267

Reconnaissance Social Survey (RSS), 134, 136

Redford, K., 267

Redmayne, A., 245

Reiche, C., 260

Reid, W.V., 254, 267

Reij, Chris, 249, 267

Reijntjes, Coen, 256, 267

reliable
  generalisation, 22; results, 55

Renganayaki, K., 265

Research Assistants (RAs), 36, 42-3, 54-5, 67, 77

research quality, 53, 55-6

Retrospective Community Mapping (RCM), 166

Rew, A., 267

Reyna, S.P., 267

Rhoades, Robert E., 51, 76-7, 83, 186, 196, 252, 254, 262, 267

Richards, Paul, 89, 98, 174, 210, 264, 267

Richardson, S.A., 98, 250

Riches, C.R., 268, 270

Ridge, P.E., 249

Rijssenbeek, Winfried, 253

Riley, B.W., 268

Rio spirit, 19

rituals, 3, 124, 156, 245, 253

Rivers, Yolanda M., 243

Roa, Jose Ignacio, 243

Roach, Steven A., 268

Robb, C., 274

Robertson, D., 271, 274

Rocheleau, D., 271

Röling, Niels, 268

roof catchment, 219-21

Roos, M., 134, 205, 268

Rose, D., 244

Rosenthal, R., 103, 268

Rossini, F.A., 72, 248

Rothman, T., 268

Royal Botanical Gardens Kew, 239

Rubin, D.B., 103, 268

Ruddle, Kenneth, 268

Rundstrum, R., 129, 268

Russell, John F.A., 248

Russell, T., 200-1, 268

Rusten, E.P., 268

Sadomba, W.Z., 165-6, 268

Sahn, D.E., 145, 268

Salman, A., 259

Sandor, Jonathan A., 264

Sands, R.G., 12, 17, 71, 269

Sano, H.O., 113, 267

Saouma, Edouard, 269

Sardan, O., 249, 269

Schafer, J., 269

Scheuermeier, U., 269

Schneider, J., 269

Schoepfle, G.M., 24, 26, 276

Schoffeleers, J.M., 269

Scholes, J., 110, 248

Schuman, H., 105, 269

scientific
technical information, 17; technocrats, 13

Scoones, I., 36, 92, 100, 238, 241, 260, 265, 269

Scott, C.A., 269

seasonal
activities, 145; calendar matrices, 154; calendars, 62, 66, 71, 109, 147, 152, 154, 187, 219; climatic fluctuations, 144; migration of labourers, 145; pattern charts, 142, 145, 148, 152-3

sector-wide approaches, 86

seed, 186, 193, 198, 200-1, 208

Seeley, J., 119-20, 269

Seidel, John, 229

Selener, Daniel, 269

Sellers, T., 269

Semali, L.M., 269

Semali, Ladi, 258

Semali, Ladislaus, 270

Sen, G., 270

Sen, S., 258

Senegal, 168

Senge, P.M., 110, 270

Serrano, Rogelio C., 270

Sexual Health Clinic, 132

Shah, M.K., 254

Shah, Tushaar, 270

sharecroppers, 19, 207

Sharland, R.W., 270

Shaw, R., 267

Shaxon, L.J., 268

Shaxson, L., 57, 270

Sherington, J., 260

Shiva, V., 270

SHOGORIP, 270

Shore, C., 242

short time frames, 10, 21, 24, 30, 50, 56, 68-9

Shulman, A.D., 249

Shyamsundar, P., 270

sickness, 7, 117, 145-6, 151

Siedel, J., 270

Sikana, P., 270

Sillitoe, Paul, 16, 57, 61, 64, 68, 97, 158, 225, 230, 239, 242-3, 245, 250, 265, 270-1

Sinclair, F.L., 57, 234-5, 271-4

Singh, V.P., 259

Sittenfeld, A., 267

Slaybaugh-Mitchell, Tracy L., 271

Slikkerveer, L. Jan, 3, 239, 241, 243, 247-8, 251-2, 255, 259, 261-4, 266-74, 276

Slikkerveer, Mady K.L., 271

Slocum, R., 271

Smith, L.T., 271

Sneddon, D., 245

Snyman, Ina, 263

social
alienation, 15; capital, 75, 90, 115, 176; differentiation, 112, 117; indices, 90, 145; learning, 96; scientists, 8, 20-1, 35, 42-3, 64, 66, 69, 88-9, 91, 93, 100, 108, 233, 262; stratification, 114, 120; survey, 98, 103-5, 120

Social, Technical, Economic, Political Sustainability (STEPS), 189

socio
cultural change, 18; cultural tradition, 3; economic categories, 48, 137, 176

sociologist, 35, 41-2, 62, 64-5, 69, 233

soil(s), 2, 19-20, 23, 25, 29, 36, 39, 43, 45, 57, 67, 84, 98, 116, 124, 127-8, 133-5, 137-8, 140, 156, 158, 160, 162, 198, 206, 209, 228-31, 234-5, 237, 245, 249, 252, 255-6, 262, 264, 266, 269-70, 277; erosion, 25, 57, 137, 228, 230, 245; fertility, 19, 23, 230, 266; management, 67, 98, 209, 256; scientists, 19-20, 45, 84, 234

Sombroek, W.G., 271

South Africa, 115-6, 128-9, 246, 255

Spanish, M.T., 182, 262

Spradley, J.P., 24, 26, 271

Springle, S., 108, 271

Srinivas, Nidhi, 271

Srinivasan, L., 263, 271

Ssembajja, F., 269

Stabinsky, Doreen, 246

staff types, 36, 55, 67, 69, 71

stakeholder(s), 1, 10, 16, 19, 21, 28, 47, 85-7, 90, 93, 95, 105, 110, 120, 131-3, 136, 148, 152, 158-61, 170, 176-9, 184-5, 187, 189, 192-3, 199-201, 204-10, 214-9, 221, 228, 233, 237, 251

standard of living, 7, 112

starvation, 7

Statistical Services Centre (SSC), 108, 241

Stevenson, M.G., 271

Stiles, Daniel, 274

Stirrat, R.L., 254, 271

Stocking, M., 245

STRAP
framework, 72-3; scores, 74

Strauss, A.L., 94, 110, 253

Strengths, Weaknesses, Opportunities and Threats (SWOT), 36

Strengths, Weaknesses, Opportunities, and Constraints (SWOC), 36-7, 137, 185, 188-90; analysis, 36, 188-90; matrix, 36-7

structured interview, 11, 61, 64, 68, 70, 96, 98-9, 101, 103, 109-10, 143, 165, 196, 214, 227

Subramanian, S., 265

Sudarshan, G., 268

Sumberg, James, 264, 271

survey questionnaires, 91, 105-6, 179, 184

sustainable interventions, 13

Sutherland, A., 50, 74, 76, 81, 272

Swedish International Development Cooperation Agency (SIDA), 114, 245

Swift, J., 272

Syers, J.K., 72, 272

Sylhet, 44

Tabor, Joseph A., 264

Tamil Nadu, 158, 265-6

Tamilmani, B., 263

Tang, L., 245

tanning industry, 127

Tanzania, 114, 117, 124, 126, 245, 251, 260, 264, 266, 276; Ngorogoro Conservation Area in, 63

taxonomy(ies), 49, 62-3, 66, 88, 94, 130, 154-6, 158, 192, 195, 211, 246, 266, 277; of soil types, 63

Taylor, L., 269

team
communication, 30, 47, 76-81; leader, 50, 65, 78, 83; management, 33, 71-3, 78

technically focused data, 50

technological
adaptations, 15; alternatives, 11, 14; interventions, 10, 102; possibilities, 11; solutions, 14, 186

technology
database of, 20; participative technology analysis, 62, 66, 187; shift, 187; transfer of, 5, 8, 10, 20, 97, 103, 186, 201

Terms of Reference (TORs), 32-3, 67

Thaker, Aswin M., 260

Thapa, B., 160, 272, 274

Theis, J., 272

Thirtle, C., 251

Thomas, D., 170, 272

Thomas-Slayter, B., 271

Thomas-Slayter, F., 252

Thompson, John, 92, 100, 118-9, 238, 241, 260, 265, 269, 272-3

Thorne, P.J., 57, 272

Thrupp, Lori Ann, 243, 248, 257, 268, 272

Thurston, H. David, 272

Tibbetts, P., 272

Tick, Akke W., 273

Tierney, A., 272

Titilola, S.O., 247-8, 268-9, 272, 276

Tomei, Manuela, 265

top-down approaches, 10

Torres, V., 244

Total Quality Management (TQM), 185-6

Townsend, J., 241

traditional healer, 131

Training and Visit (T&V), 14, 155, 186

transcript(s), 43, 182, 225-31, 234

transcription services, 55

transect, 76, 127, 138-42, 159, 163-4, 170, 175, 183; walks, 76, 127, 139, 141, 175

transfer of technological packages, 20

Transfer of Technology (ToT), 103, 186, 201

translation distortion, 58

Tripp, R., 272

Trujillo, J., 244

trustworthiness, 32, 47, 53

Tung, Ly, 270

Turner, B., 253

Turner, G.S., 274

Uganda, 119-20, 250, 269

Ulluwishewa, Rohana, 273

unforeseen factors, 51

United Nations Development Programme (UNDP), 111-2, 240, 271, 273

United Nations Educational, Scientific and Cultural Organisation (UNESCO), 239-40, 273

United States Agency for International Development (USAID), 20, 179

unstructured interviews, 96, 98, 100-1, 105, 109-10

Uphoff, N., 273

Urry, J., 89, 258

Valentin, C., 254

values, 4, 7-8, 41, 59, 76, 88, 96, 100, 156, 169, 192, 194, 196, 198, 213, 217, 222-4, 271

van Binsbergen, W., 245

van den Breemer, J.P.M., 246

van der Kamp, J., 255-6

van der Ploeg, J.D., 260, 273

van Maanen, J., 273

van Ufford, P.Q., 273

van Veen, Tjaart W. Schillhorn, 242, 258, 260-1

van Veldhuizen, Laurens, 273

van Willigen, John, 275

Vaughan, M., 262

Vayda, A.P., 259, 273

Venn diagram(s), 110, 133, 216, 221, 238

Venn diagramming, 133, 221, 238

verbatim transcripts, 42

veterinary science, 2

Vilareal, M., 260

village chairman, 61

Village Resource Management Plan (VRMP), 211, 219

village workshop, 102, 131, 178, 182-3, 211, 218

Villarreal, M., 242

Von Liebenstein, Guus, 273

vulnerability ranking, 85, 90, 105, 117, 122

Wagemakers, A., 268

Wahab, Waheed Bolanle, 252, 273-4, 276-7

Walker, D.H., 57, 62, 234-5, 271-4

Walker, Peter J.C., 274

Wallman, S., 274

Walter, M.F., 269

Wamalwa, B.N., 274

Warner, K., 274

Warner, M., 274

Warren, D. Michael, 3, 221, 239, 243-4, 246-7, 251-2, 254-5, 258-9, 261-71, 273-6

Warren, D., 239, 243, 248, 256, 272, 274-6

Warren, M., 245

waterbodies, 19, 207

Waters-Bayer, Ann, 255-6, 267, 273

Watters, R.F., 276

wealth ranking, 62, 66, 90, 105, 107, 114-5, 117, 119-21, 123, 125, 134, 136, 145, 148, 177, 205, 216, 241, 254, 265, 268; approaches, 119-20

wealth
    characteristics of, 113; criteria for, 114; standard of, 91

webbing, 49, 145, 158, 160, 205, 214

Weber, R., 182, 276

Weiner, D, 129-30, 241, 255

Welbourn, A., 249

well water, 175

Wellard, Kate, 249, 254

Werge, R., 267

Werner, Oswald, 24, 26, 243-4, 246, 256, 262, 276

Westerby, M., 269

western
    science, 5; scientists, 6

Whickam, T.W., 276

White, H., 118, 247, 255, 276

Whiteford, Michael B., 266

Whorf, B.L., 155, 276

Wignaraja, P., 115, 276

Wilken, G.C., 276

Willcocks, Theo. J., 249, 276

Willet, Anthony B.J., 264

Williams, G., 276

Willmer, A., 125, 276

Wiltgen, Beverly, 276

Winch, P., 88-9, 97, 192, 276

Winslow, Donna, 276

Wolfe, J., 5, 276

Wolff, Norma H., 277

Women in Development (WID), 88, 139, 148, 150

women, 3, 11, 37-8, 89, 94, 101-2, 104, 115-9, 124, 126, 131, 136, 139, 142, 145, 148-50, 153-5, 158, 176, 187-90, 192-4, 197, 205-6, 208, 210-1, 215, 217-8, 223, 242, 250, 255, 276; in Malawi, 104; married, 145; of South Africa, 116; pregnant, 203; vulnerability of, 118

Wood, A.W., 277

Wood, Adrian P., 258

Wood, G.D., 277

Woolgar, S., 92, 259

work practices, 11

World Bank (WB), 82, 111, 118, 123, 239-40, 245, 247-9, 255, 260-1, 263, 266, 275, 277

World Wide Fund (WWF), 82, 239, 248, 277

Wright, S., 249, 251, 257, 260, 263, 277

Zambia, 156, 200, 253, 258, 262, 276

Zapata, G., 269

Zimmerer, K.S., 57, 277

Zuberi, M.I., 244

Zurick, D.N., 277